Labour Women i

Paula Bartley

Labour Women in Power

Cabinet Ministers in the Twentieth Century

Paula Bartley
Stratford-upon-Avon, UK

ISBN 978-3-030-14287-2   ISBN 978-3-030-14288-9   (eBook)
https://doi.org/10.1007/978-3-030-14288-9

Library of Congress Control Number: 2019932971

Cover images: Margaret Bondfield © GL Archive/Alamy Stock Photo; Barbara Castle © Keystone Pictures USA/Alamy Stock Photo; Judith Hart © Keystone Pictures USA/Alamy Stock Photo; Ellen Wilkinson © Chronicle/Alamy Stock Photo; Shirley Williams © Trinity Mirror/Mirrorpix/Alamy Stock Photo
Cover design by Fatima Jamadar

This Palgrave Macmillan imprint is published by the registered company Springer Nature Switzerland AG
The registered company address is: Gewerbestrasse 11, 6330 Cham, Switzerland

For Dóra, Kata and Réka Dudley; and Eva and Kate Karalius.

ACKNOWLEDGEMENTS

Every historian is indebted to archivists and librarians whose specialist knowledge smooths the way for researchers. I am especially grateful to Emma Pizarro, Gemma Read and their colleagues at the LSE library; Carole Jones and the staff at the library and Modern Records Centre, University of Warwick; Jess Dunnicliff at Stratford-upon-Avon public library; Sophie Welsh and Nicola O'Toole at the Special Collections, Bodleian Libraries; Debbie Horner and the library staff at the British Library. Judith Hart deposited her constituency papers in Glasgow which would have been impenetrable, but for the help, I received from Michael Gallagher and Barbara McLean at the City Archives. The archivists at the People's History Museum, especially Darren Treadwell and Julie Parry were, as ever, exemplary, always welcoming, always helpful, always knowledgeable about their splendid collections. Dean Rogers at Vassar College Archives and Special Collections Library not only helped me find my way around its archive on Margaret Bondfield but helped me with my hotel and travel plans and told me about another collection held at President Franklin D. Roosevelt's Library. Thanks to Patrick Fahey, archive technician at FDR Presidential Library for forwarding letters between Margaret Bondfield and Eleanor Roosevelt. Thanks too to the staff at the National Archives who have digitised its collection of Cabinet papers making the life of this researcher a lot easier. Lastly, I am grateful to Terry George for his technological help.

I would like to thank Robert Dudley, Karl Sabbagh, Kathy Stredder and the three anonymous reviewers who usefully commented on my book proposal. Thanks to Emily Russell and Oliver Dyer at Palgrave for their patience and for seeing the book through to completion. Thanks to the many historians who have helped in various ways, including Maggie Andrews, Diane Atkinson, Lucy Bland, Lucy Delap, Richard Carr, Anna Davin, Neil Fleming, Hilda Kean, Janis Lomas, Kate Murphy, Angela V. John, Stephanie Mair, Jenny Mathers, Mary Jane Mossman, Paul O'Leary, June Purvis, Mari

Takayanagi and Stephanie Ward. My long conversations with Sue Morgan have been most enlightening, and I thank her for her insightful analysis. Thanks to Keith Jenkins and Peter Freeman for their comments on the chapters on Judith Hart; to Cathy Hunt for her comments on Margaret Bondfield; and to Cathy Loxton and Dawn Rumley for their comments on the entire book. Finally, thanks to Réka Dudley for helping me with the statistics.

Special thanks to Clare Short for her interest and her abundant generosity. She was always willing to share her insights into life at the political top, recommended books I should read on overseas aid, read the manuscript in full and made many useful suggestions to improve the text. She introduced me to Peter Freeman who in turn introduced me to Maggie Sidgreaves and Peter McLean, all of whom worked closely with Judith Hart when she was Minister for Overseas Development: their insights into her character were inestimable in helping me understand what she was like both as a person and as a Minister. Clare Short also introduced me to the late Rodney Bickerstaffe, former General Secretary of UNISON, who worked tirelessly all his life to improve the lives of low-paid workers, most of whom were women, and convinced me by his actions that trade unions and women's equality were interlinked. Thanks also to Jane Clarke and Rachel Reeves who put me in contact with Steve Hart and to Shirley Williams for letting me read an unpublished account of her life as a female MP. Steve Hart shared some of his memories about his mother, and I am grateful to him for this.

Labour Women in Power could not have been written without the sterling work of others. I have drawn on the work of scholars working in a variety of fields, in particular women's history, Labour history, political history, political biography, religious history, political science and the history of Empire. I am grateful to all the historians and political scientists mentioned in this book for their research and for their insights into—for me—sometimes unfamiliar areas. Historians rely on conferences too: I am grateful for the comments made by delegates at the various Women's History Network Conferences and the Vote 100 Conference 2018.

I could not have researched this book without financial support. Thank you to The Society of Authors' Foundation for awarding me a research grant to visit the various archives and to Professor Ronald Patkus and colleagues for awarding me the Vassar College Archives and Special Collections Library grant which was sponsored by Charlotte Hall.

As ever, I am most grateful to my husband, Jonathan Dudley. He accompanied me on my research trips to London, Manchester, Glasgow and New York and helped me with my work on each trip, the only reward being a glass of wine or a plate of pasta in the evening. He was always willing to listen to my ideas, always happy to read and comment upon my drafts. However, it is his unwavering support of me, his joyous sense of humour and his love which I value most. The book is dedicated to the younger generation of our family.

Contents

LIST OF FIGURES

CHAPTER 1

Introduction

In 1997, when Tony Blair became Prime Minister, he appointed as many women to his first Cabinet as there had been in all previous Labour Governments.[1] Until then only five Labour women had attained Cabinet status: Margaret Bondfield, Ellen Wilkinson, Barbara Castle, Judith Hart and Shirley Williams. During the same period, nearly one hundred men were appointed to Labour Cabinets.[2] This is a lamentable statistic. Why did this happen? In her spirited manifesto, *Women and Power*, Mary Beard argues that it was generally believed that women had no right to occupy powerful positions and that the 'shared metaphors we use of female access to power – "knocking on the door", "storming the citadel", "smashing the glass ceiling", or just giving them a "leg up"' underline women's lack of entitlement.[3] Beard's judgement may strike a chord, though one needs to look at women's lack of power with a more focussed historical lens: there are specific reasons why women found it hard to achieve high political status in the twentieth century. Labour Party women aspiring to reach the pinnacle of Cabinet Minister faced a triple handicap: they had to be elected as MPs; they needed a Labour Party in government; and they needed a Prime Minister sympathetic to women's advancement. The combined impact of these three obstacles made it tough for Labour women to reach high office for most of the twentieth century.[4] Conservative women politicians faced similar obstacles but fared worse: until 1979, only two women, Florence Horsburgh and Margaret Thatcher, were appointed to Cabinet posts.[5]

As Krista Cowman and others point out, women came to the parliamentary scene very much later than men.[6] For hundreds of years, Parliament had consisted of men only: well over 600 of them in each House of Commons. In 1918, women won the right to stand for Parliament but few chose to do so. As the above chart shows, throughout the twentieth-century women from all political parties were seriously under-represented in the House of Commons: until the late 1980s, they consisted of fewer than 5% of all MPs (Fig. 1.1).

© The Author(s) 2019
P. Bartley, *Labour Women in Power*,
https://doi.org/10.1007/978-3-030-14288-9_1

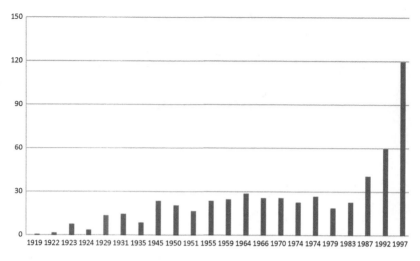

Fig. 1.1   Women MPs in twentieth-century Britain

There were a number of reasons for the scarcity of women MPs. First of all, as the charts below show, only a small number of women from across the political spectrum ever stood as parliamentary candidates in all the 23 general elections in the twentieth century.[7] In December 1918, the first election where women were eligible to stand, only 17 women out of a total of 1623 candidates put themselves forward.[8] Four were Labour. It did not improve significantly until the 1990s (Figs. 1.2 and 1.3).

Out of these candidates, only one woman was elected: Constance Markievicz who had won her seat in a Dublin constituency for Sinn Fein, a party campaigning for Irish independence.[9] However, Sinn Fein refused to recognise the authority of the British Parliament and Markievicz declined to take her seat in the House of Commons. In November 28, 1919, the American born Nancy Astor became the first woman to take her seat in Parliament when she was elected Conservative MP for Plymouth. In 1923, the first three Labour women were elected: they were the first women who had either not replaced their husbands or were unmarried to sit in Parliament.[10] At the next general election in October 1924, all three were defeated. A new Labour woman—Ellen Wilkinson—was elected, the only woman on the opposition benches.[11] In the 1929 general election, just after women over 21 were enfranchised, nine Labour women won seats, only to lose them two years later in a catastrophic electoral defeat.[12] In 1935, only

1918	1922	1923	1924	1929	1931	1935	1945	1950	1951	1955	1959	1964	1966	1970	1974	1974	1979	1983	1987	1992	1997
17	33	34	41	69	62	67	87	127	77	92	81	90	81	99	143	161	216	280	329	571	672
1606	1408	1412	1387	1661	1230	1281	1596	1741	1299	1307	1455	1657	1616	1738	1992	2091	2360	2298	1996	2378	3052

Fig. 1.2   Number of female and male candidates standing for election from all parties

1918	1922	1923	1924	1929	1931	1935	1945	1950	1951	1955	1959	1964	1966	1970	1974	1974	1979	1983	1987	1992	1997
4	10	14	22	30	36	35	45	42	39	43	36	33	30	29	40	50	52	78	92	138	156
359	404	413	492	539	480	568	517	575	551	577	585	595	591	595	583	573	570	555	541	494	483

Fig. 1.3 Number of Labour women and men standing for election (Compiled from David Butler and Gareth Butler's *Twentieth Century British Political Facts, 1900–2000*, Macmillan, 2000)

one Labour woman was returned.[13] The general election which was due to take place in 1940 was not held because of the Second World War.

In the post-war general election of 1945, the twenty-one Labour women who were elected entered Parliament on a wave of optimism.[14] Labour had won more seats than ever before in its history and many looked forward to a smooth upward rise of women politicians. The success of 1945 was not repeated.[15] When the Suffrage Act 1969 gave votes to those over 18, there were high hopes that more Labour women might be elected by a younger electorate but it in fact the number of women dropped to ten in the subsequent election.[16]

Why was it so difficult for a woman—whatever her political persuasion—to become an MP and take the first step towards being a Cabinet Minister? Was it merely social convention? Certainly, there was a strong conviction that women should not take part in public life: Britain in the twentieth century was a much more masculine-dominated country than that of the early twenty-first century. For much of the last century, women were expected to be in their own house—with a small h—looking after their families not in the House of Commons—with a big H—looking after the country. Whether they were Tory, Liberal or Labour, women were expected to marry, take care of their husbands, run the household, do the shopping, cook, make the beds and clean the house, or else supervise others to do so. Trade unions even campaigned for the family wage—that is a man's wage high enough to support his wife and children—to enable wives to stay at home. Undoubtedly, large numbers of men were chauvinistic, reluctant to encourage women to join their public sphere of work, reluctant to share political power. There were of course exceptions: several Labour MPs such as Keir Hardie, Arthur Henderson, George Lansbury, Herbert Morrison, and Harold Wilson were committed to women's equality and helped boost their careers. Nonetheless, women needed to be particularly brave to stand for Parliament as they were, after all, challenging the prevailing norms of domesticity and maternity. Only a very few exceptional women were confident or committed enough to overcome these conventional expectations. Predictably, the early women MPs were often single and if married, child-free; those who married stressed how important it was to have a supportive husband.

It was doubly difficult for women with children, trying to balance their role as a mother with parliamentary responsibilities and not feel guilty either of neglecting their children or of neglecting their constituents.[17] In the mid-twentieth century, a leading child psychologist John Bowlby suggested that a warm and continuous relationship with a mother was essential to a child's psychological health: women who went out to work risked irretrievably damaging their child emotionally, socially and intellectually.[18] The general acceptance of such theories meant that it was problematic for women, and especially women with children, to participate even in well-regulated paid work, let alone in the parliamentary world of the twentieth century with its erratic and unsocial working hours. In the 1960s, Bowlby's views were challenged by women journalists and novelists,[19] and later in the 1970s by the Women's Liberation Movement, but these newer understandings took some time to be widely accepted. Perhaps more significantly, the absence of affordable childcare for most of the century barred women from seeking any kind of paid work: Tory women like Nancy Astor could afford a large retinue of support staff; Labour women relied on family and friends.

Undoubtedly, the masculine culture of parliamentary politics discouraged women. The House of Commons was emphatically male for most of the twentieth century: over 600 men and at times only a handful of women on the benches. It was a men's club with bizarre hours of business and a year 'dictated by the urge to rise every August for the start of the shooting season'.[20] Historians often comment on the problems facing women in Parliament, pointing out how tough and unwelcoming the place could be. Certainly, the adversarial tone of the House of Commons ran counter to the educational and social values that women were expected to promote. Women, socialised to be demure and co-operative, required a certain level of assertiveness to take part in politics. Members of parliament were expected to be competitive, articulate, opinionated and argumentative, virtues that were considered vices when they were held by women.

Once a woman decided on a parliamentary career her first challenge was to be selected by the local constituency party to stand as its candidate. Not surprisingly, given societal constraints and the political atmosphere in the Commons, very few women ever came forward for selection. And when a woman was determined enough to do so, she would find an in-built prejudice on the part of selection committees: being a woman was not a political asset. The Labour Party was dedicated to women's equality—it had been the first political party to commit to votes for women—but it had another entrenched ethos, sometimes fostered by its links with the trade unions, in which women were expected to be wives and mothers. In some trade union circles, it was viewed as 'normal' to hold an unsympathetic attitude to women's political participation.[21] A number of mining communities had what has been termed 'princes in waiting', leading miners who saw it as their given right to be selected for a Labour constituency.[22] As a consequence, like all the political parties of the time, women were grossly under-represented and especially so in Wales.[23]

These attitudes found their most discriminatory expression in selection interviews where female candidates—regardless of political party—were asked about their family situations, whether they had children, whether they had a supportive husband. The underlying assumption here was that women would need to look after the children and therefore would not be up to the job.[24] Moreover, there was a latent anxiety that it would be more difficult for women to win parliamentary seats because of the attitudes of the voters. The selection committee's ideal candidate was a young married man with a couple of children not a spinster or a married woman, certainly not one with children. In addition, Labour Party selection committees feared that women candidates were often too feminist in their convictions, believing that such beliefs would further alienate the electorate. Ironically, prospective female candidates had to convince the selection committee that they were well assimilated into the Labour Party and would not frighten the voters by too much vocal commitment to female equality.

Perhaps more importantly, Labour constituencies chose candidates from two distinct lists. The first showed candidates who were sponsored by a trade union—the so-called A list. Trade union sponsored candidates would not only keep the party 'rooted in working-class experience' but the sponsoring trade union would, of course, pay their candidate's election costs.[25] The second list—the so-called B list—was provided by local groups or organisations such as the Co-op or the Fabians which usually expected their preferred candidate to meet some if not all of their own election expenses. Funding an election was expensive: in 1922, each candidate had to provide a £150 deposit—roughly the equivalent of a man's annual wage—and pay their own election expenses which could be even more considerable. The Labour Party, always desperately short of funds, could not afford the vast expense necessary to fight elections just from members' subscriptions. As a result selection committees were deterred from adopting candidates unless they were fully funded, which generally meant favouring candidates from the A list.[26] During the interwar years, only two female candidates contested elections 'as sponsored candidates of Labour-affiliated trade unions' and both were officials of trade unions with a large female membership.[27]

In addition, when they were selected female candidates were all too often adopted to stand in less safe seats. Indeed, as Martin Pugh points out, for most of the twentieth century over four-fifths of the female candidates of all parties were given hopelessly unwinnable constituencies.[28] Labour's heartlands namely the manufacturing and mining districts were regions where there was a great deal of prejudice about women working and so men were usually selected to contest these seats. If women were selected they had to 'nurse' their constituencies by making themselves known in the area, visiting schools and hospitals, opening bazaars and jumble sales, knocking on constituents' doors and holding meetings, often in draughty halls with just a few people in the audience. Again, women without trade union sponsorship or a private income were handicapped as it was an expensive business tending to a constituency, particularly as many did not live in the area in which they hoped to be elected.

Once elected MPs needed to decide where they should live. Parliament convenes in London but most constituencies were outside it, many hundreds of miles away from the House of Commons. MPs were expected to be in London during the week, travelling home on Thursday or Friday to their constituencies to look after their electorate. Marriage and children added another complication. Would the husband move to his wife's constituency? Where would the children live? The considerable pressures on a married woman MP, living away from home in London for a large part of the week, travelling to their constituency at weekends combined with long erratic hours in the House of Commons, made a sympathetic husband essential.

Since women had not been expected to be members of parliament there were no facilities for them in the House of Commons. It was a male space. The first women MPs had to squash into one small dressing room which contained a washstand, a tin basin, a jug of cold water and a bucket—a situation they naturally found intolerable. Ellen Wilkinson called it 'The Tomb'. Even so they rarely complained, partly because they were just glad to be in the building. These women soon found that they were not welcome in certain areas of the House namely the bars, the smoking rooms and the members' cloakroom. Either because they feared giving offence or were intimidated they tended to stay away from these places. The animosity of some male MPs had the unexpected effect of making the first few female MPs stick together in solidarity. Moreover because the three main parties—Conservative, Liberal and Labour—failed to take up women's issues, the first few women MPs often worked across party lines to promote gender equality on issues such as equal pay, for reform of the prostitution laws and for equal opportunities more generally.

Class, not just gender, was an issue. There were few if any domestic servants, factory workers, agricultural workers or hairdressers in the twentieth-century Parliament. From 1945 onwards female MPs, as with their male counterparts, were increasingly drawn from the professional classes: most had worked in public service, in the co-operative movement, the trade unions, local government or the Labour Party.[29] In 1979, the Labour Party issued a 'private and confidential' memo which showed that the 37 new female parliamentary candidates at the 1979 election were indisputably middle class.[30]

Once elected, women walked into a space that was both masculine and upper-class. The Palace of Westminster was an intimidatingly grand building with its panelled walls, high ceilings, crystal chandeliers, vast halls and chambers, heraldic symbols and statues of dead white men, and especially so for those who had not grown up in a big house, been to public school or to Oxbridge.[31] Not surprisingly many women, especially those from less privileged backgrounds, found it nerve-racking to speak in the august chamber of the House of Commons. It was particularly daunting for a woman to make her maiden speech when the response to 'each maiden speech by a woman was sometimes just a polite veneer with which the parliamentary misogynists covered their resentment'.[32] It took a great deal of courage to stand up in this masculine assembly and express views, especially the unorthodox ones usually put forward by Labour. Edith Summerskill remarked that 'Parliament with its conventions and protocol seems a little like a boys' school which has decided to take a few girls'.[33] Behaviour in the House of Commons hit a new low in the evening when an even more masculine atmosphere prevailed as male MPs became more rowdy and animated after dinner, largely because they had had too much to drink. These men were elected Members of Parliament, the public face of British politics; many governed the country, passed laws which affected millions of people, set taxes, decided on how to deliver public services such as education and health and conferred with foreign countries.

Suffragists and suffragettes had hoped that once women achieved the vote they would make a distinctive contribution to the political arena by 'feminising' politics. It was hoped that women would bring special skills to Parliament which would make the confrontational style of party politics disappear in favour of politics based on courtesy and respect. This hope was unrealised. Throughout the twentieth century, the House of Commons remained a male privileged institution dominated by men. They dominated numerically and also in their style of doing politics. The election of such a few women MPs did not bring about a new age nor did it feminise the political process: the new female MPs generally adapted to the masculine style of the House of Commons by assuming an equally adversarial style rather than challenge the way business was conducted.

Male MPs across the political spectrum were openly hostile to women. When Nancy Astor took her seat in the House of Commons, a number of MPs made it clear that they would 'rather have a rattlesnake in the House of Commons than me'.[34] Winston Churchill hoped to freeze her out. Jenny Lee spoke of Labour Scottish mining MPs whose 'faces curdled up like a bowl of sour cream whenever we accidentally collided'[35]; Leah Manning was hurt by the 'cold contempt of old ILP friends such as Jimmy Maxton who treated me as a criminal for having dared stand, let alone win'.[36] Some were sexist. Leah Manning complained about the lewd comments that Ben Tillett, the dock-leader and Labour MP, shouted at her and other women MPs both in the Chamber and in the bars[37]; some showed their disrespect in other ways. In 1973, Labour MP Leo Abse commented that 'essentially many of our women politicians are aberrant women, doubtless not dissimilar from the women upon whose disorders Freud made his construct of femininity'.[38] Of course, not all male MPs shared these beliefs and many women were encouraged by colleagues committed to women's equality.

The negative attitudes of some MPs were shared by the press. Newspaper reporters, mostly men, often trivialised women by emphasising what they looked like rather than what they said. Given all these downsides, it may seem surprising that women ever put themselves forward as parliamentary candidates, or even became involved in politics at all. Some women wanted to climb higher: to be a member of Cabinet was a key aspiration for those who wanted to experience real power.[39] All Cabinet Ministers according to

Anthony King were made of 'stern political stuff', career politicians deeply committed to politics, deeply committed to changing the face of Britain and the world.[40] Politics was their life. They breathed, ate, drank, slept and probably even dreamt politics.[41] All had to be willing to be subjected to the closest scrutiny with their actions being constantly judged by the Prime Minister, Cabinet colleagues, Labour MPs, the House of Commons, civil servants, the press and the electorate. The few women who did reach the top became personally involved in dealing with world-wide economic melt-down, war-time bombing, the collapse of the British Empire, and the possible withdrawal of Britain from the European Economic Community: comments about their looks were a minor irritant.

It was extraordinarily challenging to climb to these heights, particularly as women MPs were often unable to follow the conventional route to a Cabinet post by first becoming a Parliamentary Private Secretary (PPS), then a junior minister. Ministers were reluctant to accept a woman as their PPS, generally seen as an apprenticeship for a ministerial post, because until the latter part of the century women were often made unwelcome in the bars, the smoking rooms and the members' cloakroom, all places where MPs congregated to gossip, plan and conspire. This had implications for promotion for it was in the House of Commons bars that the PPS could learn—unofficially and off the record—information that might be useful for her Minister. When Ministers declined to take on a woman for this post, this training route to Cabinet was cut off.

Of course, in order to have a Cabinet post, the Labour Party needed to be in government—quite a rare achievement in the twentieth century as the above chart shows (Fig. 1.4). It was a new party, founded in 1900 by trade unionists as the Labour Representation Committee (LRC) to represent working men and women in Parliament.[42] In 1906, with the election of 29 LRC MPs it adopted the name 'The Labour Party'. For the first half of the century, the party remained small, fragile and exceedingly fractious. It formed its first (minority) government under Ramsay MacDonald in 1924 and the second between 1929 and 1931. In 1945, it enjoyed its first majority government under Clement Attlee. After that Labour held power from 1964 to 1970 under Harold Wilson and again from 1974 to 1979 under Wilson and later James Callaghan. Labour had to wait until 1997, under Tony Blair, to form its next government. Consequently, whether male or female, being a Labour Party MP often meant sitting on the Opposition benches—clearly not a helpful experience for a woman aspiring to become a Cabinet Minister.

The Prime Minister's power to appoint his (there has yet to be a female Labour Prime Minister) Cabinet is 'largely unfettered'.[43] Prime Ministers can appoint and dismiss 'more or less whomever they like. The decisions are theirs, and they can make them on more or less whatever basis they like'.[44] Nonetheless, as Anthony King points out, Prime Ministers tend to be circumspect in their choice: they would be aware of the need to include senior figures within their Cabinet, MPs who enjoyed a substantial following both

Election	PM	Party	Majority
1918	David Lloyd George	Coalition	238
1922	Andrew Bonar Law	Conservative	74
1923	Ramsay MacDonald	Labour	-98
1924	Stanley Baldwin	Conservative	210
1929	Ramsay MacDonald	Labour	-42
1931	Ramsay MacDonald	National	492
1935	Stanley Baldwin	Conservative Nat*	242
1945	Clement Attlee	Labour	146
1950	Clement Attlee	Labour	5
1951	Winston Churchill	Conservative	17
1955	Anthony Eden	Conservative	60
1959	Harold Macmillan**	Conservative	100
1964	Harold Wilson	Labour	4
1966	Harold Wilson	Labour	98
1970	Edward Heath	Conservative	30
1974 (Feb)	Harold Wilson	Labour	-33
1974 (Oct)	Harold Wilson***	Labour	3
1979	Margaret Thatcher	Conservative	43
1983	Margaret Thatcher	Conservative	144
1987	M Thatcher****	Conservative	102
1992	John Major	Conservative	21
1997	Tony Blair	Labour	179

*The outbreak of war in 1939 meant there was no election. Baldwin was replaced in 1937 by Neville Chamberlain who in turn was replaced in 1940 by Winston Churchill.
** In 1963 Alec Douglas-Home replaced Macmillan.
***In 1976 James Callaghan replaced Wilson.
****In 1990 John Major replaced Thatcher.

Fig. 1.4 Governments formed following general elections

inside and out of Parliament; of the need to balance the various groupings within the party, from the extreme left-wing socialists to those on the centre right; and of the need to have a balance between the intellectuals, the trade unionists, the sensible safe pair of hands and the radical thinkers. In addition, they would be wise to pick MPs with high-level communication skills, an ability to master a brief quickly, an ability to lead their departments, and with a clear vision for what they wanted to achieve.[45] Today, gender matters. For most of the twentieth century when women were appointed to Cabinet it made headline news because it was considered so innovative, by the beginning of the twenty-first century, it was expected that women would be appointed to Cabinet posts.

Between 1929 and 1979 five Labour women MPs broke through the political glass ceiling and became Cabinet Ministers. They had survived the selection process, been elected to Parliament, and fulfilled the criteria for

Cabinet office. However, it is argued that once women reached these heights they faced a glass cliff. This theory, put forward by Ryan and Haslam,[46] implies that women who reach the top are often appointed to leadership positions which are doomed to fail. Women's leadership positions, they argue, tend to be more precarious than those of men and 'when that failure occurs, it is then women (rather than men) who must face the consequences and who are singled out for criticism and blame'.[47] However, the suggestion that there are top jobs which have an inbuilt capacity to fail can be said of every Cabinet post, regardless of who holds it.

More significantly perhaps no Prime Minister—Labour or Conservative—appointed women as Chancellor of the Exchequer, Home Secretary or Foreign Secretary, the three major Cabinet posts. Harold Wilson who favoured women far more than any other Prime Minister offered this explanation. 'The Home Office lives in the last century; the Treasury contains a load of mandarins; and the attitudes of the Foreign Office officials are moulded by the years they have spent among the Arabs'.[48] No Prime Minister wanted to upset these powerful ministries too much. Consequently, women tended to be offered posts thought to be extensions of the home and family such as health and social services, education, prices and consumer affairs, an assumption based on the fact that women would deal better with these areas.

Historiography

Feminist historians are very aware that women who have made huge historically significant contributions can simply disappear, no ripple, no trace. To some extent historians, keepers of the bygone flame are responsible. Certainly, political historians tend to focus on male politicians: there are various biographies of twentieth-century Labour figures. For instance, Ramsay MacDonald,[49] Clement Attlee,[50] Stafford Cripps,[51] Hugh Dalton,[52] Herbert Morrison,[53] Aneurin Bevan,[54] Ernest Bevin,[55] Roy Jenkins[56] and Michael Foot[57] have all been the subject of historical attention. If women were absent from political histories, politics used to be absent from women's history. Feminist historians who focussed on the absence of women from the historical record and sought to redress this imbalance had little wish to replicate the traditional history of 'high politics, war and diplomacy' and initially preferred to focus on the history of the underprivileged and of ordinary unknown women rather than one-time celebrities. Consequently, politics was defined more widely than parliamentary politics and historians sought to uncover the lives of women immersed in local and grass-roots politics,[58] in social and political movements,[59] in women's organisations,[60] and in one-issue campaigns.[61] Others have explored the lives of Labour Party women more generally. Pamela M Graves' *Labour Women* focusses on how women in both the Labour and Co-operative Movement sought to make Labour policy more woman-friendly and demolishes the often-held perception that the Labour Party was really for male trade unionists.[62] For an understanding of how left-wing women formed their political opinions in the early years of the socialist movement, June Hannam's and Karen Hunt's path-breaking book *Socialist Women* demonstrates how socialist women's identities were influenced by gender and how this in turn led to a re-appraisal of socialism.[63]

A number of books have examined women's role in parliamentary politics: Pamela Brookes', *Women at Westminster*,[64] Krista Cowman's, *Women in British Politics, C1689-1979*,[65] Melville Currell, *Political Woman*,[66] Joni Lovenduski and Pippa Norris' *Women in Politics*,[67] Jean Mann *Women in Parliament*,[68] Melanie Phillips, *The Divided House*,[69] and Elizabeth Vallance's *Women in the House*[70] remain vital sources for understanding the possibilities and problems faced by any woman who wanted a political career, not just those who reached the heights of their profession. More recently, Iain Dale's and Jacqui Smith's *The Honorable Ladies, Profiles of Women MPs 1918–1996* which contains short biographies of every woman MP during this period makes a most useful contribution to political history.[71] Rachel Reeves *Women of Westminster: The MPs Who Changed Politics*[72] will also add to our understanding of women politicians. Individual biographies—like those of Patricia Hollis' *Jennie Lee*[73] and Rachel Reeves', *Alice in Wonderland: The Political Life of Alice Bacon*[74]—of many of these women would be both fascinating and instructive.

Three of the five Cabinet Ministers have been well served by biographers: to date there are four biographies of Ellen Wilkinson,[75] two of Barbara Castle[76] and one of Shirley Williams. However, at the time of writing there is no decent biography of Margaret Bondfield and Judith Hart has been completely ignored. Full length, academically creditable biographies of these two women are long overdue. *Labour Women in Power* draws upon these as well as a number of specialties, most notably women's history, historical biography more generally, Labour history, political science and studies of Empire.

There is an early biography, largely hagiographic, of Bondfield written by one of her contemporaries, the Labour MP Mary Hamilton[77] which examines her life before she became a Cabinet Minister. Tony Judge's recent independently published biography of Margaret Bondfield covers most of her life, though contains little original research.[78] Fortunately, there are a number of excellent articles about Bondfield, namely Marion Miliband's in the *Dictionary of Labour Biography*.[79] In addition Margaret Bondfield wrote her own autobiography *A Life's Work*[80] which recounts her rise from a humble background to become the first British woman to achieve Cabinet rank. Her life as a shop assistant, her role as a trade union official and her life in Parliament are vividly described. Bondfield comes across as a thoroughly decent human being, a team player rather than an individualist, someone who was painstaking and thorough, a deeply religious person whose Christian beliefs informed her politics. Reviews were less adulatory. Harold Nicolson thought her book 'ill-composed and badly proportioned. ... She is deficient both in historical perspective and a sense of proportion. She will thus devote many pages to her dull visits to Switzerland or the United States, and dismiss in a few sentences the very significant part which she played in the 1931 crisis'.[81]

Fortunately, Bondfield left a large personal archive, now housed in Vassar College Library. This archive disappeared for a while: it had been transferred to the care of Helen Lockwood, a Professor of English at Vassar College. It is remarkable that Margaret Bondfield's papers ended up in an elite women's college in Poughkeepsie, New York, but it was a gift explained by Bondfield's love of America and of her friend. Bondfield and Lockwood probably became close during the Second World War, met whenever possible and wrote to each other regularly. Their letters are affectionate, starting with 'my beloved Margaret' or 'my dear Helen', and ending with either a 'lovingly Margaret' or 'my love to you always, Helen'.[82] These were unusual terms of endearment from Bondfield who was generally very formal, addressing women as 'Dear Miss or Mrs' rather than by their first name. In the 1950s, the two worked together on a manuscript of Bondfield's travels and 'talked a great deal about what remained to be done'. When her friend died, Lockwood hoped to 'carry out her wishes', by working with Bondfield's executors to write a memoir.[83] Bondfield's nieces who were the executors gave her 'full freedom' to use the papers.[84] Dutifully, Lockwood wrote to the left-wing publisher Victor Gollancz about publishing her friend's recollections of her leisure time—Bondfield had already published her autobiography about her working life—but Gollancz turned down the proposal. When Lockwood died in 1971 the papers, consisting of 14 boxes of biographical material, family material, Labour Party material including her election campaigns, trips to Russia and America and miscellaneous material including unpublished manuscripts of poems and stories by Margaret Bondfield, were donated to Vassar College where they remain, still largely unread.[85] I supplemented these sources with the unpublished manuscript of Ross Davies' biography of Bondfield held at the LSE: he could not finish his biography because Bondfield's archive had gone missing. Material held at the People's History Museum, Manchester also helped.

I have drawn heavily on my own biography *Ellen Wilkinson: From Red Suffragist to Government Minister* (Pluto Press, 2014) for the chapters on Ellen Wilkinson. Since then two full-length biographies of Ellen Wilkinson, one by Matt Perry (*'Red Ellen' Wilkinson*, MUP 2014); the other by Laura Beers (*Red Ellen*, Yale 2016) have been published. Barbara Castle has been well served by both Anne Perkins (*Red Queen: The Authorized Biography of Barbara Castle*, Macmillan, 2003) and Lisa Martineau (*Barbara Castle: Politics and Power*, Andre Deutsch, 2000). Both biographies of Castle capture their subject's character: the rebellious parliamentarianism; the glittering champagne socialist; the loyal and hardworking Cabinet Minister in four separate ministries; the captivating speaker; and the incorrigible self-publicist. Both books chart Castle's remarkable journey from sales demonstrator to Cabinet Minister, from rebel left-winger to controversial trade union reformer; from campaigner against the Common Market to Member of the

European Parliament. Fortunately for historians, Barbara Castle was an inveterate diarist and a writer. Her diaries, typed up from her shorthand notes, are distinctive, not just because they broaden and enrich the reader's understanding of the period but because they discuss Cabinet meetings from an altogether unusual perspective: that of an immensely capable left-wing politician—and a woman. In her diaries, Barbara Castle writes about her feelings, about her hopes and fears, her delights and disappointments and shares her plans and her intentions. Importantly for the historian, Castle's diary captures all the drama, the determination and commitment in the face of opposition, the joys of success and the moments of despair. Barbara Castle also wrote an autobiography *Fighting All the Way* (Macmillan, 2002) which is less fiery and more measured than her diaries but which is stronger on her early life and political career. I have drawn on all these books, supplementing them with material from archives, Hansard and newspapers.

Judith Hart has been served less well. Apart from a largely unsympathetic article by Duncan Sutherland ('Judith Hart', *Oxford Dictionary of National Biography*, 2008) and an entry by Ann Rossiter in the *Dictionary of Labour Biography* (2001), there is nothing yet written about this extraordinary woman. Fortunately, Judith Hart like Margaret Bondfield left a historical treasure trove in two archives: at the People's History Museum, Manchester consisting of 138 boxes; the other in Glasgow City Archives consisting of 38 boxes of constituency papers. A few of these sources are labelled SECRET and should have been returned to the Government Office of origin. Such an act was not surprising: Judith Hart was always willing to break with convention.

A number of books written by or about Shirley Williams have been most useful in helping me appreciate the complex life of a still-living politician. Shirley Williams' autobiography[86] is less acerbic than Castle's as everyone almost without exception—from her parents to her political opponents—is shown in a positive light: there seem to be few demons and no dark side in the life of Shirley Williams. Certainly her autobiography shows what an unfailingly nice person Williams is—it is beautifully written and recounts the story of her life with sensitivity and precision. Williams' *Politics is for People*[87] which puts forward suggestions for the way Britain should develop and *God and Caesar*[88] which discusses the impact of her Catholic faith on her secular beliefs together provide insights into her political identity. Her authorised biography by Mark Peel, *Shirley Williams, The Biography*[89] reveals Williams' guilt about her privileged background, her reluctance to be nasty or fight nasty (often considered a prerequisite for a successful politician) because of her enduring humanity. Others such as *Making the Difference, Essays in Honour of Shirley Williams*[90] and Vera Brittain's often largely autobiographical novels have also helped.

Labour Women in Power draws on this archival evidence and published work to provide a survey of the political experiences of these not-always-so-famous five women Cabinet Ministers. It charts their ideas, their character

and formative influences; it provides an account of their rise to power, anal-
yses their contribution to policy making and assesses their significance and
reputation. These women were not a homogeneous group: they came from
diverse family backgrounds, entered politics in their own discrete way and
held divergent political beliefs. They rose to power at different times: the
early years of the twentieth century were quite different from those of the
early years of the twenty-first and it is important not to oversimplify women's
lives by imagining a seamless continuity. By the end of the twentieth century,
the world of politics had been turned upside down but like an upturned photograph it was nonetheless recognisable. Despite their personal diversity and
the times in which they lived these women shared one thing in common: they
all functioned in a male world, even though that world changed dramatically
over the course of the century. More importantly, they were all committed to
improving the lives of the working-class, and often brought a woman's perspective to politics. Naturally, some were more successful than others as the
following chapters will show.

NOTES

1. In 1997, Ann Taylor, Harriet Harman, Clare Short, Margaret Beckett, and
   Mo Mowlam were appointed. In 1998, Baroness Jay was appointed. Harriet
   Harman leaves the Cabinet.
2. W. Adamson, C. Addison, Lord Amulree, A. Alexander, J. Barnett, A. Benn, W.
   Benn, A. Bevan, A. Booth, A. Bottomley, H. Bowden, G. Brown, N. Buxton,
   J. Callaghan, J. Clynes, F. Cousins, A. Creech-Jones, S. Cripps, A. Crosland,
   R. Crossman, H. Dalton, E. Dell, J. Diamond, Lord Elwyn Jones, D. Ennals,
   M. Foot, T. Fraser, H. Gaitskell, Ld. Gardiner, P. Gordon-Walker, W. Graham,
   A. Greenwood, J. Griffiths, R. Hunter, G. Hall, V. Hartshorn, R. Hattersley,
   D. Healey, A. Henderson, D. Houghton, C. Hughes, Lord Inman, G. Isaacs,
   D. Jay, R. Jenkins, T. Johnston, Lord Jowitt, G. Lansbury, J. Lawson, F. Lee,
   H. Lees-Wood, H. Lever, Earl Listowel, R. Marsh, R. Mason, H. McNeil, R.
   Mellish, B. Millan, J. Morris, H. Morrison, F. Mulley, P. Noel-Baker, S. Orme,
   D. Owen, Lord Pakenham (Longford), Lord Parmoor, Lord Passfield, F.
   Peart, Lord Pethick-Lawrence, R. Prentice, M. Rees, A. Robens, W. Rodgers,
   W. Ross, Lord Sankey, Lord Shackleton, T. Shaw, H. Shawcross, Lord
   Shepherd, E. Shinwell, P. Shore, E. Short, J. Smith, F. Soskice, Vt. Stansgate,
   M. Stewart, R. Stokes, P. Snowden, G. Thomas, J. Thomas, Lord Thomson,
   G. Thomson, G. Tomlinson, C. Trevelyan, E. Varley, J. Westwood,
   T. Williams, H. Wilson, A. Woodburn.
3. Mary Beard, *Women in Power*, 2017, Profile Books, pp. 56–57.
4. See Pamela Brookes, *Women at Westminster,* Peter Davies, 1967 for a good
   analysis of why it was difficult for women to be successful in politics.
5. After 1979 three women were appointed: Baroness Young, Virginia Bottomley,
   and Gillian Shephard.
6. See Krista Cowman, *Women in British Politics*, c1689–1979, Palgrave, 2010.
   Earlier works include Pamela Brookes, *Women at Westminster*, Peter Davies,
   1967; Joni Lovenduski and Pippa Norris, *Women in Politics*, OUP, 1996; Jean

Mann, *Women in Parliament*, Odhams, 1962; Melanie Phillips, *The Divided House*, Sidgwick and Jackson, 1980; and Elizabeth Vallance, *Women in the House*, The Athlone Press, 1979.

7. For example, between 1918 and 1970 just over 1000 women representing all the political parties stood for election compared to 22,000 men. Elections were held in 1918, 1922, 1923, 1924, 1929, 1931, 1935, 1945, 1950, 1951, 1955, 1959, 1964, 1966, 1970, February 1974, October 1974, 1979, 1983, 1987, 1992, and 1997.

8. Only four of them were Labour: Mrs Emmeline Pethick Lawrence (Manchester Rusholme), Mrs Charlotte Despard (Battersea North), Mrs H. M. Mackenzie and Mrs Mary McArthur (Stourbridge).

9. At the time of the election, Constance Markievicz was in Holloway prison on suspicion for conspiring with Germany in the First World War. She had earlier been sentenced to death for her part in the Easter Rising 1916 when she allegedly killed a member of the Dublin police and wounded a British soldier. The sentence was commuted to life in prison because she was a woman. In 1917, Constance Markievicz was released, allowing her to stand for election.

10. Arabella Susan Lawrence (East Ham North), Dorothea Jewson (Norwich) and Margaret Bondfield (Northampton).

11. In 1926, Susan Lawrence (East Ham North) and Margaret Bondfield (Wallsend) were returned to Parliament in by-elections. They were later joined by Ruth Dalton (Bishop Auckland) and Jennie Lee (North Lanark) who also won their seats in a by-election. Jennie Lee, aged 24, became the youngest woman to enter the Commons, a record which remained unbeaten until 1969 when 21-year-old Bernadette Devlin was elected.

12. These were Susan Lawrence, Margaret Bondfield, Ellen Wilkinson, Jennie Lee, Dr Ethel Bentham, Mrs Mary Agnes Hamilton, Lady Cynthia Mosley, Dr Marion Phillips and Edith Picton-Turbervill.

13. By 1939 four other Labour women had joined Wilkinson, winning their seats in by-elections Mrs J. L. Adamson (Dartford), Mrs A. Hardie (Glasgow), Mrs L. Jeger (Holborn and St Pancras), and Edith Summerskill (Fulham West).

14. Mrs J. L. Adamson (Dartford), Alice Bacon (Leeds), Mrs E. M. Braddock (Liverpool), Miss. G. M. Colman (Tyneside), Mrs F. Corbet (Camberwell), Mrs C. S. Ganley (Battersea South), Mrs Barbara Ayrton Gould (Hendon North), Margaret Herbison (Lanark North), Mrs L. Jeger (Holborn and St Pancras), Jennie Lee (Cannock), Mrs J. Mann (Coatbridge and Airdrie), Mrs E. L. Manning (Epping), Mrs L. Middleton (Plymouth, Sutton), Mrs M. W. Nichol (Bradford North), Lady Noel-Buxton (Norwich), Mrs F. Paton (Rushcliffe), Mrs J. L. Adamson (Dartford), Mrs M. Ridealgh (Ilford North), Mrs C. M. Shaw (Ayr), Dr Edith Summerskill (Fulham West) and Mrs E. A. Wills (Birmingham, Duddeston). Barbara Castle entered Parliament for the first time; Ellen Wilkinson was made a Cabinet Minister.

15. In 1950, only fourteen Labour women were elected; in 1951, it dropped further to eleven before increasingly slightly in 1955 to fourteen; in 1959 thirteen; in 1964 eighteen; in 1966 nineteen.

16. In February 1974, it reduced further to nine and fell to a shameful low of seven a few months later. In 1979, when Margaret Thatcher became the first female Prime Minister, eleven Labour women MPs were elected.

17. See Carol Dyhouse, *Feminism and Family in England, 1880–1939*, Blackwell, 1989; Viola Klein, *Britain's Married Women Workers*, Routledge, 1965; Alva Myrdal and Viola Klein, *Women's Two Roles Home and Work*, Routledge, 1956; Elizabeth Wilson, *Only Half-Way to Paradise, Women in Postwar Britain: 1945–1968*, Tavistock, 1980 for broad-ranging surveys of women's lives.

18. See John Bowlby, *Maternal Care and Mental Health*, World Health Organisation, 1951. He alleged that the consequences of maternal deprivation included an inability to form attachments in later life; an inability to feel remorse; delinquency; and problems with cognitive development.

19. For instance, Betty Friedan's, *The Feminine Mystique*, W.W. Norton, 1963; Hannah Gavron's, *The Captive Wife*, Penguin, 1966; and Juliet Mitchell's, *Woman's Estate*, Verso, 1986 argued that women were imprisoned by home life.

20. Martin Pugh, *Women and the Women's Movement in Britain*, 2000, p. 190.

21. Sarah Perrigo 'Women and Change in the Labour Party, 1979–1995', in Joni Lovenduski and Pippa Norris, *Women in Politics*, 1997.

22. I am grateful to Siân James, former MP for Swansea East, VOTE 100 Conference, September 2018 for this information.

23. In 1950, Eirene Lloyd Jones was elected for Flintshire and Dorothy Rees was elected MP for Barry. Rees was defeated in 1951 and White stood down in 1970. Between 1970 and 1984 no female Labour MP represented Wales. In 1984, Anne Clwyd won a seat in the Cynon Valley, the first woman to represent the valleys. She remained the only woman in a Welsh seat until 1997.

24. Elizabeth Vallance, *Women in the House*, The Athlone Press, 1979, p. 48.

25. See James Parker, *Trade Unions and the Political Culture of the British Labour Party, 1931–1940*, PhD thesis, Exeter University, 2017, p. 120 for an excellent in-depth examination of the relationship between trade unions and Labour.

26. In the 1924, Parliament 58% of Labour MPs were trade union sponsored; in 1970, 39% were. Powerful unions like the Miners' Federation (MFGB) and the Amalgamated Engineering Union (AEU) were male-only and only sponsored male candidates, usually those who had worked in their respective industries. But not all unions were male-dominated: the National Union of Distributive Trades and Allied Workers and the Shop Assistants' Union had large female memberships and sponsored women candidates.

27. James Parker, *Trade Unions and the Political Culture of the British Labour Party, 1931–1940*, 2017, p. 146.

28. Martin Pugh, *Women and the Women's Movement in Britain*, Macmillan, 2000, p. 159.

29. Pamela Brookes, *Women at Westminster*, Peter Davies, 1967, p. 153.

30. There was 1 barrister, 1 solicitor, 1 accountant, 1 secretary, 1 student counsellor, 1 childcare officer, 1 careers officer, 2 social workers, 6 lecturers, 9 teachers, 3 trade union officials, and 4 researchers. The other six classified themselves as housewives, yet of these six, four were university graduates. See *Women Candidates May 1979—General Election*, NEC July 25, 1979, HART/12/21.

31. Thanks to Priscilla Pivatto and Emma Peplow at the VOTE 100 conference for these insights.

32. Martin Pugh, *Women and the Women's Movement in Britain*, Macmillan, 2000, p. 190.

33. Edith Summerskill quoted in Elizabeth Vallance *Women in the House*, The Athlone Press, 1979, p. 6.
34. Nancy Astor interview, Woman's Hour 1957. Two of the MPs were Arthur Balfour and Lloyd George.
35. Quoted in Helen Jones, *Women in British Public Life, 1914–1950*, Longman, 2000, p. 139.
36. Leah Manning, *A Life for Education*, Victor Gollanz, 1970, p. 87. Leah Manning was elected in 1929 and lost her seat in 1931.
37. Helen Jones, *Women in British Public Life, 1914–1950*, Longman, 2000, p. 139.
38. Quoted in Melanie Phillips, *The Divided House*, Sidgwick and Jackson, 1980, p. 154.
39. The Cabinet comprises of between 21 and 24 senior members of government, appointed by the Prime Minister. This is the decision-making body of Parliament, featuring publicly recognisable figures, their views sought by the press and other media. Each Minister holds the office of Secretary of State for a particular governmental department and each is held responsible for the actions, successes and failures of their department. All Cabinet members are made Privy Counsellors and can use the title Right Honourable.
40. See Anthony King, 'The Rise of the Career Politician in Britain—And Its Consequences', *British Journal of Political Science*, Vol. 11, No. 3, 1981.
41. Ibid.
42. Trade unions helped shape party policy, particularly in employment law. Both the TUC and the Labour Party shared a physical space at Transport House until the 1950s making it easier for trade unionists and MPs to discuss issues and events.
43. See Anthony King and Nicholas Allen, '"Off with Their Heads": British Prime Ministers and the Power to Dismiss', *British Journal of Political Science*, April 2010.
44. Ibid., p. 250.
45. See Anthony King and Nicholas Allen, '"Off with Their Heads": British Prime Ministers and the Power to Dismiss', *British Journal of Political Science*, April 2010.
46. Michelle K. Ryan and S. Alexander Haslam, 'The Glass Cliff: Exploring the Dynamics Surrounding the Appointment of Women to Precarious Leadership Positions', *Academy of Management Review*, Vol. 32, 2007, pp. 549–572.
47. Ibid., p. 550.
48. Quoted Melanie Phillips, *The Divided House*, Sidgwick and Jackson, 1980, p. 152.
49. David Marquand, *Ramsay MacDonald*, Jonathan Cape, 1977.
50. John Bew, *Citizen Clem*, Riverrun, 2013.
51. Peter Clarke, *The Cripps Version: The Life of Sir Stafford Cripps*, Allen Lane, 2002; Erick Estorick, *Stafford Cripps. A Biography*, The John Day Co, 1949; Colin Arthur Cooke, *The Life of Richard Stafford Cripps*, Hodder and Stoughton, 1957; and Christopher Bryant, *Stafford Cripps: The First Modern Chancellor*, Hodder and Stoughton, 1997.
52. Ben Pimlott, *Hugh Dalton*, Macmillan, 1986.
53. Bernard Donoughue and G. W. Jones, *Herbert Morrison*, Phoenix Press, 2001.

54. For example: John Campbell, *Nye Bevan: A Biography*, Hodder and Stoughton, 1994; Michael Foot, *Aneurin Bevan*, Vol. 1 and 2, Davis-Poynter, 1973; and Nicklaus Thomas-Symonds, *Nye: The Political Life of Aneurin Bevan*, I.B. Tauris, 2016.
55. For example, Alan Bullock, *The Life and Time of Ernest Bevin*, Heinemann, 1960; Peter Walker, *Ernest Bevin*, Routledge, 1981.
56. Andrew Adonis and Keith Thomas, *Roy Jenkins: A Retrospective*, OUP, 2004; John Campbell, *Roy Jenkins*, Vintage, 2015.
57. Kenneth O. Morgan, *Michael Foot: A Life*, Harper Perennial, 2008; Mervyn Jones, *Michael Foot*, Victor Gollanz, 1994.
58. For example, Vicky Randall, *Women in Politics*, Macmillan, 1987.
59. For example, Beatrix Campbell and Anna Coote, *Sweet Freedom: The Struggle for Women's Liberation*, Blackwell, 1987.
60. For example, Maggie Andrews, *The Acceptable Face of Feminism: The Women's Institute as a Social Movement*, Lawrence and Wishart, 1997.
61. For example, Jill Liddington, *The Long Road to Greenham: Feminism and Anti-Militarism in Britain Since 1820*, Virago, 1989.
62. Pamela Graves, *Labour Women*, CUP, 1994.
63. June Hannam and Karen Hunt, *Socialist Women*, Routledge, 2002.
64. Pamela Brookes, *Women at Westminster*, Peter Davies, 1967.
65. Krista Cowman, *Women in British Politics, c.1689–1979*, Palgrave, 2010.
66. Melville Currell, *Political Woman*, Croom Helm, 1974.
67. Joni Lovenduski and Pippa Norris, *Women in Politics*, OUP, 1996.
68. Jean Mann, *Women in Parliament*, Oldhams Press, 1962.
69. Melanie Phillips, *The Divided House*, Sidgwick and Jackson, 1980.
70. Elizabeth Vallance, *Women in the House*, The Athlone Press, 1979.
71. Iain Dale's and Jacqui Smith's invaluable *The Honorable Ladies, Profiles of Women MPs 1918–1996*, Biteback, 2018.
72. Rachel Reeves, *Women of Westminster: The MPs Who Changed Politics*, I.B. Tauris, 2019.
73. Patricia Hollis, *Jennie Lee: A Life*, OUP, 1997.
74. Rachel Reeves, *Alice in Wonderland: The Political Life of Alice Bacon*, I.B. Tauris, 2017.
75. Betty D. Vernon, *Ellen Wilkinson*, Law Book of Australasia, 1982; Paula Bartley, *Ellen Wilkinson: From Red Suffragist to Government Minister*, Pluto, 2014; Matt Perry, *Red Ellen, Wilkinson*, MUP, 2014; Laura Beers, *Red Ellen*, Yale University Press, 2016.
76. Anne Perkins, *Red Queen: The Authorized Biography of Barbara Castle*, 2003; Lisa Martineau *Barbara Castle: Politics and Power*, Macmillan, 2000.
77. Mary Hamilton, *Margaret Bondfield*, Leonard Parsons, 1924.
78. Tony Judge, *Margaret Bondfield*, Athlone Press, 2018.
79. Marion Miliband, 'Margaret Bondfield', *Dictionary of Labour Biography*, Vol. 11, 1974.
80. Margaret Bondfield, *A Life's Work*, Hutchinsons, 1948.
81. Harold Nicolson, 'Labour Leader', *Observer*, December 25, 1949.
82. Helen Lockwood to Margaret Bondfield, August 13, 1950. Margaret Bondfield papers, Vassar College, Box 2, Folder 19.
83. Lockwood to Murphy, April 26, 1954, Bondfield papers, Vassar College, Box 2, Folder 23.

84. Lockwood to Victor Gollanncz, August 25, 1954, Bondfield papers, Vassar College, Box 2, Folder 23.
85. Cameron Hazlehurst and Sally Whitehead with Christine Woodland, *A Guide to the Papers of British Cabinet Ministers, 1900–1964*, CUP, 1996, pp. 57–58.
86. Shirley Williams, *Climbing the Bookshelves*, Virago, 2009.
87. Shirley Williams, *Politics Is for People*, Penguin, 1981.
88. Shirley Williams, *God and Caesar: Personal Reflections on Politics and Religion*, Continuum, 2003.
89. *Shirley Williams, The Biography*, Biteback, 2013.
90. *Making the Difference*, Biteback, 2010.

CHAPTER 2

A Woman in a Man's World: Margaret Bondfield's Early Career, 1873–1929

Margaret Bondfield was just over 152 cm (5ft) tall with 'merry brown eyes and bright red cheeks', a great sense of humour and an infectious laugh (Fig. 2.1).[1] This tiny woman achieved a number of firsts in her lifetime: she was the first woman to chair the Trades Union Congress, the first woman to hold a ministerial post and the first woman to be a Cabinet Minister. These were impressive achievements particularly from someone from her background. Margaret was born on March 17, 1873, in her parents' cottage in Chard, Somerset, the tenth of eleven children. Her father William had started work at the age of 8 as a bobbin boy and had worked himself up to be foreman in the local lace factory until he was made redundant; her mother Anne took care of the house, the cooking, the garden and the many children. When Margaret was about six years old, she was sent away to her grandmother's because her newborn sister was not well and her mother found it too stressful to look after young Margaret as well as her sickly baby. After two years away from home, Margaret fell ill and lost her memory, a nervous disorder which would often come back to affect her at times of stress. In a later interview on BBC radio, Margaret maintained that her early experience taught her many things, but chiefly 'to play the game and take hard knocks without whining'.[2]

Christianity played a large part in Margaret's political development. As Congregationalists her parents belonged to a non-Conformist religion with roots set as firmly in the temporal world as in the afterlife. Theirs was a serious, socially committed religion which attracted leading Labour Party figures such as Keir Hardie.[3] For them, religion was not Marx's 'opiate of the people' but a remedy which gave them courage to help cure social ills. For Congregationalists, Christianity was as much about caring for the underprivileged, for prisoners, for widows and orphans as it was about spirituality, mysticism and praying. 'We could not think religion' Margaret said 'yet not think of the needs of the poor'.[4] All her life Margaret Bondfield remained deeply religious, taking daily communion when possible and attending church

© The Author(s) 2019
P. Bartley, *Labour Women in Power*,
https://doi.org/10.1007/978-3-030-14288-9_2

regularly. Her diaries speak of her need to 'press forward towards the spiritual life' which was 'being constantly threatened by petty sins, vices – sloth, pride, jealousy and anger constantly tripping me up'.[5] She prayed to be good and do good. However, she was often plagued by self-doubt and tended to be far too critical of her perceived inadequacies. Sometimes her 'prayers became vain repetitions until it seemed a most senseless chattering', and she became despondent.[6] She asked God to 'make me steadfast lest from inconstancy or weariness I give up the work I have begun'.[7] Despite her wobbles, her faith sustained and fired her, affording a framework for her political convictions as well as for her spirituality. Throughout her life, there would always be a strong theological relationship with her socialism.

In addition, Brian Harrison argues, religion provided young Margaret a gateway to a different world and presented her with the chance to rise above her class and gender by giving her 'the ability to read, write, speak and organise, the self-discipline to make the most of opportunity – and at the same time impelled her towards the welfare reforms'.[8] Moreover, its spiritual authority lay in the congregation rather than in the priesthood, making it easier for women to take on public roles.[9] On December 14, 1883, the ten-year-old Margaret made her speaking debut at the Congregational Church annual Christmas tea.[10] From then on, she performed each year in the Christmas concerts, learning all the time to enunciate her words, modify her regional accent and speak 'Standard English', breaking through what has been termed the 'cut-glass ceiling'.

On August 23, 1886, just before her 13th birthday, Margaret Bondfield was appointed pupil teacher at Chard Boys' School and put in charge of 42 'young imps'[11] who were often rowdy and unmanageable. It was not a job she enjoyed, even though the school inspectors thought her a competent teacher, remarking that 'considering the crowded state of the room and the large number of half-timers, the order is good. With the exception of some of the reading, the Elementary subjects are quite satisfactory and the two class subjects are quite good'.[12]

A Young Shop Assistant

When she reached 14, Margaret moved to Hove to work in a quieter and altogether different environment in Mrs White's drapery store. Here, as an apprentice, she learned how to sew and smock 'lovely silks for babies' frocks'. Fortunately for Margaret, Mrs White was a friend of the family and she was well treated in a business where exploitative practices were commonplace. However, when Mrs White retired early Margaret, now aged 17, was without work. Her next job gave her an unpleasant shock: she was appointed to the outfitting department at Hetherington's, a large Brighton store where she stayed for three and a half years, learning window dressing, stock-keeping and selling techniques. Margaret had been accustomed to the friendly intimate atmosphere at Mrs White's and found the large impersonal space of Hetherington's a bleak contrast.[13]

It was a harsh existence. For £15 a year, Margaret was required to work from early in the morning until 10 p.m. on weekdays and until the last few minutes before midnight on Saturdays. Margaret's life took a better turn when she met Louisa Martindale at the local Congregationalist church which they both attended. Martindale was a Liberal, a lifelong suffragist and campaigner for better conditions for shop workers. She took a number of these underprivileged young women under her wing, one of whom was Margaret Bondfield. Louisa's daughter Hilda described Margaret as an 'eager, attractive and vividly alive girl of sixteen' who 'needed sympathy, and was ready to talk'.[14] Here, Margaret began her political journey, mesmerised by the charm and graciousness of her new friend, later saying that Louisa Martindale was a 'most vivid influence in my life, the first woman of broad culture I had met. She seemed to recognise me, and make me recognise myself, as a person of independent thought and action'.[15] Mrs Martindale lent her protégé books and encouraged her to read about social issues, all of which prepared Margaret 'to take my proper place in the Labour Movement'.[16]

A few years later, Margaret moved to London. She nearly starved trying to find a job. There was no social security, no unemployment benefit, no housing allowance for her to claim, and once her savings were spent, she only had the workhouse, domestic service or prostitution as a way out of her poverty trap. Margaret remembered 'tramping up and down the streets of London and going into every place that seemed a likely place to hire labour'.[17] One day she walked the entire length of Oxford Street going into every shop in the hope of a vacancy. Finally, she found work in a little shop of the North End Road before moving to a department store in Westbourne Grove. She later confessed that her first months in the 'great City searching for work carry the shadow of a nightmare'.[18]

Once again her church helped. The Pastor at the Congregational Church where she worshipped believed that the City of God on earth was more likely to be built by Socialists than by Liberals or Tories. He encouraged Margaret to join the Ideal Club, a club which aimed to bridge class barriers, and which had G. B. Shaw, Beatrice and Sidney Webb, Gertrude Tuckwell, Sir Charles and Lady Dilke and Margaret MacDonald, Ramsay MacDonald's wife, as members. Here, the young shop worker experienced 'such rich and varied fare to feed the mind ... where I had the chance to listen to conversation, brilliant, profound and sometimes silly, about social and political questions of the day'.[19] Margaret began reading about 'children in mines, in mills, in bakers, where sometimes the children employed slept in the oven'[20]; she deepened her religious convictions by reading biographies of Julian of Norwich, Catherine of Siena, the Quaker saints, and Josephine Butler— all the time she was reinforcing the religious foundations of her socialism. Margaret joined the Social Democratic Federation, a Marxist organisation, but quickly tired of its emphasis on 'bloody class war' and moved over to the recently formed Independent Labour Party (ILP) and the Fabian Society. Her socialism, as with so many Labour leaders, 'owed more to Methodism than Marxism'.[21]

Margaret's contacts at the Ideal Club found her work. Margaret MacDonald ran the Women's Industrial Council (WIC), an organisation which campaigned against the poor wages and conditions of women workers. In 1896, Margaret was employed by the WIC to carry out a two-year investigation into the pay and conditions of shop workers. She worked undercover, changed her name to Grace Dare—the names of her grandmother and great-grandmother—and spent her two years investigating London shops. Her articles published in the union journal *The Shop Assistant* describe in graphic detail the awful meanness and exploitation of shop assistants. They describe how shop work was characterised by low pay, long hours and poor conditions and how employees became locked into a circle of poverty and deprivation. Shop assistants suffered petty tyrannical regimes: they were fined for giving the wrong change, breaking goods, chatting with colleagues, sitting down, coming late to work, making a noise, being cheeky to a superior, using bad language, bringing matches or newspapers to the premises, letting a customer leave without a purchase and even addressing a customer as Miss instead of Mrs. One firm had 176 rules, including one which covered 'any mistake not before mentioned'.[22]

Shop assistants who worked in large department stores were expected to 'live-in' with the cost of accommodation and food deducted from their meagre wage. Margaret, along with over 60% of shop workers, experienced being under her employer's lock and key, knew what it was like not go out when she wished, 'locked up in a peculiar segregated life'.[23] She described how this led to gross mistreatment as employers controlled all aspects of their assistants' lives: their work, their free-time and even their sleep. The living-in system, Bondfield insisted, not only robbed the assistant of independence, it was humiliating and degrading as assistants had to obey petty house rules even after the shop was closed: to go to bed at a time dictated by the employer, to put out candle-lights at 11 p.m., not to stay out overnight without permission, etc. The living-in system, she argued, had many other disadvantages. Firstly, assistants frequently lived many miles from home which meant that if they no longer worked at the shop they were on the streets, often unable to find the fare to return home.[24] Secondly, sleeping arrangements were 'altogether inadequate'.[25] Shop workers commonly slept in dormitories which were 'dingy, ill-ventilated, sparsely furnished, cold in winter, intolerably hot in summer, unbearably stuffy at all times'.[26] In many cases, twenty or twenty-five assistants slept 'in a single room of the barest and most barrack-like kind'.[27] All too often 'the bedrooms are like barns, with water trickling down the walls … and we cannot sleep for the cold'.[28] Strangers shared double beds; in at least one establishment sheets were only changed every three months. Many prohibited employees making their room a little more homely: no pictures, photos were allowed to 'disfigure the walls',[29] no flowers were allowed to be placed in water glasses or bottles. All clothes and personal property had to be kept in a trunk underneath the bed or else be confiscated. Thirdly, washing facilities were inadequate. Few shops had bathrooms and assistants were expected to wash themselves in a small hand basin in front of other girls. Margaret knew how difficult it was to keep clean: in one of her jobs, she was forced to use the public baths which were only open after work once a week and she had to make 'a dash from the shop and run at top speed for about ¾ of a mile. We could then reach the baths in time to have exactly a quarter of an hour to undress, bath and dress again, before the attendant had to turn us out'.[30]

Finally, Margaret reported, food was generally monotonous, unappetising and 'the nourishment is not sufficient for a growing youth or girl doing a long day's work.[31] One London store provided the same weekly menu for years—Monday: hot roast mutton, potatoes; Tuesday: Cold roast beef, potatoes, boiled pudding; Wednesday: stew; Thursday: cold salt beef, potatoes; Friday: hot roast beef, potatoes, boiled pudding; Saturday: cold roast beef, potatoes, bread and butter pudding'. All too often, 'a girl found on going down to breakfast in the morning that the menu was "doorsteps and scrape". This translated as 'bread and butter and tea. … There was nothing stimulating in this, so the assistant was obliged to go out and buy an egg or a rasher of bacon. Then for dinner there was badly-cooked vegetables and meat drowned in "sloshy" gravy. For tea, bread and butter again turned up, probably the old friend from the breakfast table'.[32] Sometimes the food was inedible, so putrid and rotten that she could not touch it.[33] Not surprisingly shop assistants spent their meagre wage on food to supplement their diet.[34]

Margaret's study of shop assistants brought her into close working contact with people well outside her social sphere like Emilia Dilke, a leading figure in the WTUL and her husband Sir Charles, a radical Liberal MP. It was Margaret's exposure to shop working conditions which provided the material for Charles Dilke's 1889 Shop Bill, a Royal Commission and other changes in the law.[35] Over time she helped abolish the living-in system and the humiliating practice of fines and deductions; she campaigned for the payment of fair wages, adequate time for meals and a reduction in the hours of labour.[36] Yet however much she liked the Dilkes, her experiences turned her into an 'ardent socialist', rather than a Liberal.[37]

JOINING A TRADE UNION

One evening as she walked along the street eating fish and chips from a newspaper—the food provided at her place of work was inadequate—she read an advert for a meeting of the National Union of Shop Assistants, Warehousemen and Clerks (NAUSAW&C), a trade union founded in 1891 and generally known as the Shop Assistants Union.[38] Margaret, who was working around 76 hours a week for a wage of £1 a month, went to the meeting, joined the union and began organising a branch in her shop. This was a pivotal moment in her life, one that would change it dramatically. She later commented that it was 'the most important step in my career, because practically every other step was almost consequential. My Union gave me the chance to learn about economic theories; how to work for reforms by education, and through political parties. ... It opened doors of knowledge which no University could teach'.[39] In 1898, now aged 25, she was appointed assistant secretary to the Shop Assistants Union with an enormous pay increase—a wage of £2 a week. For ten years, she worked unceasingly to improve the wages and conditions of shop workers, conquering her 'dislike of canvassing in shops' to recruit new members.[40] Visiting a shop during opening hours was a risky business as it might mean instant dismissal for the shop assistant and 'impotent fury' by the shop owners towards Margaret. She drew strength from her religion as 'everyday Trade Union work took on a deeper significance. The doing of ordinary everyday things became lit up with that inner light of the Spirit which gave one strength and effectiveness; strength to meet defeat with a smile; ... to be willing to do one's best without thought of reward'.[41] In her view, the love of God was a 'principle of action', demanding that 'we do something, not merely talk or feel sympathetic'.[42]

Women were reluctant to join unions for reasons other than fear of dismissal. For one thing, trade unions were all too often male-only and made women feel unwelcome: in 1921, 60% still refused to allow women to join. Ben Tillett, founder of the dockers' union, maintained that women would undercut male wages by working for lower wages. He particularly disapproved of married women working, arguing that they threatened the peace of married life. It was therefore not surprising that Margaret was often treated with 'suspicion and hostility' by male union representatives.[43] Indeed, Margaret found that in a great many trades women were paid such 'disgracefully low wages' that they could not afford to pay the high union fees.[44] It was even difficult to collect union dues from women as large numbers worked in shops, small workshops or domestic service, places where the employer was almost always in close proximity. A number of women shop workers believed that belonging to a trade union was 'beneath their dignity'.[45] Some saw themselves as superior to other workers because they wore smart clothes, worked in smart establishments and met smart shoppers. These were 'white-blouse' workers who preferred to be drawn into a world in which gentility and respectability took the place of a decent wage. Margaret called them 'paltry artificial dolls' who were 'empty headed, selfish, boastful, with no room in their miserable, shrivelled-up little souls for one thought of the toiling millions'.[46] Predictably Margaret Bondfield found it hard to recruit women to her union: at a meeting held in the home of Charlotte Despard no one turned up; at another held at the Albert Hall only a dozen or so were present at the start of the meeting and only gradually did the audience reach a respectable number.[47] Nonetheless, Margaret persisted in her recruitment drive, increasing union membership from 3000 in 1898 to 7500 in 1900. By the time she left the Shop Assistants' Union in 1908 membership had increased to 20,000, largely because she had persuaded assistants that the Union was 'doing its best to improve the conditions of the workers by abolishing fines, references, and the system of living in, which is held to be so degrading to the independence and freedom of the workers'.[48]

Margaret's union work was a turning point in her life for it gave her the training she needed to take a leading political role and it gave her a nation-wide profile too. In 1899, the 26-year-old Margaret attended her first TUC conference. She was the only female delegate; the other 382 were men. To her surprise, she was asked to move a vote of thanks to the foreign delegates present and 'before a half-a-dozen sentences were uttered curiosity was changed into close attention and admiration'.[49] Her thank you speech made such an impact that she was asked to support a resolution calling for the setting up of a Labour Representation Committee (LRC): the leaders of trade unions were well aware they needed their own representatives in Parliament to make life better for the working class. Miss. Bondfield did so 'with great conviction', concluding her speech 'on the necessity for further labour representation in the House of Commons' to make sure that laws were passed which were favourable to working people. Margaret Bondfield's talk was considered the 'feature of the day and the discovery of the day. ... She is only a girl in years, and as she stood up amongst the bronzed, hard-handed workmen, her slight girlish figure, clad in a simple grey frock, made her look younger and even more girlish than she is. But her voice, as clear as it was unostentatious, was heard distinctly in every part of the hall ... There was no trace either of nervousness or conceit. It was a striking picture, this slip of a girl, standing out and lecturing 300 or more men'.[50] She was thought to be a natural orator and emerged from the conference a national figure; she had come a long way from her early days embroidering children's smocks. In addition, her speech convinced the TUC to take action. In February 1900, the LRC was set up to sponsor MPs who would promote working-class interests in Parliament[51]; in 1906, the LRC morphed into the Labour Party.

Margaret Bondfield felt comfortable in the male-dominated union world but she was aware that many male trade unionists were suspicious and hostile towards women and that in turn most women found the masculine nature of trade unionism disagreeable. She became active in the Women's Trade Union League (WTUL), originally founded in 1874 to promote trade unionism among women.[52] The WTUL recruited women who were previously unorganised: rope-makers, confectioners, purse and pocket makers, artificial flower makers, feather-dressers, shawl-makers, brick-makers, paper-makers, box-makers, bag-makers, glass-workers, tobacco workers, jam and pickle workers, rag-pickers, small metal workers, munition workers, typists, domestic servants and shop assistants.[53] Emilia Dilke was a leading activist and once again Margaret found herself working with the Dilkes.

In 1906, Margaret Bondfield helped Mary Macarthur set up the National Federation of Women Workers (NFWW), a women's union which combined the smaller unions under one roof and offered low subscription rates and financial backing for strikes. The Federation, it is clear, 'provided vital publicity for women's trade unionism and forced men – politicians, civil servants, union leaders and members – to take notice of it'.[54] The NFWW emerged at a time of great industrial, social and political unrest: rebellion in Ireland, an intransigent House of Lords, the women's suffrage movement and increased strike action, particularly by unskilled workers. Undoubtedly, the NFWW and Bondfield contributed to this unrest by supporting women who took strike action. For example, on March 1906 between four and five hundred girls stopped work at a metal-box firm, Betts and Company factory, City road, London because their employers cut their piecework rates by more than half: women in the embossing department had their rates reduced from 5d a thousand to 2d a thousand.[55] Their case was taken up by Margaret Bondfield and Gertrude Tuckwell, 'which after prolonged negotiations with the Management, was settled on the girls' own terms'.[56]

In October 1908, just a few months after her 35th birthday, Margaret Bondfield resigned from her job in the Shop Assistants Union. She had been an active member for fourteen years and a paid official for ten 'slogging years'.[57] She left because she felt 'drained of vitality and realised the need for a complete change'[58] and 'because she felt the call of a wider sphere'.[59] It was, she felt, both 'a grief and deliverance'.[60] In fact, her departure coincided with one of her recurrent breakdowns. There was little time to recover as Margaret was 'immediately overwhelmed' by requests as a lecturer and soon became involved 'in the big formative currents that were making and changing opinion'.[61] From 1908 to 1912, she earned a living speaking at meetings organised by the ILP, the WTUL, the NFWW, the WIC and the Women's Labour League. Margaret Bondfield worked hard in the NFWW's fight to obtain a minimum wage, speaking at meetings all around the country and working with the Anti-Sweating League to put pressure on the Liberal Government to reform the law. They had a small but significant success. In 1909, the Trades Board Act set up four boards empowered to fix minimum wages in chain making, lace making, paper box making and bespoke tailoring. However, a minimum wage for all workers was a long way off.

In 1910, the WIC employed Margaret to research married women's work in the Yorkshire textile mills. Here, she reported cases of child abuse: of girls who had children by their brothers and of children sold into prostitution. In 1912, she found work at the Women's Co-operative League, helping its investigation into maternity care which led to the publication of *Maternity: Letters from Working Women Collected by the Women's Co-operative Guild*, 1915, a moving volume of letters outlining the experiences of working women. 'The life stories', she recalled in later years, 'of 400 women were given in their own words … Of these 400 women, 26 were childless, and 26 did not give definite figures; the remaining 348 had 1396 live children, 83 still births and 218 miscarriages. In an extreme case we find a woman married at 19, having 11 children and 2 miscarriages in 20 years'.[62] The mortality rates were shocking and so too was the health of those who survived: 'miserable draggle-tailed anaemic children with defective teeth, defective eyesight'. Margaret Bondfield railed against the high level of infant mortality among the working class which stood at 67.67 per thousand. 'Did it occur' she cried 'to the mother weeping over her babe that it might have been a singer, a poet or a great statesman? Dead, because of conditions which were alterable; dead, because of insanitary dwellings and other causes. Had it ever occurred to them it was communal murder, it was the slaughter of the innocents'.[63] The inside knowledge she obtained 'of the appalling conditions in the homes of women wage-earners' she claimed 'turned me into an ardent socialist'.[64]

Towards the Vote

In 1906, the LRC won 29 seats in Parliament and changed its name to the Labour Party. It was not enough to make a difference as its MPs were overwhelmed by 397 Liberals, 156 Conservatives and 83 Irish Nationalists. Obviously, the newly created Labour Party needed more voters to vote for it. However, the Labour Party faced a problem as only roughly 40% of working-class men could vote; no women were enfranchised. Women's suffrage organisations were set up to campaign for votes for women. The two main ones were the nineteenth-century National Union of Women's Suffrage Societies headed by Millicent Fawcett and the Women's Social and Political Union founded in 1903 by Emmeline Pankhurst. Margaret Bondfield did not agree with either group. Her experience as a shop assistant and union organiser compelled her to take up the cause of adult suffrage—that is votes for all people, men and women, over the age of 21—rather than the women's suffrage cause which only campaigned for the vote on the same terms as men, a vote which excluded about 40% of the male population. 'There are' Bondfield told one reporter 'about 250,000 women connected with the Union, very few of whom would get a vote without adult suffrage'.[65] She insisted that she had never been 'able to approach the question from the standpoint of *women's rights*' since she was opposed to 'the idea of a limited franchise on a property basis, because it seemed to me that it was tipping the scales against the workers by strengthening the political power of the propertied classes'.[66] In her view, votes for women on the same terms as men was an elitist measure which would be detrimental to the Labour Party because it would increase the political power of the propertied class by giving the vote to middle-class women. It was obvious, Bondfield insisted, that the lives of working women were hardly likely to be remedied by a franchise from which they would be still excluded. For her 'the real antagonisms are not those of sex but of class'.[67]

Margaret Bondfield was committed to gender equality but she wanted gender equality for her class: she was in effect a socialist feminist, conscious of the fact that neither male nor female shop assistants, the people she represented, had or would gain the vote because the living-in system meant they did not qualify as a rate-payer or householder. Shop workers, she told her audience, were known to be 'a vote-less class, the men as well the women – political nonentities'.[68] And if women gained the vote on the same terms as men, both male and female shop workers would remain disenfranchised. Bondfield wanted to 'sweep away the existing franchise and substitute one man one vote, one woman one vote, on a short residential qualification'.[69]

Margaret Bondfield joined and led a number of adult suffrage societies. In the early years of the twentieth century, she joined the People's Federation Society founded by Charles Dilke to campaign for adult suffrage; in 1905, she helped found the Adult Suffrage Society and later became its President; in 1916, Bondfield along with George Lansbury and Mary Macarthur set up a new National Council for Adult Suffrage; and she joined the People's Suffrage Federation which had as its motto 'One Man One Vote; One Woman One Vote'. In 1918, the Representation of the People Act gave the vote to women over the age of 30; under the Qualification of Women Act 1918, women over 21 were eligible to be elected MPs. Margaret thought the first Act a 'mean and inadequate little Bill'[70] and campaigned for equal franchise. The idea that a woman could become an MP at 21 but could not vote was clearly ridiculous.

In 1908, all too aware that the Labour Party was overwhelmingly male in its membership and masculine in its outlook, Bondfield helped Margaret

MacDonald set up the Women's Labour League, a pressure group affiliated to the Labour Party which encouraged women to take part in politics. When Margaret MacDonald died, Margaret Bondfield took over as Secretary of the Women's Labour League, only to be replaced by Marion Phillips[71] when she herself became ill. In August 1912, Bondfield, her friend Maud Ward[72] and Mary Macarthur resigned from the Women's Labour League because they found Marion Phillips much too abrasive and difficult. Bondfield later claimed that for the first time in her life she had met someone with whom she could not work.

Gradually, over the years Margaret had carefully built up significant political experience. In 1910, she stood for election on the London County Council but then in 1911 she was appointed organising secretary for the WLL on the death of Margaret MacDonald. It was a job too much. In a tour of Lancashire, she collapsed in the middle of a speech and completely broke down. Her mind went completely blank, a repeat of her recurring illness. It was, she cried, a 'terrible experience. I felt lost'. She was taken home and ordered complete rest by her doctor. She spent some time being looked after by a friend and obeying her doctor's orders 'to live like a cabbage, not to read, or write, or talk'. For the first few months, she 'was haunted with the sense of deserting my post; worrying about how the work was going on – a kind of inflated egotism, which makes one feel indispensable, but at the end of two months I had gone to the other extreme, I was not thinking or caring much about anything'.[73] In April 1912, she returned to London but at one of her first meetings she felt 'tired and excited before. Tired and depressed after'.[74] She asked for another leave of absence and returned to the country to recuperate completely.

Two years earlier Margaret Bondfield had enjoyed her first speaking tour of the USA, accompanied by Maud Ward with whom she shared a house in Hampstead. In a later radio broadcast, she spoke of seeing chain gangs making roads in Georgia, witnessing a strike at Hart, Schaffner and Marx in Chicago, a campaign to protect immigrants by 'my very dear friend Jane Addams'[75] and a demonstration in support of a strike of textile workers.[76] She made friends with a number of leading trade unionists, notably Rose Schneiderman.[77] Margaret grew to love America, a country where she found none of the class-based patronising attitudes that she experienced back home. Whereas in Britain her spinsterhood was pitied, in America it seemed more acceptable for women to remain single, have close female friends and be active politically. Her talks attracted—largely female—audiences in their thousands and she became quite a celebrity, later meeting Eleanor Roosevelt, Frances Perkins[78] and other luminaries of the Democratic Party

THE FIRST WORLD WAR, 1914–1918

On August 4, 1914, Britain declared war on Germany. It was a moral shock to Margaret Bondfield, coming 'suddenly, unexpectedly, as a surprise'.[79] In Bondfield's view, the war was unjustifiable, a 'negation of Christianity'.[80]

Most women, she believed, hated war or any other 'method of destroying human life; they are interested in the preservation and nurture of human life, not its destruction'.[81] She had taken a pacifist position during the Boer Wars and was 'still more of a pacifist at this date'.[82] In her view, one of the great scandals of the war was 'the attitude of mind which regarded human life as the cheapest thing to expend. ... "To militarise" the worker meant to turn him into unskilled cannon fodder'.[83]

Bondfield joined leading Labour politicians such as Keir Hardie and Ramsay MacDonald in speaking out against the war. She opposed conscription and helped set up the Women's Peace Crusade, a socialist and feminist organisation which campaigned across the UK to stop the war. Now a leading pacifist she was invited to an International Conference of Women in The Hague organised by a group of Dutch women who 'felt strongly that at a time when there is so much hatred among nations, we women must show that we can retain our solidarity and that we are able to maintain a mutual friendship'.[84] However, the government refused to let Bondfield travel and she was left marooned at Tilbury Docks. Undeterred, she travelled to Berne Switzerland later in the month for a secret international conference of Socialist and Labour women organised by the German revolutionary, Clara Zetkin.[85] Secrecy was essential because it was feared the women might once more be forbidden to travel. Four British delegates, including Margaret Bondfield joined 24 other women representing Germany, France, Russia, Poland, Holland, Switzerland and Italy.[86] Delegates called for a speedy end to the war, urged that no humiliating conditions be imposed on defeated nations, and upheld the rights of nationalities to self-determination.[87] The British delegates also proposed that 'the menace of the armament interests and their huge international organisation' be curtailed.[88] Margaret Bondfield made a courageous decision to make her pacifism public since most people in Britain were swept away by jingoistic patriotism. When she spoke at a woman's peace demonstration in Lancashire, she 'could scarcely be heard owing to the opposition, the jeering, and the singing of patriotic songs. Some sods were thrown, and the meeting had to close'.[89]

During the war, Margaret was a wartime organising secretary for the NFWW, and then in 1918 became Chief Assistant Secretary.[90] The war created a new problem for trade unionists. In the first few months, women were made redundant in a wide range of industries but particularly in the cotton and textile industries and the clothing trade. Queen Mary invited a number of labour organisations to join her to alleviate this. On August 19, 1914, the Queen's Employment Advisory Committee on Women's Employment was formed: Mary Macarthur, Susan Lawrence, Marion Phillips and Margaret Bondfield all agreed to act on its Advisory Committee. It was the first-ever all-woman committee to be endorsed by the Cabinet. The Advisory Committee's mission was to find alternative employment for women made redundant by war.[91] Queen Mary's Workshops were set up to engage women, mostly from the textile trade and the 'distressed sections of the community'.

Bondfield refused to allow workers to be badly treated and she became involved in 'a great fight ...on behalf of the women employed in the Queen's workrooms. They are asking for a rise of a half-penny an hour. At present the rate of pay is 3d an hour, with a maximum of 10s a week. Everyone will admit this was only a bare subsistence rate before the rise in prices; now it is starvation pure and simple'.[92] An unlikely bond sprang up between Queen Mary and Margaret Bondfield: years later the Queen would send telegrams commiserating with Margaret on the death of her sister,[93] or on the loss of her parliamentary seat or on an accident or illness that had befallen her. The Queen even invited her to the King's Silver Jubilee.

By early 1915, there was a shortage of labour as more and more men joined the armed forces. In March, the Board of Trade asked women to register at the Labour Exchange, a request which Bondfield considered to be ill-considered because it 'threatened to flood the labour market with volunteers willing to take employment on any terms'.[94] War offered working-class women an alternative to the grossly exploitative job of domestic service or sweated labour. Women went into engineering, agriculture, transport and government offices. They replaced men as bus drivers, window cleaners, chimney sweeps, coal deliverers, electricians and fire-fighters. The number of female bus conductors rose from half a dozen to about 2500 during the war. Munitions showed the biggest increase in female labour: in 1914, the Woolwich Arsenal employed 125 women; by 1917, the number increased to over 25,000. However, the wages paid to most women, from munition workers to chimney sweeps, were far lower than those paid to men. Margaret Bondfield was at the forefront of the campaign to protect these new women workers from being underpaid and from working in poor conditions. In order to safeguard them, she and other trade unionists put forward five basic proposals: that all women registering for war service join a union; that women receive equal pay for equal work; that no woman be employed on less than a living wage; that women be given suitable training; and that after the war men should get their jobs back. These proposals were followed by a vigorous campaign to enrol women into the unions, to secure equal pay for those taking the jobs of men at the front and a living wage for all employed women. In 1915, they reached an agreement with the Amalgamated Society of Engineers—which would not allow women to be members of the union—for a £1 a week minimum wage for women who had replaced men.

It was tough fighting for workers' rights in wartime, particularly when the government claimed that war made it necessary to erode all manner of rights. In 1915, a Munitions of War Act made it a penal offence for workers to leave their job without the consent of their employer. It also forbade strikes and lockouts. Bondfield 'protested against the tyrannical way in which the Munitions Act was being worked and instanced cases where the liberty and civil rights of the working people were being filched'.[95] In a speech to the 1916 Labour Party Conference, Bondfield moved a resolution demanding a 'drastic revision of the Munitions Act with a view to preventing the pretext of war being used for the greater coercion and subjection of Labour; to that end the Conference demands the restoration of individual right of contract, and the abolition of the system of leaving certificates'.[96] She saw that the excuse of war was being 'used for many reactionary purpose for the curtailment of the freedom of speech and writing, for the growth of child labour, for the rendering null and void of labour protective laws, for the spreading of industrial compulsion'[97] As a result of Bondfield and the work of the NFWW, a basic wage for munition workers was secured, even though equal pay was a long way off. In 1919, with the war safely over, the Munitions Act was repealed.

In October 1917, the Bolsheviks seized power and attempted to create a socialist state in Russia. Bondfield, like many others on the left, initially welcomed the Russian Revolution. In May 1920 as civil war raged, she visited the country as part of a Labour delegation[98] appointed to inquire into the economic and social conditions under the Soviet regime. Margaret kept a diary, detailing every visit, and every interview. During her, trip she met many of the revolutionary celebrities such as Lenin, Kamenev, Kropotkin and Inessa Armand, visited farms, schools, electricity works, tool shops and aeroplane factories as well as the ballet and opera. On May 26, she spent the morning with Kamenev discussing the structure, composition and function of the Soviet government; in the afternoon, she met Lenin at the Kremlin. Bondfield thought Lenin 'was very frank—was quite prepared to recognise that they had made mistakes ... No one could possibly accuse Lenin of wishing to mislead ... as to the nature of his Government, or the ruthlessness of his policy in dealing with the opposition'.[99] There were no freedoms 'either of Press or speech for the enemies of the Revolution'.[100] Bondfield was impressed when she attended a lecture by Angelica Balabanoff on the aims and ideals of the Communist Party. She thought it 'was a wonderful experience to see that audience of young and old faces, young boys and girls from fifteen or sixteen years to grizzled haired old men, with quite a large sprinkling of soldiers, who listed with rapt attention'.[101] However, this was idealistic propaganda. When Bondfield spoke with some cooperative workers, they revealed the terrible sufferings of the previous winter where people had no overcoats when the temperature plummeted; feet and fingers were frozen off.[102] On a visit to a village school, she was told that there were no books, no pencils, no pens or ink. Lavatories were primitive, just earth closets with no flush or drain and no washing facilities. She learned that 8500 people had been shot for opposing the regime. When she visited St Petersburg, now newly named Petrograd, she was struck by the clean streets which had an 'air of lifelessness' about them, the people seemed 'thin and hungry looking' and soldiers were dressed in 'all sorts of nondescript clothes' and wore straw or felt shoes.[103] The great shopping precincts in cities had boarded-up windows and the Soviet shops which were open had limited goods. When she returned the group wrote a report for the Labour Party and on the basis of its evidence Labour decided against closer links with the Communist Party of Great

Britain. Margaret Bondfield was 'profoundly thankful' when the attempt to find some mutual agreement between the two parties was abandoned.

Margaret was a Christian socialist, not a Marxist. Politics, she believed, should be used to bring the reign of God to earth, arguing that it was not possible that this 'could come through a capitalist system of government ... which sanctioned the enslavement of any individuals or groups'. In her opinion, 'politics was a department of the Church ... and social developments as the march of the human race towards the Kingdom of God'.[104] The Kingdom of Heaven on earth, she maintained, could only be brought about through a 'juster distribution' of wealth and opportunity since inequality did not sit happily with Christianity.[105] The atheistic nature of Russian Marxism did not appeal to her. Moreover, Bondfield's personality made it unlikely for her to espouse revolutionary politics and violence—she always preferred quiet diplomacy and negotiation to fiery rhetoric.

During the First World War, the Labour Party grew in strength and popularity. When it was founded in 1900, it had just a couple of MPs but by the end of the war this number had grown to 57. As Bondfield noted, 'we had entered the war period a comparatively humble and small party of idealists entirely taken up with domestic social reform. We emerged from it with the organisation, the policy and the principles of a great national party committed to the pursuit of international ideals of democracy and justice'.[106] In 1918, the Labour Party adopted a new constitution which included Clause IV,[107] closer links to trade unions and permission for people to join as individual members.[108]

After the war, the NFWW amalgamated with the National Union of General Workers (GMW) and the WTUL was absorbed as the Women's Department of the TUC General Council.[109] For the next 18 years, Margaret Bondfield was employed as Chief Woman Officer at the newly amalgamated GMW. She was very popular. 'No worker in any Movement' wrote Margaret Llewelyn Davies 'ever had a colleague who was more single-minded, generous, and loyal. She is in many ways the type of what all labour women should be – unflinchingly staunch to her cause, fair to her opponents, radiating good will to all'.[110] In 1923, Bondfield became the first woman Chair of the TUC, the spokesperson for six million workers. In her address, Bondfield regarded this appointment 'as a very signal proof of the reality of the claim made by Labour that they believe in equality of opportunity for women'.[111] Congress elected her to office, not because she was a woman but because she was seen to have a 'forceful and indomitable spirit and a remarkable power of speech, combined with a wide experience of the industrial movement'. There were few women, it was maintained who had the same gifts and perhaps 'not one capable of more electrifying eloquence and moral passion'.[112]

It was a difficult time to lead the TUC. The post-war slump and its resulting unemployment had both depleted union membership and with it union funds making effective action more difficult than it had been before the war. One of the first crises that Bondfield handled was that of a strike of several months standing in the shipbuilding industry which affected 70,000 men. She was asked to resolve the dispute, and it was here that her pragmatism and conciliatory manner came to the fore. In her usual careful, rigorous and calm manner, she made a thorough investigation, discussed the issue with the various unions involved and then called the trade union representatives and employers to a conference. Within a month, almost single-handedly, she settled the dispute.[113] The ending of the strike drew her to national prominence. She maintained it was a triumph for Trade Union diplomacy; it was certainly a triumph for Bondfield. It was her negotiating skills, her willingness to listen, her clarity of vision that had helped bring the strike to a close.

BEGINNING A PARLIAMENTARY CAREER

Meanwhile Bondfield's political reputation was growing. In 1918, she was sponsored by her trade union and placed on Labour's list of parliamentary candidates; in 1920, she was adopted for Northampton, a seat held by Charles McCurdy, a high-ranking well-regarded Liberal holding a safe majority.[114] In April, McCurdy was promoted to the Cabinet, and according to parliamentary rules of the time, he had to seek re-election. In the by-election which followed Bondfield was supported by the 'full resources, platform and propaganda of the Labour Movement'[115] but no one expected her to win the safe Liberal seat. George Bernard Shaw wrote 'why Northampton? You are the best man of the lot and they shove you off to a place where the water is too cold for their dainty feet ... and keep the safe seats for their now quite numerous imbeciles'.[116] Bondfield worked hard canvassing votes, often speaking at six meetings a day. Her eloquence was thought to rise 'higher and higher. The women are her devoted disciples. The men come to hear "this woman" and go away captivated and in thrall. ... She is the very incarnation of the Spirit of Labour. Her voice is the voice of Labour'.[117] Despite her oratorical skills, Bondfield lost the election even though she increased the Labour vote. The next year was a year of 'spiritual darkness ... being constantly thwarted by petty sins and vices - sloth, pride, jealousy and anger constantly tripping me up'.[118] Her melancholy was exacerbated by the death of her very close friend Mary Macarthur who died of cancer in January 1921 at the age of 41.

Another opportunity came two years later when a general election took place. By now Bondfield's depression had lifted and 'the light returned and I had great happiness – I could pray once more with a sense of reality'.[119] She knew that Northampton was still a safe Liberal seat and once again was not expected to win. Bondfield's election addresses tried to convince voters that the Labour Party was a safe choice. 'You will be told' she said 'that Labour is out for violence and destruction because it is a revolutionary party. I am opposed to all forms of violence. ... I believe in the policy of a peaceful revolution – a revolution of the mind and heart – a substitution of service for self-interest, co-operation for competitive individualism, of putting the public well-being before individual privilege and profits'.[120] For a second time, Margaret Bondfield lost the election but was gradually increasing her share of the vote, gaining 13,729 votes to McCurdy's 16,650. Labour did better nationally, rising from 59 to 142 MPs and becoming the official Opposition party. Bondfield thought it a 'landmark in our history. We had arrived'.[121] She was partly responsible for Labour's success, having co-written the Labour Party manifesto.

In December 1923, there was another general election when Stanley Baldwin succeeded Bonar Law as Prime Minister and asked for a mandate to secure his premiership within the Conservative Party. Labour was clear about who they represented: the person without employment, the workers 'toiling for dwindling and uncertain wages, the mother whose life is a long martyrdom of suffering and self-sacrifice in trying to feed and clothe her little ones'.[122]

Unexpectedly Baldwin lost, Ramsay MacDonald became Prime Minister of the first Labour Government[123] and Margaret Bondfield succeeded in replacing the Liberal as MP for Northampton. She was one of the first three female Labour MPs, 'elected to the House entirely on their own merits'.[124] When it was announced in Northampton that Margaret Bondfield had won 'coloured bonnets were thrown into the air; women started dancing in the street; men broke into song'. The cries of 'Maggie, MP, Maggie MP, Good old Maggie; Maggie's done it!' reverberated through the streets, as did 'We Gave Our Votes To Margaret Bondfield, and she is our MP' to the tune of John Brown's body. The newly elected MP was hustled away by 'jubilant supporters' and helped into a wagon which was pulled by hundreds of men through the constituency and followed by crowds singing, dancing and cheering, people lining the pavements and mothers lifting up their babies to admire the sight.[125] Their cheers, commented one newspaper 'almost drowning the strident notes of the local colliery jazz bands' which accompanied them. Margaret Bondfield was presented with a magnificent victory cake with an iced inscription saying 'Maggie MP' by the housewives of a tenement block of flats.[126] 'Our Maggie' was considered a safe Labour candidate, 'a homely looking woman of early middle age – the sort of woman, one thinks on seeing her, whom one would choose for the part of the middle-aged mother in the film drama who saves the family fortune when everything else goes wrong'.[127] Nonetheless, it was quite clear that the Labour vote needed to be increased if her seat was to be held.

Margaret Bondfield was aged 53 when she entered Parliament. Eight women—three Labour, three Conservative and two Liberal—were elected, swamped by nearly 600 men. In these circumstances, the new female MPs felt they had much in common, entering a male enclave in which large numbers were unsympathetic to women taking any part in politics, let alone becoming MPs. The Conservative MP Nancy Astor hosted a dinner to celebrate their success and all eight women attended. It was agreed that 'no party politics will be obtruded ... though upon some legislative proposals the women are in complete agreement'.[128] The women needed to stick together as sexism was prevalent. The Liberal MP Margaret Wintringham complained that she had heard a couple of male politicians discussing one of the new women MPs in the lobby of the House of Commons 'What is she like?' 'Oh', replied the other 'not much to look at'. Wintringham hoped that 'the day would soon come when women's politics were more important to their fellow-members than their looks or dress'.[129]

Margaret Bondfield's first impressions of Parliament were 'decidedly mixed'.[130] The new Honourable Member for Northampton found herself lost in the labyrinthine corridors of the House of Commons even though she was treated with the 'utmost courtesy' from the officials who took 'endless trouble to help the new Member'.[131] Years later Margaret Bondfield was interviewed by the BBC about the daily life of a politician.[132] It was evident that MPs needed a robust constitution, an ability to exist on less sleep than the average individual and a quick wit to respond to the inevitable jibes and personal insults. Bondfield revealed that the House loved 'an exhibition of quick-witted analysis, deft turning of the tables in argument, witty rejoinder or the apt interjection', that only a very confident, articulate individual could hope to accomplish.[133] Bondfield had no wish to challenge the adversarial atmosphere, believing that women 'got fair play'. She argued that a woman MP had 'quite properly, to take her chance in debate with the other members; she must be willing to grin and bear it when the joke is on her; she must be able to keep her temper under provocation. . She must cultivate an external calm in dealing with callers, no matter how exasperating'.[134] The House of Commons had no set hours and all-night sittings were common. Instead of criticising it, Bondfield believed that women should conform to established traditions.

At 8 a.m. a 'fairly heavy post' arrived at her home, letters which she skimmed over and sorted out during breakfast 'into piles of varying urgency'.[135] There were even more letters to read when she arrived at the House of Commons. Many of these meant a visit to another department, a letter to a Minister or some 'patient research' in the reference library. Bondfield saw these as all part of her day's duty when they were from constituents but found it rather a chore when the letter was from someone outside her constituency writing to her simply because she was a female MP. Her morning was busy, either attending a Party Committee, or meeting—mostly female—constituents 'who came in ever-growing numbers' to see how Parliament worked.[136] These constituents had travelled from Northampton, were keen to make the most of their visit and expected their MP to show them round and explain the rituals of the House, not at all mindful that their MP might have more pressing work. Bondfield did her duty even though she was always more at ease with a task to complete, a talk to deliver, a report to write than with acting as a tour guide to a group of women.

At 2:45, the ushers cry of 'Hats Off' was heard everywhere: it was the start of the parliamentary business. Black Rod, the Mace, the Speaker and the Chaplain entered the Chamber and doors were shut for prayers. After ten minutes, the public business began. A few weeks after being elected Margaret Bondfield made her maiden speech, a speech sandwiched between two commanding politicians, the Conservative grandee Austen Chamberlain and the leading Liberal Sir John Simon.[137] Her speech, which dealt mainly with the suffering of unemployed women, was packed full of statistics and facts. As a speaker she had always avoided rhetoric, preferring to appeal to people's conscience rather than emotions.[138] It was definitely a sensible speech but was considered somewhat rambling, bore no relevance to what Chamberlain had said previously and was ignored by the next speaker. Margaret Bondfield was known to be a compelling orator with a wonderful speaking voice but she was nervous and had forgotten an important principle: the need to tailor her speech and modulate her voice to each audience. She was more accustomed to speak in large halls and open places, places which demanded a loud voice whereas the acoustics of the House demanded a voice less severe, more gentle and persuasive. Obviously tense and carrying the weight of being one of the first female Labour MPs, Bondfield spoke at an 'excessive speed, and when such speed is added to loudness of tone the result is a harsh cascade of sound'.[139] In her next speeches, she overcame her nerves, adopted a new tone and was soon regarded as the 'best speaker of all the women MPs'.[140]

The formation of a Labour Government brought new opportunities for Margaret Bondfield. On January 23, 1924, Margaret was summoned by the newly appointed Minister of Labour Tom Shaw and asked to be his Under-Secretary of State. Within a month of taking her seat, the girl from Somerset had been catapulted into a ministerial post: she was the 'First British Woman Minister'.[141] It was a meteoric rise for a woman who had just been elected as an MP and was regarded as 'a tribute to Miss Margaret Bondfield that nobody seems to question the fitness of her selection'.[142] Some newspapers reported that her appointment was one more 'step in the advance of women towards the full participation in the governance of the country, which was begun with the granting of the franchise'.[143] Labour women were jubilant but at least a couple of influential Tory women were more critical. Nancy Astor thought it disgraceful that Bondfield was not in the Cabinet. 'I am certain that if any man had done as much work for his party as Miss Bondfield he would have had a place in the Cabinet. Some people say that she has been omitted because she has had no Parliamentary experience. I know the Cabinet pretty well, and there are some men in it whose Parliamentary experience is not to their credit. ... Every woman in the country, whatever her party, had been hoping that Miss Bondfield would get a place in the Cabinet, and we are all bitterly disappointed'.[144] Another Tory grandee, Lady Rhondda expressed the regret felt by many women that Margaret Bondfield was not given a Cabinet post. 'For the first time', she said 'we get a Government which has always stated that it is in favour of sex equality. It is unbelievable that a man who had done the work that Miss Bondfield has done ... would not have been given a place in the Cabinet'.[145]

Bondfield felt that the tasks facing the new government were ones 'which nobody in their sober senses would take up. ... There are some of us who will lose our reputation ... There are some who will throw us to the wolves'.[146] When Labour took office, it took over a 'bankrupt concern ... the coffers were empty; industrial anarchy was in full swing; ... the financial crisis in Europe germinating and the figures of unemployment were steadily rising. Nearly all the leading figures in the financial world were out of sympathy with the Socialist programme, and knew how to be politely obstructive'.[147] The Labour Government was committed to a large programme including the nationalisation of land, of transport, plans for unemployment, education, pensions, health and maternity services, and reform of the Factory Acts. It was an unachievable agenda as all legislation had to be agreed by Liberal MPs if it was to have a chance of securing a majority when it passed through the House of Commons. Even so Labour provided £9 million a year to build council houses, increased Old Age Pensions and unemployment benefits, reintroduced scholarships to university, allocated £28 million to public works and cut taxes on basic foods such as tea and sugar.

The work of a Minister is demanding for experienced politicians let alone for someone who had only been an MP for a few weeks. Margaret Bondfield likened the new post as 'going on a strange adventure'[148] as 'we were a new team, most of us having to learn the rules of the House as well as master the details of Departmental business, with a gigantic mass of papers to be read'.[149] On February 18, barely a month after she had been elected, Margaret Bondfield made her second contribution in the House of Commons, this time as a member of the government. It was a speech on the Unemployment Insurance Bill, a Bill which was to remove the three week period in which unemployed workers were ineligible for benefit. This time Margaret Bondfield appeared more self-assured, answering questions in a 'resounding voice, and with a confident manner that won her a round of cheers from all parties'.[150] The Bill passed its second reading and was referred to a Standing Committee. By the end of the parliamentary session, Bondfield had contributed to nearly 100 debates, often making significant speeches, all the time growing in confidence. During her term of office, she tried to extend the power of trade boards to fix wages, improve conditions in industry, help disabled men and juveniles, arbitrate in trade union disputes and oversee work permits for German music-hall performers. Margaret Bondfield now had no time to ramble, no time for nerves.[151] Indeed, the MP for Northampton showed command of the often unruly benches of the House of Commons which demonstrated, according to one newspaper, that her 'precocious ability to keep little boys in order, acquired in the Board School at thirteen, had not rusted over the years'.[152]

Bondfield's high-profile work on the front bench was only part of the work of a junior minister. Much of her job was administrative, answering queries from other MPs, listening to appeals and responding to pleas for help. It was in this work that Margaret Bondfield felt comfortable: she was efficient, friendly, good-tempered and extraordinarily conscientious. She was thought to have a 'firm hold on common life, had never forgotten her own roots, and always understood, remembered, and respected the speechless majority'.[153]

The position of the Labour Government remained precarious. In October 1924, MacDonald faced a surprise vote of censure and was forced to dissolve Parliament. A few days before the election the *Daily Mail* published a letter allegedly from Zinoviev the head of the Russian Comintern to British communists in which he gave advice to his British comrades on how to promote revolution. The letter was a forgery but its publication fed into people's anxiety about the Soviet Republic and created a mood of panic and conviction among the electorate that the Russians—helped by the Labour Party—were coming to take over the British Isles. The Conservatives won a resounding victory gaining 415 seats at the expense of Labour's 152 and the Liberals' 42. The government had only survived for 10 months.

Losing Her Northampton Seat, October 1924

When the election was called, Margaret Bondfield was 6000 miles away in Canada, as a member of the British Government Delegation investigating child migration.[154] It was a bad time to be away. Bondfield lost her seat, handicapped by being allotted an unsafe constituency. She had held her Northampton seat for less than one year. Both Lawrence and Jewson lost theirs too, though the defeat of Bondfield was considered the biggest loss as 'there was perhaps no other woman whom so large a section of the public, irrespective of party, desired to see in the House'.[155] Only four women were elected: three Conservatives and one new Labour MP, Ellen Wilkinson.

Margaret Bondfield returned to her union work and more industrial challenges. She was on the General Council of the TUC on Monday, May 3, 1926, when it called a General Strike in sympathy with the miners who were striking against an increase in their working day and a reduction in their pay. Within 24 hours all the buses, trams and trains stopped running, the docks were paralysed, the iron and steel industries shut down. No newspapers were published. Bondfield drove around the south-west of England addressing meetings, meeting the local Strike Committees and collecting information about responses to the strike. Everywhere she visited the strike was solid. She witnessed the 'loyalty, disciple and efficiency' of trade unionists and found that people widely agreed that the miners should have a fair deal and that mine-owners were incompetent. It was also thought that the government 'blundered hopelessly and seems quite incapable of securing peace in industry'.[156] Even so, Bondfield approved of the decision by the TUC to call off the strike, and everyone, apart from the miners, returned to work. The miners who campaigned for 'not a penny off the pay, not a minute off the day' remained on strike for a further six months.

MP FOR WALLSEND, JULY 1926–OCTOBER 1931

At midday on a hot summer's day in July 1926, a crowd of some 20,000 people milled outside Wallsend Town Hall waiting for the by-election results. The previous Labour MP, Sir Patrick Hastings, had resigned to allow Bondfield the opportunity to return to Parliament. Margaret Bondfield won a resounding victory: winning 18,866 votes to the Conservatives 9839. At last, she had been given a safe seat and was now MP for Wallsend, a ship-building and mining town on the north bank of the River Tyne in North East England. In her view, the Wallsend electorate had sent an indignant message to the government about its handling of the coal crisis, a warning which the government should 'ignore at its peril'.[157]

This time, Margaret Bondfield had left little to chance, proving an 'indefatigable electioneer' with a full programme of meetings. Her campaign augured well: she had a 'most wonderful body of helpers' who organised meetings in the colliery villages where sometimes the whole village turned up, complete with a miner's band.[158] Her trade union the General and Municipal Workers contributed £500 towards her election expenses, though asked her to do her 'level best in keeping down the expenditure'.[159] She thought it the 'most wonderful fight I have ever been engaged in. It is strenuous work, but the feeling her is magnificent. They have adopted me with a real North Country spirit, and the meetings appear to be a triumphal procession of unanimous votes of confidence'.[160] The women were thought to be as determined as the men, sometimes walking miles in the rain to hear her speak.[161]

The by-election took place in the middle of the miners' strike. Bondfield's uncompromisingly socialist message resonated in the mining villages: her election leaflets accused the Tories of mishandling the coal crisis, of failing to 'curb the Coal-owners in their unjust demands', of wantonly wrecking the peace efforts of the TUC and precipitating the General Strike by its intransigence.[162] She condemned the Tory government for its 'retrogressive and anti-social measures' in its support of coal-owners against the miners, for its discrimination of the working class in favour of the rich, for the cutting of social services, for lavishly handing out millions of pounds to the wealthy by reducing their taxes.[163] The government, she insisted, 'was deliberately supporting the rich against the poor'.[164] Later on, in her autobiography, Bondfield argued that the miners stuck too tenaciously to their demands, thus preventing a settlement. In her opinion, 'the result of that rigidity was to leave the miners in a much worse position than before the strike was called'.[165]

When the MP for Wallsend took her seat in the House of Commons she brought 'a little colour to the array of grey or black suit on the front Opposition Bench. As she stood at the bar waiting to take her seat she made a pretty picture dressed in a one-piece costume of stripped biscuit-coloured satin and at her breast a dark red rose'.[166] Some newspapers took the art of physiognomy to a ridiculously new level, arguing that her physical appearance engendered trust: her black hair, parted in the centre of her forehead and twisted in a big knot behind her head was thought to mark that of a sensible woman. Margaret Bondfield 'looked the part, with no trace of fanaticism in either her appearance or her personality: the world for her was not made up of political tendencies and factions but human beings with human problems which she would try to resolve'.[167] Labour MPs, many of whom had put a red flower in their button-hole to mark her return, gave her a loud welcoming cheer.[168] She was one of the most popular Labour women, respected by most MPs 'despite her penchant for a flaming red blouse'.[169]

Bondfield's time on the opposition benches confirmed her status as a serious-minded, conscientious, politician who was punctilious in her approach, carefully gathering up her evidence to make a reasoned professional statement or to ask a pertinent question. Her speeches in the House of Commons focussed on domestic policy, demonstrating a concern for the hours of shop workers, sick leave for women, overcrowding in houses, slum clearances, maternity welfare, unemployment and unemployment benefits. In 1927, a newly confident Conservative Government passed the Trades Disputes Act which restricted workers' rights, made sympathetic strikes illegal, banned civil servants from joining unions affiliated to the TUC, protected black-legs, and made picketing almost impossible. In the House of Commons, Bondfield sneered that the 'profession of friendship on the part of the Conservative party for the working men and women of this country is simply a hollow sham'.[170]

Some accused her of insincerity. Just before she was elected, Bondfield's commitment to the Labour movement was tested and found defective. In 1925, the Conservative Government had set up a Select Committee under the chairmanship of Lord Blanesburgh to examine unemployment and the ways in which the unemployed received benefits. Margaret Bondfield was invited to serve on the committee in a private capacity: she had a good claim to be included since she had had 30 years of experience as a trade unionist and had studied the unemployment question for many years. More importantly for the Tory government, Bondfield was known to be fair-minded, sensible, steady and unflappable, a trade unionist and a Labour Party representative who could be relied on to compromise and negotiate, not a firebrand who might cause trouble. In 1927, less than a year after the General Strike and only months after the defeat of the miners, the Blanesburgh Report was published: it recommended lowering benefits including cutting benefits for single women from 15s a week to 8s and making them payable only to those 'genuinely seeking work'. The ever-conciliatory Bondfield had signed the Report, convinced that she had got the best deal available. Firstly, she convinced the committee that despite popular sentiment and press opinion there was no evidence of unemployment abuse and thus those claiming benefits were justified in doing so. Secondly, she helped reconcile the two conflicting schools of thought on unemployment: one which thought that unemployment insurance should only be paid to those who contributed to it; another which thought that provision should be made for all unemployed people regardless how long they were unemployed. Margaret Bondfield favoured the latter but compromised to avoid the possibility of an even more limited insurance programme: she was all too aware that policy is largely based on concessions from both sides.

She faced an avalanche of criticism for her action: her union disowned her; a conference of Socialist Women condemned her; party activists in Wallsend demanded her resignation and the TUC censured her actions by a vote of 1,836,000 votes to 1,419,000. There was so much criticism in the Labour movement about her work on the Blanesburgh Committee that the Wallsend Labour Party held an emergency meeting and the National Joint Council, a body which represented the TUC, the Labour Party and the PLP, convened a special conference to discuss the whole subject.[171] The 'savage criticism' of the report meant 'a very exhausting campaign throughout the country' defending her decision to sign it.[172] Margaret Bondfield believed that criticism of her was 'the work of an embittered minority who had no firm ground at all on which to base their objections'.[173] The Labour movement, she maintained, 'was in an angry and restless mood, sensitive to the slightest suggestion of enmity, or even of neglect. ... The Labour Movement is like all human movements – full of little wars, wrestlings, disagreements and minor disputes, which need skill and tact to deal with. What now arose was something on a very different model. Expert hands moulded a series of deceptive misrepresentations of fact, and plausible untruths'[174] which she found 'dangerous and unpleasant'. She blamed the Communist Party for it all. At the Labour conference, Bondfield showed courage in the face of criticism, made a 'very vigorous defence' of signing the Report and convinced delegates of her sincerity. In the end, delegates were persuaded that she had acted wisely and she was cleared of operating against the interests of the working class. Nonetheless, her signing of the Report and her defence of doing so confirmed her place on the right-wing of the Labour Party. More importantly, the seeds sewn by Blanesburgh would grow into a dangerous crop that Bondfield would later have to cut down. And if Labour militants and trade unionists had known about her friendly relationship with Lord Blanesburgh and how she had joined him and other members of the committee at a celebratory dinner at a West End Club on May 18—they would have been more aghast.[175]

In 1928, Margaret, despite having signed the Blanesburgh Report, criticised the Tory government's Unemployment Insurance Bill for introducing means testing. She told of how in her own constituency 'people have lost every penny that they had saved ... They have parted with such articles of furniture as had any saleable value'.[176] Bondfield tried to ameliorate the poverty experienced by children living in areas of high unemployment. On December 4, 1928, she introduced a Bill sponsored by women MPs from across the political spectrum—Nancy Astor, Mrs Runciman, Mrs Phillipson, Susan Lawrence, Countess of Iveagh and Ellen Wilkinson—which proposed that

Fig. 2.2 Kicking off a football game in her constituency (Courtesy of Vassar College)

public health and education authorities be given the right to provide footwear for children in distressed areas. Unfortunately, the Bill did not become a law because the government did not provide sufficient time for it to pass through Parliament.

The MP for Wallsend was also active in her constituency, talking to groups, opening fairs and even kicking off a game of football (Fig. 2.2). More crucially, she helped resolve some of the issues that faced the local population. Most of the problems were about lack of money: constituents asked for her help when they faced eviction, when claiming benefits and pensions, when a daughter got pregnant or when a teenage boy disappeared from home and ended up in Australia. She was even asked to help to squash a murder conviction.[177] In 1927, she was asked to persuade the courts to amend the sentence of two young boys, aged 11 and 12, who had been given long sentences in a Reformatory Ship. Both had had three previous convictions for breaking and entering, for shop breaking and for stealing. On the first conviction, they were put on probation; on the second, they were subjected to three strokes of the birch, on the third to four strokes. At their fourth offence, they were given a custodial sentence: they had stolen milk. Bondfield was unable to help.

In 1929, Parliament came to its natural end and a general election took place. The Labour Party Manifesto was a 'clarion call to the people to rally to the polls' in order to give the party a majority and a clear mandate to 'tackle those social and economic ills which, under Tory misrule, are rapidly reducing our country to chaos'.[178] The Labour campaign in Wallsend was officially opened on May 13 when Margaret Bondfield addressed a meeting in the Miners' Hall.[179] Bondfield campaigned forcefully: between May 13 and 19 she addressed 61 meetings in Wallsend alone, many of which were outside. She also toured the constituency holding five or six meetings a day.[180] As ever, money was short—there were no 'heaped up coffers at Transport House, no hefty bank balance to vie with the cash from the Carlton Club' but fights waged with 'workers' coppers, carefully collected—poor pennies against prouder pounds'.[181] She informed Will Thorne that there had been great difficulty in getting in trade union fees, and in particular, there had been a 'terrible drop in the miners' fees. In previous years their contribution has been anything from £140 to £200 a year to the local party, but this year it has dropped to £65'.[182]

She was fighting on the party programme contained in *Labour and the Nation* and in the manifesto. Her own leaflet promised schemes of work for the unemployed and more 'generous maintenance to the genuinely unemployed'.[183] She affirmed that 'Labour policy is practical application of Christian teaching'. At one of the meetings, she was presented with a bag 'every stitch worked by the women, in the Party colours of black and amber'.[184] The actress Sybil Thorndike wrote that she 'should unhesitatingly vote for her, as I believe she is the sort of woman who ought to have a hand in the affairs of the country'.[185] It was the first election in which women over the age of 21 could vote. Margaret Bondfield 'with very profound pleasure' had supported the Bill to give women equal voting rights as men.[186] The press suggested that any 'Party which wins the Election will feel itself obliged to include at least one woman in the Cabinet. Both the Conservative and Labour Parties are now in the position of having in their ranks women MPs who have served apprenticeships in departmental administrations and Front Bench responsibility'.[187]

On May 30, 1929, the great electoral fight was over and 'the political judgement of the people' delivered.[188] Labour overturned the great Conservative majority, winning 288 seats and emerging as the largest single party in the House of Commons. The newly enfranchised female electorate took the credit. It seemed, Noreen Branson argues, that the 'prophecies that the flapper vote would lead to the downfall of the Conservative Party had come true'.[189] The number of female MPs rose from 4 to 14, nine of them Labour: Cynthia Mosley,[190] Ellen Wilkinson, Jenny Lee, Susan Lawrence, Marion Phillips, Mary Agnes Hamilton, Ethel Bentham, Edith Picton-Turbervill and Margaret Bondfield. Six of these nine women were middle or upper class, a sign that the Labour Party was moving away from its roots in the trade union movement. Margaret Bondfield, however, was a working-class woman with strong connections to the trade union movement and a proven commitment to making life better for women of her class. The next chapter will examine how Bondfield once in power tried to put her principles into practice.

NOTES

1. *Liverpool Evening News*, July 24, 1926.
2. Margaret Bondfield, *Rungs of the Ladder*, BBC Radio Broadcast, June 6, 1932.
3. This tradition continued. Tony Benn's mother was the first President of the Congregational Federation when it was formed in 1972.
4. Margaret Bondfield, *A Life's Work*, Hutchinsons, 1948, p. 353.
5. MB diary January 1921–1922, Archives and Special Collections Library, Vassar College Libraries, Box 12, Folder 5.
6. Ibid.
7. MB diary 1927, Archives and Special Collections Library, Vassar College Libraries, Box 12, Folder 5.
8. Brian Harrison, *Prudent Revolutionaries, Portraits of British Feminists Between the Wars*, Clarendon Press, 1987, p. 129.
9. I am grateful to Prof Sue Morgan for her insights on Congregationalism in the nineteenth century.
10. *Western Gazette*, December 14, 1883, p. 7.
11. Margaret Bondfield, 'Rungs of the Ladder—V', *The Listener*, June 1932, p. 869.
12. Chard School Board Log Book, August 23, 1886, Margaret Bondfield Papers, Archives and Special Collections Library, Vassar College Libraries, Box 3, Folder 9.
13. Margaret Bondfield Papers, Archives and Special Collections Library, Vassar College Libraries, Box 9, Folder 13.
14. Margaret Bondfield, *A Life's Work*, 1948, p. 26.
15. Letter from Bondfield to Hilda Martindale quoted in Hilda Martindale, *From One Generation to Another*, 1944, p. 34, in Margaret Bondfield, *A Life's Work*, 1948, p. 26.
16. Letter from Bondfield to Hilda Martindale quoted in Hilda Martindale, *From One Generation to Another*, 1944, p. 34, in Margaret Bondfield, *A Life's Work*, 1948, p. 26.
17. Quoted in Mary Agnes Hamilton, *Margaret Bondfield*, p. 47.
18. Margaret Bondfield, 'From Counter to Cabinet', broadcast published in *The Listener*, February 1938, p. 2.
19. Margaret Bondfield, *A Life's Work*, 1948, p. 353.
20. Ibid., p. 46.
21. Morgan Philips, General Secretary of the Labour Party between 1944 and 1961.
22. Quoted in Pamela Cox, Pamela and Hobley Annabel, *Shopgirls*, Arrow Books, 2014, p. 37.
23. Mary Agnes Hamilton, *Margaret Bondfield*, Leonard Parsons, 1924, p. 68.
24. Margaret Bondfield, 'Conditions Under Which Shop Assistants Work', *The Economic Journal*, June 1899, p. 278.
25. *London Daily News*, April 11, 1901, p. 6.

26. Mary Agnes Hamilton, *Margaret Bondfield*, p. 43.

27. *London Daily News*, April 11, 1901, p. 6.

28. Letter to Margaret Bondfield quoted in Margaret Bondfield, *Socialism for Shop Assistants*, 1909, p. 4.

29. Margaret Bondfield, 'Conditions Under Which Shop Assistants Work', *The Economic Journal*, June 1899, p. 278.

30. Margaret Bondfield, 'In the Days of My Youth', *Cassell's Weekly*, January 12, 1927, p. 430.

31. *London Daily News*, April 11, 1901, p. 6.

32. *Preston Herald*, August 18, 1906, p. 13.

33. Letter to Margaret Bondfield quoted in Margaret Bondfield, *Socialism for Shop Assistants*, 1909, p. 4.

34. *Preston Herald*, August 18, 1906, p. 13.

35. For example, the Shop Hours Act 1904 and the Shop Act 1911 which gave a half-day holiday to shop workers and a maximum working week of 60 hours. The Shop Act 1906 decreed the end of 'living in'. She also helped organise an exhibition of the 'Sweated Industries' which led to the Trade Boards Act, 1909 which regulated the work of a number of trades.

36. *South Wales Daily News*, October 29, 1898, p. 6.

37. Margaret Bondfield, 'From Counter to Cabinet', broadcast published in *The Listener*, February 1938, p. 2.

38. In 1946, it merged with NUDAW to form USDAW.

39. *Fifty Years in the Labour Movement*, unpublished manuscript notes for a BBC broadcast, Margaret Bondfield Papers, Archives and Special Collections Library, Vassar College Libraries, Box 9, Folder 13.

40. Margaret Bondfield, *A Life's Work*, 1948, p. 51.

41. *Myself and Life*, transcript of a radio broadcast, March 29, 1939, Margaret Bondfield Papers, Archives and Special Collections Library, Vassar College Libraries, Box 9, Folder 13.

42. Ibid.

43. H. Tracy (ed.), *The Book of the Labour Party, Its History, Growth, Policy and Leaders*, Vol. III, Caxton Publishing Company, 1925.

44. Dorothy Kirby, Margaret Bondfield, *The Labour Magazine*, October 1923, Margaret Bondfield Papers, Archives and Special Collections Library, Vassar College Libraries, Box 9.

45. See Christopher Hosgood, '"Mercantile Monasteries": Shops, Shop Assistants, and Shop Life in Late-Victorian and Edwardian Britain', *Journal of British Studies*, July 1999, Vol. 38, No. 3, pp. 322–352.

46. Grace Dare, aka Margaret Bondfield, 1898, p. 66.

47. *Derby Daily Telegraph*, April 26, 1905, p. 2.

48. *The Daily News*, November 22, 1901, p. 7.

49. *Dundee Courier*, September 7, 1899, p. 7.

50. *The Shop Assistant*, 1899, p. 71.

51. Margaret Bondfield did not attend the first meetings even though she had advocated its foundation (Labour Party Foundation Conference and Annual Conference Reports, 1900–1905).

52. It was first called the Women's Protective and Provident League but changed its name in 1889.

53. Margaret Bondfield, *A Life's Work*, 1948, p. 58. In 1920, the WTUL became the Women's Department of the TUC.
54. Cathy Hunt, *The National Federation of Women Workers, 1906–1921*, Palgrave Macmillan, 2014, p. 2. Hunt's book provides an invaluable historical survey of the NFWW. In 1921, the NFWW merged with the National Union of General Workers, becoming the National Union of General and Municipal Workers in 1924.
55. *Dundee Evening Telegraph*, March 14, 1906, p. 5.
56. WTUL Annual Report, 1906. I am grateful to Cathy Hunt for this quote and reference.
57. Margaret Bondfield, *A Life's Work*, 1948, p. 81.
58. Ibid.
59. Agnes Mary Hamilton, *Margaret Bondfield*, p. 71.
60. Margaret Bondfield, *A Life's Work*, 1948, p. 81.
61. Mary Agnes Hamilton, *Uphill All the Way*, Jonathan Cape, 1953, p. 70
62. Margaret Bondfield, 'Women and the Factory System, Conditions—Past and Present', *Labour*, July 1934, p. 255
63. *Burnley Express*, August 5, 1908, p. 3.
64. Margaret Bondfield, *A Life's Work*, 1948, p. 45.
65. *London Daily News*, February 17, 1906, p. 7.
66. Margaret Bondfield, *A Life's Work*, 1948, p. 82.
67. Quoted in Agnes Mary Hamilton, *Margaret Bondfield*, 1953, p. 84.
68. Margaret Bondfield and Teresa Billington-Greig, Sex Equality versus Adult Suffrage, Verbatim Report of Debate, December 3, 1907, p. 15. In the debate, Bondfield reminded the audience that Millicent Fawcett supported a limited suffrage because it was an effective barrier to the 'dangerous demand for Adult Suffrage', that is for working-class men.
69. Margaret Bondfield, *Shop Workers and the Vote*, The People's Suffrage Federation, 1911, p. 9.
70. Margaret Bondfield, *A Life's Work*, 1948, p. 87.
71. Marion Phillips (1881–1932) was Secretary of the Women's Labour League and became Labour's first chief Women's Officer. She was MP for Sunderland between 1929 and 1931.
72. Margaret Bondfield and Maud Ward were good friends and shared a house. Ward accompanied Bondfield on her early trips to America.
73. Margaret Bondfield, *A Life's Work*, 1948, p. 126.
74. The meeting took place at Woolwich Town Hall. Margaret Bondfield, *A Life's Work*, 1948, p. 126.
75. Jane Addams (1860–1935) is known as the 'mother of social work'. She founded Hull House, a centre of research and debate. Hull House had an adult night school, children's clubs, a music school, a library, and employment bureau and a bath-house.
76. *Lessons I have learned in America*, WNYC broadcast, January 15, 1939, Margaret Grace Bondfield Papers, Archives and Special Collections Library, Vassar College Libraries, Box 7 Folder 8.
77. Rose Schneiderman (1882–1972) was born in Poland, the eldest child of working-class religious Jewish parents. In 1890, the family moved to America. In later life, Schneiderman served as President of the American

Women's Trade Union League. In 1933, Roosevelt appointed her to the Labor Advisory Board, the only woman. Between 1937 and 1943, she was secretary of the New York State Department of Labor. She coined the term 'bread and roses'.

78. Perkins was an American sociologist and workers-rights campaigner who became the first woman appointed to the US Cabinet. She was Secretary of Labor between 1933 and 1945.

79. Margaret Bondfield, *A Life's Work*, 1948, p. 137.

80. MB Notebook, undated, Archives and Special Collections Library, Vassar College Libraries, Box 12, Folder 16.

81. Margaret Bondfield, *A Life's Work*, 1948, p. 137.

82. Ibid., p. 138.

83. Ibid., p. 152.

84. *Daily Herald*, March 6, 1915, p. 3.

85. Clara Zetkin (1857–1933) was born into a Protestant German family. She was a socialist feminist, one of the leading figures of the far-left, a co-founder of the Independent Social Democratic Party of Germany and later a member of the German Communist Party. She was forced to leave Germany when Hitler came to power and went to the USSR.

86. The others were Marion Phillips, Mary Longman and Ada Salter.

87. *The Scotsman*, April 6, 1915, p. 8.

88. *The Scotsman*, April 10, 1915, p. 3.

89. *Evening Despatch*, August 13, 1917, p. 7.

90. I am grateful to Dr Cathy Hunt for this information.

91. *Manchester Courier and Lancashire General Advertiser*, August 20, 1914, p. 4.

92. *Daily Herald*, February 13, 1915, p. 1

93. Telegram from Queen Mary to Margaret Bondfield, July 27, 1934, Archives and Special Collections Library, Vassar College Libraries, Box 2, Folder 18.

94. Margaret Bondfield, *A Life's Work*, 1948, p. 144.

95. *Dundee Courier*, December 6, 1915, p. 5.

96. Margaret Bondfield, Labour Party Conference, Bristol, 1916.

97. *Daily Express*, January 28, 1916, p. 6.

98. The delegation also included Ethel Snowden, Mary Macarthur, Mr H. Skinner, Mr A. A. Purcell, Robert Williams, Clifford Allen and Mr R. C. Wallhead.

99. Margaret Bondfield's Russian diary, May 7–30, 1920, Margaret Grace Bondfield Papers, Archives and Special Collections Library, Vassar College Libraries, Box 5A, Folder 2.

100. Margaret Bondfield, *A Life's Work*, p. 194.

101. Margaret Bondfield's Russian diary, May 26, 1920, Margaret Grace Bondfield Papers, Archives and Special Collections Library, Vassar College Libraries, Box 5A, Folder 2.

102. Margaret Bondfield's Russian diary, May 27, 1920, Margaret Grace Bondfield Papers, Archives and Special Collections Library, Vassar College Libraries, Box 5A, Folder 2.

103. Margaret Bondfield's Russian diary, May 7–30, 1920, Margaret Grace Bondfield Papers, Archives and Special Collections Library, Vassar College Libraries, Box 5A, Folder 2.

104. *Manchester Guardian*, November 24, 1924, p. 3.
105. *Manchester Guardian*, March 8, 1927, p. 13.
106. Margaret Bondfield, *A Life's Work*, 1948, p. 161.
107. The clause was 'to secure for the worker by hand or by brain the full fruits of their industry and the most equitable distribution thereof that may be possible upon the basis of the common ownership of the means of production, distribution and exchange, and the best obtainable system of popular administration and control of each industry or service'.
108. Margaret Bondfield Papers, Archives and Special Collections Library, Vassar College Libraries, Box 9, Folder 3.
109. I am grateful to Dr Cathy Hunt for this reference.
110. Margaret Llewlyn Davis to Miss MacArthur, May 7, 1918, Bondfield papers, Box 3 Folder 2, Vassar Archives.
111. Quoted in Agnes Mary Hamilton, *Margaret Bondfield*, 1953, p. 194.
112. 'Makers of the Labour Movement', *Labour Magazine*, January 27, 1973.
113. *Sunday Sun*, February 3, 1963, p. 4.
114. In 1918, women over 30 were given the vote; women over 21 were allowed to stand for Parliament.
115. *Manchester Guardian*, March 31, 1920, p. 6.
116. George Bernard Shaw quoted in Elizabeth Vallance, *Women in the House*, 1979, p. 52. Apparently, Shaw wrote a similar letter to other unsuccessful women candidates.
117. *The Labour Outlook*, March 31, 1920, p. 3.
118. MB Diary, January 1921–1922, Margaret Bondfield Papers, Archives and Special Collections Library, Vassar College Libraries.
119. MB Diary January 1922, Margaret Bondfield Papers, Archives and Special Collections Library, Vassar College Libraries.
120. Election address, 1922 quoted in Margaret Bondfield, *A Life's Work*, 1948, p. 244.
121. Margaret Bondfield, *A Life's Work*, 1948, p. 246.
122. *Northampton Labour Gazette*, November 24, 1923, p. 1.
123. Labour increased its number of MPs from 144 to 191; the Liberals won 158 seats while the Conservatives declined to 258 MPs.
124. *Manchester Guardian*, December 8, 1923, p. 6. The Conservative and Liberal women MPs had all taken over their husband's seats. The two other Labour women were Susan Lawrence and Dorothy Jewson.
125. *The Manchester Guardian*, December 10, 1923, p. 8.
126. *Sunday Sun*, February 3, 1963, p. 4.
127. *Western Gazette*, December 14, 1923, p. 10.
128. *Leeds Mercury*, January 15, 1924, p. 8.
129. *The Scotsman*, January 11, 2924, p. 9.
130. Notes on Northampton, Margaret Bondfield Papers, Archives and Special Collections Library, Vassar College Libraries, Box 7, Folder 9.
131. Ibid.
132. Unabridged transcript of broadcast sent to the BBC, November 1928, Margaret Bondfield Papers, Archives and Special Collections Library, Vassar College Libraries, Box 9, Folder 10.
133. Ibid.

134. Ibid.
135. Ibid.
136. Ibid.
137. Hansard, January 21, 1924, Vol. 169, cc32–685.
138. Mary Sutherland, *Labour Woman*, July 1953, p. 152.
139. J. Johnston, *A Hundred Commoners*, Herbert Joseph, 1931, p. 110.
140. Unpublished manuscript, *The Feet of Young Men* by 'The Janitor', February 1928, Vassar College, Box 12, Folder 24.
141. *Western Times*, January 25, 1924, p. 12.
142. *Yorkshire Evening Post*, January 24, 1924, p. 6.
143. *Dundee Courier*, January 14, 1924, p. 4.
144. *Nottingham Evening Post*, January 24, 1924, p. 1.
145. *Manchester Guardian*, January 25, 1924, p. 8.
146. *Manchester Guardian*, February 18, 1924, p. 11.
147. Margaret Bondfield, *A Life's Work*, 1948, p. 247.
148. Ibid., p. 256.
149. Ibid., p. 256.
150. *The Daily Express*, February 19, 1924, p. 7.
151. See Hansard, February 18, 1924.
152. Undated and unattributed newspaper report, Ross Davies collection.
153. Agnes Mary Hamilton, *Margaret Bondfield*, p. 171.
154. Election leaflet, Bondfield papers, Box 3, Folder 2, Vassar Collection.
155. *Manchester Guardian*, October 31, 1924, p. 12.
156. Margaret Bondfield, *A Life's Work*, 1948, p. 269.
157. Margaret Bondfield, *The Manchester Guardian*, July 23, 1926, p. 12.
158. Letter from Margaret Bondfield to L. M. Hewitt, July 6, 1926, Margaret Grace Bondfield papers, Archives and Special Collections Library, Vassar College Libraries, Box 3, Folder 3.
159. Will Thorne to Bondfield, June 30, 1926, Margaret Grace Bondfield papers, Archives and Special Collections Library, Vassar College Libraries, Box 3, Folder 11.
160. Letter from Margaret Bondfield to Miss Elliot, July 8, 1926, Margaret Grace Bondfield papers, Archives and Special Collections Library, Vassar College Libraries, Box 3, Folder 3.
161. Letter from Margaret Bondfield to her brother Frank, July 6, 1926, Margaret Grace Bondfield papers, Archives and Special Collections Library, Vassar College Libraries, Box 3, Folder 3.
162. Election leaflet, 1926, Margaret Grace Bondfield papers, Archives and Special Collections Library, Vassar College Libraries Box 3, Folder 1.
163. Ibid.
164. Margaret Bondfield, *A Life's Work*, 1948, p. 269.
165. Ibid., p. 269.
166. *Northampton Mercury*, July 30, 1926, p. 5.
167. *Shepton Mallet Journal*, July 30, 1926, p. 6.
168. *Shepton Mallet Journal*, July 30, 1926, p. 6.
169. *Nottingham Evening Post*, July 23, 1926, p. 4.
170. Hansard, June 13, 1927, Vol. 207, cc681–814.
171. *Gloucester Citizen*, April 30, 1927, p. 4.
172. Unpublished manuscript, Box 4, Folder 2.

173. Margaret Bondfield, *A Life's Work*, 1948, p. 274.
174. Ibid., p. 271.
175. Lord Blanesburgh to Bondfield, Margaret Grace Bondfield Papers, Archives and Special Collections Library, Vassar College Libraries, Box 3, Folder 7.
176. Hansard, April 30, 1928, Vol. 216, cc1347–1477.
177. Wallsend Constituency cases, Margaret Grace Bondfield Papers, Archives and Special Collections Library, Vassar College Libraries, Box 3, Folder 5.
178. *Daily Herald*, May 1, 1929, p. 4.
179. *The Herald*, May 1929, p. 1.
180. Berwick, Hartlepools, Hexham, Middlesbrough, North Shields, Whitley Bay, Seaton Sluice and Newcastle. *The Herald*, July 1929, p. 3.
181. *The Dawn and Day Is Coming*, unpublished manuscript, Margaret Grace Bondfield Papers, Archives and Special Collections Library, Vassar College Archives, Box 3, Folder 1.
182. Margaret Bondfield to Will Thorne, January 30, 1929, Margaret Grace Bondfield Papers, Archives and Special Collections Library, Vassar College Archives, Box 3, Folder 10.
183. Election leaflet, 1929, Margaret Grace Bondfield Papers, Archives and Special Collections Library, Vassar College Archives, Box 3, Folder 1.
184. Margaret Bondfield's Labour Election Special, Margaret Grace Bondfield Papers, Archives and Special Collections Library, Vassar College Archives, Box 3, Folder 1.
185. Sybil Thorndike to Margaret Bondfield published in Margaret Bondfield's Labour Election Special, Margaret Grace Bondfield Papers, Archives and Special Collections Library, Vassar College Archives, Box 3, Folder 1.
186. Hansard, June 16, 1928, Vol. 215, cc1359–1481.
187. *Gloucester Journal*, September 22, 1928, p. 5.
188. *The Bath Chronicle and Herald*, June 1, 1929, p. 4.
189. Noreen Branson, *Britain in the Nineteen Twenties*, Weidenfeld and Nicolson, 1971, p. 208.
190. Cynthia Mosley was one of the wealthiest women in the UK. The daughter of Lord Curzon, she met her husband Oswald Mosley while campaigning for the Conservative Lady Astor. Oswald Mosley later joined the Labour Party and so did she. However, she had no sympathy for his later fascism. She died in 1933.

CHAPTER 3

Over the Glass Cliff: The First Female Cabinet Minister, 1929–1953

On June 5, 1929, Margaret Bondfield returned from a few days rest at Brighton to be met at Victoria with a telegram which asked her to see Ramsay Macdonald, newly elected as Prime Minister of a Labour minority government.[1] When the two met, he offered Bondfield a Cabinet post as Minister of Labour at the considerable salary of £2000 which made her one of the country's top female earners.[2] When asked to take the post, Margaret Bondfield hesitated before modestly pointing out 'that a brilliant group of women had been returned … and asked him if he was quite sure he had made the best choice'.[3] Ramsay MacDonald reassured her that he was quite certain, though he was economical with the whole truth. He was uncomfortable with strong assertive women, preferring to talk to his female MPs about the weather and his silver collection rather than about politics.[4] In fact, Bondfield was appointed because Arthur Henderson,[5] 'a loyal supporter of women's emancipation',[6] had persuaded the Prime Minister that 'it would be a popular thing to do and would be especially popular among the women'.[7] MacDonald could have chosen Susan Lawrence, possibly the most competent, the most intellectual and the most able candidate for the post, but Bondfield fitted the trade union bill better and would act as a 'useful counter to the patrician intellectual wing of the Party'[8] epitomised by Lawrence. Certainly, MacDonald wanted his Cabinet to contain a mix of trade union officials and intellectuals in order to placate the various wings of the Labour Party. Furthermore, Miss Bondfield was considered more malleable and easier to work with than the acerbic too-clever-by-half Miss Lawrence.[9] Bondfield was no ideologue with good intentions; she was a team player, a realist who would not hesitate to compromise to get things done. She was thought 'kindly and honourable – a Christian gentlewoman. In a Cabinet she might be a poor counsellor but she would be a good colleague'.[10] MacDonald, of course, could have appointed both but preferred to appoint male mediocrities

© The Author(s) 2019
P. Bartley, *Labour Women in Power*,
https://doi.org/10.1007/978-3-030-14288-9_3

Fig. 3.1 Margaret Bondfield, the first woman Cabinet Minister, 1929 (© Chronicle/Alamy Stock Photo)

to other Cabinet posts, considering his appointment of one woman to his Cabinet sufficiently novel and innovative (Fig. 3.1).

For Bondfield, it was a momentous achievement. Wherever her future career might lead, Margaret Bondfield would always hold the unique distinction of being the first British woman Cabinet Minister and the first woman Privy Councillor.[11] She was now the Rt Honourable Margaret Bondfield, making a huge crack in the political glass ceiling. Her appointment was a landmark for women, even though she was not given a high-status ministry. Indeed, the Minister of Labour was considered to be an 'arduous and unpopular office' even in economically bountiful times'.[12] Moreover, Leah Manning heard more than one MP claim that she was only 'given the job because no one else would take it and because she's sure to make a mess of it'.[13] Nonetheless, Bondfield recognised the historical significance of her appointment, later commenting 'that it touched much more than merely my own self – it was part of the great revolution in the position of women which had taken place in my lifetime and which I had done something to help forward'.[14] Even King George V was impressed. When Bondfield went to Windsor to accept office he 'broke the customary silence to say "I am pleased to be the one to whom has come the opportunity to receive the first woman Privy councillor". His smile was cordial and sincere'.[15]

If anyone had been asked to describe what the first female Cabinet Minister would be like, commented the journalist Hamilton Fyfe, they would have portrayed her as a 'stern, hard-faced, intellectual-looking person, cold and competent and masculine in her ways',[16] which was probably a sketch of Susan Lawrence. In contrast, Margaret Bondfield was warm, friendly, rather plump and womanly. She was a popular figure, considered a careful, reliable politician, never one to make rash, emotional judgements, never one to make a quick thoughtless comment, someone who would listen, negotiate and compromise to achieve a result. Nonetheless, Bondfield had a 'quick wit and a tart tongue' honed in the trade union movement and was never at a loss for a reply to any heckler.[17] Her colleagues considered her a hard worker, practical and realistic. No one, claimed one newspaper, 'can listen to her speeches without being struck by their quality of common sense. They are singularly free of hyperbole; they deal always with the actualities of the situation'.[18] She was thought to have one of the 'finest speaking voices in the British Labour movement – clear as a bell, yet utterly without the strident quality that makes many women orators tiresome'.[19] Bondfield was thought to be widely read and knowledgeable from experience unlike the 'stale stereotyped knowledge of the so-called intelligentsia'. The new Minister of Labour was certainly seen as a safe pair of hands: she was an experienced trade unionist, a loyal party member and a well-respected expert on labour issues who could be relied on to be reasonable. She was now 56 years old, an age at which each measure would be carefully weighed and considered rather than approached with the revolutionary zeal of later colleagues like Ellen Wilkinson and Jenny Lee.

The Rt Hon Miss Bondfield received enormous piles of congratulations, especially from women's organisations. Messages flooded in from all over the world—from China, Peru, Asia, Africa, America, Canada, Australia, from the Dominions and the Colonies—all celebrating her success as the first Cabinet Minister. Lord Blanesburgh sent 'heartiest congratulations... it is all a delight'.[20] Many of the leading women of the day across the political spectrum—Emmeline Pethick-Lawrence, Margaret Llewelyn Davies, Nancy Astor, The Duchess of Atholl, Mrs Corbett-Ashby and the Marchioness of Londonderry—wrote personally to congratulate her. Oswald Garrison Villard, editor of the *New York Evening Post*, wrote that 'it will amuse you to know that Herbert Hoover now says he intended to appoint a woman in his Cabinet but he could not find anyone to measure up to the office'.[21] Bondfield read all her letters 'with a queer jumble of pride and humility. ... Pride that I should occupy this historic place, humility in the certain knowledge that uncounted numbers of pioneers had a greater right to it than I could claim'.[22] The National Union of Societies for Equal Citizenship hosted a lunch for the new Minister and the other female MPs to celebrate their success and the successes of the women's movement. Eleven of the fourteen women MPs joined a group of eminent feminists: Bondfield sat next to the Liberal Millicent Fawcett who sat next to the Conservative Nancy Astor, party politics forgotten in the euphoria of celebrating the progress of the women's movement.

Others were less eulogistic. The far left viewed her not as a skilled negotiator but as someone who would make too many concessions to capitalism.
For them, she was never going to be the heroine of working-class women.
The first step taken by Ramsay MacDonald, according to Wal Hannington,
the leader of the unemployed workers in the 1920s and 1930s, 'to assure
the ruling class that the treatment of the unemployed was safe in the hands
of Labour ... was the appointment of Margaret Bondfield as Minister of
Labour'.[23] Hannington remembered that Bondfield had been a member of
the notorious 1927 Blanesburgh Committee which reduced the payment of
unemployment benefits and brought in stricter rules for claimants. He had
his views confirmed when Bondfield refused to meet deputations from the
National Unemployed Workers' Movement (NUWM) insisting that no 'useful purpose could be served' by meeting them as the organisation was controlled by communists.[24] When the NUWM representatives refused to leave,
Margaret Bondfield called for the police to eject them.

Bondfield appeared unruffled by both the praise and criticism. She enjoyed
being Cabinet Minister: she had, she maintained, a natural inclination for
teamwork so when asked if she felt nervous she could truthfully answer
'No'.[25] Margaret Bondfield knew her own worth. In public, she claimed that
'the Blanesburgh Report ... had drawn attention to some of the qualifications for office which I possessed. ... I was known to be a person proved by
practice to be capable of defending a thesis, of answering questions on the
spur of the moment, and of facing without nervousness the hostile critics who
sought to trip me up. All the trials I had suffered in that detestable episode
now proved to be so many testimonials to my advantage'.[26] Privately, she was
plagued by doubts, confiding to her diary that all the congratulations she
received 'did not fit my mood which was one of depression. All yesterday and
today I have been oppressed by the complexity and difficulty of this post'.[27]

Margaret Bondfield joined a Cabinet of twenty men which included Arthur
Henderson (Foreign Secretary), Philip Snowden (Chancellor), J. H. Thomas
(Lord Privy Seal responsible for unemployment) two Conservatives, three
Liberals and a token left-winger, George Lansbury. It has been suggested that
she must have been lonely in the male-dominated Cabinet, but Bondfield was
used to being the only woman in far larger gatherings and was well able to
hold her own in discussions and parliamentary debates.

On her first morning, the new Minister of Labour was 'at work in her
office before 10 o'clock, the usual starting hour. She had the various officials introduced to her, and then plunged straight into the duties of the
Department'.[28] She had hobbled into her office on crutches due to a sprained
ankle. Immediately Bondfield set to work putting her ideas into practice. On
her first day, she notified the International Labour Organisation that Labour
would ratify the Washington Convention, a Convention that sought an
8-hour working day and a 48-hour week. In its election manifesto 'Labour
and the Nation', the party had promised to build bridges, roads and houses,
clear slums and employ people on public works. In reality, neither Miss

Bondfield nor the Labour Government was in a position to fulfil any of its promises. Once again it was a minority government, winning 287 seats to the Conservatives 260, and dependent on the goodwill of the 59 Liberals for its survival: Labour was in office, not in power.

POLITICAL AND ECONOMIC CHALLENGES

Margaret Bondfield realised that she would struggle with her new job, all too aware that the Labour Government had taken office at a critical moment.[29] In 1918, Britain had ended a war in which 'thousands of millions of pounds had first been borrowed, and then blown away in military operations'.[30] She knew only too well that Britain was in financial difficulties, faced with a large national debt and an increasingly lopsided balance of payments. The previous Conservative Government, under Stanley Baldwin, had left the country a legacy of 1.16 million unemployed, a government deficit, loans from international bankers and high interest rates. The outgoing Chancellor, Winston Churchill, gleefully informed Philip Snowden that 'he'd had not left a penny in the till!'[31] The new Minister of Labour had agreed to take on what was to be an impossible job: to find money for the rising unmanageable costs of unemployment benefits. Her Secretary in the civil service thought that no Minister had a rougher passage, maintaining that Bondfield showed great courage in taking on the role at a time of heavy unemployment.[32] Understandably, she occasionally felt 'oppressed by the complexity and difficulty of this post'.[33] Ramsay MacDonald had placed her at the edge of the glass cliff, and it would only take a small push for her to fall off into political oblivion.

Unfortunately, the Labour Government was too faint-hearted, too inexperienced and too ill-informed to offer new economic strategies to alleviate the situation. Margaret Bondfield later claimed that she had had little respect for the Prime Minister, believing that behind MacDonald's 'learned eloquence and charm' there was a weak man who never really understood the trade unions and who was too quick to appease those who opposed him. Certainly, MacDonald relied far too much on the Chancellor of the Exchequer Philip Snowden to direct policy. Snowden was an orthodox economist who believed in balanced budgets and ruled out 'every constructive option, arguing that major economic innovation and reconstruction was an unaffordable luxury'.[34] He convinced most of the Cabinet that economic retrenchment, rather than expansion, would restore confidence and prosperity to Britain, even using the budget to pay off the national debt rather than investing in public works. Unfortunately, Margaret Bondfield's term in office coincided with the economic strategy pursued by Snowden: she had responsibility, but little else.

Unfortunately, MacDonald did not organise his Cabinet efficiently. He placed Margaret Bondfield in charge of unemployment *benefits* but made overall unemployment the responsibility of J. H. Thomas, Oswald Mosley, George Lansbury and Tom Johnston. This group was considered to be an 'ill-assorted and ill-qualified team: Thomas had no stomach for hard work, Lansbury was politically illiterate, Johnston a lightweight, while Mosley had the useful but disruptive quality of being a young man in a hurry'.[35] As Bondfield later noted, the arrangement of separating responsibility for unemployment and responsibility for unemployment benefit never worked and later claimed that she thought it 'rather astonishing that anyone should have expected it to do so'.[36] In her view, J. H. Thomas was too opinionated, out of his depth in economics, unable to offer sensible solutions to the escalating unemployment and certainly not equal to the tremendous task that faced him.[37] Moreover, the four men were 'not suited by temperament to make an effective committee'[38]; their appointments, Bondfield maintained, were a strategic mistake. She was not surprised that the quartet soon broke apart. In January 1930, Oswald Mosley presented Cabinet with a set of proposals to reduce unemployment: investing in roads and other public works; imposing tariffs to protect British industry from international competition; and nationalising the main industries. Lansbury and Johnston supported his proposals whereas Thomas was vehemently against them. On February 3, the Cabinet had an inconclusive and incoherent discussion about Mosley's memorandum and referred it to a committee consisting of Snowden, Shaw, Greenwood and Bondfield. Snowden was undoubtedly the ruling figure in the committee and his ideas dominated. Bondfield and the committee rejected Mosley's ideas, and he resigned from the Cabinet; in February 1931, he left the Labour Party and formed the New Party which later merged with the British Union of Fascists.

Almost immediately Margaret Bondfield was confronted with the troublesome question of unemployment benefits. At the time she took office, the unemployment fund had a deficit of £36,870,000, nearly up to its statutory borrowing limit of £40,000,000.[39] Her first job was to safeguard the fund, find enough money to finance unemployment benefit and to check any abuse of the system. She set to work with her usual efficiency, carefully and pragmatically examining the evidence before making a judgement. First of all, Bondfield reviewed the whole system of unemployment insurance, toured the country to find out how it worked in practice and focussed on funding unemployment benefit adequately.[40] She aimed to end the policy of government borrowing to finance unemployment benefit: her upbringing made her dislike debt. Her view was not shared by the left-wing of the Labour Party who accused her of treating the unemployed as if they were criminals.[41] Unfortunately, as Brian Harrison points out, Bondfield 'was not in charge of the government's economic strategy, and all she could do was keep a cool head, administer her department efficiently, and hope that things would improve'.[42] *The Guardian* reported that any Minister of Labour would have a thankless task as 'the holders of the office are apt to become the whipping boys of governments. Miss Bondfield is proving no exception, and has been assailed with much vehemence and a good deal of unfairness by the backbenchers of her own party'.[43]

In July 1929, Bondfield introduced her first Unemployment Insurance Bill, an interim measure which increased the fund's limit to £49 million and set up local boards to assess the credibility of those claiming benefit. There was tense excitement in the House of Commons as the new Minister, 'with every eye upon her' and showing no signs of nervousness, rose from the crowded Bench.[44] Bondfield remained 'quite unruffled ... quietly and clearly stating her case, marshalling facts and figures to show the reasons for the decisions'[45] as she faced those on the opposition benches eagerly awaiting an opportunity to pick holes in the Bill. Occasionally, there was an outburst from the opposition benches 'expressing dissent, protest, doubt or possibly even ridicule. These are ignored as she serenely proceeded with her speech'.[46] 'Masterly Maggie', as she was now called, was in control, aware that she had faced much more hostile audiences in her time as a trade union organiser.

Unfortunately, for Margaret Bondfield the economy worsened. The Labour Party had only been in office for a few months when on October 29, 1929, the Wall Street Crash precipitated a worldwide economic crisis. The Labour Government had to choose: it could either cut expenditure or spend its way out of recession. The Chancellor of the Exchequer Philip Snowden convinced most of the Cabinet that economic retrenchment rather than expansion would restore confidence and prosperity to Britain.

By November 1929, unemployment was rocketing and the Unemployed Insurance Fund was bankrupt. It was against this background that Bondfield introduced her second Unemployment Bill which proposed changes in the rates and conditions of benefits in order to cut costs. On Thursday night, November 21 'that little body with a mighty heart' faced her critics 'with the same alert confidence that must have been hers ... when she sold silks and linens over a draper's counter'.[47] She appealed to reason rather than emotion, reading her speech 'with clearest utterance and at amazing speed'.[48] Her Bill tried to please all and ended up by alienating both parties. On the one hand, it displeased the Tories: it removed the anomaly under which children leaving school at 14 found themselves excluded for two years, it raised benefits for juveniles and other sections of the unemployed, and it amended the 'not genuinely seeking work' clause by allowing claimants to refuse unsuitable job offers. On the other hand, it displeased Labour: it put a limit on the time that benefits could be paid and restricted the categories of those who could apply. Bondfield defended her Bill by stating that 'like a housekeeper, she had not enough money to do what she wanted to do, having inherited a bankrupt estate from the Tories'.[49]

The publication of the Bill drew sharp criticism from a number of Bondfield's Labour colleagues and the trade unions. They insisted that the standard rate of benefit be increased, that agricultural workers and domestic servants be included in the scheme, that the waiting period for insurance be reduced from six days to three and—most significantly—that the 'not genuinely seeking work' clause be repealed completely. One of Labour's leading left-wing figures James Maxton gave an impassioned plea that the country had a 'duty' to see that the unemployed had the right to 'be maintained decently and in decent physical conditions'.[50] The attack on the Bill from trade unionists was not surprising. Union leaders had helped formulate the Labour Party Manifesto which promised to amend the Unemployment Insurance Acts 'so as to afford more generous maintenance for the unemployed' and the removal of those qualifications which 'deprived them of payments'.[51] Labour they felt had them down. Moreover, they had been offended when Bondfield refused their offer to help draft the Insurance Bill. A stand-off between trade unions and a member of the government was worrying as unions were the backbone of the Labour Party and it would not help Margaret Bondfield to upset her financial sponsors.

By way of contrast, Chancellor Philip Snowden paid tribute to Bondfield's efficiency in undertaking the 'difficult and often unpleasant task' of office and displaying a 'thorough acquaintance of the Unemployment Insurance Acts'. In his view, she was 'thoroughly competent'.[52] Moreover, Snowden considered that she was 'treated with a shameful lack of courtesy and with unfair criticism by the Left-Wing section of the Labour Party'.[53] The attack, according to Snowden, was an 'exhibition of disloyalty and of the lack of the team spirit which has so often exposed the Labour Party to the jeers of its opponents and caused dismay among its supporters in the country'.[54] The Labour Party, he believed, was 'still harbouring the illusion that there was an inexhaustible source of revenue to be drawn upon by further taxation of the rich'.[55] In his opinion, Maxton and the left-wing had not appreciated the crisis facing the nation, nor the fact that the economic situation meant that it was 'impossible to carry out a policy of increased expenditure which might have been possible when trade was booming and revenue was expanding'.[56] Snowden may have been critical of the left-wing opposition to Margaret Bondfield in his memoirs but at the time neither he nor others on the Front Bench gave her much support. Indeed, as one colleague noted, 'they seemed content to sit back and leave her to take the brunt of the attack. ... As the first woman to hold cabinet rank, and with unsympathetic colleagues, she had unusual difficulties to contend with, in circumstances which would have daunted any Minister, however competent'.[57]

As a result of pressure from MacDonald and Snowden who in turn had been coerced by the trade unions, Bondfield withdrew the offending 'not genuinely seeking work' clause. When Bondfield's amended Bill passed its second reading, there was a 'great roar of cheering' from the Labour MPs who had crowded into the House of Commons.[58] However, Bondfield's withdrawal of the offending clause made the government 'appear mean, incompetent and pusillanimous all at once'.[59] Margaret Bondfield's capitulation was regarded as spineless, and she was accused of surrendering to the extremists of the Labour Party. She had pleased no one: in putting the Bill forward she had first of all offended the left-wing of the Labour Party; in retracting it she had offended the rest. The Conservatives attacked her for her being much too generous, claiming that unemployment benefit enabled 'work-shy's to live in idleness on public money'[60] and allowed undeserving shirkers to enrich themselves at the expense of the workman. The Tories had obviously forgotten that they had left the Unemployment Insurance Fund nearly bankrupt with a deficit of £36,000,000, just 4 million short of its maximum. Even a section of the left-wing press expressed concern about the spiralling costs of unemployment benefit. *The Guardian* argued that unemployment relief had 'become surrounded with an insidious undergrowth of abuse' and that reform was essential. In its opinion, there were 'ridiculous anomalies by which quite high-paid casual workers received supplementary benefits'.[61]

Margaret Bondfield had another problem: in this case the person in charge of unemployment policy, J. H. Thomas. He had rejected Mosley's recommendations and still had done little to alleviate the growing unemployment. As a consequence, Bondfield's job was becoming ever more stressful: with numbers out of work increasing, the unemployment fund was once again running out of money. By the end of 1930, the economy was in free fall and as unemployment figures climbed towards 2 million Margaret Bondfield had the unenviable task of asking Parliament to increase the borrowing limit of the government. In April 1930, she asked to increase the limit to £50 million, in July 1930 to £60 million, in December 1930 to £70 million.[62] Bondfield found the stress unbearable, especially when the leading left-wing intellectual Harold Laski criticised her in a widely read newspaper. In January 6, 1931, she wrote a note to the Prime Minister 'written after considerable thought and with the sole desire to serve in the best way open to me – It is obvious that feeling has been working against me inside the Party – Laski's article in today's *Daily Herald* merely expresses the kind of criticism which has been going around in private conversation'.[63] She offered to resign. Ramsay MacDonald replied 'My dear Miss Bondfield, Your letter offering to resign came to me yesterday. I grieve very much at the causes. You have had a hard and thankless task and your critics have been heartless, as jealous people must be. Laski was not too helpful. But don't think of doing anything at present. You have my sympathy and support. Always'.[64] Margaret Bondfield was persuaded to remain in post while the situation worsened. As unemployment approached two and a half million in February 1931, she pleaded for the unemployed insurance to be raised to £90 million. In June 1931, with the unemployed now totalling 2,713,000, Bondfield asked for £131 million. It was, in the view of the Cabinet Minister and trade union leader J. R. Clynes, 'like trying to stop an incoming tide with a sand barrier'.[65] The House of Commons put pressure on Bondfield to justify these increases. She defended her policy by saying that she did not support 'the idea of further borrowing because I believe that it is right, or because I believe that it is a good principle. I say that in the world situation in which we find ourselves it is the only possible course'.[66]

The Conservatives demanded a drastic reduction in national expenditure. Applicants for unemployment benefits were suspected of claiming falsely or unjustifiably. In Bondfield's home of Chard, it was claimed that a farm worker 'who had been drawing a dole of 3s a week ... had refused farm work' because work was not worth it.[67] Married women, short-term workers and seasonal workers were all accused of abusing the system by claiming benefits to which they were not entitled. Unemployment pay, it was alleged 'encouraged abuse of the dole by the work-shy'.[68] Day after day, stories of alleged misuse appeared in the national press. Cases were reported of girls 'leaving their employment one day to be married, and, the day after the marriage ceremony, applying for unemployment benefits'.[69] Poor Law Guardians in Tiverton declared there was a 'scandalous abuse of unemployment benefits'. Homeless men, they alleged, were getting free board and lodging at the workhouse, claiming benefits and returning to the workhouse 'the worse for drink'.[70] Some of the allegations were patently ludicrous: the *Nottingham Guardian* accused a sixteen-year-old girl of obtaining £150 in benefits for one year, a charge rebutted by Margaret Bondfield who declared that the girl 'must have maintained not only herself but a husband or parent and at least 23 children' to be awarded such a large sum.[71] The attacks on unemployment benefit were part of a general demand to cut back on government expenditure and 'scarcely a day would pass without some industrialist or Chamber of commerce being quoted as prophesying doom if the Government did not bring to a halt the ruinous expenditure on the social services'.[72] The government, it was argued, must curtail its expenditure and drastically reduce taxes if prosperity was to be restored. Predictably, the right-wing press blamed the unemployed and the Labour Government for the failure to balance the budget rather than the fact that the capitalist system had broken down in the Western world and that Britain was in the middle of the deepest and most prolonged depression in modern history.

In December 1930, the Labour Government had appointed a Royal Commission under the direction of Judge Holman Gregory to enquire into the provisions and workings of the Unemployment Insurance Scheme and alleged abuses of the system.[73] Ramsay MacDonald thought it was a way of the government securing more borrowing for the insurance fund, and 'to tide things over for the next ... six months'.[74] He knew that Royal Commissions take years to complete, making it attractive for governments like MacDonald's to use them to postpone decision-making. Margaret Bondfield was delegated to persuade the TUC Walter Citrine and other Trade Union representatives to join the Commission. After much persuasion, only two Labour MPs agreed to be on it: Citrine and the trade unions were suspicious, believing the Commission to be a government plot to justify future reductions in unemployment pay. Moreover, they particularly mistrusted Margaret Bondfield, remembering her signature of the Blanesburgh Report and her attitude towards those accused of 'not genuinely seeking work'. Their fears were well founded: Bondfield provided the Commission with examples of the way in which benefit was being misused: of steel and coal workers who worked for three days a week and claimed benefit for the remaining days; of women who worked part-time of their own accord and claimed benefit; of market workers who only worked on market days and claimed benefit for the rest of the week.[75] On June 4, 1931, the Commission published its provisional decisions, recommending limiting benefits to 26 weeks a year, reducing benefits by approximately 12% for adults,[76] withdrawing benefit for those considered to be 'not genuinely seeking work' and introducing a means test. It also tightened up the regulations for those in intermittent, casual or short-time work, seasonal workers and married women—the so-called anomalies. The two Labour MPs refused to sign it and issued their own minority report.

Left-wing opposition to the report was unanimous: on June 7, the TUC announced preparations for massive demonstrations against it; on June 9, the *Daily Herald* denounced it as a 'malicious attack on the already poverty-stricken conditions of the unemployed'[77]; on June 11, about 100 trade union-sponsored MPs declared it was 'wholly unacceptable'. MacDonald caved into this pressure and promised not to reduce benefits, increase contributions or shorten the period of benefit.[78] Realising that she was in the minority, Bondfield changed her mind and now spoke out against cuts, declaring that it was 'not the time to single out one class, and that the class which can least afford it, for a serious reduction in the already low level of subsistence which has been secured for it. Our country is not so poor that it cannot afford to maintain its unemployed at least sufficiently well to preserve them from physical deterioration'.[79] She went on to say that it was 'a gross libel on the working classes to suggest that any substantial number of them prefer unemployment to work', arguing that 'so long as our modern civilisation continues to permit the extremes of wealth and poverty ... we cannot abandon the unemployed victims of modern industrialism and let them sink below a level of bare subsistence'.[80] In the end, the Labour Government rejected the recommendations of the Royal Commission and agreed not to reduce benefits or impose any drastic tests for those seeking benefits.

The unemployment crisis remained. Bondfield proposed increasing borrowing to £150 million to finance the unemployment fund, yet had to persuade the House of Commons and the bankers to do so. Bondfield was a team player, always willing to compromise, always seeking to appease, always willing to listen to the other point of view, always willing to negotiate and always trying to find a solution. She realised the need to pacify the Conservatives and Liberals who were clamouring for cuts, otherwise Parliament would not agree to increase the funding of unemployment benefits. Bondfield also had to convince the bankers to provide further loans to the government. There was no secret, claimed the New York *Morning Post* that 'Wall Street dislikes the dole, which it regards as a sort of premium on shiftlessness and a practice encouraging idleness'.[81] Bondfield was pressurised to reduce the escalating costs of unemployment benefits: she could either make a general reduction in benefit rates or exclude certain groups from claiming benefits. In the end, Bondfield took what she thought was the least offensive option and brought in an Anomalies Bill which focussed on the alleged inconsistencies in unemployment benefit. Her new Bill which aimed to remedy anomalies in Unemployment Insurance was designed to save an estimated £5 million a year. It was nowhere near enough to solve the nation's economic problems and was viewed as merely a humiliating gesture to pacify those clamouring for cuts.

Unfortunately, it was mostly women who suffered: short-time, part-time and seasonal workers were excluded. And all married women were to be denied benefit. It was a tough decision: Bondfield was a feminist and had spent all her life fighting for the rights of working-class women. The Cabinet was divided and wanted to postpone making a decision. This time Bondfield was unusually obdurate. On July 1, she wrote to MacDonald telling him about her 'serious apprehension at the possibility that the Anomalies Bill may be postponed ... If it is now decided to postpone any action until the autumn, my own position will be impossible and we shall be open to the accusation that we obtained the consent of the House to further borrowing on false pretences'.[82] The Prime Minister wrote back that he had been surprised 'that you yourself did not seem to press for the immediate enactment of the measure' in the Cabinet.[83] It seemed as if neither Bondfield nor MacDonald wanted to shoulder the responsibility for such a controversial proposal.

In July 1931, Margaret Bondfield brought in the last Bill she was to pilot through the House. By now, she had alienated a number of trade union leaders, particularly those in areas of high unemployment by her willingness to cut expenditure. She had also alienated feminists by her exclusion of married women from benefits and by her suggestion that unmarried unemployed women should retrain as domestic servants. Once again, Bondfield faced overwhelming criticism from her colleagues leading to an internecine conflict between various sections of the Labour Party. The Conservative and Liberal parties withdrew 'from this painful spectacle of civil war'[84] and left the Labour radicals and the government to battle it out. Under the leadership of James Maxton, the Independent Labour Party (ILP) tabled ten pages of amendments to Bondfield's Insurance Anomalies Bill. The gloves, according to the *Manchester Guardian*, were off as the ILP's 'carefully planned campaign of obstruction against the Bill' forced votes on each amendment.[85] On July 15, the ILP group kept the House sitting from 2:15 p.m. until 10:00 a.m. There were 33 Divisions. MacDonald complained that the left-wing harried the Bill 'unmercifully in an all-night session, when tempers ran high, and furious accusations were flung across the floor'.[86] 'The real attack' Bondfield believed 'laid in the steady and irreconcilable hostility of the ILP members of the House. ... I was compelled to keep the House sitting until I got through the Committee stage of the Bill – and that was at 9am in the morning'.[87] As the night wore on, MPs began to fall asleep; at 8:45 a.m., the smell of eggs and bacon began to pervade and the Chamber 'thinned considerably' when MPs were tempted by breakfast.[88]

At 4 a.m., the clause that would disqualify 180,000 married women from claiming benefits was discussed. For a woman to cut women's benefits was too much for some of the feminists in the Chamber. A group of Labour women (Jenny Lee, Cynthia Mosley and Ellen Wilkinson) worked with the Independent MP Eleanor Rathbone and the Conservative Nancy Astor to oppose the policy of the female Minister who planned to make the lives of other women even more difficult. In Ellen Wilkinson's view, it raised 'the old, bad principle of discrimination against women, which the whole women's movement has been fighting against since about 1870'.[89] Outside Parliament, Rebecca West and Emmeline Pethick-Lawrence voiced their objections too. Their cries remained unheeded. The Bill was carried by 221 to 20 votes and a large tranche of married women were removed from the unemployment register on the basis that they were not 'genuinely seeking work'. Bondfield's economies did little as unemployment continued to rise and borrowing continued to increase. As a consequence, Bondfield 'got the worst of both worlds: she failed to impose her policy and at the same time undermined her political base'.[90] Many thought that the unemployed had been punished enough by being thrown out of work and 'to victimise them all over again, in order to find a way out of a crisis which was none of their making, would be to make a mockery of everything the Labour Party stood for'.[91] Nonetheless, some like Leeds Council favoured the Bill, pleased to save £1000 a week when 1700 local women were disqualified from claiming benefits.

Meanwhile, another committee was about to cause havoc for the Labour Party and its handling of the British economy. In February 1931, Snowden had set up a Committee on National Expenditure under Sir George May to see what economies could be made in national expenditure. He wanted ammunition for his proposed budget cuts and particularly for Margaret Bondfield's proposed reductions in unemployment benefits. When it reported on July 31, the 'five rich men on this committee'[92] advocated that the £120 million budget deficit forecast for 1932–1933 should be bridged by cuts of £97 million made up of cuts in benefits and pay: £67 million from a reduction of 20% in unemployment benefits; 20% from a reduction in teachers' salaries; 12.5% from a reduction in police salaries; and 10% from a reduction in the armed services. It was a report, A. J. P. Taylor argues, consisting of 'prejudice, ignorance and panic'.[93] More importantly, it made Britain's economic position seem much more precarious than it actually was, a position not refuted by Snowden or the government.[94]

The May Report was allegedly read by every banker 'and by the frugal, prudent, investing public of these great Powers … (who) unanimously asseverated over the morning coffee or grapefruit that they would never, never, ever lend a penny to the Bank of England, nor invest a penny in British industry'[95] until the Budget was balanced. Certainly, following the publication of this report, and the negative press it received, foreign investors lost confidence both in the British economy and the Labour Government.

Shareholders and financiers did not believe that the Labour Government would implement the recommended cuts and sold their sterling. As Bondfield later pointed out, 'things were already tumbling. Foreign depositors were withdrawing their money from London, and demanding gold. The Bank of England reserve was melting. ... The whole thing was irrational and perverse but the stampede had been started, and nothing seemed able to stop it'.[96]

When the report was published, Parliament was in recess. Ministers were called back from their holiday. In the next few days, the political pace quickened. On August 19, a full Cabinet meeting discussed the collapse of sterling and the need to restore confidence in British economy: the New York Federal Reserve Bank had refused to advance a loan unless cuts were made. At a later meeting, MacDonald told his Cabinet that 'foreign lenders regarded the heavy financial burdens ... of the Unemployment Insurance scheme as impairing the security of their loans'.[97]

At 7 p.m., Sunday, August 23, 1931, after a number of very tense meetings, the Cabinet gathered to reach a crucial decision: cutbacks of around £68 million were detailed including limiting benefit to 26 weeks, introducing a means test, removing the 'anomalies' and reducing unemployment pay by 10%. There were proposals for a 15% reduction in teachers' salaries and for pay cuts in the armed forces and the police. MacDonald urged his Cabinet to agree to the cuts, arguing that if 'the Cabinet were unable to accept them, then it was clear that the loan which was essential to avert the crisis would not be forthcoming and it was unthinkable that the Government could remain in Office'.[98] Bondfield agreed to the proposed reductions 'in the belief ... that a 10% cut would be a far less hardship to the unemployed' than the consequences a likely freeze on benefits and government spending.[99] However, MacDonald was unable to persuade all of his Cabinet, and it divided 12:9 in favour of the economies.[100] Since the minority consisted of some of the leading ministers who carried great weight within the Labour Party, the resignation of the Labour Government was largely inevitable.

At 10.00 a.m., Sunday, August 24, 1931, Ramsay MacDonald went to the Palace: King George asked MacDonald to form a National Government. By now the economy was in free fall and the misery of those already unemployed, underemployed and poorly paid was set to worsen. Later that day, MacDonald told his Cabinet that because it had failed to 'reach agreement on the previous day, the financial position had greatly deteriorated, and the situation was now one of the gravest possible character'.[101] He stated that in view of the gravity of the situation he proposed to tender the resignation of his government. The Cabinet resigned. The Labour Government was no more.

THE NATIONAL GOVERNMENT, AUGUST 1931

On August 25, MacDonald became Prime Minister of a National Government; in effect, he was a man without a party, a figurehead for and a prisoner of the Conservatives.[102] MacDonald insisted that if he had agreed

to stay as Labour Prime Minister and defy the bankers, 'a perfect tor-
rent of credit' would leave the country every day and the Cabinet would
have been overwhelmed by it all. Furthermore, he argued 'the day you met
Parliament you would have been swept out of existence. ... the rank and
file have not always the same duty as the leaders'.[103] MacDonald accused
his former Labour Cabinet for destroying 'all we have done. Had the Govt.
done its duty there would have been little interruption in that work. They
ran away and left everything unprotected. If this is the best Labour can do,
then it is not fit to govern'.[104] Moments after the Labour Government had
resigned, confidence in sterling recovered and international financiers offered
unlimited credit to the Bank of England. A new credit of £80 million was
arranged, even before the new government had discussed its budget. Ramsay
MacDonald insisted that there had been no 'bankers' ramp' nor a conspiracy
against the Labour Government. Few in the Labour party believed him.

Only three Cabinet Ministers—Philip Snowden, J. Thomas and Lord
Sankey—agreed to serve in MacDonald's National Government; three junior ministers and 13 backbenchers joined them. Earl Winterton nicknamed
it the 'Government of the unburied dead'.[105] Margaret Bondfield's immediate response was that 'Mr MacDonald ... has decided to sacrifice himself to
save the country from financial chaos'.[106] She wrote to MacDonald expressing approval for his decision and to 'assure you of my deep sympathy in and
admiration for the decision you have taken. May God give you the strength
you need and the success you deserve in bringing the nation through this
crisis'.[107] He replied on August 25 thanking her for 'all that you have done',
and claiming that he was 'trying to involve very few of my friends in the new
Government because so far as I can see it means their political death, and if
we are to have a small Cabinet the available offices are very few'.[108] It was
clear that Margaret Bondfield would not be offered a job in the new government, even though she had supported MacDonald's proposals to cut government expenditure. Whether she would have accepted a post if asked is an
unanswerable question.

In the end, Bondfield refused to cross the floor to join MacDonald. She
told one American friend, the labour activist Elizabeth Evans that there 'was
no choice at all. I stand by the organised Labour movement; I have grown
up with it, and I owe it practically all that I am; and whether our policy was
wise or unwise, that was the road that I had to travel'.[109] Bondfield's departure was mourned. She received a pile of letters from unexpected sources.
Eleanor Rathbone, who had fought against the Anomalies Bill, wrote how
sad she was about Bondfield's departure, praising her for her 'fine work at the
Ministry amidst great difficulties and antagonism'.[110] One former civil servant
wrote 'to thank you on my own account for all the kindness and considera-
tion which you have shown us. You encouraged us to tell you frankly the facts
as we knew them ... you gave us prompt decisions and you stood up for your
policy and your department with a courage which won our hearts. Any civil
servant must regret parting from such a minister'.[111] Two others wrote that

'to us as women the appointment as Minister of Labour of the first woman to hold Cabinet rank was a source of the keenest pride and satisfaction. ... Your presence in the department was a very real encouragement and inspiration'.[112] Later Bondfield confessed that her post as Minister of Labour was an unsatisfactory job 'with more kicks than thanks because we were heading for the big depression with millions unemployed for whom no work had been planned. Not glory, but hard work and deep anxiety, was my portion'.[113] In effect, Margaret Bondfield was in the wrong place at the wrong time.

Labour opposition to MacDonald's newly formed National Government soon made itself heard, particularly when the new government agreed to implement the cuts in public expenditure. On August 26, the trade unions, the parliamentary party and the National Executive issued a joint statement agreeing to 'vigorously oppose' the new government. The TUC praised the actions of Bondfield and those who had resigned from the Cabinet maintaining that they had 'acted as Labour Ministers would be expected to act by the Labour Movement'.[114]

On September 8, 1931, Parliament re-assembled. It presented a 'new and strange appearance'[115] with the Labour Party now on the opposition benches facing the combined strength of the Liberal and Conservative parties, a dozen Labour MPs and its previous leader, Ramsay MacDonald. Margaret Bondfield was not there: she was in a nursing home in Tunbridge Wells suffering from fibrosis, a chronic extremely painful autoimmune condition which affected her central nervous system, stiffened and weakened her muscles and brought about sudden painful spasms. It made her skin painful to touch and produced unremitting tiredness. Margaret Bondfield lost a stone in weight and was ordered to bed. She wrote to a friend that it was 'one of the most horribly painful things that anybody can have – it is not the least interesting or romantic'.[116] She had completely collapsed after her defeat: Margaret Bondfield had had a physical and nervous breakdown, brought on by stress, fatigue and over-work combined with the grief of watching all she had worked for disappear.[117] There are many letters of sympathy. Philip Snowden wrote to 'My dear Margaret' offering his sympathy and 'best wishes for a speedy and complete recovery', saying he was 'not surprised at your breakdown in view of the very strenuous and worrying time you have had during the last two years. ... I know too that I have your sympathy in my own unpleasant task. Believe me, yours affectionately'.[118] Even the King and Queen sent a telegram expressing regret about 'your indisposition'.[119]

Margaret Bondfield had every right to be cast-down: over many years, she had helped to create the parliamentary Labour Party, she had helped build it up from a handful of MPs to over 100, she had enabled it to gain office, and she had been part of government. Now she witnessed the Labour movement disintegrate, all within a few days. Moreover, she beheld the incompetent Thomas, the man who had helped make her job as Minister of Labour untenable, appointed to a Cabinet post. Margaret Bondfield drew upon her religious beliefs to give her the strength to carry on. In a speech to the Central

Club, Bondfield claimed that 'we are living in a world which is not Christian – that our economic system is not Christian – that our political system is not Christian. ... Jesus came to teach us that we are to be saved through love ... love of our fellows ... of our neighbours'. As ever, she had a radical interpretation of Christianity based on temporal not just spiritual action.[120] She had wanted the Kingdom of God on earth, thought Labour was the only party that could deliver a theological socialism and was devastated to watch her ideals be obliterated by those she had once esteemed.

On his first day as leader of the National Government, MacDonald faced a storm of criticism from his former colleagues. Arthur Henderson, the new leader of the Labour Party denied the claim of MacDonald to call his government a National Government when it did not contain the majority of Labour MPs; James Maxton ironically declared that 'Great Britain is ... going to be the great, wonderful country ... It is going to have its great future as the financial centre of the world by succumbing to the meanest, greediest, most grasping, least patriotic section of the community and by imposing sacrifices upon women and children who have known nothing but sacrifice during all their lives'.[121] Winston Churchill felt as if he was 'listening to a family quarrel, to a bitter dispute which was going to break up a happy home'.[122]

On September 11, MacDonald presented the government's National Economy Bill, introducing economies of £70 million. It cut the wages of teachers, it cut the wages of civil servants, it cut the wages of soldiers, sailors and airmen, and it cut unemployment benefit. On October 14, a general election took place. The election campaign 'was a political whirlwind without parallel',[123] fought during the biggest world financial crisis the world had ever known. Nearly 3 million people were now out of work. MacDonald appealed for a 'doctor's mandate' to remedy the economic situation, called for national unity and charged the Labour Party with absconding from governmental responsibility. Snowden urged 'the country to show its condemnation of the cowardice and untrustworthiness of men who ran away from their national duty in the hour of crisis'.[124] The National Government had the mainstream press on its side: only the *Daily Herald*, Labour's paper, the *Manchester Guardian* and *Reynold's News* remained sympathetic.

The Labour Party, now without its more Conservative leaders, moved to the left. Its new manifesto advocated state control of the banks, of transport, steel, electricity, gas and coal, a programme which Snowden denounced as 'Bolshevism run mad'. L. C. B. Seaman makes the point that the idea of the Labour Party bereft of MacDonald and Snowden, 'carrying into effect a programme as ambitious as this after its sorry performance in the two previous years was risible in the extreme'.[125] Moreover, funds for fighting the election declined dramatically: Labour had almost £20,000 less to spend on election expenses.[126] Bondfield got up from her bed, broke off her treatment for fibrosis and still unwell, fragile and in pain began to campaign in her constituency. As soon as the election was over, she went back to bed.

LOSING HER WALLSEND SEAT, OCTOBER 1931

In the last election, Bondfield spoke at 61 meetings, quite a large proportion of them in the open air.[127] This time she had to get out of bed and break off her treatment to canvass voters and the number of meetings she held dropped to 37. Her efforts were ineffectual, and she lost her seat to the Conservative candidate, Irene Ward. In 1929, Bondfield had won her seat by a majority of 7105; in 1931, she lost by 7606 votes. The safe Labour seat was no more. She was not alone: Labour only won a humiliating 52 seats. 91% of MPs now owed allegiance to MacDonald's new Ministry, making it an unbalanced House of Commons, a Conservative Government in all but name. Over 70% of the electorate from 'all political parties, all religious denominations, all vocations, all social grades and especially both sexes' had voted against the Labour Party programme.[128] There was no effective opposition left. As the TUC stated, the first Labour Government had been destroyed by a 'Red Letter and the second by a Bankers' Order'.[129] Bondfield 'lost in good company. ... Such a landslide carried away the Labour Party ... All the members of the Labour Government except George Lansbury lost their seat'.[130] No Labour women were left in Parliament: thirteen Conservative women, one Liberal and one Independent now sat on the benches. Bondfield felt that 'we had not been outreasoned, nor overcome in matters of principle – we had been outmanoeuvred by unscrupulous tacticians'.[131] In this respect, Bondfield shared the disconsolate and recriminatory mood of the Labour Party, all of whom blamed Ramsay MacDonald for their collective defeat.

In fact, Bondfield was partly responsible for her own loss. Her election leaflets claimed that she had 'endeavoured to ease the lot of the unemployed' but the electorate disbelieved her, remembering her actions as Minister of Labour in putting forward the Anomalies Bill and initially supporting the cuts recommended by Snowden.[132] She was so distrusted that a number of dissatisfied and disillusioned Labour voters actively campaigned against their local MP.[133] At the time of the election, the industrial depression hung like a cloud over Wallsend and showed no signs of lifting. Unemployment in the North East was high and the wages of those employed 'shockingly low'.[134] Her agent had earlier warned her that the effect of 'long continued unemployment, under-employment and low wages' upon the life of the local party was bad'.[135] It did not help that there were no longer generous contributions from trade unions towards electoral expenses: the Miners Association's donation dropped to £20. Moreover, the combination of ministerial duties and illness had meant that Bondfield was absent a lot from her constituency: she had ignored one of the important lessons for any politician, that is the need to take care of her political base. In contrast, her Conservative rival, the younger, healthier Irene Ward was most assiduous in nurturing the constituency at all times. After the election was over, Margaret Bondfield returned to the nursing home.

The new House of Commons looked odd: there were only about 50 Labour MPs rattling about on the opposition benches while the government of over 500 sat packed on the other side. The Labour Party had lost nearly all its leaders, making the opposition unequal to the 'task of using the Opposition instrument and without it the Parliamentary institution itself cannot be worked'.[136] Moreover, it meant that the newly elected government could proceed to carry out its policy without being challenged: the unemployed had their benefit reduced by 10%, and cuts were made in social services, the pay of teachers, the armed services and the police. Means testing was introduced. It foreshadowed a bleak future: the people of the UK were about to face one of the worst economically challenging periods of modern times.

Bondfield was now 58, a little too young to retire and a little too old to start a new career. Nonetheless, she had been forged in the fire of trade union politics, had fought hard to gain her seats in Parliament and had struggled against strong opposition in her ministerial roles. In 1935, she contested Wallsend again only to be defeated for the second time by Irene Ward who beat her by 2379 votes. It must have been particularly frustrating to see a younger rival like Ellen Wilkinson who also lost her seat in 1931 sit once more on the opposition benches, now as MP for Jarrow, a neighbouring constituency.

Margaret Bondfield was a single woman, dependent on her own resources to pay her rent and bills, buy her food, clothe herself and have money left for travel and entertainment. Being an MP was a financially precarious existence for those without a private income, a husband or a trade union to support them. After the loss of her seat, Margaret returned to her old post as Chief Woman Officer at the National Union of General and Municipal Workers, back to a job which paid much less and which involved 'constant travelling, often in the cold and rain, sleeping in a different hotel every night, giving up leisure hours, evening and Sundays to speak at Labour and trade union meetings'.[137] But now she was much older, had been very ill and no longer had the energy of youth to help her cope with the demands of her job. Out of office, and back in the trade union movement Bondfield grew more radical. At the 1932 TUC conference, she proposed that 'this Congress views with alarm the position of unemployment' and asked that Congress support a 40-hour week. She drew wry comments from colleagues sceptical about her re-discovered commitment to workers' rights. Hugh Dalton thought she had 'cheek to make speeches now in favour of a forty-hour week, when, in office, she couldn't put through a forty-eight hour week'.[138] Bondfield also faced criticism at the 1932 National Conference for Labour Women for the part she played as Minister of Labour; one delegate even shouted out that Miss Bondfield 'was not in sympathy with the workers or the unemployed'.[139] Bondfield worked hard to regain her socialist credibility. In 1935, at the Conference for Labour Women she put forward a resolution condemning the family Means Test, arguing that it involved 'degradation and intolerable hardship on the unemployed and employed alike and is the means of breaking up homes and families'.[140] She also protested against the 'inadequacy of existing rates of unemployment benefit for all men and women'.[141] At the conference the following year, Miss Bondfield went further, 'recognising that the social-isation of the means of production, distribution and exchange, is ulti-mately the only secure guarantee for an adequate standard of living'.[142] But Bondfield's political standing remained low. Trade unionists were particularly unforgiving of her work on the Blanesburgh Committee and her unemploy-ment policies when she held power: she never regained a seat on the General Council of the TUC.[143]

For the most part, she seemed adrift, trying to find a cause in which she could make a difference. In 1936, the 63-year-old Bondfield was endorsed by the NEC as prospective candidate for Reading, ready for the next election to be held in 1940. When the scheduled election was postponed because of the Second World War, Bondfield withdrew her candidature, fulfilling 'the pledge I had given myself not to stand again for Parliament after I had reached the age of seventy'.[144] The press dubbed her a 'forgotten woman', someone who had been a household name who was now out of the lime-light. In February 1936, she helped form the Over-Thirty Association with Gertrude Denman and Margaret Wintringham to help women over 30 find work; in 1938, they founded the Over-Thirty Housing Association to provide homes for poorly paid workers.[145] She continued to write articles for Labour journals on social issues. One article, 'Killing the Killer', argued that tubercu-losis spread because of 'insufficient nourishment, unventilated rooms, alco-holism, worry, overstrain, insufficient rest, and lack of domestic and personal cleanliness. Many of these conditions are subscribed under the broad heading of poverty, but poverty is not the main ally' she thought but ignorance.[146] In March 1938, now aged 65, Margaret Bondfield retired from her post of chief woman officer of the National Union of General and Municipal Workers which she had held since 1920. Overall, she had been a trade unionist for 48 years. In April 1938, she packed her bags, booked a passage on a ship and went on a twenty-one thousand mile, ten-month lecture tour/holiday of the USA, Canada and Mexico. At last, she could breathe freely.

Margaret Bondfield was at her happiest in America. She felt cherished by her trade union friends like Rose Schneiderman who was 'terribly excited at the news' of her visit and could not 'begin to tell you how much it will mean to have you with us again. ... There is so much to discuss with you'.[147] On April 24, she was guest of honour at the Women's Trade Union League Annual Meeting, a meeting with 2000 delegates. The organisers had fixed the date at a time she could attend, a reflection of how well regarded she was in the USA.[148] It gave Margaret Bondfield 'much pleasure to meet really effi-cient women who treat their jobs seriously as do the best men'.[149] She had visited in 1933, a trip that coincided 'with the birth of Roosevelt's New Deal and it will be my inspiration to remember that the day I reached Washington was the day on which child labour under the age of 16 was abolished'.[150] In 1938, she was 'deeply impressed' by the success of the New Deal and the way it pumped money into the economy and reduced unemployment. The New Deal was a similar strategy as that advocated by Oswald Mosley, a strategy which had been rejected by Bondfield and the Labour Cabinet. She met other friends too such as Frances Perkins who had been appointed by Roosevelt as Secretary of Labour, the first woman to hold a Cabinet position in America.[151]

It was a dark and stormy August night when Margaret Bondfield drove out to meet Leon Trotsky in a house just outside of Mexico City provided by the radical artist, Diego Rivera.[152] She spoke of her experience in heightened prose, describing how her group was squashed into seven large cars 'which splashed their way through the silent roads till we were halted outside a house which appeared to be in complete darkness; ... we lowered our voices and quietly went through a dark doorway into a dimly-lit yard, where an attendant, wearing a revolver, checked us in. The door was then locked and we were taken through patios and passages to an inner room where armed attendants covered the two doorways'.[153] Natalia Sedova, Trotsky's wife came in looking worn and tired with grief 'ash-grey hair and eyebrows, eyes that could weep no more. ... in came Leon Trotsky looking singularly unchanged since I last saw him in 1920 ... neatly dressed, not a hair out of place ... the same clear mocking glance ... the same assurance that he had no doubts about the rightness of his way – a vital personality'.[154] Trotsky's capacity for 'uttering the biting phrase and of puncturing pretentiousness' was seen to be as great as ever. Two years later Trotsky was murdered with an ice-axe by a NKVD agent whom he had befriended.

On Labor Day weekend, September 3, Margaret Bondfield went on holiday 'no conferences, no meetings for a month! O! frabjous joy!'[155] She seemed to come to life, taking a boat to Vancouver to stay with friends and go camping. In early December, she travelled to Toronto to speak at a lunch party of over a thousand women eager to meet the first woman Cabinet Minister. All this travel, staying in various hotels and often sharing a bathroom resulted in athlete's foot, a fungal infection, a 'horrid nuisance'.[156] She was 'thankful to have come through such a journey with only one infected toe'. She returned to the USA and to her last lecture at New York Town Hall on January 7, 1939, to an audience of 2000, most of whom were women with 'just a sprinkling of men'.[157] On January 18, she had a last lunch with her 'intimate and oldest friends ... It was a parting from my family, though not blood, but our work, our hopes and experiences made us kin'.[158] Shortly after, she caught a boat back to the UK.

THE SECOND WORLD WAR AND AFTER

Bondfield was back in Britain when the Second World War broke out. The 66-year-old was working in her garden when a telephone call came asking her advice on how women could help their country.[159] Miss Bondfield left her garden to attend a conference organised by the National Council of Social Services held to discuss the evacuation of women and children. At the conference, the *Women's Group on Problems Arising from Evacuation* was formed with Margaret Bondfield as its first Chair. This organisation aimed to promote understanding between town and country people, devised welfare schemes for mothers and children evacuated from the towns and provided clothing and free milk for the evacuated children. In September 1939, millions of children, sometimes with their mothers, were evacuated from the cities to the countryside. Soon, there were complaints about the behaviour and flea and lice-ridden state of the new arrivals. Even though Bondfield knew that there were problem families which existed 'like a hidden sore, poor, dirty and cruel in their habits',[160] she helped defend the evacuees against complaints about their dirtiness, their verminous condition and insanitary habits and encouraged host families to be as sympathetic as possible. In a broadcast, she appealed for 'a more imaginative use of the goodwill in reception areas', stating that evacuees 'needed comforts, warm clothing to supplement the Government allowance, and plain, honest-to-God kindness expressed in practical ways. ... The children needed extra clothing, chocolates and toys'.[161] In 1940, the organisation which now consisted of representatives from 46 national organisations changed its name to the 'Woman's Group on Public Welfare' when it became clear that evacuation was not the only problem affecting women. It published a number of pamphlets such as *Our Towns—A Close Up* with a preface written by Bondfield which was used by the government to frame policy.

A day after Britain's declaration of war, the government set up the Ministry of Information, a department responsible for publicity and propaganda. It had a threefold function: to manage news; to publicise the war effort at home; and to promote sympathetic coverage overseas. Margaret Bondfield, now referred to as a homely little woman with greying hair, regularly spoke at meetings organised by the Ministry of Information on subjects such as 'The War and Our Social Purpose' and 'Home Defence and Anti-rumour Week'. Bondfield also undertook several lecture tours in Canada and America on behalf of the British Information Services, a department of the Foreign and Commonwealth Office which provided information on British politics to North American audiences.

In 1946, exhausted by her war effort she contracted shingles.[162] Nonetheless, now in her early seventies, she remained politically active. She was involved in the YWCA, helped set up the second Mary Macarthur Holiday Home for women in Blackpool, became President of Hillcroft College, a college for working women and published her autobiography. In February 1948, she was made Companion of Honour; in April, the Northampton County Council named a new road, Bondfield Avenue as a tribute to her.[163] In June 1949, she returned to her favourite country, the USA, where she stayed with her friend Helen Lockwood, lunched with Eleanor Roosevelt who lived nearby and conferred undergraduate degrees at Vassar. Undoubtedly, Margaret Bondfield felt at home in America. She had visited the country many times: in 1910, in 1933, 1938–1939 and in 1942–1943. Each time she had enjoyed the experience, glad to be away from a class-ridden male-dominated Britain, glad to be with women who championed women's rights.

In April 1951, Margaret Bondfield 'an elderly woman, a fur cape drawn about her shoulders, leaning heavily on a stick as she walks slowly through the trees'[164] was almost 80 years old, largely forgotten, living in a bedsitting room at Woodcote Nursing Home in Surrey run by the Friends of the Poor Society. She confessed that she had 'had very little private life. Between 14 and 60 I had no real home'.[165] She had chosen to go to Woodcote because it aimed 'to bring happiness to the over 70s who have to retire and have no relations to look after them. I was in that position last year and it drove me distraught'.[166] Bondfield was isolated and lonely—the price she paid for being 'one of the new women'.[167] She was frail, very religious and soon began to lose her mind. The manager of the Home reported that she was 'in a mental mist suspended between earth and heaven ... vague, she is at one time perceptive, sometimes unconsciously demanding. But as lovable'.[168] Helen Lockwood was warned that Woodcote would not be able to cope if her state deteriorated any further.[169]

On June 16, 1953, Margaret Bondfield died at Verecroft Nursing Home. She was cremated at Golders Green Crematorium on June 22, and her ashes were removed by the Funeral Director and later scattered over the family grave in Chard.[170] No memorial was erected to her in the cemetery.[171] A few weeks later, a Memorial Service was held at St Margaret's Westminster, the parish church of the House of Commons.[172] Clement Attlee gave the eulogy. Bondfield left £6063 to be divided equally between her four nieces after a bequest of £200 to the Mary Macarthur Holiday Home was honoured.

CONCLUSION

Margaret Bondfield outlived most of those who had served in the 1929 Labour Cabinet,[173] five of the nine women MPs elected that year[174] and all of her siblings.[175] The lives and achievements of the politicians, like those of Bondfield, have been largely forgotten or in the case of MacDonald and Snowden, vilified. Bondfield was maligned when she was alive and by the time she had died had largely been forgotten. It was felt that her compromise on the Blanesburgh Committee and her role as Minister of Labour damaged her reputation irreparably and with it her chance of becoming a working-class and feminist heroine: years later, Barbara Castle even refused to write a forward to a Fabian booklet about Bondfield.

However, Bondfield achieved much, having the quadruple distinction of being the first woman in British history to become Chair of the TUC, the first woman to be a member of a British Government, the first female Cabinet Minister and the first female Privy Councillor. In 1929, she received an honorary doctorate from Bristol University; in 1930, the Freedom of Chard and in 1948 was awarded a CBE. These are all notable achievements but perhaps Bondfield was at her best before the First World War, building up trade unions for women, making a name for herself as a competent, resourceful organiser. She was called the 'shop-girl princess of politics', the champion of every girl behind the counter, fighting to get rid of the living-in system, the iniquitous fines and inhumane working conditions. She was also a key player in campaigns for unemployment insurance, more effective Factory Acts, higher wages and reduced hours of work. The Trades Boards Act which provided minimum rates of pay in four female-dominated industries was largely Bondfield's work. Undoubtedly, joining a trade union was a turning point in her career, providing a route out of shop work. She rose to the very top of the trade union movement, the spokesperson for six million workers, most of whom were men. Her union also gave her the opportunity to become a politician by sponsoring her as a Labour candidate. As soon as she was elected to Parliament, she was catapulted into power, becoming Under-Secretary of State at the Ministry of Labour.

The years after the First World War, although she achieved high office, were much less successful as her reputation as a socialist and a feminist disintegrated with the onset of the Depression. Both Bondfield and the MacDonald Government were thought to be woefully inadequate in dealing with the impact of a world crisis, and it was thought that Bondfield's 'experience in fighting for improved conditions in the workplace was no match for dealing with the complexities of international finance which confronted the Labour Government'.[176] Indeed, her intellectual grasp of the economic situation was considered to be wholly defective.[177] She was believed to have been promoted beyond her ability and 'lacked any flair or wider sense of political strategy. ... Her career cannot be said to have promoted the cause of women ministers in the Labour Party'.[178] These are harsh assessments. Margaret Bondfield was unfortunate to have served under a Prime Minister and Chancellor who were both accused of betraying the working class. Moreover, she had been given what turned out to be one of the most important ministerial posts of the Labour Government yet without any of the resources to make a success of it. Margaret Bondfield was known as a negotiator who believed in the politics of the possible and was only defeated by the most challenging economic period of modern times. The worldwide depression had led to a dramatic increase in unemployment and no one was competent to tackle the problem: Thompson who was in charge of it was ineffectual; Mosley's ideas based on Keynesian economics were dismissed. Bondfield was left to pick up the pieces. Her colleague, Leah Manning, believed that there was never 'in any one Parliament such a large number of distinguished women. Margaret Bondfield was the star'.[179]

Furthermore, unlike her successors, Margaret Bondfield never enjoyed being in a majority government. She served in the 1929 minority government and not surprisingly found herself in great difficulties, trying to overcome intractable problems that even the most experienced of politicians would be unable to solve. Labour overall, not just Margaret Bondfield teetered on the edge of a glass cliff. And slipped off.

It would take a majority Labour Government to achieve some of the ideals of parliamentary socialism held by Margaret Bondfield. The next Cabinet Minister Ellen Wilkinson, who like Bondfield was a single working-class trade unionist with roots in non-conformism, would help to realise the dreams held by her predecessor, maybe because she lived in more propitious times. By 1945, Britain was ready for a radical Labour Government; in 1929, it was decidedly not.

NOTES

1. MB Diary, June 5, 1929, Margaret Grace Bondfield Papers, Archives and Special Collections Library, Vassar College Libraries, Box 3, Folder 8.
2. The average wage was around £150 per annum. I am grateful to Dr Mari Takayanagi for providing me with the salary of Margaret Bondfield.
3. Margaret Bondfield, *A Life's Work*, Hutchinsons, 1948, p. 277.
4. Martin Pugh, *Women and the Women's Movement in Britain*, Macmillan, 2000, p. 203.
5. Henderson was a major Labour figure, one of the first Labour MPs, the first Labour Cabinet Minister under Asquith's war-time coalition. In 1924 he was Home Secretary, in 1929 Foreign Secretary.
6. Margaret Bondfield, *Becoming the First Female Chancellor*, Interview with BBC Radio, circa 2919.
7. Philip Viscount Snowden, *An Autobiography*, Vol. 2, Ivor Nicolson and Watson, 1934, p. 759.
8. Ross Davies, unpublished biography of Margaret Bondfield, Women's History Library, LSE, p. 130.
9. Arabella 'Susan' Lawrence (1871–1947) was one of the first three Labour women MPs. In 1923 she was appointed PPS to the Board of Education; in 1929 she was given a ministerial post as Parliamentary Secretary to the Ministry of Health. Susan Lawrence who according to Beatrice Webb 'despised' Margaret Bondfield would not have been that delighted. (Beatrice Webb Diary, January 30, 1928.)
10. Beatrice Webb Diary, January 30, 1928.
11. Alexandra Kollontai was the first female minister in the world, appointed in 1917 by the Russian government; in 1919 Constance Markievicz was appointed Minister for Labour in the First Dáil Éireann. In 1933 Roosevelt appointed Frances Perkins Secretary of the Department of Labour, the first woman to be appointed to a Cabinet post. Other female firsts include: in 1936, Federica Montseny Mané, Spain; in 1947 Mabel Howard, New Zealand; in 1947 Amrit Kaur, India; in 1949 Enid Lyons, Australia; in 1949, Golda Meir, Israel; in 1957 Marga Klompé, Netherlands; in 1957 Ellen Fairclough Canada; in 1962 Hikmat Abu Zayd, Egypt; in 1963 Isabel Teshea, Trinidad and Tobago; in 1971 Turkân Akyol, Turkey; in 1974 Simone Weil, France; in 1978 Tina Anselmi, Italy; 1in 1984 Elisabeth Kopp, Switzerland; in 1995, Nyiva Mwendwa, Kenya; in 2005 Massouma al-Mubarak, Kuwait.
12. Philip Viscount Snowden, *An Autobiography*, Vol. 2, 1934, p. 759.
13. Leah Manning, *A Life for Education*, Victory Gollanz, 1970, p. 90.

14. Margaret Bondfield, *A Life's Work*, 1948, p. 276.
15. Margaret Bondfield's Diary, June 5, 1929, Margaret Grace Bondfield Papers, Archives and Special Collections Library, Vassar College Libraries, Box 3, Folder 8.
16. Hamilton Fyfe, *Britain's First Woman Cabinet Minister*, unnamed, undated newspaper, Margaret Grace Bondfield Papers, Archives and Special Collections Library, Vassar College Libraries, Box 10, Folder 11. Fyfe was editor of the *Daily Mirror*, then of the *Daily Herald*.
17. Unnamed, undated newspaper, Margaret Grace Bondfield Papers, Archives and Special Collections Library, Vassar College Libraries, Box 3, Folder 6.
18. *The New York Times*, June 16, 1929, Margaret Grace Bondfield Papers, Archives and Special Collections Library, Vassar College Libraries, Box 3, Folder 5.
19. Unnamed, undated newspaper, Margaret Grace Bondfield Papers, Archives and Special Collections Library, Vassar College Libraries, Box 3, Folder 6.
20. Lord Blanesburgh to Margaret Bondfield, June 8, 1929, Margaret Grace Bondfield Papers, Archives and Special Collections Library, Vassar College Libraries, Box 3, Folder 5.
21. Villard to Margaret Bondfield, June 11, 1929, Margaret Grace Bondfield Papers, Archives and Special Collections Library, Vassar College Libraries, Box 3, Folder 5.
22. Margaret Bondfield, *A Life's Work*, 1948, p. 278.
23. Wal Hannington, quoted in the *Morning Star*, August 20, 2014, p. 10.
24. *Manchester Guardian*, July 24, 1929, p. 12.
25. Margaret Bondfield, *A Life's Work*, 1948, p. 353.
26. Ibid., p. 276.
27. MB Diary, June 5, 1929, Margaret Bondfield Papers, Archives and Special Collections Library, Vassar College Libraries, Box 1, Folder 2.
28. *Daily Herald*, June 11, 1929, p. 1.
29. Margaret Bondfield, *A Life's Work*, 1948, p. 292.
30. Ibid., p. 292.
31. Philip Snowden, extract from autobiography, Margaret Bondfield Papers, Archives and Special Collections Library, Vassar College Libraries, Box 9, Folder 11.
32. Letter from Harold Emmerson to Ross Davies, dated, June 6, 1975, in Ross Davies' file.
33. Margaret Bondfield, *A Life's Work*, 1948, p. 277.
34. Martin Pugh, *Speak for Britain: A New History of the Labour Party*, Vintage, 2011, p. 209.
35. L. C. B. Seaman, *Post-Victorian Britain 1902–1951*, Methuen and Co., 1966, p. 212.
36. Margaret Bondfield, *A Life's Work*, 1948, p. 297.
37. Ibid., p. 297.
38. Ibid., p. 297.
39. Margaret Bondfield, Hansard, December 1, 1930, Vol. 245, cc1827–1952.
40. Brian Harrison, *Prudent Revolutionaries: Portraits of British Feminists Between the Wars*, Clarendon Press, 1987, p. 137.
41. *Manchester Guardian*, October 1, 1929, p. 15.

42. Brian Harrison, *Prudent Revolutionaries: Portraits of British Feminists Between the Wars*, 1987, p. 137.
43. *Manchester Guardian*, October 21, 1929, p. 8.
44. *The Outlook*, December 1935, p. 239.
45. Ibid., p. 239.
46. Ibid., p. 239.
47. *Daily Herald*, November 22, 1929, p. 1.
48. Ibid., p. 1.
49. Ibid., p. 1.
50. Hansard, December 16, 1929, Vol. 233, cc1083–1145.
51. *Manchester Guardian*, November 16, 1929, p. 12.
52. Philip Viscount Snowden, *An Autobiography*, Vol. 2, 1934, p. 844.
53. *The Daily Telegraph*, June 8, 1953.
54. Philip Viscount Snowden, *An Autobiography*, Vol. 2, 1934, p. 846.
55. Ibid., p. 845.
56. Ibid., p. 896.
57. Letter from Harold Emmerson to Ross Davies, dated, June 6, 1975, in Ross Davies' file.
58. *Daily Herald*, November 26, 1929, p. 1.
59. David Marquand, *Ramsay MacDonald*, Jonathan Cape, 1977, p. 525.
60. Margaret Bondfield, *A Life's Work*, 1948, p. 295.
61. *The Manchester Guardian*, December 2, 1930, p. 8.
62. Margaret Bondfield, Hansard, December 1, 1930, Vol. 245, cc1827–1952.
63. Pencilled draft of letter by Margaret Bondfield to Ramsay MacDonald, January 6, 1931, Margaret Grace Bondfield Papers, Archives and Special Collections Library, Vassar College Libraries, Box 3, Folder 7.
64. Ramsay MacDonald to Margaret Bondfield, February 10, 1931, Margaret Grace Bondfield Papers, Archives and Special Collections Library, Vassar College Libraries, Box 3, Folder 5.
65. J. R. Clynes, "The Years 1929–31" quoted in Herbert Tracey, *The British Labour Party: Its History, Growth, Policy and Leaders*, Caxton Publishing Company, 1948, p. 170.
66. Margaret Bondfield, Unemployment Insurance Bill, Hansard, Vol. CCLIV, June 26, 1931, Col 773.
67. *Exeter and Plymouth Gazette*, October 30, 1931, p. 16.
68. *Exeter and Plymouth Gazette*, December 18, 1929, p. 4.
69. *Hull Daily Mail*, February 12, 1931, p. 4.
70. *Western Times*, August 28, 1931, p. 16.
71. *Nottingham Guardian*, September 18, 1930, quoted in Robert Skidelsky, *Politicians and the Slump: The Labour Government of 1929–1931*, 1967, p. 234.
72. Robert Skidelsky, *Politicians and the Slump: The Labour Government of 1929–1931*, Macmillan, 1967, p. 235.
73. When a government is faced with intractable and controversial problems it often sets up a Royal Commission, an ad hoc committee usually chaired by an eminent individual (such as a judge) who consults with experts both inside and outside of government before issuing its report.
74. Ramsay MacDonald quoted in Robert Skidelsky, *Politicians and the Slump: The Labour Government of 1929–1931*, 1967, p. 263.

75. *Manchester Guardian*, May 19, 1931, p. 11.
76. I am grateful Réka Dudley for working out these percentages. So many historians, including myself in the past, have worked them out incorrectly.
77. Quoted in Robert Skidelsky, *Politicians and the Slump: The Labour Government of 1929–1931*, 1967, p. 318.
78. It was finally published in 1932 and formed the basis of the National Government's National Insurance Act 1934, the 21, Act to deal with unemployment since 1920.
79. Margaret Bondfield, unpublished manuscript, Margaret Bondfield Papers, Archives and Special Collections Library, Vassar College Libraries, Box 4, Folder 1.
80. Ibid.
81. William Gillies, 'The Crisis', *Labour Magazine*, u/dated, p. 5, Margaret Bondfield Papers, Archives and Special Collections Library, Vassar College Libraries.
82. MacDonald Papers, file 6, Unemployment Insurance quoted in Robert Skidelsky, *Politicians and the Slump: The Labour Government of 1929–1931*, 1967, p. 319.
83. Ibid.
84. *Manchester Guardian*, July 16, 1931, p. 8.
85. Ibid.
86. MacDonald Papers, file 6, Unemployment Insurance quoted in Robert Skidelsky, *Politicians and the Slump: The Labour Government of 1929–1931*, 1967, p. 320.
87. Margaret Bondfield, *A Life's Work*, 1948, p. 302.
88. *Manchester Guardian*, July 17, 1931, p. 14.
89. Unemployment Insurance Bill, Debate on Clause 1, Provisions with respect to benefit in the case of special classes of persons, Hansard, July 15, 1931, Vol. 255, cc485–715.
90. Martin Pugh, *Women and the Women's Movement in Britain*, Macmillan, 2000, p. 205.
91. David Marquand, *Ramsay MacDonald*, Jonathan Cape, 1977, p. 623.
92. A. J. P. Taylor, *English History, 1914–1945*, Penguin, 1965, p. 362.
93. Ibid.
94. Charles L. Mowat, 'The Fall of the Labour Government in Great Britain, August 1931', *Huntingdon Library Quarterly*, Vol. 7, No. 4, August 1944, pp. 353–396.
95. William Gillies, 'The Crisis', u/dated, Margaret Bondfield Papers, Archives and Special Collections Library, Vassar College Libraries, Box 3, Folder 12.
96. Margaret Bondfield, *A Life's Work*, 1948, p. 304.
97. CAB 23/67/19, August 22, 1931.
98. Ibid.
99. Margaret Bondfield, unpublished manuscript, Margaret Bondfield Papers, Archives and Special Collections Library, Vassar College Libraries, Box 4, Folder 11.
100. Those accepting the cuts were Ramsay MacDonald, Philip Snowden, Lord Sankey, Herbert Morrison, Lord Parmoor, William Wedgwood Benn, Thomas Shaw, Lord Amulree, Hastings Lees-Smith and Margaret Bondfield;

those against were Arthur Henderson, John Robert Clynes, William Graham, Arthur Greenwood, Albert Victor Alexander, George Lansbury, Thomas Johnston, William Adamson, and Christopher Addison.

101. CAB 23/67/22, August 24, 1931.
102. Charles L. Mowat, 'The Fall of the Labour Government in Great Britain, August 1931', *Huntingdon Library Quarterly*, Vol. 7, No. 4, August 1944, pp. 353–396.
103. MacDonald to Mary Hamilton, quoted in David Marquand, *Ramsay MacDonald*, 1977, p. 651.
104. MacDonald quoted in David Marquand, *Ramsay MacDonald*, 1977, p. 653.
105. Quoted in L. C. B. Seaman, *Post-Victorian Britain 1902–1951*, Methuen and Co., 1966, p. 221.
106. Unpublished memo, Margaret Bondfield, August 25, 1931, Bondfield Papers, Box 4, Folder 11.
107. Bondfield to MacDonald, August 24, 1931, MacDonald Papers, NA 30/69/1314 quoted in *Dictionary of Labour Biography*, p. 120.
108. Ramsay MacDonald to Margaret Bondfield, August 25, 1931, Margaret Bondfield Papers, Archives and Special Collections Library, Vassar College Libraries, Box 3, Folder 7.
109. Margaret Bondfield to Elizabeth Glendower Evans, November 11, 1931, Margaret Bondfield Papers, Archives and Special Collections Library, Vassar College Libraries, Box 3, Folder 7. Elizabeth Glendower Evans had first met Margaret on a trip to the UK in the early twentieth century to study the socialist movement.
110. Eleanor Rathbone to Margaret Bondfield, October 29, 1931, Margaret Bondfield Papers, Archives and Special Collections Library, Vassar College Libraries, Box 3, Folder 7.
111. J. Barlow to Margaret Bondfield, August 28, 1931, Margaret Bondfield Papers, Archives and Special Collections Library, Vassar College Libraries, Box 3, Folder 7.
112. B. M. Power and Dora Jefferson to Margaret Bondfield, September 22, 1931, Margaret Bondfield Papers, Archives and Special Collections Library, Vassar College Libraries, Box 3, Folder 7.
113. *Fifty Years in the Labour Movement*, unpublished manuscript notes for a BBC broadcast, Margaret Bondfield Papers, Archives and Special Collections Library, Vassar College Libraries, Box 9, Folder 13.
114. Quoted in David Marquand, *Ramsay MacDonald*, 1977, p. 646.
115. Philip Viscount Snowden, *An Autobiography: 1919–1934*, Vol. 2, Ivor Nicolson and Watson, 1934, p. 965.
116. Margaret Bondfield to Mrs Hamilton, October 14, 1931, Margaret Bondfield Papers, Archives and Special Collections Library, Vassar College Libraries, Box 3, Folder 7.
117. *Gloucester Citizen*, September 30, 1931, p. 6.
118. Philip Snowden to Margaret Bondfield, September 22, 1931, Margaret Bondfield Papers, Archives and Special Collections Library, Vassar College Libraries, Box 3, Folder 7.
119. Telegram to Margaret Bondfield, Balmoral Castle, September 29, Margaret Bondfield Papers, Archives and Special Collections Library, Vassar College Libraries, Box 3, Folder 7.

120. Central Club, February 12, 1933, *Fifty Years in the Labour Movement*, unpublished manuscript notes for a BBC broadcast, Margaret Bondfield Papers, Archives and Special Collections Library, Vassar College Libraries, Box 9, Folder 13.
121. James Maxton, Hansard, September 8, 1931, Vol. 256, cc13–135.
122. Winston Churchill, Hansard, September 8, 1931, Vol. 256, cc13–135.
123. Sydney Webb, *What Happened in 1932: A Record*, The Fabian Society, 1932, p. 10.
124. Philip Snowden, Letter to National Labour candidates, *Manchester Guardian*, October 17, 1931, p. 11.
125. L. C. B. Seaman, *Post-Victorian Britain 1902–1951*, 1966, p. 225.
126. Margaret Bondfield Papers, Archives and Special Collections Library, Vassar College Libraries, Box 9, Folder 11.
127. *The Herald*, July 1929, p. 3.
128. Sydney Webb, *What Happened in 1932: A Record*, 1932, p. 11.
129. *A Call to the Workers*, Trades Union Congress General Council leaflet circa 1931.
130. Margaret Bondfield, *A Life's Work*, 1948, p. 314.
131. Ibid., p. 315.
132. Margaret Bondfield Election leaflet, 1931, Margaret Bondfield Papers, Archives and Special Collections Library, Vassar College Libraries, Box 3, Folder 1.
133. *Manchester Guardian*, October 22, 1931, p. 13.
134. Claude Dunscombe (election agent) to Bondfield, April 28, 1930, Margaret Grace Bondfield Papers, Archives and Special Collections Library, Vassar College Libraries, Box 3, Folder 10.
135. Ibid.
136. *Manchester Guardian*, October 30, 1931, p. 8.
137. Unnamed newspaper, Margaret Grace Bondfield Papers, Archives and Special Collections Library, Vassar College Libraries, Box 3, Folder 7.
138. Hugh Dalton, *The Fateful Years, Memoirs 1931–1945*, Frederick Muller, 1957, p. 25.
139. *Manchester Guardian*, June 16, 1932, p. 12.
140. National Conference of Labour Women, Sheffield, May 15–17, 1935, p. 21.
141. Ibid.
142. National Conference of Labour Women, Swansea, May 19–21, 1936, pp. 86–87.
143. *Manchester Guardian*, September 9, 1932, p. 4.
144. Margaret Bondfield, *A Life's Work*, 1948, p. 338.
145. *Manchester Guardian*, March 6, 1938, p. 10.
146. Margaret Bondfield, 'Killing the Killer', *Labour*, July 1937, p. 258.
147. Rose Scheidemann to Bondfield, February 14, 1938, Margaret Grace Bondfield Papers, Archives and Special Collections Library, Vassar College Libraries, Box 2.
148. American Diary, u/dated, Margaret Grace Bondfield Papers, Archives and Special Collections Library, Vassar College Libraries, Box 6, Folder 8.
149. American Diary, January 12, 1939, Margaret Grace Bondfield Papers, Archives and Special Collections Library, Vassar College Libraries, Box 6, Folder 8.

150. Statement made by Bondfield sent to Eleanor Roosevelt at her request, August 14, 1933, Eleanor Roosevelt Papers, White House Correspondence, 1933–1945, Personal Letters—1933, Box 584. I am grateful to Patrick F. Fahy for sending me this source.
151. Perkins had visited Britain in 1931 to see how Bondfield's unemployment insurance worked.
152. Rivera was an atheist Jewish communist. He married Freda Kahlo. American Diary, August 1938, Margaret Grace Bondfield Papers, Archives and Special Collections Library, Vassar College Libraries, Box 6, Folder 8.
153. American Diary, August 1938, Margaret Grace Bondfield Papers, Archives and Special Collections Library, Vassar College Libraries, Box 6, Folder 8.
154. Ibid.
155. Ibid.
156. American Diary, p. 252, Margaret Grace Bondfield Papers, Archives and Special Collections Library, Vassar College Libraries, Box 6, Folder 8.
157. American Diary, January 7, 1939, Margaret Grace Bondfield Papers, Archives and Special Collections Library, Vassar College Libraries, Box 6, Folder 8.
158. American Diary, January 18, 1939, Margaret Grace Bondfield Papers, Archives and Special Collections Library, Vassar College Libraries, Box 6, Folder 8.
159. *The Women's Group on Public Welfare*, November 1948, p. 1. Central Committee on Women's Training and Employment, Margaret Bondfield Papers, Archives and Special Collections Library, Vassar College Libraries, Box 7, Folder 9.
160. Ibid.
161. *The Times*, November 8, 1940, p. 2.
162. Elizabeth Magee to Margaret Bondfield, August 14, 1946, Margaret Grace Bondfield Papers, Archives and Special Collections Library, Vassar College Libraries, Box 3, Folder 7.
163. Letter from Northampton Town Clerk to Bondfield, April 6, 1948.
164. *Reynolds News*, u/dated, Margaret Grace Bondfield Papers, Archives and Special Collections Library, Vassar College Libraries.
165. *Fifty Years in the Labour Movement*, unpublished manuscript notes for a BBC broadcast, Margaret Bondfield Papers, Archives and Special Collections Library, Vassar College Libraries, Box 9, Folder 13.
166. Margaret Bondfield to Helen Lockwood, April 15, 1951, Margaret Grace Bondfield Papers, Archives and Special Collections Library, Vassar College Libraries, Box 2, Folder 22.
167. *Daily Mirror*, June 18, 1953, p. 4.
168. Winifred Midgley to Helen Lockwood, September 12, 1951, Margaret Grace Bondfield Papers, Archives and Special Collections Library, Vassar College Libraries, Box 2, Folder 22.
169. Winifred Midgley to Helen Lockwood, October 23, 1951, Margaret Grace Bondfield Papers, Archives and Special Collections Library, Vassar College Libraries, Box 2, Folder 22.
170. Note of family tree, Margaret Grace Bondfield Papers, Archives and Special Collections Library, Vassar College Libraries, Box 1, Folder 2.
171. I am grateful to Viv, Golders Green Crematorium for this information. Bondfield's cremation number was 112245. The funeral directors were E. C. Butt.

172. Memorial Service leaflet, July 9, 1953, PHM.
173. Ramsay MacDonald (1937), William Adamson (1936), John Robert Clynes (1949), Stafford Cripps (1941), Arthur Henderson (1935), George Lansbury (1940), Philip Snowden (1937), William Graham (1932), Thomas Shaw (1938), James Henry Thomas (1947), Lord Thomson (1930), Sydney Webb (1947), and Lord Sankey (1948) had all died.
174. Ethel Bentham (1931), Susan Lawrence (1947), Cynthia Mosley (1933), Marion Phillips (1932), and Ellen Wilkinson (1947) were all dead.
175. Hand-written note by Bondfield, undated, Margaret Grace Bondfield Papers, Archives and Special Collections Library, Vassar College Libraries, Box 3.
176. Fred C. Hunter, 'Margaret Bondfield', in Joyce C. Bellamy and N. J. Gossman's, *Biographical Dictionary of Modern British Radicals*, Vol. II, Harvester Press, 1974, pp. 102–106.
177. Marion Miliband, *Dictionary of National Biography*, Vol. II, 1974, p. 44.
178. Martin Pugh, *Women and the Women's Movement in Britain*, 2000, p. 205.
179. Leah Manning, *A Life for Education*, Victor Gollanz, 1970, p. 90.

CHAPTER 4

The Mighty Atom:
Ellen Wilkinson, 1891–1945

Ellen Wilkinson had a great heart in a little body. She may have been 'small in stature, but there were occasions when she dwarfed her colleagues by the tenacity with which she stood up for the principles she held to be right'.[1] Like Margaret Bondfield, Ellen did not enjoy a privileged childhood. She was born on October 8, 1891, in a tiny two-bedroomed-terraced house with no bathroom or inside lavatory, at 41 Coral Street in a grimy overcrowded district of industrial Manchester. Maybe the damp conditions in this environment contributed to the debilitating bronchial problems and lung disease which were to trouble her throughout her life. Yet despite this infirmity and despite her background, this 4ft11″ redhead became one of the most famous female politicians in the first half of the twentieth century. 'Little Nell', one of her early nicknames, was quite a different character from Miss Bondfield: she was hot-blooded rather than cool; emotional rather than impassive; friendly and subjective rather than detached or objective; left-wing rather than moderate. Ellen judged with her heart, often rushing headlong into issues and events without thinking. This sometimes led her to form inappropriate relationships with married men and make friends with Russian Soviet spies and controllers. Margaret Bondfield would never have dreamt of behaving in such a way (Fig. 4.1).

Ellen's parents were poor but they wanted a better life for their daughter. Her father in particular encouraged 'Nell' to read widely and engage with current affairs. Her religion helped in her journey too, as did her education and her early commitment to politics. Ellen was brought up as a Methodist, a faith which like Congregationalism, expects its followers to do good works here on earth. Methodists believed in the basic Christian principles of social justice and egalitarianism which, as with other Labour figures, helped shape

Much of this chapter is from Paula Bartley, *Ellen Wilkinson: From Red Suffragist to Government Minister*, Pluto Press, 2014.

© The Author(s) 2019
P. Bartley, *Labour Women in Power*,
https://doi.org/10.1007/978-3-030-14288-9_4

Fig. 4.1 Ellen Wilkinson as a young trade unionist (Courtesy of People's History Museum)

Ellen's later political thinking. As Harold Wilson later commented, Labour owed more to Methodism than Marxism. Ellen undoubtedly appropriated the millenarian, emotional, sentimental rhetoric of Methodism: her later speeches at street meetings, on upturned package cases and other hastily constructed platforms, were delivered with all the fervour and passion of a Methodist Minister.

Ellen was clever. She won a scholarship to grammar school but would struggle to reach university and have a good career since there were few educational and professional opportunities for women, especially for those from the working class. Most girls from her background left school at 14 and became factory workers, domestic servants or shop assistants. Teaching, the most obvious career choice for intelligent girls, involved either a degree course at a university, a two-year course at a teacher training college or, for those less financially secure, a combination of pupil teaching and training college. At the age of 16, Ellen enrolled at the Manchester Pupil Teacher's Centre, spending half the week teaching younger pupils and the other half studying; three years later, Ellen won the Jones Open History Scholarship to Manchester University. Here she learned the research skills and the clear analytical, factually accurate writing she later used in her parliamentary work.

It was here too that she developed her political voice. Ellen worked hard on a range of projects, all the time testing and refining her emerging beliefs: she helped found the University Socialist Federation and later became vice-chair[2]; she organised meetings such as those addressed by Mary Macarthur the radical trade unionist, feminist and friend of Margaret Bondfield; in 1912, she joined the Manchester Society of Women Suffrage (MSWS) and ran the local branch of the Fabian Society; in 1913, she joined the Tyldesley branch of the Women's Labour League; and she graduated. She had already joined the Independent Labour Party (ILP).

Towards a Political Career

As a teenager, Ellen wanted to enter that 'magic sphere of politics', confirmed by the speech at the Richard Pankhurst Memorial Hall of a 'small slim woman, in a plain woollen frock of a soft blue, her hair simply coiled into her neck'[3]: Katherine Bruce Glasier, a prominent figure in the Labour movement.[4] It was 1909. Suffragettes were smashing windows, chaining themselves to railings, organising mass demonstrations and going on hunger strike; others were campaigning for adult suffrage. But it was Glasier who became Ellen's role model, not the leader of the suffragettes, Emmeline Pankhurst, nor the adult suffrage leader, Margaret Bondfield. In July 1913, now aged 21, Ellen took the first step in her political career when the MSWS,[5] a branch of the suffragist National Union of Women's Suffrage Societies (NUWSS), appointed her 'assistant organiser in training' at a salary of two guineas a week, a decent wage for a young woman just out of university. She was expected to speak at open-air meetings in Manchester and the nearby towns, all the time learning how to capture the attention of often hostile audiences, who sometimes threw stones and other objects at the young suffragist. Ellen was a minor figure in the MSWS but she was learning fast. As a paid suffrage worker she read the suffragist newspaper, *The Common Cause*, listened to suffrage speakers, discussed suffragist aims and strategy, gained experience in public speaking, developed organisational skills and consolidated her emerging feminism.

It was a dream job for an aspiring politician at that time. In 1912, the Labour Party pledged support for votes for women—the first political party to do so—and in turn the NUWSS offered to help them get elected. To her delight, Ellen was able to combine her emerging feminism and socialism when she was asked to liaise with the Labour Party over the best way forward for votes for women.[6] The Labour Party, impressed by Wilkinson's political acumen, asked her to sit on a committee set-up to get Labour candidates into Parliament.[7] Ellen, a strong Labour supporter, had not only found her natural home but she was learning about the inner workings of a constituency.[8] Ellen saw that getting elected was a long-term process, and that constituencies needed to be 'nursed' by candidates and their supporters. All the time she was developing her understanding of the craft of politics.

On August 4, 1914, Britain declared war on Germany. The MSWS unanimously agreed to stop suffrage activity. Ellen was without a job. At first, she organised volunteers for the war effort and later worked for the Women's Emergency Corp. In July 1915, now aged 23, she found another post, more suited to her politics, ideals and temperament: she became a national organiser for the Amalgamated Union of Co-operative Employees (AUCE), with special responsibility for organising women shop assistants and factory workers. From now on, the AUCE would form an important part of Ellen's life. It would further her political education, help her form alliances within the Labour movement, consolidate her skills in organising, finance her politics and make it possible for her to become an MP.

In October 1917, the Bolsheviks seized power and attempted to create a socialist state in Russia. Ellen Wilkinson, as with many on the left, was thrilled by the Russian Revolution and became excited by the possibility of socialism in the UK. In the summer of 1920, she joined the newly created British Communist Party. However, the Labour leadership regarded communism as ideologically incompatible with parliamentary democracy. Communists wanted a 'Dictatorship of the Proletariat' by armed revolution whereas Labour believed in the parliamentary, not the revolutionary, road to socialism. Consequently, Ellen's membership of the Communist Party (CP) was not to last. In 1924, realising that the Labour Party would soon make it a proscribed organisation, Ellen formally resigned from the CP. Yet Ellen remained sympathetic to the CP's aims and policy, and repeatedly set up or joined communist-front organisations. From now on, balancing the tensions between the two ultimately incompatible political paths of revolutionary and democratic socialism would dominate her life until the outbreak of war in 1939.

Gradually Ellen became aware that parliamentary democracy, not just revolution, could improve lives for the majority. In November 1923, now in her early 30s, Ellen was sponsored by her union, now renamed National Union of Distributive and Allied Workers (NUDAW) to stand as parliamentary candidate for Gorton. It was not easy for a woman to be selected as a Labour Party candidate and even with generous funding from NUDAW Wilkinson failed in her first attempt. Undeterred Ellen sought another seat to contest and only a week later the Ashton-under-Lyne Labour Party selected her as its parliamentary candidate largely because Ellen's union agreed to pay her electoral costs, costs which the impoverished local Labour Party could ill-afford. Ellen's election addresses were popular: the halls were packed full of supporters as well as those intrigued by a woman standing for election in a heavy manufacturing town. Of course, those who attend meetings may not be representative of the electorate: Ellen Wilkinson lost, coming third. The Labour Party in general did better, forming its first minority government with Ramsay MacDonald the first Labour Party Prime Minister.

Fortunately, Ellen did not have to wait long to put herself forward. In October 1924, Ramsay MacDonald dissolved Parliament and announced another general election. It was the third general election in as many years. This time Ellen Wilkinson, again sponsored by her union, was selected as Labour candidate for Middlesbrough East, an iron, steel and shipbuilding town situated on the River Tees in North East England. It was a hard-fought contest, especially challenging when four days before the election the British press published a letter allegedly from Grigory Zinoviev, now one of the most powerful figures in the Soviet Union, calling for increased communist agitation in England. The letter was later pronounced a forgery except the damage had been done: the Labour Party lost 40 of its MPs, including Margaret Bondfield, Susan Lawrence and Dorothy Jewson. Ellen Wilkinson, however, won her seat.

MP FOR MIDDLESBROUGH EAST, OCTOBER 1924–OCTOBER 1931

Ellen Wilkinson was delighted with her victory. This tiny young woman now 'represented the heftiest men in England', that is the steel, iron and shipyard workers of Middlesbrough.[9] She was lonely: the only woman on the opposition benches and one of only 4 women in the grey masculine House of Commons, her feet dangling six inches from the floor because the high benches were built for taller men. The uniqueness of her position generated a lot of media coverage, though as she commented in *The New Dawn* 'for the Labour Party to have only one woman in Parliament is not something to be interested in, but something to be ashamed of'.

On December 10, 1924, on the second day of the parliamentary session, Wilkinson made her first speech. 'A really wise member of Parliament', she acknowledged, 'always waited seven years... I didn't think that Middlesbrough had sent me to the House of Commons to wait seven years ... I couldn't wait any longer because I was so indignant' about the injustices in Britain.[10] The frisson of a young attractive female MP addressing the House for the first time was too exciting for most of the male MPs and a considerable number packed into the House of Commons. The new MP for Middlesbrough did not disappoint. It was customary for maiden speeches to be inoffensive and devoid of political content but Wilkinson had little time for this type of convention. In her maiden speech, this less-than-demure redhead displayed complete self-possession and an assured speaking style. In one great sweep of a speech, she put forward the need for votes for women on the same terms as men, increased unemployment benefits, improved insurance protection and factory law reform, all issue close to her heart. The House of Commons, very predominantly male and very predominantly Conservative, gave her a 'generous cheer'. She was quickly dubbed the 'Mighty Atom'.

Wilkinson's combative personality found its natural home in the belligerent and challenging atmosphere of the House of Commons. Historians often comment on the problems facing women in Parliament, pointing out how tough and unwelcoming the place could be. Wilkinson's suffrage days, when she had faced hostile crowds and been forced to react fast with witty replies to hecklers, prepared her well for the rumbustious testosterone-charged male-dominated Parliament she now inhabited. She may have been the only Labour woman in the House of Commons but her character had been forged in rough and tumble politics elsewhere. She said later that there was one absolutely necessary precaution for any woman who wanted to enjoy public work and that was to grow a spiritual hide as thick as the elephant's physical one. What is certain is that Wilkinson had to be extraordinarily resilient in order to balance the sometimes competing demands of her constituents, her union, her political colleagues and the socialists and feminists who saw her as their representative in Parliament.

The MP for Middlesbrough startled the House of Commons in other ways. Wilkinson was no wallflower demurely hiding from the glances of sexually alert male colleagues. The other three female MPs[11] dressed soberly in black suits and white blouses, or as one newspaper remarked 'Quaker' attire, in order not to attract too much attention. Being a woman, they believed, was quite enough to draw comment. Wilkinson patently did not agree. In February 1925, she broke the conventions of sober attire established by the other female members of Parliament and startled the House into 'murmurs of admiration' when she wore a vivid green dress. Wilkinson believed she had the right to wear what she liked. Nancy Astor, clearly worried that Ellen Wilkinson's dress detracted from what she said, took her aside, talked to her in 'a motherly fashion and begged her to dress "dull". You are not here to excite an assembly already superheated on every occasion'.[12] Wilkinson took notice of Astor's words and reverted to the dull black and white dress adopted by other women MPs much, according to the *Empire News*, to the 'great disappointment of about 600 honourable members'.

Wilkinson was audacious, quite happy to break into the male enclaves of the House of Commons. The three other female MPs, either because they feared giving offence or were intimidated, did not use the bars, the smoking rooms or the members' cloakroom. Wilkinson however confronted the exclusively masculine culture and claimed the space for women, fully aware that these were spaces 'where a whispered word may sometimes have more effect than an hour's speech in the debating chamber',[13] spaces where informal gossip—so useful to politicians—took place.

Wilkinson's first year as MP was hectic. There was no official job description and therefore no limits placed on the amount of work she could take on. The Labour MPs' day, she said, started 'at 10am with party meetings, following on to Committees, getting through masses of correspondence when and where they could, interviewing delegations and constituents and in some cases dashing off to address large demonstrations'.[14] In her constituency, Wilkinson was expected to hold weekly surgeries, speak at local party meetings, visit local schools, factories and businesses, attend local functions and other events, promote the interests of her constituency in Parliament and be part-time social worker and charity distributor. In her first few weeks, she tried 'to cope with my 1,394 letters and telegrams' from people who wanted advice of some sort. Ellen Wilkinson stated she needed a wife who collected her letters 'drafted answers and typed them ... give a hand with bazaars and when I got home fagged out would have ready a delicious meal'.[15] As with Margaret Bondfield, there was no significant other to help out. Fortunately for Ellen her sister Annie often took care of her, especially during her frequent bouts of illness. Throughout her life Miss Wilkinson remained resolutely single, stating that she had no wish to be a traditional wife herself.[16]

What is striking is the way in which Ellen Wilkinson, and indeed women MPs in general, worked closely with feminist groups outside Parliament. Some even became parliamentary spokeswomen for feminist reform: for instance Ellen Wilkinson and the Conservative MP Nancy Astor cared passionately about the rights of women and established links that cut across party lines. They were said to share two traits 'a booming voice and the ability to annoy the male members of the Commons'. Certainly, the two women continually protested against the unfair treatment of women. They campaigned for equal pay, for an end to unjust laws against prostitutes, for the reform of the Aliens Act, for fairer pensions for women and the vote on the same terms as men. It was a double act which regularly exasperated male MPs on both sides of the House. Indeed Wilkinson's commitment to women's rights sometimes made her an uncomfortable colleague particularly when she sided with the right-wing Astor against her own party.

Unusually for a woman MP, Wilkinson often spoke in economic debates, maintaining a fierce criticism of the Tory Government's economic strategies which adversely affected the poorer sections of society. In her view, the banks and the bankers were much more powerful than the Houses of Parliament and controlled government policy. Britain, she argued, paid a 'very high price for the smiles of the financiers of America'[17] as the bankers' interests ran counter to the interests of ordinary people.

Wilkinson continued helping NUDAW, writing for left-wing newspapers and journals and getting involved in strike action. On Monday, May 3, 1926, the TUC called a General Strike. Millions of workers stopped work in support of the coal miners who had had their wages reduced. For those fateful nine days Wilkinson, along with her married lover Frank Horrabin, was one of several flying squads of speakers who drove cars around the country, holding meetings in each town, attracting large numbers, sometimes of men and women who walked ten or fifteen miles to hear her speak. Nine days later, to her surprise and disgust, the TUC called off the strike and everyone, apart from the miners, returned to work. The miners demanding 'not a penny off the pay, not a minute off the day' remained on strike for a further six months. Wilkinson later helped immortalise the strike in two books. Her co-authored *A Workers History of the Great Strike* is an emotionally charged account of the nine days of the Strike and her autobiographical novel *Clash* captures the atmosphere, excitement and frustration of the strike, its officials and grass-roots supporters. In December, six months after the General Strike had ended, the hungry miners, beaten into submission, were forced to return to work on the owners' terms which meant longer hours, lower pay and the victimisation of strikers. Unlike Bondfield who thought the miners too intransigent, Wilkinson blamed the defeat on TUC officials and Labour Party timidity, endorsing her reputation as 'Red Ellen'.

In 1927, the Conservative Government passed the Trades Disputes Act which restricted workers' rights even further. It made sympathetic strikes illegal, banned civil servants from joining unions affiliated to the TUC, protected blacklegs and made picketing almost impossible. 'Red Ellen' fiercely insisted that the Conservative Government was working steadily, and deliberately, in the interests of a very few rich people. In the same year in recognition of her growing parliamentary reputation, Wilkinson was elected to the National Executive of the Labour Party (NEC). She was on her way to becoming a key figure in the party and in a good position to help shape party policy. At the Labour Party Conference that year, the MP for Middlesbrough appealed to delegates to make the party's programme a 'very bold programme' because the working classes wanted an unflinching radical lead 'to deal with the situation, the terrible situation of poverty and destitution in which they found themselves'. She urged that socialism was 'something that could be attained in their time if only they had the will, the passion, and the determination to put it through'.[18]

In May 1929, Ellen Wilkinson fought her second general election. As a member of the NEC's Press and Publicity Department, she was responsible for writing, editing and distributing election literature: leaflets, pamphlets, posters, speakers' notes, election specials and even lantern films and helping to write the manifesto outlining Labour policy. The election, fought against a background of rising unemployment and memories of the General Strike, returned a minority Labour Government for the second time. On June 4, Ramsay McDonald once more became Prime Minister. By now, thanks to the efforts of Wilkinson and other sympathetic MPs,[19] all women over the age of 21 were eligible to vote in what was condescendingly called the 'Flapper Election'. Fourteen women MPs were elected, 9 of whom were Labour. Wilkinson, who increased her majority by 3199, was overjoyed.

Ramsay MacDonald, perhaps mindful of the increased female electorate, promoted women to ministerial posts. Ellen Wilkinson was appointed Parliamentary Private Secretary to Susan Lawrence. Beatrice Webb confided to her diary that Ellen, whom she considered to be 'far more efficient and more popular than either Susan or Margaret', was 'becoming moulded for office'.[20] Wilkinson continued to work extraordinarily hard. Each day she got up at 6 a.m., wrote her articles until 9 a.m. and then spent the rest of the morning working through one of the heaviest postbags of any MP. As well as dealing with constituency issues, her new job involved looking after Susan Lawrence, helping with her correspondence, meeting her visitors, receiving deputations and sitting behind her boss in the House of Commons ready with information. It was known to be self-sacrificing and self-obliterating work with one saving grace—it was viewed as an apprenticeship for a ministerial post.

On October 29, 1929, as Chapter 3 has shown, the Wall Street Crash precipitated a worldwide economic crisis. Wilkinson knew exactly where to place the blame for this economic catastrophe: the greed of the bankers. In her view, the City of London had loaned money in order to reap immense, and ultimately unsustainable, profits but instead 'had been caught out with heavy losses in speculation'. 'We are told' she thundered 'that the Budget doesn't balance, that there are going to be terrible things happen unless you are prepared to accept cuts—cuts everywhere except in the dividend of the Bankers'.[21] The squeeze, the Governor of the Bank of England had urged, was essential for restoring the economy to health; nationalising the Bank of England, countered Ellen, was essential for restoring the country's wealth. The government's austerity programme strategies, she argued, hit the poorer sections of society the hardest.

Still enthralled by the Soviet Republic and still a Marxist at heart, Ellen echoed the current socialist belief that a planned economy was the only real solution to the economic crisis. Capitalism, she maintained, was an unworkable, wicked system. She was in favour of public control of the banking system and nationalising the 'commanding heights of industry'. For Ellen, nationalisation and planning were the means of introducing order and stability to a roller-coaster economy. Ellen Wilkinson, who never baulked at upsetting anyone if the cause was justified, joined forces with Eleanor Rathbone, Jennie Lee and Cynthia Mosley, to champion the rights of women against her own party's leadership and that of other Labour Party feminists such as Margaret Bondfield and Marion Phillips. The big test of Labour loyalty came with Margaret Bondfield's Anomalies Bill. At 5 a.m. on July 15, 1931, when Bondfield proposed a clause which would disqualify 180,000 married women from claiming benefits, Wilkinson vehemently objected. In her view, the clause raised 'the old, bad principle of discrimination against women, which the whole women's movement has been fighting against since about 1870'.[22] Her cries, we know, remained unheeded and the Labour Government passed the clause on the basis that married women were not 'genuinely seeking work'. As stated in the previous chapter, a large minority of the Labour Cabinet opposed the cuts, forcing MacDonald to resign as Prime Minister. He formed a National Government to oversee the economic cutbacks.

Not surprisingly, Ellen, along with the TUC and most of the Labour Party, disagreed with the stringent measures put forward by MacDonald and his National Government. Time and time again, Wilkinson reiterated her belief that bankers' greed, not the unemployed, was responsible for the crisis. Ramsay MacDonald keen to consolidate his power, called for new elections. The campaign in Middlesbrough was rough. On one occasion, Ellen's car window was broken, the lamp smashed and the Labour Party ribbons torn off; she herself was attacked by a number of women and only escaped with the help of a few young men who came to her rescue.[23]

When Parliament opened on November 10, 1931, Ellen Wilkinson was not there to oppose the government. She was one of over 200 Labour MPs who had lost their seats. Only 52 Labour MPs remained. The *Guardian* mourned her departure, reporting that women's organisations 'will miss the help that Miss Ellen Wilkinson has always given fully in and out of Parliament, while the House of Commons will miss an energetic, vivid and provocative personality'.[24] The whole framework of Wilkinson's life suddenly crumbled. Devastated by her defeat, she spoke of how it was 'too painful to look at the Labour benches and remember the men and women who were not there'.[25] She insisted that the Labour Party lost the election not because it was socialist 'but because it was not Socialist enough' and blamed the Press, the BBC and the church for its defeat. In her view, the Labour Party had lost its direction. Wilkinson maintained it was better to have 'a small disciplined party that knows what it wants than a huge mass of people whose allegiance to Labour is little more than a vague humanitarian sentiment. If this defeat is the cause of the Labour Party facing facts, and cutting away a lot of the pretence of the last two years, the sacrifice of so many fine comrades will not have been in vain'.[26]

Between 1931 and 1935, Ellen Wilkinson was out of Parliament, years that were challenging for the independent 40 year old. As with Margaret Bondfield, Ellen Wilkinson needed to earn her own living and she resumed full-time work for NUDAW, she lectured, wrote articles for leading newspapers and journals and developed her reputation as a writer. She published a number of books including *The Division Bell Mystery* (1932) a crime novel set in the House of Commons, as well as co-authoring political treatises such as the *The Terror in Germany* (1933), *Why Fascism?* (1934), *Why War?* (1934) and the *Condition of India* (1934). During this period, her politics remained uncompromising and her role as the party's left-wing conscience reinforced. She wrote uncompromisingly radical and deliberately provocative articles for the popular press. The range of her activities was breathtaking, despite her recurring bronchial and lung infections: she remained committed to women's equality, fought for the rights of the working class and unemployed and devoted much of her boundless energy into a vigorous campaign against fascism.

A COMMUNIST FELLOW-TRAVELLER

Ellen's naturally rebellious and dissident temperament was uninhibited, whether she was an MP or not. Although no longer a member of the official CP, she joined communist-led organisations and publicly agreed with much of CP propaganda. In company with many on the left, she ignored the voices of those warning about conditions in the Soviet Union. More worryingly for British security, Ellen Wilkinson became friends with some Russian spies, notably Willi Munzenberg and Otto Katz. In 1919, Munzenberg was put in charge of the Soviet Union's propaganda operations in the West.[27] Soon a large number of groups and hundreds of individuals—Ernest Hemingway, Bertolt Brecht, Dorothy Parker, Kim Philby, Guy Burgess, Anthony Blunt … and Ellen Wilkinson—came under his influence. Undoubtedly, Willi Munzenberg and Wilkinson were friendly and worked together closely. On February 10, 1927, at the Palais d'Egmont in Brussels, while still the MP for Middlesbrough, she and Munzenberg met with 174 other delegates to discuss 'colonial oppression and imperialism' and to set up the League Against Imperialism (LAI). On April 7, 1927, the first meeting of the LAI took place in a House of Commons Committee Room, a room probably booked by Wilkinson; Willi Munzenberg was elected International Secretary.

Munzenberg recruited Otto Katz who worked at the OGPU, the Soviet Secret Intelligence Service, to help. Katz was trained as an 'illegal', that is 'an agent operating under false names and identities', and used a number of aliases such as Andre Simon and Paulo Breda, to become a 'vital part of Soviet infiltration and intelligence-gathering'.[28] 'Illegals' as they were called 'worked as couriers, transporting secret documents and hoards of cash to finance their global network; they ran other agents and formed secret units and spy rings for penetration and surveillance; they worked as forgers and falsifiers of captured documents; they pushed propaganda and gathered information; they learned to dispose of anyone who threatened the well-being of the Party'.[29] Otto Katz was about 5ft7" tall, of medium build, with blue eyes, black hair and a fresh complexion, marked by a scar on his face from nose to chin.[30] He was a handsome man who was very attractive to women, and a man willing to use his looks and natural magnetism to further his political cause. He even managed to charm Hollywood: Otto Katz and his wife Ilse were immortalised as Victor Lazlo, the Czech leader of the anti-fascist underground network, and Ilse Lazlo in the film *Casablanca*.

Wilkinson worked closely with Katz, helping him with visas to come to Britain, writing to the various authorities when he was forbidden entry,[31] helping to publish his book on the terror in Germany and generally acting as his factotum. Katz encouraged his acolyte to raise funds for the World Committee, provide help for his anti-fascist campaigns and introduce him to a number of high-ranking figures such as Lloyd George, Lady Rhondda and the Duchess of Atholl. Otto Katz organised at least three of Ellen's visits to Spain during the Spanish Civil War. He was, in effect, her controller: she was his inadvertent spy and maybe his lover. Indeed, some of her colleagues assumed the two were lovers, a fact which Ellen denied. She wrote to Isobel Brown that 'it has come to my knowledge that Harry (this was probably referring to Harry Pollitt, later leader of the Communist Party) is under the impression that Katz and I have been having an affair. I would not like it to be thought that the work I have done … was motived by my personal interest … the rumour has been carefully told to someone whom I do happen to think rather a lot about and it is causing a good deal of complication and unhappiness. I should be really grateful, therefore, if when you do hear this rumour you would sit on it firmly. It is so very wide of the mark'.[32] The

lady may have been protesting a little too much. Certainly, MI5 whose opera-
tors followed both Katz and Wilkinson believed there were 'good grounds for
assuming that Miss Wilkinson is infatuated with Katz'[33] and noted that the
spy sometimes spent the night at her flat. Undoubtedly Katz used his good
looks and charm to woo Ellen, and maybe in true spy fashion to seduce her.[34]

FIGHTING FASCISM WITH KATZ AND THE COMMUNISTS

Katz tapped into Wilkinson's distress about the growing menace of Fascism
and encouraged her to fight against it. No longer constrained by her parliamentary duties she became involved in anti-Nazi activity. In January 1933,
Hitler became Chancellor of Germany and called for new elections. Six days
before they took place, on the night of February 27, the German Parliament,
the Reichstag, was set on fire: a lone Dutchman, the former communist Van
der Lubbe, was discovered on the premises. The Nazis, keen to uncover
Soviet complicity, accused him and the CP of torching the building. As
soon as the Reichstag had burned down, Wilkinson reported, Nazi leaders
announced that a real terror would begin and with it the systematic hunting
down of every socialist, every communist, every Jew and every left-leaning
intellectual. 'There can be no mercy', said Goering, 'Every Communist func-
tionary will be shot wherever we find him. The communist deputies must be
hanged this very night. Everyone in alliance with the Communists is to be
arrested'.[35] The *Daily Herald* published Wilkinson's horrific accounts of how
leading socialists, such as the Deputy of the Reichstag and the ex-Minister of
the Interior, had their houses broken into and everything breakable smashed,
how they were arrested and taken to a prison where the Nazis 'amused themselves by doing all the things they could think of – and they had unpleasant minds – finishing by giving a quarter litre of castor oil'.[36] Berlin, she
reported, was a city in which everybody was afraid.

Four leading communists, as well as Van der Lubbe, were charged with
setting fire to the Reichstag. At once Munzenberg and Otto Katz sprang into
action and used Ellen Wilkinson to help them. On May 18, 1933, Otto Katz,
dressed in a dark grey suit, dark grey overcoat, dark grey hat, red and white
striped shirt, red and white bow tie and looking every inch like a rich busi-
nessman, went to the Russell Hotel to meet his agent.[37] He and Wilkinson
were being watched. The Security Services tailed Otto Katz, noting how
much time he spent with his quarry. One report spoke of how he 'spent the
next day meeting various people until the evening when he returned in a
motor car owned by Ellen who was at the wheel. ... The two then drove back
to Ellen's Wilkinson's home' at No. 18, Guildford Street, WC1 where Special
Branch noted that he stayed the night.[38] In addition, Katz used Wilkinson's
union office as his official address. Evidently, she enjoyed the subterfuge.
When her car was trailed by detectives, Ellen did her best to outmanoeuvre
them. As a consequence, the Special Branch were not always able to monitor Otto Katz's movements as 'they were carried out in the main by means

of Miss Wilkinson's car, which was able several times to out-distance the motor cabs in which he was followed'.[39] It was an intrigue straight out of a Le Carré novel, though more frightening because it was real: Katz's activities were those associated 'with a very highly placed Comintern agent... We therefore think it feasible to put forward the theory that he is one of the principal means by which Moscow carries out its policy in western Europe and America, and that he is either the head, or the chief mouthpiece of a Comintern-type organisation'.[40] He was, in effect, a dangerous man. And Miss Wilkinson, former MP for Middlesbrough, later MP for Jarrow and future Cabinet Minister was thought to be much too close to him.

Otto Katz persuaded Wilkinson to invite a number of leading anti-fascists from all political parties to her tiny flat. Here they set up A *Relief Committee for the Victims of German Fascism*, another one of Munzenberg's communist fronts consisting of what George Orwell called fellow-travellers, crypto-communists and sentimental sympathisers. Kim Philby joined the organisation and was later recruited as a Soviet spy. During the summer months of 1933, the Relief Committee planned 'The Legal Commission of Enquiry into the Burning of the Reichstag', a mock trial which had no legal status but, as Ellen remarked, they wanted to judge the German Government at the 'bar of world opinion' and to put pressure on the judges in the Nazi trial due to take place two weeks later. On Wednesday, September 6, Winifred Holtby wrote to Lady Rhondda 'Ellen Wilkinson has just left. She has been here to supper. I gather that before Monday she must arrange for (a) hospitality (b) an official reception (c) accommodation at the Law Courts (d) a press – for an international committee of distinguished jurists, about to sift the Reichstag Fire evidence ... Too, too, tiresome, as she has now all the arrangements to do – has been haring about the continent without sleep for ninety-six hours. ... Life, my dear, Goes On, as they say. The spate of treason, mutiny, arson and whatnot that has flowed through this room tonight fairly makes the atmosphere hum'.[41]

Wilkinson booked the Law Society Court Room for the 'Legal Commission', a choice of venue which would give legal authority to the trial. The Foreign Office—which knew the 'trial' was 'being held under the auspices of the Comintern and at the instigation of Herr Katz, a communist agent'[42]—tried to prevent the trial taking place because it 'has caused the greatest annoyance in Germany ... These proceedings are quite ridiculous as well as provocative and do the reputation of this country no good (besides inflaming Herr Hitler). ... I really don't see why we should lend ourselves to the manoeuvres of so notorious a person as Willi Munzenberg, even if he had ... Ellen Wilkinson in his pocket'.[43] The Foreign Office tried to pressurise the Law Society to cancel Wilkinson's contract for the Court Room but it refused to do so. The FO continued to keep an eye on Miss Wilkinson through the Special Branch who furtively attended meetings of the Reichstag Trial Committee.[44]

Ellen Wilkinson, Otto Katz and the committee, aware that any hint of political intrigue might undermine the credibility of the trial, deliberately kept the proceedings formal, rigorous and legalistic. Between 14 and 18 September, the celebrated British barrister and eminent Labour Party member, D. N. Pritt and his international legal team, heard detailed evidence about the fire and the Nazi reaction to it. Several leading German politicians, writers and officials who were now refugees gave evidence. One witness (the former President of Police in Berlin who had had responsibility for Reichstag security) testified that the Nazis must have helped place the incendiary material in the building. The judges concluded that Van der Lubbe was not a member of the CP but an opponent of it; that the accused communists were all innocent; that Van der Lubbe could not have acted alone; and that the Reichstag was set on fire by Nazi leaders. Press coverage was wide and, as Ellen had hoped, electrified anti-Nazi sentiment. Meanwhile, Ellen Wilkinson helped Katz get his book, the *Brown Book of Hitler Terror*, published in Britain. It was subsequently translated into 23 languages and ran to over fifty editions.

In Germany, Nazi newspapers demanded the death penalty for anyone who gave evidence in support of the accused. Surprisingly, the German court, which was put on the defensive by the adverse publicity generated by the Legal Commission in London, acquitted and eventually released four of the defendants, the leading communists Ernst Torgler, Georgi Dimitrov, Blagoi Popov and Vasil Tanev.[45] Only Van der Lubbe, who had no CP to defend him, was found guilty and executed on January 10, 1934—Wilkinson called it 'judicial murder'. Shortly after, a very angry Hitler announced that all future treason trials would be held in a new Nazi-dominated People's Court, thus marking the end of any legal justice in Germany.

A number of German communists and socialists who wanted to flee Germany turned to Ellen for help. She gave her money from journalism to German Jewish émigrés,[46] put refugees up in her flat, acted as guarantor to others and tried to help them by publicising their plight. She was anxious about the 'unconscious growth of anti-semitism' in the UK, an atmosphere that spread through the world like 'an all-pervasive gas' and made it harder for refugees to be welcomed. In an article for the *Daily Herald* entitled 'No Home, No Country, No Hope' Ellen condemned the UK for being the most inhospitable country for refugees, and for imposing restrictions in a way that no other country bordering on Germany was doing.[47] She had one small triumph when, as a result of pressure from Katz, she persuaded the Home Secretary to give visas to 32 former communist members of the Reichstag despite objections from MI5 who regarded some of them as dangerous individuals. Tragically, some refugees like her friends Dora Fabian and Mathilde Wurm died in mysterious circumstances, possibly murdered by Nazis agents operating in England.[48]

Political action was combined with humanitarian relief. Wilkinson helped set up a children's home in the Saar for the children of Nazi victims—another

Munzenberg initiative—and led a campaign to adopt children who had lost parents in often horrendous circumstances. She even helped persuade a reluctant Home Secretary to allow German refugee children into the country and guaranteed funding to support them: the descendants of at least 150 children have Ellen Wilkinson and her colleagues to thank for their lives.

In her newspaper articles, Wilkinson continued to describe the increasing violence and anti-semitism in Germany. One article told of how Albert Einstein had his Berlin house damaged, his books scattered and his manuscripts and notebooks destroyed. He was lucky. For less prominent individuals, she reported, the treatment was worse. The Nazis 'first attention to their Jewish prisoners is to smash their noses … at one time they broke into a Jewish café, took away 4 people whom they beat unconsciously and compelled them to lick each other's wounds and the blood on the table when they regained consciousness'.[49] Fascism, Wilkinson declared, meant terror: 'it means hitting your opponent hard and not merely killing them but torturing them'. She had herself heard the awful screams of human beings in agony and had witnessed lorry loads of armed thugs dragging people out of their houses and beating them. Whips made of steel springs, 'bone-breaking instruments which tore flesh and skin, rubber truncheons which burst internal organs'[50] leaving no mark on the outside were used to break the spirit and body of Jewish people and opponents of the regime. In her view 'the contempt for civil order, for personal rights, for constitutional methods of change', was slowly engulfing Europe 'like a thick black wave of despair'.[51] Bullies, she insisted, ruled in Germany.

Ellen Wilkinson used her friendship with Lady Rhondda to write in her feminist journal *Time and Tide*. She reported that the Nazis had no use for women outside the home. Under Hitler's orders, women were dismissed from their posts in universities, from law practices, from hospitals and doctors' surgeries and all public services. She spoke of how one Nazi officer strode into a university exam hall to make sure there were no Jews and Socialists there, adding 'and the women may as well go too. Law exams won't help them bear better children'.[52] The wholesale clearance from public services of Germany's most active and devoted women, she cried, was an all-absorbing tragedy for feminists. Paradoxically, Wilkinson noted, gender difference did not apply to Jewish women who were given equality with Jewish men, i.e. they were not immune from the 'sickening Nazi savagery'. Nazi newspapers denounced her as a 'Jew of the Jews'.

Just as importantly, Ellen Wilkinson helped Spanish socialists to fight against the encroachment of Fascism: in November 1934, she and Lord Listowel were thrown out of Spain for their activities. They had been visiting the country as representatives of the Relief Committee for Victims of Fascism. Otto Katz was with them, keeping out of sight but according to the secret services, watching refugees on behalf of the GPU and murdering political opponents.[53] In 1936, Ellen's support for Spanish socialists was further tested when the army led by General Franco tried to overthrow the democratically elected government. Ellen was now back in Parliament, this time as MP for Jarrow, and argued for military help to defend the government. Neville Chamberlain thought otherwise and hid behind the principle of non-intervention; the Labour leadership and the TUC fearing that intervention might precipitate a European war took Chamberlain's side.

Providing humanitarian aid was perhaps Wilkinson's most crucial service to the Spanish Government. In 1936, she helped set up the Spanish Medical Aid Committee to send medical staff and equipment to Spain; helped co-found a Parliamentary Committee for Spain to help those in need of food, clothing and medical aid; and she was a founder member of the National Joint Committee for Spanish Relief which coordinated the work of the various groups helping Republican Spain. She was also involved with the Basque Children's Committee, the International Brigade Independents' and Wounded Aid Committee and the Tyneside Food Campaign.

In April 1937, she travelled once again to Spain, this time with a cross-party section of women, the Independent MP Eleanor Rathbone, the Conservative MP Duchess of Atholl and Dame Rachel Crowdy.[54] Otto Katz, who had arranged the visit, accompanied them. At the time, there were reports of Soviet manipulation of the Republican government and attacks on fellow anti-fascists who were not communists, reports that Wilkinson heavily influenced by Katz, chose not to believe. Instead, she concentrated on reporting the atrocities of Franco, stating that 'shells from rebel six inch guns, smashing in the street outside, tearing through the roof of a theatre blew mangled bodies of women and children'[55] through the doorway of the hotel where she was lunching with the other members of the delegation. Their car was standing nearby. Before they could drive away, the body of one of the victims had to be wiped off it, a gruesome reminder of the reality of war. These experiences made an impact on all four women and they returned with a new commitment to organise relief schemes and convince the British Government that Franco and his army were being assisted by German and Italian forces. One of their notable successes was persuading the government to allow nearly 4000 Basque children to come to Britain as refugees. Ellen Wilkinson was successful in getting her Union, NUDAW, to raise a voluntary levy for a period of three months to help finance it. Soon people were calling her the 'pocket Passionara'.

Ellen Wilkinson's glowing international reputation was not matched with popularity inside the Labour Party. At the 1933 Labour Party Conference, she had faced a number of criticisms. First of all delegates accused her of misusing money collected for German political refugees by giving it to communist groups. She denied the charge. Secondly, Ellen Wilkinson was rebuked by Herbert Morrison. In his pamphlet, *The Communist Solar System*, Morrison drew up a list of proscribed organisations and Wilkinson belonged to a number of them. Characteristically, she defended her membership. In a debate about communists and their role in the Labour Party, the two confronted each other. She accused Morrison of 'going on the defensive', and that his pamphlet *The Communist Solar System* was 'a magnificent advertisement of the energy and drive of the Communist Party in this country. Why have those organisations flourished like this? Because our own Executive has not acted quickly enough'. Ellen condemned the Labour Party for leaving the Reichstag Fire trial, and with it the defence of democracy, in the hands of an unofficial committee. Labour, she insisted, should have taken the lead. In reply, Morrison argued that Miss Wilkinson's 'energy and drive go into wrong channels and sometimes she is a bit of a nuisance to us ... instead of running straight over and starting an unofficial organisation in association with people whom she knows she ought not to associate with ... she would be better occupied by concentrating her undoubted energy and drive on the forward work of the Party'.[56] There was a flirtatious edge to their exchanges that was not lost on many of the delegates.

Herbert Morrison sought to purge the Labour Party of communists and communist-led sympathisers. In his view, the CP and the Labour Party were fundamentally incompatible. The aim of the Communist International was to 'organise an armed struggle for the overthrow of the international bourgeoisie and the establishment of an international Soviet Republic'.[57] In contrast, the Labour Party believed in a parliamentary road to socialism. Morrison was fully aware that the CP, forbidden to affiliate to the Labour Party, sought other ways to influence Labour politics by creating 'a whole solar system of organisations and smaller committees around the communist Party'.[58] These organisations were superficially self-governing independent bodies but in reality were subservient to the CP. The inventor of this system, Morrison argued, was none other than Willi Munzenberg, seen as the 'versatile author and producer of every piece. He chooses the titles. He is the unseen prompter, stage manager and scene shifter'.[59] In October 1934 at the Labour Party Conference, Herbert Morrison who had a visceral dislike of communism accused Wilkinson of belonging to an allegedly communist organisation: the Relief Committee for the victims of German and Austrian fascism.[60] Rather than be expelled, she resigned from the Relief Committee, though continued to work closely with communists.

At first, Ellen was a lone voice within the Labour Party, but as the Spanish Civil War escalated she was joined by some powerful men. Herbert Morrison perhaps influenced by Wilkinson was one of the first of the Labour Party's more established figures to denounce non-intervention and urge support for the Spanish legitimate government. At a NEC meeting in January 1937, Morrison proposed that Labour put pressure on the National Government to allow the Spanish Government to buy arms. The motion was defeated. By now, he shared Wilkinson's dismay and despair. He was clearly perturbed that a constitutionally elected government had been overthrown by the army and he began urging the British Government to help Spanish democracy. It was perhaps a turning point in their relationship. However, although the two agreed about Spain, they still differed on political strategy. Ellen continued to work across party lines, joined communist-fronted organisations and tried to get the Labour Party to join United Front campaigns; in contrast Herbert Morrison held stubbornly to the idea of keeping the Labour Party separate from other organisations. We now know that he was right to be worried.

The bombing of Guernica in April 1937 by the German air force changed the Labour Party's attitude towards the Spanish Government. It denounced the bombing as an 'outrage upon humanity, as a violation of the principles of civilisation, and a manifestation of the merciless and inhuman spirit' of the Nazis and Fascists.[61] At the next Labour Party Conference, Ellen Wilkinson's analysis of the situation in Spain was now, at last, accepted. The Labour Party, horrified by Guernica and embarrassed by its position of non-intervention, reversed its policy, advocated supplying arms to the Republic and organised a series of mass demonstrations in support of the Spanish Government. In October 1937, the NEC set up a Spain Campaign Committee to further its aims: Wilkinson was elected Joint Secretary. The committee called for the immediate withdrawal of foreign troops in Spain and insisted that the legitimate government be allowed to purchase weapons. After battles with her colleagues and many threats of expulsion, Ellen Wilkinson's views of Franco and the Fascists were finally accepted by the Labour Party.

However, Otto Katz remained the éminence grise, still operating behind the scenes, still influencing Ellen Wilkinson. In 1937, he arranged for Ellen Wilkinson, the Labour leader Clement Attlee, John Dugdale and Philip Noel-Baker to visit Spain. It was a demanding tour, full of incident. In Barcelona, the group stayed with the Prime Minister, Negrín, before being driven to Madrid. Here they visited the front-line trenches under artillery fire and carried out an inspection of the British Battalion of the International Brigade. They visited a school where working-class children were as 'keen as needles, but so thin, every day they had to come through falling shells or casual bullets to a school only 2½ miles from the trenches'.[62] One day, Ellen saw 1500 children line up for a cup of milk, dried powder, water and a biscuit.

Starvation threatened to undermine the Spanish Government so the main focus of Ellen's work back in Britain was organising humanitarian relief. In Madrid alone there were a million people, many of them sick and wounded, who faced another winter of war without sufficient food, of which the most urgent was seen to be lack of milk. She helped set up the milk for Spain fund and persuaded NUDAW and the Cooperative Union to get involved. Customers at the 20,000 Cooperative shops were encouraged to buy a 6d token to help towards the purchase of cost price condensed milk and milk powder to be sent to Spain. In Barcelona, for example, the Fund served 33,000 glasses of milk and a biscuit each morning to children on their way to school.

Wilkinson was fully aware that the Spanish Government needed more than milk and food to win. Everywhere she could, in the House of Commons, at conferences, public meetings, demonstrations and in newspaper articles, she spoke of the need for arms. Ellen Wilkinson, Eleanor Rathbone and the Duchess of Atholl constantly asked questions in the House of Commons about the so-called non-intervention pact, the plight of refugees and the role of Germany and Italy in providing arms to the rebel forces.

At the 1938 Labour Party Conference, Wilkinson once more called for the right of the Spanish Government to purchase arms. If the Spanish Government was given the freedom to buy aeroplanes, anti-aircraft guns, artillery and tanks, she urged, Franco's insurgents could not win. In her view, in the interests of international peace, Franco should be prevented from winning the Civil War. If Fascism triumphed over democracy, she prophesised, it would herald the destruction of Europe. Wilkinson's left-wing reputation and her work helping the Spanish legitimate government led to accusations in Parliament that she was recruiting men for the International Brigade, a charge she denied. 'My whole work', she insisted 'has been in helping to provide medical aid and supplies inside Spain and in appealing for money for the wives and dependants of those who have gone to fight'.[63] What else could she have said?

On April 1, 1939, the democratically elected government conceded defeat by Franco's Army. Almost immediately, Chamberlain recognised Franco and his Fascists as leaders of Spain. The fight was over. Ellen Wilkinson, however, insisted that those who fought to defend Spanish democracy must not be forgotten. At the Labour Party Conference that year she moved that conference 'expresses its undying admiration for the heroism of the Spanish people, who, in the face of overwhelming odds, held the Fascist invaders at bay for two and a half years ... retarded the development of Fascist aggression in Europe and helped at least to postpone the outbreak of World War ... The Spanish fight is our fight, because it is a fight against Fascism'.[64]

Ellen Wilkinson focussed primarily on fighting fascism in Germany and Spain but her commitment to fighting fascism and imperialism led her to speak against it in Austria, Hungary and elsewhere. She once commented that she had 'heard Hitler orate, talked to Gandhi in gaol, picnicked with terrorist leaders on the run in Bengal, lunched with tribal chieftains on the Khyber Pass'. In 1925, she helped set up the 'Friends of Italian Freedom': she spoke out against Mussolini and later publicised the plight of Abyssinia. In August 1932, as part of a delegation of the India League, she visited India for three months, travelling to outlying villages, staying with local people, eating Indian food, meeting Gandhi and learning the respective viewpoints of Hindus and Muslims.[65] When she returned to England, her book, co-written with Krishna Menon, Monica Whately and Leonard Matters, included details of the political repression, torture and starvation which they had encountered on their journey in India. Repression, the authors claimed, forced the spread of terrorist activity.[66] In Ellen's opinion, Britain had run India 'much in the same way as the Nazis ran Germany'[67] and should 'clear out altogether'. She argued that Britain went to India for trade, stayed for loot and remained there because 'India is very largely the great out-relief agency for the young sons of the aristocracy and the very middle class'.[68]

Meanwhile, the rise of Hitler prompted Ellen Wilkinson to re-evaluate her attitude towards peace. Her experiences in combating Fascism in Germany,

Spain and elsewhere convinced her that Fascism was more dangerous than war and that democracy was worth fighting for. In September 1936, she resigned from the Peace Pledge Union because she felt utterly unable to leave the UK defenceless in the face of what was happening abroad. In March 1938, she resigned from the Women's International League. On August 23, 1939, Hitler and Stalin signed the Nazi-Soviet Pact in which both countries secretly agreed to invade Poland. The pact, which was defended by the British Communist Party, marked both the end of Ellen Wilkinson's ideological admiration of communism and of her willingness to work with organisations identified with the British Communist Party.

By 1939, Wilkinson had become a fierce anti-Stalinist. Willi Munzenberg, now a critic of Stalin, warned her to take care when mentioning him to MI5 because 'one of his most dangerous enemies was to be found there'.[69] It was at this point that both Ellen Wilkinson and her new friend Herbert Morrison became implacable adversaries of Guy Liddell. In fact, it was Wilkinson who now 'brought an end to Liddell's previously uninterrupted rise in the British security service'.[70] Liddell was tipped to become Director General of MI5 but was passed over when Wilkinson informed Herbert Morrison that he might be a double agent: he was after all close friends with Guy Burgess and was friendly with Kim Philby and Anthony Blunt. Liddell may well have been the agent that Munzenberg feared.[71]

MP FOR JARROW, NOVEMBER 1935 TO FEBRUARY 1947

Earlier, in 1932, Ellen had been adopted as Labour candidate for Jarrow, a town with one of the worst unemployment records in England: only 100 out of 8000 skilled manual workers had work. She nursed her prospective constituency carefully, driving regularly from London in her little Austin 7 motor car (often referred to as a bath or bedpan on wheels) to attend meetings and discuss electoral strategy with her agent, a journey of 290 miles along the single-carriageway of the Great North Road. Fortunately the 20 mile an hour speed limit had been repealed in 1930, allowing Miss Wilkinson to drive as fast as her car would go. Three years later, her work paid dividends: after an absence of more than 4 years Ellen Wilkinson was returned to the House of Commons, as MP for Jarrow, helped in her election campaign by Vera Brittain. Nine women were returned to Parliament: six Conservatives, one Liberal, one Independent and one Labour—Ellen Wilkinson. Once again, she was the only woman on the Labour benches. First and foremost, Ellen Wilkinson was a local MP dedicated to the needs of her constituents: she held regular surgeries, presented prizes at local schools, attended functions, visited businesses, dealt with individual problems where she could and raised issues affecting Jarrow in the House of Commons. One newspaper reporter wrote that he met Ellen Wilkinson 'dog-tired in the small hours; midnight journeys Jarrow, back House, back again Jarrow ... Whirligig life. Never still'.[72] Like Margaret Bondfield, Wilkinson was a single, economically independent woman and could work as hard as she wished, but she had no one to share the driving, no one to help offset her workload, no one to hold her hand when politics got tough.

In July 1936, aware that all the previous deputations to publicise the plight of Jarrow had failed, David Riley, Chair of the Council, suggested a new strategy: a march of the male unemployed to London. It is highly likely that Ellen Wilkinson had planted the idea in his mind. She had helped plan hunger marches before, ones organised by the Unemployed Workers' Movement, and led by the CP. Only too aware that these communist inspired marches were easily condemned by trade unions and the Labour Party as far-left propaganda she realised that it was crucial for the Jarrow Crusade to be different if it was to have an impact. The march was kept non-political and known communists were excluded from it. On October 31, thirty days and 290 miles later, the Crusade reached London. Yet the Jarrow Crusade failed to gain help for the town and its unemployed. Soon, however, principally because of Ellen's passionate oratory, her organisational genius and her best-selling book with that evocative and provocative title *The Town That Was Murdered*, Jarrow began to be noticed. The publicity that followed the Jarrow march contributed to the town's renewal and, according to Ellen, did much to raise the question of the relationship between big business and government.

Some historians argue that by the 1930s Ellen had abandoned her feminism, though her articles and parliamentary work provide evidence of someone who remained committed to promoting the rights of women. In fact, she continued to work with feminist groups and across party lines to advance women's equality and continued to sponsor Bills, such as the British Nationality and Status of Aliens (Amendment) Bill.[73] On April 1, 1936, Ellen Wilkinson introduced a motion to the House of Commons to 'place women in the Civil service on the same scales of pay as apply to men'. Her proposal was surprisingly carried and the government defeated. However, the Prime Minister, Stanley Baldwin, refused to accept the outcome, called for a second vote, and asked that it be treated as a vote of confidence. In the next division, the government won and female civil servants had to wait another twenty years—until 1956—to receive equal pay with men.

In addition to women's rights, Ellen Wilkinson championed the needs of her Jarrow constituents and her union. Between 1935 and 1939, she continually challenged the government over its attitudes towards the unemployed, means testing and its ineffectiveness in dealing with the Depression. She asked questions in Parliament about the iron and steel works at Jarrow, equal pay for women civil servants, help for the unemployed, maternity and child welfare, malnutrition and married women's property. And she asked lots of questions about Spain. In 1937 alone Ellen took part in all the key debates about Jarrow, the Iron and Steel Industries, the Depressed Areas, Merchant Shipping, Old Age and Widows' Pensions, the Arms Industry, Factories, Education, Milk, Agriculture and Finance Bills. Wilkinson even asked whether Parliament could have a guarantee that the 'country will not be insulted' by the presence of the leading Nazi and founder of the Gestapo, Hermann Goering, at the forthcoming Coronation of George VI.[74] As she spoke, the clouds of war were gathering and Ellen would soon have to readjust her politics to suit the new challenges facing her and the country.

THE SECOND WORLD WAR, 1939–1945

On September 3 1939, Britain declared war on Germany. Neville Chamberlain was Prime Minister of a Conservative Government and Ellen Wilkinson and others plotted to get rid of him. In her view, Chamberlain had shown no desire whatever to fight fascism: he had refused to help the Republican government in Spain, had signed the Munich Agreement and had refused to negotiate with Stalin, leaving the way open for the Nazi-soviet pact.[75] She wrote a series of articles in the popular press, arguing that Chamberlain's 'halting excuses' when the Scandinavian countries fell to Germany were too painful to hear, especially since the war was a 'gloves-off fight with Fascism'.[76] Chamberlain, she insisted, needed to resign. On May 10, 1940, Winston Churchill replaced Chamberlain and Ellen Wilkinson was delighted. Certainly, the new Conservative-led coalition with Churchill as Prime Minister gave Labour an opportunity for increased influence. Churchill appointed Wilkinson to a minor Ministerial post in charge of hardship tribunals, a job she said that was 'after her own heart'. In October 1940, she was moved to work as joint Parliamentary Private Secretary to Herbert Morrison who had himself just been promoted to Home Secretary. Ellen Wilkinson proved to be a loyal, hard-working and able Private Secretary, now much closer to Herbert Morrison who was suspected to be her new lover. She shared the job with her long-time friend and former union boss, John Jagger. Ellen Wilkinson, John Jagger and Herbert Morrison faced colossal challenges as the British civilian population came under attack. In London, a series of heavy bombings—the Blitz—began on Saturday September 7, 1940, and continued until May 1941, leaving 20,000 dead and approximately 70,000 wounded. In other places too the bombardment was horrific: fifteen other cities from Plymouth to Glasgow suffered major raids. It is widely accepted that the bombing had a dreadful impact on public morale as those who survived often had lost their family, their homes, their possessions and their courage. There was often no gas, no electricity, no water and no transport. At first, Wilkinson was given special responsibility for air-raid shelters and the care of the homeless, a job that fitted her compassionate personality and her practical and problem-solving approach. Ellen vowed to do as much as she could do to keep the population safe and public morale positive but it was a tough undertaking. Part of her new job was 'to put to bed each night, outside their own homes, 1 million Londoners'. On the first evening of her new appointment she visited the East End, talked to people about their experiences and listened. According to Ellen, five-sixths of her time was spent visiting shelters: in the earliest months of her job she spent nearly every night inspecting a shelter, speaking to people and taking notes on how to improve the enforced communal life. The *Daily Express* commented that 'going round with Ellen Wilkinson there were two things I liked about her, things that give me confidence in her approach to the problem – her energy and her natural touch with these people. She talked to the wardens and would always stop to talk to some man or woman and find their points of view'.[77] People called her the 'Shelter Queen'.

In the early days of the war, Ellen needed urgently to improve the conditions of communal shelters and London underground stations. As usual, she threw herself into the challenge. She promised people, 'Safety, Sanitation and Sleep', a typical Ellen sound bite highlighting people's understandable human urge for all three. She chivvied and bullied, encouraged and threatened, ordered and charmed. On one visit to Manchester, Ellen condemned the Corporation for its damp, unhygienic and uncomfortable shelters. The Corporation responded quickly: new shelters were built, old ones were renovated and bunk beds, canteens and sanitation were provided in the shelters. By the spring of 1941, thanks partly to the efforts of Ellen, Londoners were sheltering underground in some relative comfort. Ticket systems of entry were established, over 200,000 bunks were installed and allocated to regular users of the shelters, canteen facilities were set up, chemical lavatories, ventilation, lighting and running water were provided. And in some shelters night classes, films and other activities were made available.

In April 1941, Herbert Morrison restructured the fire services. Ellen Wilkinson was asked to help and her new role demanded that she quell any protest from firemen. At the beginning of the war, Britain's fire services were made up of professionals and volunteers, largely under the control of local authorities. The service was not efficient enough to respond swiftly to fire outbreaks so Morrison merged them and put them under the control of a new Fire Service Council. At the end of May, 1400 local fire brigades were forced to amalgamate down to 32. Ellen was on the Council and her job was to convince firemen to accept the changes.

On New Year's Day 1941, Morrison established compulsory fire-watching and put Ellen Wilkinson in charge of it. Trade unions insisted that fire-watchers be paid for their time and accused the government of violating the wartime consultation process. Wilkinson, who in the past might have led the protest, was forced to endorse the government's position: the needs of the whole country she now believed, overruled the rights of a section of it. Moreover, she knew only too well that if Fascism won life would significantly worsen for the working class. More compromise followed. In January 1941, the viscerally anti-communist, Herbert Morrison, banned the CP's newspaper, the *Daily Worker*, after a number of inflammatory articles in the paper had called for 'revolutionary defeatism'. In the past, Wilkinson would have undoubtedly criticised such a ban but faced with the necessity of overcoming Fascism she justified it and accused the *Daily Worker* of undermining the war effort. By this time, Ellen was altogether exasperated by the irresponsible and unstable character of the British Communists. When she was asked about this she replied. 'I not only worked with the Communists but I risked my political career because of them' and now their policies appalled her. The communists, in turn, hated Ellen, possibly because she knew too much about them.[78] Ellen Wilkinson, who had spent her life voting for rights for women, also put aside these beliefs during the war: for instance she voted against an amendment to the 1939 War Injuries Act which had set women's compensation for war-related injuries at 33% less than men's, a legal anomaly that all the women MPs found unacceptable. In November 1942, Mavis Tate seconded by Edith Summerskill moved an amendment to the Act: all the women backbenchers voted for Tate's amendment but Ellen Wilkinson remained loyal to the government and voted against. Tate's amendment failed.

Some believe that Ellen's tough and unpopular commitment to civilian conscription, strike breaking and censorship undermines her pre-war reputation as a left-wing feminist. Yet, in Ellen's opinion, the end justified the means. Faced with the menace of Hitler, she was in favour of an unqualified resistance to Fascism and its advancement. Undoubtedly her role as Parliamentary Secretary to Herbert Morrison gave her a new-found respectability: she had proved herself to be a competent administrator and loyal colleague. Ellen Wilkinson was now part of the political establishment and she reaped the rewards. In June 1943, she was elected Vice-Chair of the National Executive. Ellen's rise in the political echelon was unstoppable. In January 1945, when the Chair of the NEC died suddenly, Ellen Wilkinson became Chair and Harold Laski, Vice-Chair, of the Labour Party; in the same month, she was made Privy Councillor in the New Year's Honours List. On April 11, 1945, the Right Honourable Ellen Wilkinson MA accompanied Clement Attlee, Anthony Eden and Lord Halifax to a major international conference in San Francisco to help set up the United Nations. The exigencies of war, her fierce opposition to Fascism and her role as Private Secretary combined to make Ellen Wilkinson a much more mature politician, fully at ease with responsibility. The next chapter will examine how Wilkinson put her socialist ideals into practice as the war drew to a close and how, despite ill health, she helped change the British education system.

NOTES

1. Violet Markham and Miss Ellen Wilkinson: The Tributes of Three Women, Margaret Bondfield papers, Vassar College, Box 1, Folder 20.
2. *The New Dawn*, April 1923.
3. Quoted in Paula Bartley, *Ellen Wilkinson*, p. 4.
4. Katherine Bruce Glasier (1867–1950) was brought up as a Congregationalist and became involved in the Labour Churches. She edited the *Labour Leader* and helped found the ILP. She was elected to the ILP's first Council.
5. Minutes of the MSWS Executive Committee, September 2, 1913.
6. Ellen was sent to help J. R. Clynes and others in the forthcoming election.

7. MSWS Executive Report, March 31, 1914.
8. *The Common Cause*, October 10, 1913, p. 469.
9. Ellen Picton-Turberville MP, *Windsor Magazine*, March 1931.
10. Quoted in Paula Bartley, *Ellen Wilkinson*, p. 29.
11. The Conservative Nancy Astor, Mabel Philipson and the Duchess of Atholl were the three MPs.
12. Nancy Astor, *Evening News*, February 12, 1925.
13. Ellen Wilkinson, *The Division Bell Mystery*, 2nd edition, British Library, 2018, p. 93.
14. *The New Dawn*, June 20, 1925, p. 8.
15. *Empire News*, February 15, 1925.
16. See Katherine Holden, *The Shadow of Marriage: Singleness in England, 1914–60*, Manchester University Press, 2010 for the first major history of the lives of single women and men.
17. *Hansard*, May 5, 1925, Vol. 183, cc797–835.
18. Labour Party Conference, October 3, 1927, p. 183.
19. Ellen Wilkinson fought both inside and outside of Parliament for votes for women on the same terms as men. By now, Margaret Bondfield supported votes for women and the two spoke on the same platform at a large demonstration in 1926 in support of equal franchise.
20. Beatrice Webb Diaries, May 1929. Webb was referring to Margaret Bondfield.
21. *North East Daily Gazette*, September 28, 1931, p. 6.
22. *Hansard*, July 15, 1931, Vol. 255, cc495–715.
23. *North East Daily Gazette*, October 20, 1931, p. 25.
24. *Manchester Guardian*, October 28, 1931, p. 13.
25. *Daily Express*, February 16, 1932, p. 9.
26. *The New Dawn*, November 7, 1931, p. 554.
27. In 1937, Munzenberg fell into disgrace because he took the view that Communism should be propagated democratically rather than in a dictatorial or revolutionary manner. In 1938, he was expelled from the Central Committee of the Communist Party, dismissed from his post as communist representative in Western Europe, expelled from the Third International and accused of being in contact with Trotsky. In October 1940, he was found dead underneath a tree near Grenoble with a rope round his neck. See Stephen Koch, *Stalin, Willi Munzenburg and the Seduction of the Intellectuals*, HarperCollins, Bantam Books, 1995, p. 5.
28. Jonathan Miles, *The Nine Lives of Otto Katz*, 2011, p. 101.
29. Ibid.
30. MI5 Memo, November 18, 1933, KV2 1382/2.
31. The British Government, quite rightly, were very wary of Otto Katz and tried to prevent him visiting Britain. Each time, Ellen intervened and the ban was overturned: Ellen was still helping him when she became MP for Jarrow. For instance, Katz was allowed into Britain in August 1936 and then paid six further visits, all at Ellen Wilkinson's request. In March, July and October 1937 and January, February, and April 1938 he claimed he needed to visit to see his publisher. 'It is difficult to believe' stated security records 'that his publishers in this country can have needed his presence for six weeks in the first four months of this year and there is presumably some other purpose behind his visits. In any event his "exclusion" from the United Kingdom is for all practical

purposes nullified if this sort of thing is to go on and it seems desirable to reconsider the whole affair before the next inevitable request arrives from Miss Wilkinson' (KV2/1384 May 20, 1938).

32. Ellen Wilkinson to Isobel Brown, September 29, 1933, letter intercepted, KV2/1382.
33. KV2/1384 June 24, 1938.
34. MI5 took a great interest in Ellen Wilkinson's movements and stalked her. Apparently the MI5 file on Wilkinson was destroyed, probably when she became Cabinet Minister.
35. Goering, Prussian Interior Minister, quoted in Sean McMeekin, *The Red Millionaire: A Political Biography of Willi Munzenberg, Moscow's Secret Propagandist*, Yale University Press, 1974, p. 58.
36. *Daily Herald*, March 27, 1933, p. 4.
37. Special Branch Memo, May 18, 1933, KV2 1382/2.
38. Special Branch Report, July 4, 1933, KV2 1382/2.
39. Ibid.
40. Memo to Miss Bagot, August 25, 1948, KV2/1384.
41. Winifred Holtby to Lady Rhondda, Wednesday, September 6, 1933 L WH/5/5/24/04/05a.
42. 'Unofficial Commission of Enquiry into Nazi Murders and Kidnapping', July 9, 1935, quoted in Charmian Brinson, *The Strange Case of Dora Fabian and Mathilde Wurm: A Study of German Political Exiles in London During the 1930s*, Verlag Peter Lang, 1996, p. 342.
43. Ibid.
44. Letter from F. A. Newsam to G. A. Mounsey, November 27, 1933, FO 371/16755. The actual reports are missing and were probably destroyed.
45. Torgler was a leading figure in the German Communist Party. The other three were Bulgarian communists known to the police as Soviet undercover agents; Dimitrov was a leading figure in the Comintern, the other two his lieutenants.
46. *Daily Express*, February 23, 1934, p. 10.
47. *Daily Herald*, February 11, 1936, p. 3.
48. See Charmian Brinson, *The Strange Case of Dora Fabian and Mathilde Wurm: A Study of German Political Exiles in London During the 1930s*, 1996.
49. *Daily Herald*, March 27, 1933, p. 4.
50. *Daily Herald*, July 1, 1933, p. 3.
51. *Daily Express*, April 20, 1933, p. 4.
52. *Daily Mirror*, May 22, 1933, p. 4.
53. Secret Service Report, December 1940, KV2/1384.
54. Rachel Crowdy had been Commander of the Voluntary Aid Detachments in the First World War, Head of Social Questions and Opium Traffic Section in the League of Nations.
55. *Sunday Referee*, April 18, 1937, p. 5.
56. Labour Party Conference, Hastings, October 1933, p. 221.
57. Herbert Morrison, *The Communist Solar System*, Labour Publications, 1933.
58. Ibid.
59. Ibid.
60. *Daily Express*, October 2, 1934, p. 10.
61. NEC Manifesto, April 28, 1937.

62. C. R. Attlee, Ellen Wilkinson, Philip Noel-Baker and John Dugdale, *We Saw in Spain*, Labour Party, 1937.
63. *Hansard*, July 28, 1938, Vol. 338, cc3305–3307.
64. Labour Party Conference Report, Southport, May 1939, pp. 256–257.
65. *The Daily Telegraph*, October 10, 1934.
66. Ellen Wilkinson et al., *Condition of India—Being the Report of the Delegation Sent to India by the India League in 1932*, Essential News, 1932, p. 507.
67. *Birmingham Town Crier*, September 24, 1937, p. 5.
68. *Western Daily Press*, March 2, 1932, p. 6.
69. Stephen Koch, *Stalin, Willi Munzenburg and the Seduction of the Intellectuals*, HarperCollins, 1995, p. 309.
70. Ibid., p. 309.
71. Academics believe that Liddell was naïve in his friendships rather than a spy. Morrison and Wilkinson also knew that Liddell had worked closely with the Nazi authorities before the war trying to counteract communism.
72. Paula Bartley, *Ellen Wilkinson*, p. 86.
73. In 1948, after 34 years of campaigning, women were eventually granted the right to their own nationality regardless of marital status.
74. *Hansard*, February 22, 1937, Vol. 320, cc1612–1618.
75. AUCE Annual Delegate Meeting, 1939, p. 10.
76. *Tribune*, May 10, 1940.
77. *Daily Express*, October 11, 1940, p. 6.
78. *Leader*, March 3, 1945, p. 11.

CHAPTER 5

The First Female Minister of Education, 1945–1947

On April 30, 1945, Hitler committed suicide. A few days later Germany sur-rendered and the war officially ended in Europe. No more bombs would be dropped, no more houses destroyed, no more families made homeless, no more people killed or injured and no more need for shelters or fire-watchers. Ellen collapsed in a relief-fuelled exhaustion but there was little time to recuperate. On May 23, the Coalition Government was replaced by a Conservative 'Caretaker' Government; on May 28, Churchill hosted a fare-well cocktail party at which Ellen, along with others, said their goodbyes; on June 15, Parliament was dissolved. On July 5, new elections took place (Fig. 5.1).

During the war, Ellen had held enormous responsibility for the lives of people. This, according to the *Daily Herald*, added new qualities to her per-sonality with her junior ministerial experience reinforcing her quick brain and warm heart by adding 'dignity to her wit'.[1] Ellen was now a 'cool woman, quietly but dapperly dressed … an occasional spark in the frank eyes, hints that somewhere inside the young student who used to argue hotly about Votes for Women is still alive and giggling'.[2] She continued to produce her familiar trenchant witticisms, once commenting that the House of Commons was a 'place full of ex-future Prime Ministers'.[3]

Now that Fascism had been vanquished, and the war had ended in Europe, the class war was about to resurface. Ellen Wilkinson had no desire to uphold wartime anti-women and anti-union measures and quickly returned to her old, deeply held socialist ideals. By now, she was firmly estab-lished as a key figure in the Labour Party and a senior member of the NEC. She was a member of the Policy Sub-Committee, the policy-forming body

Some of this material is from Paula Bartley's *Ellen Wilkinson: From Red Suffragist to Government Minister*, Pluto 2014.

Fig. 5.1 Ellen Wilkinson in the Labour Cabinet, 1945 (Courtesy Peoples History Museum)

responsible for developing the economic and social agenda for the 1945 Labour Government. She took part in all the key discussions. At the time, the NEC supervised policy development and Ellen played a pivotal role, helping to direct policy and undoubtedly arguing for Labour to be more radical. The Committee stressed that 'the ultimate aim of the Movement was socialism, which we believe can only be attained on the basis of democracy'.[4] Ellen Wilkinson wrote *Plan For Peace*, a plan for 'a new world to be created, out of the ruins of the old' in which she stated that Labour's plan was 'the same as the wartime plan – to meet the needs of the nation. ... In place of vast armies of tanks, fleets of warships and bombers, we shall need vast numbers of houses, schools, hospitals, health centres ... it will be a plan – not for destruction, but for reconstruction of a new and finer country which we can be truly proud to hand on to our children'.[5]

In April 1945, the NEC printed 100,000 copies of *Let Us Face the Future*, a document which embodied the thinking of two decades and years of work by the NEC.[6] Ellen co-authored the manifesto with Michael Young, Herbert Morrison and Patrick Gordon Walker—who wrote each section is difficult to ascertain, as it was definitely a collaborative effort that had been well honed in discussions in the Policy Committee. *Let Us Face the Future* was a passionate, expressive, radical manifesto which had Ellen's core beliefs and principles written all over it. The manifesto reminded readers that the Conservatives had handled the pre-war depression badly because 'Big Interests had things all their own way'. And Churchill's famous aphorism was turned on its head: 'Never was so much injury done to so many by so few'. The manifesto declared that the 'Labour Party stands for freedom – for freedom of worship, freedom of speech, freedom of the Press ... But there are certain so-called freedoms that Labour will not tolerate: freedom to exploit other people; freedom to pay poor wages and to push up prices for selfish profit; freedom to deprive the people of the means of living full, happy, healthy lives'.[7]

The nation, the manifesto went on to say, needed a tremendous overhaul, 'a great programme of modernisation and re-equipment of its homes, its factories and machinery, its schools, its social services'. The Labour Party pledged itself to full employment. 'No more dole queues in order to let the Czars of Big Business remain kings in their own castles. The price of "economic freedom" for the few is too high if it is bought at the cost of idleness and misery for millions'.[8] One can almost hear Ellen Wilkinson speaking when the manifesto stated it would raise the level of production as 'firstly ... over production is not the cause of depression and unemployment; it is under-consumption that is responsible ... Secondly, a high and constant purchasing power can be maintained through good wages, social services and insurance, and taxation ... thirdly planned investment in essential industries and on houses, schools, hospitals and civic centres'.[9]

The Chair of the Labour Party had long believed that 'to nationalise the banks is to attack the very citadel of capitalist supremacy', a commitment made in the manifesto when it declared that the Bank of England must be brought under public ownership. And in recognition of Clause IV in the 1918 Labour Party Constitution—in hardly the words of Herbert Morrison—the manifesto stated 'The Labour Party is a Socialist Party, and proud of it. Its ultimate purpose at home is the establishment of the Socialist Commonwealth – free, democratic, efficient, progressive, public-spirited, its material resources organised in the service of the British People'.[10] The transformation of society that Ellen had worked for all her life now seemed possible. Socialism would be achieved the parliamentary way: Red Ellen's youthful aim of a revolutionary road to socialism was now well and truly relinquished.[11]

On May 21, 1945, at the 44th Annual Conference of the Labour Party held in Blackpool, Ellen Wilkinson presided over the largest Labour Party Conference ever held. She was now at the pinnacle of her power, sitting centre stage on the conference platform. In her opening remarks, she spoke of how people must decide 'whether Britain will put itself again under the rule of Big Business, or whether we will advance towards a society in which the whole resources of the country are efficiently used in the interests of the community'.[12] We want, she informed her audience, millions of houses, jobs for all, social security, educational opportunity for all and a real state health service. The conference, under Wilkinson's guidance, went on to debate *Let Us Face the Future*.

In her concluding speech, Ellen Wilkinson reminded delegates that they were fighting the 'Party of the rich, the Party of the powerful, the Party of big business, the Party that controls the great industries, the cartels and very largely the Press. These are our enemies'.[13] She concluded by saying 'Fight,

fight clean, fight hard, and come back with a solid majority for a Labour Government'. It was a rousing, socialist speech and a strong rebuttal to those who castigated Ellen for sliding to the right. Her Union was proud of the fact that one of its officials should have presided and prouder still that 'she discharged that responsibility with such outstanding success'.[14] It was, claimed a colleague, Ellen's finest hour. 'No one will ever forget the nerve, the verve, the wit, the confidence and the joyful challenge with which she led the Conference from its brilliant opening to its triumphant close'.[15] Ellen herself said 'This is the proudest moment of my life'. Margaret Bondfield moved the vote of thanks to Ellen. She was surprisingly muted in her tribute, merely complimenting Ellen Wilkinson for her work as Chair of the NEC and the 'agreeable and able manner in which she has conducted and guided the business of the Conference'.[16] In fact, Ellen Wilkinson had electrified the conference. But by this time, Ellen's star was shimmering whereas Margaret Bondfield's had waned.

Ellen was undoubtedly happy. She and Herbert Morrison were close, especially after working together during the war. At the social evening at the end of the conference, Ellen and Herbert Morrison danced the last waltz, 'canoodling in a rather obvious manner'.[17] It was the first time that the two had shown any amorous feelings about each other in public, their inhibitions swept away by the euphoric conference atmosphere. Wilkinson's love of her wartime boss clouded her judgement and she began a campaign to oust Attlee and replace him with Morrison. Shortly after the conference, Ellen Wilkinson attacked Attlee in the *Sunday Referee*, a scurrilous popular paper devoted to social gossip. Attlee, she reported, was a quiet London member who should be replaced by 'that superb political organiser', i.e. Herbert Morrison. In an anonymous and even more unguarded criticism of Attlee in *Time and Tide*, she maintained once more that Morrison was Labour's 'biggest personal asset. He has great achievements to his credit. His work is known all over the country ... Mr Attlee does not command that authority'.[18] Hugh Dalton noted in his diary that a row was rumbling in the Labour Party. Some people were 'going about swearing that they would have Ellen's head on a charger'. At the NEC meeting, the new Chair and former ally Harold Laski raised 'with regret' Ellen's article and rebuked her for expressing a lack of confidence in the Labour leader just before an election. Hugh Dalton noted that 'the discussion which followed was angry and confused. She was not popular with most of the men at the best of times, and on this occasion she had infuriated three sections: Greenwood's friends, the loyal Attleeans and a number of members who simply rallied to the side of a sick man. She did not make a very good defence and she did not counter-attack'. A vote of 'severe condemnation' of Ellen was proposed, though later withdrawn when it was realised that opinion was divided on the question. Instead, the NEC passed a vote of confidence in Clement Attlee. Ellen abstained.

Ellen Wilkinson went into the election with weapons loaded with socialist ammunition, committed to attack the Tory Party at every opportunity.

She was part of a special Campaign Committee, including Clement Attlee and Herbert Morrison, which directed the election. She hectored, wrote and spoke to as many as she could, reminding each audience of the bitter period of 18 years of interwar Tory rule. One of nine celebrity MPs who broadcast to the nation, Wilkinson hit out against the proposed deregulation of price controls. If controls were taken off, she argued, it would be 'a polka to perdition' and the 'biggest gamblers' clean up in history', just like the 'mad orgy of uncontrolled capitalism' after the First World War. The Conservatives talked about protecting nest eggs, she said, but it would be 'scrambled nest eggs' if they had their way.

The Labour Party won a sweeping victory, winning an overall majority of 146. Labour took 393 seats, the Conservatives 213 and the Liberals only 12. Twenty-one female Labour MPs were elected, one of whom was Barbara Castle. For the first time in its history, Ellen Wilkinson's party was in control. The future, she believed, could now be faced full-on. A sense of optimism prevailed: Michael Foot called it 'the blissful dawn of July 1945'. Hopes were very high that the Labour Government would not only solve the problems of post-war reconstruction but would make life considerably better for the working class. Certainly large numbers of the electorate, who still remembered the privations of the Conservative-dominated Depression years, had posted a vote of no confidence in the past and showed their preference for a British-style socialist revolution.

Ellen was returned to Parliament with a greatly increased majority of 11,007. On October 11, 1945, the London Co-operative Branch threw a victory party for all the NUDAW-sponsored MPs. The hall echoed to the 'noise of such an excited, happy throng as that which waltzed, foxtrotted and jittered ... over 1,200 people twirled and whirled, danced and sang in expression of their warm welcome to the NUDAW contingent to the first Labour Government in power. ... Here was our Ellen, looking well and vigorous, enjoying an evening's respite'.[19] The union which had been critical of their delegate during the war now took pride in the achievement of its celebrity MP.

Appointed the First Female Minister of Education

On August 3, 1945, Ellen, aged 53, became the first female Minister of Education, the second woman in Britain to become a Cabinet Minister and the only woman in a Cabinet of twenty. Two other women were elected to ministerial office: Mrs J. L. Adamson as Parliamentary Secretary, Ministry of Pensions, and Dr Edith Summerskill as Parliamentary Secretary, Ministry of Food. Ellen Wilkinson was part of a government, which apart from Aneurin Bevan, Emanuel Shinwell, Stafford Cripps and herself held firmly to the centre-ground of the Labour Party. Figures like Clement Attlee (Prime Minister), Herbert Morrison (Lord President), Ernest Bevin (Foreign Secretary) and Hugh Dalton (Chancellor) dominated. Despite these difficulties, the Labour Government held to its electoral promise of reform. It created the National Health Service, introduced a more comprehensive system of national insurance, nationalised the Bank of England and key industries like coal and iron, repealed anti-union laws and reformed the education system. Ellen's hopes for her country seemed to have materialised.

Historians have expressed astonishment that Clement Attlee gave 'Red Ellen' such an important post especially when she had tried to depose him as leader, but this underestimates both Attlee's management skills and Wilkinson's importance.[20] The political scientists Anthony King and Nicholas Allen argue that prime ministers make 'some kind of cost-benefit analysis' in their appointment choice.[21] In their view, prime ministers look for four criteria: government competence, political utility, presentational capacity and policy compatibility. The first priority for every prime minister was *government competence*. Some historians question Wilkinson's appointment, arguing that the post required someone with exemplary administrative skills and an ameliorative way with officials, qualities they believed were missing in the new Minister of Education. However, Attlee thought otherwise. He knew that the new Minister had proven administrative skills, could master a brief quickly, could deal with officials, could negotiate with outside agencies and would contribute effectively in Cabinet. She was, after all, a Senior Member of the Labour Party, had been Chair of the National Executive Committee, had co-written the manifesto and had proven her competence sitting on various committees during her parliamentary career. Attlee knew that Wilkinson was proficient, having previously demonstrated the requisite skills of framing legislation and placing it on the statute books. Moreover, during the war her efficiency as a junior Minister had been well established and she was thought to have 'worked magnificently in her subsidiary role at the Ministry of Home Security'.[22] It would have been inconceivable for the Prime Minister to ignore her. Indeed, Attlee had first put Wilkinson down for Minister of Health, though later crossed out her name and replaced it with Aneurin Bevan's.[23] The Minister of Education fulfilled Attlee's faith in her: her civil servants, according to Leah Manning, thought very highly of her.[24]

Secondly, prime ministers consider the '*political utility*' of their choice, what standing the prospective minister had in the party and the general public, of whether they brought with them a political constituency. Ellen Wilkinson had come a long way from her suffragist and revolutionary past and was now the most important woman in the Labour Party. She was a well-known politician, almost regarded as a national treasure. Attlee shrewdly wanted a Cabinet balance of middle-class MPs and trade unionists and knew that Ellen represented both: she held a master's degree and was clearly one of the most able and articulate trade union-sponsored MPs. Attlee also wanted a woman in his Cabinet in order to confirm Labour was a progressive, modern party; Wilkinson was the obvious choice.

Thirdly, prime ministers choose people who have '*presentational capability*'. Attlee knew that Wilkinson performed well in the House of

Commons and was someone who would reach out to voters. The *Daily Herald* believed that Miss Wilkinson's 'sincerity, her brilliant personal gifts and her knowledge of working-class problems well fit her to become Minister of Education at an hour when education is taking new strides in the direction of democracy'.[25] As well as an adroit public speaker, Ellen knew how to write for a popular audience. She had already written two novels, four non-fiction books, co-authored a number of books, tracts and pamphlets and regularly contributed to journals and newspapers. Fourthly, King and Allen argue, prime ministers look for '*policy compatibility*', that is compatibility with the views of the prime minister. Attlee knew that during the war Wilkinson had proved her loyalty as a junior minister and was now considered a safe pair of hands. She was no longer a member of the 'awkward squad'. In addition, each prime minister had to consider the composition of their Cabinet as a whole, having 'to take into account the balance of ideological and factional forces within the governing party'.[26] Attlee was aware that the left was entitled to its share of government and bringing in Ellen would appease, and hopefully restrain, them. Moreover, the principle of collective responsibility gave Attlee an incentive to include political opponents in Cabinet in order to contain potential criticism. Ministers were expected to tow the Cabinet line. Finally—crucially—personal affection came into play. Attlee respected and liked Wilkinson, having a huge regard for those like her who had an inspiring vision of socialism and a visceral detestation of poverty.[27]

Many feared, and some hoped, that Ellen's instinctive radicalism might sit uneasily with her ministerial brief. She was certainly still in contact with old communist friends: in March 1946, she wrote asking Morgan Phillips, the General Secretary of the Labour Party, for 'a special favour'[28] and smooth the way for Otto Katz who wanted to visit Britain. Katz had been initially refused leave to land in Britain but 'in view … of the interest which Miss Wilkinson appears to have in KATZ, the case was referred to H M Superintendent (Mr Spinks) for further instructions'.[29] The ban was overturned and Katz was allowed to stay for 14 days.[30]

On occasions, the newly appointed Cabinet Minister remained irrepressible and there were glimpses of the old reckless and indiscreet Ellen Wilkinson. In a characteristically off-the-cuff remark to an audience at Jarrow, she urged the dock workers on strike to return to work because bread might be rationed if the current strike continued as ships sent over to fetch grain would not reach Canada before the winter freeze.[31] The Prime Minister was furious about this lack of protocol and recalled Wilkinson to London. Something needed to be done, the *Western Mail* urged, about the habit Ministers had of making unauthorised pronouncements that seem to be unannounced Cabinet decisions. The doctrine of collective responsibility, it advised, needed brushing up. When Ellen Wilkinson was questioned in Parliament about her statements, a great crowd of MPs assembled in the Common to hear her and the mood was jovial. MPs of all parties entertained each other with caustic jibes before giving Ellen a rousing cheer and settling back to enjoy the prospect of her familiar ripostes. They were disappointed: her speech was not humorous at all. Instead, Ellen stood up 'very pale, dressed in black, looking smaller and more slender than ever'[32] and speaking in a very serious manner, apologised for her mistake and promised to be careful in future. As a Cabinet Minister, Ellen Wilkinson could no longer afford to be entertainment fodder for the House of Commons. By now, she knew that 'if I make one slight remark off the point, I may find myself the centre of embarrassing attention the next day'.[33]

MINISTER OF EDUCATION, AUGUST 1945–FEBRUARY 1947

As a Cabinet Minister, Ellen was responsible for the work of her department, she was its spokeswoman in Parliament, and represented it to the outside world. Her main task as Minister was to implement 'Rab' Butler's 1944 Education Act which set out a controversial tripartite system of grammar schools for the most intellectually gifted, modern schools for the majority and technical schools for those with a technical or scientific aptitude. To assess which pupils should attend which schools all pupils who wished to attend a state school took an exam when they were eleven years old, known as the 11+. Those who passed went to the grammar school, whereas those who failed went to secondary moderns. At the time, the principle of selection was widely accepted—Ellen Wilkinson saw it as a fairer system, a meritocratic system, rewarding the cleverest rather than those with money by abolishing fees in maintained schools and ensuring that entry to those schools was on the basis of intellectual ability. The next female Labour Secretary of State, Shirley Williams disagreed and overturned Wilkinson's policy by changing most of the grammar schools into comprehensives.

It was set to be Wilkinson's last big challenge. In her own lifetime, educational acts such as the Fisher Act had been passed and not put into effect either through a lack of will or a change of government. Colleagues congratulated Ellen on her boldness and decisiveness in rescuing the Act when it 'looked as though it were drifting into the doldrums'.[34] It was nothing less, Ellen claimed, than an overhaul of the entire system of state education. Regrettably, she was required to deliver an Education Act she had not written. *The Tribune* believed that 'we do not doubt that she will strive to instil into it the maximum socialist content, but it is not the Act which she would have fashioned if she could have started afresh'. Many thought it would be impossible to introduce any measure of educational reform at a time of economic constraint; Ellen complained to Harold Laski that she had 'a hell of a job here because of the shortage of everything and the difficulty of ever getting the Ministry of Works to do anything to time'.[35] Certainly, Britain's severe post-war difficulties meant that it was hardly a propitious time for expansion. The country was on the verge of bankruptcy, had lost approximately one-quarter of its wealth, lost many of its overseas assets and was dependent on the USA for loans. Ellen set about persuading a reluctant

Cabinet to provide the money for reform, chivvying the building industry and training the new teachers. 'But I never doubted', commented Susan
Lawrence 'that in spite of all the frightful obstacles – want of teachers and
want of buildings – that Ellen would find a way, and she did, where a weaker
Minister might well have shrunk from all the lions in the path'.[36]

Ellen Wilkinson was motivated by a belief that education was a force for
social change and a way to increase social capital. Investment in people's education, she thought, was the key to economic, social and political advancement. Her aim was to provide equal opportunity for all children based on
their ability and aptitude, irrespective of the means of the parent. When she
went to the Ministry of Education, she said 'I had two guiding aims, and
they come largely out of my own experience. I was born into a working-class
home, and I had to fight my own way through to the University. The first of
those guiding principles was to see that no boy or girl is debarred by lack of
means from taking a course of education for which he or she is qualified ...
the second one was that we should remove from education those class distinc-
tions which are the negation of democracy'.[37]

Given her radical past, many hoped that Ellen would eradicate the elitism
central to the British educational system, particularly the public and private
school system. She did not. Her aim was to 'make the schools provided
by the State so good and so varied that it will just seem to be quite absurd
not to send the children to the schools'.[38] Using a booklet written by the
previous Conservative regime, *The Nation's Schools*, Ellen and her team re-
affirmed Labour's commitment to the Act. The left-wing of the Labour Party
was outraged, condemned the pamphlet and asked that the Socialist Minister
of Education 'burn it'.[39] William Cove, a member of the National Union of
Teachers' and Labour MP for Aberavon, attacked her at the Labour Party
Conference, describing the pamphlet as a 'reactionary document riddled with
class distinction and class privilege'.[40] He disapproved of Labour's secondary education policy, in particular grammar schools, and started an 'Ellen
must go' campaign. Cove, along with a number of left-wing MPs, favoured
comprehensive schools. In July 1946, in a Commons debate on education
he demanded that Ellen Wilkinson's salary be reduced by £100 as a token
of dissatisfaction, arguing that the education world was disappointed at her
performance.[41] Other Labour MPs leapt to Ellen Wilkinson's defence. The
chair of the Labour Party's education group deplored Cove's vituperative
remarks; another asserted that the NUT believed she was doing her best.
Leah Manning MP for Islington East later wrote that Cove's campaign was
caused by jealousy and that 'his unwarranted attacks on Ellen could only have
been motivated by her success'.[42] The Scottish MP Jean Mann provided sympathy when 'just after receiving a barrage from the Labour benches, Ellen
came down to the Ladies Members' Room, shaking and upset. In the ruthless
attack on her there were no holds barred and no regard made for the fact that
Ellen was suffering from extreme physical disability'.[43] This was a reference to
Ellen's chronic bronchial disease.

Ellen Wilkinson had been educated at a grammar school and she had a strong loyalty to the elitist system which had helped her succeed. She drew support from Mr Evans, President of the National Federation of Class Teachers, who believed that the new Education Act was the 'first great social measure' and 'offered great opportunities', arguing that the dynamic personality and enthusiasm of Ellen Wilkinson would ensure that the Act would become a 'living thing'.[44] Not everyone shared this belief. The most cogent criticism was made by Margaret Herbison, a Labour MP and former secondary school teacher who argued that segregation would deny equality of opportunity, that it would not be possible to determine a child's aptitude at 11 years, and that the best brains would go to the grammar school, the next best to technical schools and the rest to secondary moderns. Herbison wanted every child to go to the same type of school and be given a liberal arts education.[45] Ellen Wilkinson, however, argued for the tripartite scheme. She envisaged that there would be parity of esteem between the three school systems, a hope which never materialised. Technical schools were expensive to manage and local education authorities (LEA) were therefore reluctant to build them. The education system imagined by Ellen was bipartite one rather than tripartite. And the bipartite system was deeply flawed. Ellen appealed to LEAs and teachers never to regard secondary modern schools as dumping grounds for children. Her words went largely unheeded. LEAs remained unwilling to build more grammar schools resulting in fierce competition for places. Only 20% of school pupils passed the 11 plus examination; the rest who had 'failed', the majority of working-class children, went to the secondary moderns. The damage to the self-esteem of the 11-year-olds who failed was considerable.

Ellen Wilkinson was commended by the left-wing of the Labour Party when she raised the school-leaving age from 14 to 15. Raising the school-leaving age was an ambitious task as the Blitz had destroyed a great many schools and teachers were in short supply. It required every ounce of determination Ellen could muster to do this. First, she had to find 5000 additional classrooms, pay for all the extra desks, chairs, blackboards and textbooks needed and train 13,000 more teachers for the expected extra 390,000 pupils. Second, she had to defend her policy to both Conservative and Labour politicians. Some newspapers argued that raising the school-leaving age would take too many out of the labour market, a criticism that Wilkinson rebuffed by arguing that an extra 12 months of school would make young people better suited to work as 'British industry does not depend on a swarming mass of illiterate hands … what it needs is a skilled work-force'.[46] The Labour Cabinet, hard-pressed by post-war financial limitations, was disinclined to allocate sufficient money. In several Cabinet meetings, and with Clement Attlee's support, she fought against three heavyweights, and friends, Hugh Dalton, Stafford Cripps and Herbert Morrison, to gain the necessary funding for raising the school-leaving age. After a series of battles, she threatened the Cabinet that if it refused to back her, she would campaign outside

Parliament. 'As a trade union official', she insisted, 'I am quite fully prepared to use my union, public platforms and the press to argue the case'.[47] The Cabinet, fully aware of her previous campaigns, conceded.

There were not nearly enough classrooms to accommodate the pupils who profited from the raising of the school-leaving age. As Minister of Education, Ellen had to oversee a very large school building programme. There was no money to build new schools or new extensions to existing buildings so the pragmatic Ellen devised special prefabricated huts to accommodate the new pupils. She defended these huts from critics by saying 'I know that some of these huts look very functional...but they generally are much cleaner, more sanitary and more weatherproof than many of the picturesque old buildings... They are not disused Army huts, they are proper huts, well designed for their job'.[48] The last remaining 'temporary' school hut was demolished in the Wirral in 2012.

Ellen Wilkinson also had to overcome a shortage of teachers. She set up a one-year Emergency Training Scheme: generous grants were given to ex-service men and women between the age of 25 and 30 to train as teachers. Twelve new training colleges were set up, housed in hastily improvised buildings 'which ranged from a Duke's castle in Northumberland to groups of munition works near Wednesbury'.[49] She faced complaints from Labour MPs and others who feared that the emergency training scheme would produce hordes of ill-trained teachers to work in schools.[50] Interestingly, the NUT did not protest.

She joined forces with the Secretary of State for Scotland to advocate free milk and free school meals for children in grant-aided primary and secondary schools. In a joint memorandum, the two argued for the need for free milk and school dinners.[51] Together, they convinced the Cabinet to support free school milk reminding them that before the war, when malnutrition was rampant, the Tories had refused to give milk and school meals to children because Winston Churchill believed it undermined parental responsibility.[52] Her success in providing free milk was an important achievement. A number of working-class and poorer children did not eat adequately, were malnourished and often left home without breakfast. It is said that generations of children grew up stronger and healthier because of this measure. It more or less remained in force until Margaret Thatcher was ordered to abolish it by the Chancellor when she became Education Secretary in 1970.[53] Free school meals for all children never became law.

The expansion and improvement of technical education were high on Ellen's list of priorities. In her view, a better technical education was needed for Britain's industrial reconstruction and the revival of the export trade. Ellen aimed to promote new schemes in more than 20 industries including mining, building and the motor trade. Her policy operated on three levels: national, regional and local, words widely used today but which were refreshingly new at the time. She opened the College of Aeronautics at Cranfield which provided a residential two-year post-graduate course for

50 aeronautical science and engineering students. Money again was limited so instead of a brand new purpose-built college the government converted the site of a former RAF base: the Airmen's Dining Hall was divided up for a library, a lecture hall, two common rooms and a staff room; the barrack blocks were transformed into laboratories; and the Sergeant's Mess into a hall of residence. The College eventually developed into a highly successful graduate centre for science, engineering, technology and management: Cranfield University.

EDUCATION INTERNATIONALLY

As Minister of Education and committed anti-fascist, Ellen took an interest in what was happening in post-war Germany. In October 1945, Clement Attlee and the Foreign Secretary, Ernest Bevin, asked her to visit Berlin and the British Zone in Germany to get a general sense of what was going on politically, and to review the educational facilities there. Both men knew about Ellen's pre-war involvement in Germany, knew that she was respected in socialist circles and believed that she had the ability to see, comment upon and advise on its reconstruction. It was a whirlwind tour with visits to Hamburg, Munchen-Gladbach, Dusseldorf, Buckeberg and Berlin where she met the Central Commission, old socialist and communist friends in the Social Democratic Party (SPD) and the Communist Party of Germany (KPD) and visited a number of German schools. It was expected that, as well as reporting on educational issues, Ellen Wilkinson's pre-war anti-fascist activities would encourage German socialists to trust her and enable her to gather evidence on the general reconstruction and de-nazification in Germany.

In a secret, and long, memorandum which was circulated in the Foreign Office and the Criminal Investigation Department (CID), Ellen outlined the problems and possibilities of rebuilding a post-war Germany. She used a measured, academic and neutral tone to describe conditions in Germany which must have surprised the detectives in CID who had spied on her before the war. When Britain first overran Germany, she wrote, it was an 'administrative desert' with no industry, no communications, no electric power and no local government. As in most defeated countries, there was a shortage of food, shortage of coal, shortage of manpower and a shortage of accommodation. 'Typhus and typhoid', she noted, were 'under control. Diphtheria has been bad in some areas and so had tuberculosis, and venereal disease has been rampant'. Added to which there were, in the British zone alone, some 2¼ million displaced persons, 2½ million German troops living in open fields and masses of refugees from the East entering the zone at a rate of some 9000 a day. And as she stated in her report, life in post-war Germany was dangerous for a lot of people as 'there were naturally many cases of murder and rape (even though) there were no attempts at massacre of the German population on any considerable scale'.[54] Ellen warned that the Germans seemed unwilling or unable to think independently, accentuated by the fact that most of the opposition—including many people she knew—had been murdered by the Nazis.

By now, Ellen was completely disillusioned with Soviet Russia and with the German Communist Party (KPD) which was under Russian control. She condemned the Russians for 'not worrying very much about what happens to the Germans and in particular how many of them die or contract diseases during this winter ... Russians are stripping the zone which they occupy of as much material and plant as they can carry away to Russia'.[55] She spoke of the difficulties of establishing democracy in Germany, especially when the Russians and the KPD tried to undermine it. Ellen, as a former trade unionist and trade union-sponsored MP, believed that trade unions, which had been abolished by the Nazis, could act as a powerful democratising force and welcomed the fact that they were being re-built, albeit slowly. Every factory election, she wrote, was a struggle between the two main left-wing parties for control of the unions, a struggle Ellen maintained that had 'to be fought out if German democracy is to be born ... These factory struggles may throw up much-needed new leadership'.[56] Trade unions, she believed, were a necessary part of democracy.

However, Ellen's main job was to report on the educational system, seen as an important tool for the reconstruction of democracy in Germany. She gave an incisive picture of educational facilities, or the lack of them, in the occupied country. Shortage of administrative staff, shortage of schools, shortage of appropriate teaching staff and shortage of textbooks were matters of some concern. Ellen was not directly responsible for education in Germany, as this was the job of the Control Commission, though her thinking on the subject was welcomed. She saw the task as firstly to set up an efficient administration, secondly to open the schools in 'reasonably tolerable conditions' and thirdly to see that education was underpinned by democratic values. Ellen reported that teachers were vetted 'with some care', with a number dismissed for their Nazi activities.[57] There were, she noted, 'no real suitable textbooks in any subject – even introductory books for little children were sheer Nazi propaganda'.

Ellen Wilkinson was a committed internationalist. In October 1945, she had accompanied Clement Attlee to San Francisco where representatives of 50 countries met to draw up the United Nations charter. In November 1945, Ellen chaired a conference which aimed to establish 'an educational and cultural organisation' of the United Nations (UNESCO). Delegates from 45 countries ranging from Argentina through to Yugoslavia attended but no representative from the USSR was present. Ellen asked the British Prime Minister, Clement Attlee, to welcome the delegates to the conference. He agreed to do so—as long as she wrote a draft of his speech.[58] At the founding conference, Ellen suggested that science be included in the title of the organisation since 'in these days when we are all wondering, perhaps apprehensively, what the scientists will do to us next, it is important that they should be linked closely with the humanities and should feel that they have a responsibility to mankind for the result of their labours. I do not believe that any scientists will have survived the world catastrophe, who will still say that they are utterly uninterested in the social implications of their discoveries'.[59] The delegates, all too aware that the dropping of atom bombs on Hiroshima and Nagasaki had made science a very topical subject, agreed. And so the United Nations Educational, Scientific and Cultural Organisation (UNESCO) was born.

The conference split up into commissions to agree the terms of a constitution. This had originally been drafted by 'Rab' Butler and had been developed by Ellen at several meetings. The final draft certainly mirrored Ellen's style: 'that since wars begin in the mind of men, it is in the minds of men that the defences of peace must be constructed; that the great and terrible war which has now ended was a war made possible by the denial of the democratic principles of the dignity, equality and mutual respect of men, and by the propagation ... of the doctrine of the inequality of men and races'.[60] At the end of the conference, UNESCO's ultimate goal was defined: it would contribute to 'peace and security by promoting collaboration among the nations through education, science and culture'. Once the Conference was over, the Commission began to put its strategies in place. The Commission, with representatives from 14 countries, was presided over by Ellen, and on November 4, 1946, UNESCO was given official status as an agency of the United Nations. UNESCO's first official conference was held in Paris later that year: Ellen was extremely disappointed not to be there but a worsening of her bronchial condition prevented her from attending.

ANTI-IMPERIALISM

In addition, Clement Attlee asked his Minister of Education to join the India and Burma Committee, a six-member committee on which Stafford Cripps, Clement Attlee and Frederick Pethick-Lawrence served. The Committee's task was to examine the case for Indian independence and suggest ways to make it happen. The Labour Party was committed to dismantling the Empire and giving former colonial countries their independence. Ellen was a well-known anti-imperialist, counted Nehru as a personal friend, had visited India for the India League, had met Gandhi at his request and later co-wrote a book about her experiences, the *Condition of India: Being the Report of the Delegation Sent to India*.[61] She had been a founder member of the League Against Imperialism until it was made a proscribed organisation by the Labour Party. In November 1945, the India and Burma Committee recommended that a delegation be sent to India to communicate Labour's commitment to self-rule. Less than two years later, the British Government announced that it would grant full self-government to British India. Sometimes there was tension between Muslims, Sikhs and Hindus about how political power should be distributed. Ellen Wilkinson, all too aware of the tensions, believed that national unity would transcend religious sectarianism. On July 18, 1947, the Indian Independence Act received the Royal Assent, partitioning British India into two fully sovereign dominions, that of India and Pakistan. Ellen's friend Jawaharlal Nehru became the first Prime Minister of an independent India, now the largest democracy in the world and Muhammad Ali Jinnah served as Pakistan's first Governor-General. Ellen Wilkinson did not live long enough to celebrate the independence of India and Pakistan, nor did she witness the post-independence violence between the various ethnic and religious groups.

By January 1947, Ellen's health was deteriorating fast. All her life she had suffered from asthma, bronchitis, influenza and lung infections. During the war, she had been admitted to hospital at least seven times. Exhausted by the war effort, her health was undermined further by the demands of her new post. She was plagued by serious illnesses aggravated by unremitting work, smoking and an exceptionally harsh winter. Margaret Bondfield gave her 'motherly warnings about her need for rest – of mind and of nerves – which she, as cheerfully as usual disregarded'.[62] The two were not particularly friendly and rarely met each other because they belonged to different spectrums in the Labour Party: Ellen was distinctly left-wing; Margaret was not. Ellen Wilkinson ignored her advice.

One of Ellen Wilkinson's last engagements was opening, with Laurence Olivier, the Old Vic Theatre School. The school building had been bombed and at the time of opening on January 24 still had no roof. Ellen, wearing her fur coat, bore the almost sub-zero temperature and the snow with her usual fortitude, making a stirring speech saying that 'man did not live by bread alone' and she 'would like to have a nation that knew so much about the standards of good music, of great drama, and of the visual arts that those things became passionately needed necessities'.[63] Predictably, given her frailty she caught pneumonia (again) and a few weeks later, on February 6, 1947, died in a private ward at St Mary's Hospital Paddington. Herbert Morrison was also in hospital, recovering from thrombosis. The BBC agreed not to broadcast Ellen Wilkinson's death until her old friend had been told. When he heard, 'Morrison did not say anything, but suddenly looked years older'.[64]

Ellen left her whole estate of £7253 and her property to her sister Anne Elizabeth Wilkinson.[65] At 11.15 a.m., Monday February 10 Ellen was buried in the Holy Trinity churchyard at Penn. It was a private funeral with only about 20 family members and close friends present. A few days later, a memorial service was held at St Margaret's Westminster, the same church which was to hold Margaret Bondfield's, and attended by the King, Winston Churchill, Clement Attlee, most of the Cabinet and hundreds of MPs including Nancy Astor and Eleanor Rathbone, civil servants, trade unionists and overseas friends and colleagues. There were also memorial services in Jarrow and Hebben attended by local civil dignitaries and friends. Herbert Morrison did not attend any memorial: he was still in hospital.

Conclusion

Obituaries point to Ellen's personality remaining relatively unchanged throughout her life. The *New York Times* could not 'forget the amazing amount of energy and passion, gaiety and vivaciousness compressed into 4ft 9'. She was a strong-willed, empathetic, warm-hearted, generous woman who brought to 'public affairs an acute mind, an ebullient spirit and a passion for social justice, an intuitive and devoted partisanship for the poor and the weak'. Nonetheless, like so many other successful politicians, social reformers and political activists, she 'had a necessary vein of intransigence' and could be 'an uncomfortable colleague as well as a ruthless opponent'.[66] Her rebellious nature, somewhat inhibited by high office, did not disappear. In his obituary, the Communist leader Ian McKay wrote that 'she was a great fomenter of trouble, and wherever there was a row going on in support of some good – or even fairly good – cause that rebellious redhead was sure to be seen bobbing about in the heart of the tumult ... and, if she mellowed a little towards the end ... it only needed some cynical after-dinner gibe from one of the Tory diehards to rouse the old devil in her and show that behind the correct, austere façade of the Cabinet Minister there still pulsed the hot angry heart of the poor penniless but dauntless Lancashire lass who had fought her way up, past all the pomp and privileges, from the slums of Ardwick to the seats of the mighty'.[67]

If Ellen's political outlook seemed to shift to the right as she got older, it was probably because she was now in a position to get things done rather than point out what others ought to be doing. As she grew older, and some say, grew up, Ellen developed into a fully rounded politician at ease with her ministerial status and for the short time she held the post worked comfortably within the strict parameters of her new job. For sure, she faced challenges both as the first-ever female Minister of Education and as a feminist and socialist within a centre-left Cabinet. Even so, Ellen's contribution to the post-war government was perhaps not as great as she hoped, partly because of her chronic asthma and lung problems and partly because her new job commanded so much of her time. The 'heavy burden of official responsibility' maintained Mary Agnes Hamilton who had served with Ellen in the 1929 government, 'had come to her rather too late. Those who have worked as hard as she did pay a heavy penalty; the physical apparatus may betray them at the point of maximum strain'.[68] Ellen Wilkinson kept working up to her end: a few days before she died, she wrote a foreword to a pamphlet she had largely created, *The New Secondary Education*.

Ellen Wilkinson had a multiple political individuality that escapes easy definition: she was a socialist, a feminist, a trade unionist, a pacifist, a Wesleyan Methodist, a vegetarian, an anti-fascist, an internationalist, a parliamentarian and at one time, a revolutionary. Tensions inhabited each stage of her journey as she balanced the sometimes competing ties of gender and class, of fostering peace yet fighting dictatorships, of Marxist theories and religious beliefs, of revolutionary politics and parliamentary democracy, of union solidarity and wartime exigencies, of nationalism and internationalism. It proved impossible for her to construct a coherent 'version' of her life, however principled she might want it to appear, without meeting difficulties and tensions. 'Red Ellen' remained throughout her life a socialist and feminist but these were negotiated terms, not fixed.[69]

Ellen Wilkinson was fortunate to serve in Labour's first majority government, a government that transformed Britain. She was certainly one of Britain's great female politicians. Her persistence and tenacity led to the transformation of the British educational system giving working-class children opportunities they had rarely enjoyed before. Her commitment to grammar schools was questioned at the time, yet no one can deny her other educational achievements, from building new schools, recruiting new teachers, raising the school-leaving age, providing free school milk, awarding educational grants and helping set up UNESCO, all of which combine to make her one of the greatest Ministers of Education. Throughout her life, she was involved in many of the important left-wing issues of the day. So many different groups of people had reason to be grateful for her contribution to transforming their lives: young women under 30 who benefited from equal franchise; women married to foreigners who retained their citizenship; female civil servants who campaigned for equal pay; women police officers for their existence; her Jarrow constituents for alleviating unemployment; trade unionists for improvements in union law; walkers who wanted the right to roam in the countryside[70]; borrowers who bought goods on hire-purchase; wartime city dwellers for keeping them safe from bombs; Italian, Spanish and German socialists for her anti-fascist crusades; and Indian nationalists for publicising their cause. Everyone, save the bankers and other capitalists, had reason to thank Ellen for trying to safeguard their economic rights. In addition, the post-war generation are indebted to her for helping to shape the Labour programme for social, economic and cultural change.

Ellen Wilkinson's political convictions remained steadfast, though her methods of achieving them changed. Parliament she argued, not Soviets, could 'be the mighty engine of the people's liberties if the people will use its levers'.[71] By the outbreak of the Second World War, she had spent long enough in the political wilderness of the far left and had witnessed the success of Fascism and the collapse of her ideals in Soviet Russia to realise that the exercise of influence and power outside the democratic process was problematic. In the end, Ellen chose to work within the existing structure of political power, believing that parliamentary democracy was a more effective route for radical activists than criticising and organising from outside. In her view, parliamentary democracy could offer a way forward if the Labour Party would only decide to be more courageous. In post-war Britain it was, and whatever criticisms might be levelled at the first majority Labour Government it was a genuinely reforming government. And we have Ellen Wilkinson to thank for helping to make it so.

Ellen Wilkinson, like Margaret Bondfield, came from a working-class non-conformist background, worked as an official in a trade union and remained single all her life. The next chapter will examine the political development of Barbara Castle who came from a more privileged background, had no roots in either religious or working-class organisations and was to become the first married woman to be appointed Cabinet Minister.

Notes

1. *Daily Herald*, November 1, 1945.
2. Ibid.
3. Ibid.
4. Policy Committee, Points for Discussion, September 1944.
5. Ellen Wilkinson, *Plan for Peace*, issued by the Labour Party.
6. Labour Party Research Programme, October 1946.
7. *Let Us Face the Future*, Labour Party Manifesto, 1945.
8. Ibid.
9. Ibid.
10. Ibid.
11. NEC Minutes, October 29, 1944.
12. *The New Dawn*, June 6, 1945, p. 178.
13. Labour Party Conference, May 1945, p. 152.
14. *The New Dawn*, June 16, 1945, p. 178.
15. Obituary, Labour Party Conference, 1947.
16. Margaret Bondfield, Labour Party Conference, 1945.
17. quoted in Paula Bartley, *Ellen Wilkinson: From Red Suffragist to Government Minister*, 2014, p. 118.
18. Ibid.
19. *The New Dawn*, October 20, 1945, p. 330.
20. For example, David Rubinstein, 'Ellen Wilkinson Re-Considered', *History Workshop Journal*, March 1979.
21. These ideas about prime ministerial choices are from Anthony King and Nicholas Allen, "Off with Their Heads': British Prime Ministers and the Power to Dismiss', *British Journal of Political Science*, April 2010, p. 255.
22. *Daily Herald*, August 4, 1945, p. 2.
23. Attlee papers, May 18–August 13, 1945, dep. 18, fols. 67–81.
24. Leah Manning, *A Life for Education*, Victor Gollancz, 1970, p. 203.
25. *Daily Herald*, August 4, 1945, p. 2.
26. Anthony King and Nicholas Allen, "Off with Their Heads': British Prime Ministers and the Power to Dismiss', *British Journal of Political Science*, April 2010, p. 258.
27. I am indebted to Robert Pearce for this insight.
28. Letter to Morgan Phillips, March 12, 1946, PHM. I am grateful to Darren Treadwell for this reference.
29. Letter from W. H. Daw to Chief Inspector, March 7, February 1946, KV1/1384.
30. Katz returned to his home country, Czechoslovakia. He was hanged in December 1952, his body incinerated and his ashes dumped on a roadside.

Katz was convicted for his involvement in a 'Trotskyist-Zionist conspiracy', one of 250 show trials in Czechoslovakia. He was among 13 convicted, 11 of whom were Jewish. In effect, it was an anti-semitic purge.

31. *The Times*, October 29, 1945, p. 4.
32. *Daily Express*, November 11, 1945.
33. *Daily Telegraph*, November 16, 1945.
34. Letter from Tawney, September 30, 1945, Attlee dep. 23.
35. Ellen Wilkinson to Harold Laski, June 3, 1946, UDLA/21/4.
36. Susan Lawrence, *Fabian Quarterly*, March 1947.
37. Labour Party Conference, 1946, p. 189.
38. Labour Party Conference, 1946.
39. Mr Cove, Hansard, March 22, 1946, p. 2235.
40. Bournemouth Conference, 1946 reported in *The Times*, June 14, 1946, p. 8.
41. *The Guardian*, July 2, 1946, p. 6.
42. Leah Manning, *A Life for Education*, Victor Gollancz, 1970, p. 203.
43. Jean Mann, *Woman in Parliament*, Odhams, 1962, pp. 39–40.
44. Mr C. S. Evans, *Nottingham Evening Post*, September 21, 1945, p. 5.
45. *Guardian*, June 14, 1946, p. 5.
46. *Evening Standard*, January 29, 1946.
47. Cabinet Minutes, PRO ED 136/727.
48. Labour Party Conference Report, 1946.
49. Ibid., p. 191.
50. *Guardian*, July 2, 1946, p. 6.
51. Joint Memorandum by the Minister of Education and Secretary of State for Scotland, February 21, 1946, CAB/129/7.
52. *Daily Telegraph*, June 14, 1945.
53. Apparently Margaret Thatcher spoke against this move but was forced to enact it.
54. Visit to Germany, Secret Report by the Minister of Education, October 2–6, 1945, FO 371/46935.
55. Ibid.
56. Ibid.
57. Ibid.
58. Letters between Wilkinson and Attlee, Attlee papers, September 17–October 9, 1945.
59. UNESCO Conference Report, November 1945.
60. Ibid.
61. The India League, 1933.
62. Margaret Bondfield, notes on Ellen Wilkinson, Box 2, Margaret Grace Bondfield Papers, Archives and Special Collections Library, Vassar College Libraries, Box 5A, Folder 2.
63. *Guardian*, January 25, 1947, p. 5.
64. Leah Manning quoted in Donoughue and Jones, *Herbert Morrison*, Phoenix Press, 2001, p. 392.
65. *Evening Telegraph*, October 22, 1947, p. 1.
66. *Manchester Guardian*, February 7, 1947.
67. quoted in Paula Bartley, *Ellen Wilkinson: From Red Suffragist to Government Minister*, 2014, p. 134.

68. Mary Agnes Hamilton, *Uphill All the Way*, Jonathan Cape, 1953, p. 115.
69. I am grateful to June Hannam for these insights.
70. In May 1931, Ellen presented a Bill to allow 'the right of access to mountains and moorlands'. The Bill failed. The Right to Roam was not granted until March 1999.
71. *The New Dawn*, December 11, 1926, p. 11.

CHAPTER 6

A Political Apprenticeship: Barbara Castle, 1910–1964

When Ellen Wilkinson chaired the 1945 Labour Party Conference, she encouraged newly adopted Labour candidates to speak first. Barbara Castle took the opportunity to make a speech Wilkinson would have been proud of by roundly condemning the greed of landowners who might try to profit from Labour's future housing schemes. The party she urged should prohibit this kind of 'legalised robbery'.[1] Barbara a fiery red-headed socialist and conviction politician seemed set to become a second Red Ellen.

The two women may have shared a hair colour and political beliefs but their backgrounds were distinctly different. Barbara was born on October 6, 1910, at 64, Derby Road, Chesterfield to middle-class parents, Frank and Annie Betts, the youngest of three children. Unlike Ellen, Barbara never personally suffered from poverty or the ill health that resulted from it. No one went to bed hungry in the Betts household. In addition, Barbara's political character was formed in the cradle, not from lived experience. Frank Betts, a tax inspector by profession, was a leading member of the Independent Labour Party (ILP): he wrote pamphlets for the Socialist League and edited the socialist *Bradford Pioneer*. Her mother Annie was a local ILP Councillor. Barbara's parents put their socialism into practice, setting up soup kitchens for miners' children in the 1926 strike, sheltering Republican refugees from the Spanish Civil War and fostering children whose families could not afford to feed them. Barbara's father ate, slept and drank politics and his wife and children were expected to do so too. Every aspect of their lives was influenced by his political beliefs: Barbara joined the woodcraft folk instead of the girl guides, became a member of the ILP Guild of Youth and took part in ILP drama groups.

This future brazen politician professed that she was 'reared in irreverence: trained to challenge all the stale assumptions of a class-bound society'.[2] Her parents prompted her 'to speak out – to voice any disagreements, to express our own views, never to accept authority unquestioningly. There was always

© The Author(s) 2019
P. Bartley, *Labour Women in Power*,
https://doi.org/10.1007/978-3-030-14288-9_6

a great deal of political argument going on at home and I was trained that it was a virtue to hold my own'.[3] Barbara was a strong figure, encouraged by parents who believed that women were equal to men and who 'far from trying to direct me into womanly pursuits, encouraged me to go to university, encouraged me to read economics, encouraged me to do any of the things which were, at one stage in our society, not considered womanly'.[4] Her father expected his children to be clever, well-read and accomplished. His standards were high and he impressed upon his youngest daughter the need to avoid 'woolly thinking' and make her case armed with facts. Barbara knew that if she argued with her father without being prepared he would respond with 'a devastating analysis which would make me feel very small. … At first I was overawed by him, but gradually I steeled myself to disagree. And I held my own'.[5] The cut and thrust of debate encouraged by her father was the 'one reason for the impression I give of being belligerent and intransigent and all that'.[6]

Trade union leader Vic Feather, who was one of Frank Betts protégés, has said that Barbara's father expected 'her to fight and fight hard … that was one of the things he drummed into the youngsters who were always around him; that you mustn't give up, you've got to keep on trying'.[7] Feather also believed that Barbara's Yorkshire heritage helped form her personality. She was a 'Yorkshire lass' who had the Yorkshire characteristic of tenacity whereby 'you haven't got to show when you're hurt … if you're wounded, then you've got to clout back harder'.[8] Vic Feather however was jealous. He saw that Barbara lived in a comfortable home and enjoyed all the privileges bestowed on her by middle-class parents whereas he had to leave school at 14 and go out to work.

Frank Betts, worried that his children would not experience what life was like for the majority of children, sent them all to the local primary school, Love Lane. Barbara was shocked to use an outside lavatory with its unavoidable stench, to discover that her hair was full of nits and to confront her rough and unmannered classmates. It was an unsettling awakening to a parallel yet distinct world, a world that would have been familiar to Ellen Wilkinson and Margaret Bondfield.[9] Barbara did not stay long at Love Lane. The tax office regularly moved its inspectors and the family relocated several times, from Chesterfield, to Hull, to Pontefract, to Carleton and to Bradford.

When the family arrived in Bradford, it was the epicentre of Labour life, the 'pace-setter of the Labour movement'.[10] The significance was not lost on twelve-year-old Barbara. Here, she imbibed Labour's ideals, absorbed its history, believed passionately in its political philosophy and confirmed her socialist principles. Barbara, unlike Ellen Wilkinson, never struggled with her political identity: all her life she remained committed to parliamentary socialism. She attended Bradford Girls' Grammar School, full of girls from middle-class Tory and Liberal families with Barbara and the daughter of a blacksmith the only socialists. Barbara was never afraid to be in a minority. At roughly the same age as Ellen Wilkinson when she stood in her school's mock election, Barbara put herself forward as the Labour candidate. The schoolgirls were not convinced and she only polled 17 out of 600 votes.

Throughout her life, Barbara's socialism was democratic: she never ever became attracted to revolutionary communism or the Communist Party. Nonetheless, she was committed to Clause IV of the Labour Party manifesto which aimed for 'the most equitable distribution thereof that may be possible upon the basis of the common ownership of the means of production'. For Barbara, Clause IV was the 'guiding principle of socialism' so much so that in 1993 aged 83, she opposed Tony Blair's wish to be rid of it. She still believed that 'it would be wrong for the party to drop it as though it were part of a disreputable past. … It is essential not to jettison that principle now at a time when private wealth is being promoted as never before'.[11] Tony Blair took no heed and Clause IV was dropped from the Labour Party constitution.

In 1929, Barbara won a scholarship to Oxford to study French, later switching to PPE. Colleges at the time were segregated by sex and the rules were strict: female students were not allowed to go outside the college without a chaperone and had to be in by 11 p.m. The young Miss Betts reacted against the restrictions of college life. Her youthful high spirits were too boisterous to be contained and Barbara, who liked to have fun, escaped by climbing over the walls. It was at Oxford that Barbara consolidated her emerging commitment to women's rights—she was shocked by the entrenched masculinity of Oxford University, its sexism and the attitudes of a number of dons towards female students.[12] She was appalled that women were barred from joining the Oxford Union Debating Society and were expected to sit in the public gallery listening to the male undergraduates pontificating below. Barbara was confident enough, gutsy enough and feminist enough to avoid these masculine debates and instead joined the Oxford Labour Club where she took the opportunity to practise her own debating skills.

Towards a Political Career

On October 6, 1931, Barbara celebrated her 21st birthday at the Labour Party Conference in Scarborough. Her father had commissioned his daughter to report on the events for the *Bradford Pioneer*, a radical journal that he edited. Vic Feather had expected to be given the job and was naturally piqued that he had not: he probably never forgave the boss's daughter for replacing him. Barbara, who was now in her last year at university, was thrilled to cover such a prestigious event and much preferred to report on the conference than study for her finals. She obtained a third class degree, a bitter disappoint for her and her family. Barbara left Oxford just as the Tory-dominated Coalition Government cut public spending and the Depression was in full swing. Unable to find a job she returned to her parents who had now relocated to Hyde. She quickly immersed herself in local politics and became propaganda secretary of the local Labour Party, a role which gave her the opportunity to chair public meetings, learn how to speak in public and practise her skills in the marketplaces and town squares, often to unsympathetic audiences.

Barbara got a paid job as a sales demonstrator promoting sweets and dried fruit in shops. Here she met other workers and tried unsuccessfully to recruit them to the Shop Assistants' Union. She hated it. It was the Hungry Thirties, the abhorrent Means Test was being vigorously enacted and Ellen Wilkinson was leading the Jarrow March against the harshness of it all.

It was at this time that Barbara met William Mellor when he came to deliver a lecture in Hyde and was invited to the Betts' home for afternoon tea. He was her 'kind of man: tall, black-haired, erect, with a commanding presence and strong, handsome features'.[13] Mellor was clever, debonair and as editor of the *Daily Herald*, a powerful figure in Labour politics. He also loved fashion and stylish living. William embodied the characteristics Barbara admired: he was principled yet light-hearted; witty yet politically focussed; loved a bit of glitz and glamour yet was committed to ending poverty. There was one big snag: William Mellor was married, and his wife refused to divorce him. Barbara was not deterred: in 1934, she moved to London to be with him.

William Mellor offered his young lover more power and influence than women in their twenties usually enjoyed in socialist movements, introducing her to key figures in the Labour movement and employing her as a journalist. In 1932, Mellor helped found the Socialist League to encourage the Labour Party to commit to left-wing policies: Barbara was elected to the executive. At 26 years old she was the youngest member, running the League's publication department, organising conferences and other public events and learning to be super-efficient. In 1936, the League set up its own weekly newspaper, the *Tribune* with William Mellor as editor. He commissioned Barbara and Michael Foot to write the industrial affairs column, despite the fact that both were university graduates with little experience of work. Barbara also wrote feature articles and had her own column 'Barbara Betts says'. The NEC however disapproved of the Socialist League, accused it of being communist controlled, disaffiliated it in January 1937 and banned its members from belonging to the Labour Party. William Mellor's radicalism, his commitment to the Socialist League and his criticism of the Labour leadership also led to conflicts with his employers at *The Herald*. In March 1936, he was dismissed. Fortunately, Mellor was able to borrow money to set up a journal, *Town and County Councillor* aimed at Labour Party supporters who worked in local government. He put his young lover in charge of the paper.

In 1936, Barbara Betts began to look for a parliamentary seat. She went for selection at Hertford, did well at the interview, and although the selection committee applauded her speech, they gave the seat to a middle-aged man with more experience.[14] In 1937, Barbara took her first step towards political office when she was elected on to St Pancras Borough Council. Two years later when war broke out, Barbara was 29 years old without a husband, without a 'proper' job, without a decent income and still dependent on her mother for money. For her the worst thing was the loneliness especially when

William Mellor claimed he was too busy to see her. However, when William's wife and family were evacuated Barbara moved in with her lover. In 1941, she found work as an administrative officer in the Fish Division of the Ministry of Food, an experience which gave her useful insights into the workings of Whitehall. In June 1942, William Mellor unexpectedly died from an operation to remove a stomach ulcer. Jennie Lee had lost her married lover a few years before and was quick to offer support and consolation to Barbara who was distraught with grief.

The war provided Barbara with the chance to grow up politically and to shed her image as the mistress of a controversial political older man. In May 1943, she was nominated party delegate to the Labour Party Conference. Here she made the speech that changed her life. Her passionate address criticised trade unionists for their unfair dominance and their Conservative ideas and argued that Labour should be more courageous. It was the defining moment of the whole conference, especially when she announced pithily that governments always promised 'jam yesterday, and jam tomorrow, but never jam today'.[15] She became an instant heroine among the delegates. More importantly, her speech was picked up by the *Daily Mirror* and her photo appeared on the next morning's front page. As a result of this, she met the editor of the newspaper, Ted Castle. She was now in her early 30s and lonely after the death of William Mellor. At first, she was not attracted to Ted even though he possessed the well-groomed, physical attributes she usually admired. Ted pursued her for a year, gained her affection and they married on July 28, 1944, in the middle of a doodle-bug raid.[16]

By this time, Barbara was well placed to become a Labour candidate. She had proved herself to be a competent administrator, an effective public speaker and someone who could attract positive press coverage. Even so, it was hard to be selected. Men such as James Callaghan and Harold Wilson found a place straight away whereas Barbara applied unsuccessfully to Oldham, Crewe, Exeter, Stockton and Macclesfield before being adopted for Blackburn. Even here she struggled. Trade unions which funded the election expected their sponsored candidate to be selected and Barbara was not on that list. They were only thwarted when women in the Blackburn Labour Party refused to help in the election unless a woman was placed on the shortlist: consequently Barbara found herself placed alongside five male trade unionists. The selection committee thought her 'a fighter with great sincerity. Young, eloquent, and oozing with personality. Those of us who were more concerned about winning the election than with financial support warmed to this fresh breeze of womanhood'.[17] Fortunately for Barbara, Blackburn was a two-member constituency: both a trade union candidate and Barbara were selected. Immediately she was told to change her name to Castle because Blackburn electors disliked 'career women who use their maiden names'.[18] And so, the name Barbara Castle, future Labour MP and Cabinet Minister, entered the political arena.

MP FOR BLACKBURN, JULY 1945–MAY 1979

In July 1945, Barbara was elected MP for Blackburn, swept into Parliament on a wave of post-war optimism. Her constituency of Blackburn was 'shabby and down at heel'[19] with dilapidated schools and bleak terraced houses in dingy streets. It was a cotton town that had been forgotten. Undoubtedly, Barbara Castle became a first-rate constituency MP, fully committed to helping people. Before 1945, MPs were virtually able to ignore their constituencies, secure in the knowledge that their agents would do the work for them. The Labour Party changed this by introducing the idea of the constituency 'surgery' where MPs could meet their constituents and listen to their concerns. Castle's first surgery was crowded with residents keen to discuss problems they were having with housing, pensions and coping with poverty. She maintained that she would 'fight with everything I possessed' to right their wrongs. Like other MPs, she knew that constituency work involved long hours 'listening to people … every now and then you say: My heavens this is a gross injustice and I can do something about it'.[20] No case was too small. She once helped a milkman, who was threatened with dismissal because he was short-sighted and wore glasses, by harassing Ernest Marples the Conservative Minister of Transport until he changed the law.[21]

In September 1946, when a violent rainstorm flooded the streets of Blackburn, she put on her wellington boots, stepped into a small boat and, rowed by a policeman, distributed food to people trapped in the upper rooms of their houses.[22] Even years later as a Minister, Castle still dealt with her constituents' personal problems, finding time to help with what some thought relatively insignificant and unimportant personal matters because 'if she feels there's a human problem to which she can bring some help, she's prepared to do it'.[23] She also continued to hold street meetings in obscure parts of town, opened new schools and visited hospitals. Some thought that it was unnecessary for a Secretary of State with a 7000 majority to do so but Mrs Castle knew the importance of nursing her constituency, remembering that in 1955 she only enjoyed a majority of 489. Her agent commented that 'we've never had an MP like her before'.[24]

Barbara's commitment to her constituency was extraordinary. In her first years as Blackburn's MP, she spent two weeks learning about the cotton industry. The first week she attended a training school in Manchester; the second week she worked at Horrockses Mill, Preston to find out what life was like for many of her constituents. Dressed in a blue overall and flat-heeled shoes Castle began work, amazed at the clatter and din of the weaving shed. She was told by Miss Dorothy Bateson who was looking after her 'Don't worry, love, you'll soon get used to it' as she showed her MP how to manage a clacking loom.[25] During the week, she lodged at a local home and was 'surprised to find someone tapping at my bedroom window before seven o'clock. I felt like turning over, but the knocker-up must have realised that because he came back'.[26] As with the other workers, she queued for lunch in the canteen. A colleague explained to a party of astonished Italian journalists 'that the tired-looking woman in overalls ... with a milk-less cup of tea in one hand and a bun in the other, was Mrs Barbara Castle'.[27] Her time in the factory was reported in the newspapers. Even at the beginning of her career Barbara Castle was a consummate self-publicist, fully conscious of the need for positive press coverage. She was, after all, not just a woman in a man's world but a socialist with strong political convictions. At the centre of her concern was her commitment to eradicating injustice: she cared about the ordinary citizen and wanted to improve the lives of less advantaged women and men.

Barbara thought that the House of Commons was a 'relic of the days when government was run by wealthy amateurs'.[28] She had no desk, let alone an office and had to prepare her speeches in the corner of the Commons library. But Castle's delight in the reforming zeal of the new government overcame any discomfort she faced. In her view, Attlee was an unexpectedly courageous Minister appointing left-wingers like Stafford Cripps, Aneurin Bevan and Ellen Wilkinson to his Cabinet and overseeing the most left-wing government that Britain had ever experienced. Barbara Castle was fortunate in taking her seat at an auspicious time for Labour, witnessing at first hand the radical overhaul of the British economic and social system. Her views were shaped by the optimism of the 1945 Labour Government and she learned very early on about the need for political audacity. She was the youngest female MP among twenty other Labour women and one Conservative, and already receiving press attention. The *Daily Herald* reported that Barbara Castle 'has for several years been one of the most challenging members of the St Pancras Council. With a complete mastery of the subjects on which she speaks, she never uses a note and she has a remarkably effective platform manner. She is another who will liven up the new Parliament'.[29]

Immediately after the election, the Labour Government faced economic problems. The war had depleted Britain's reserves, increased the national debt and made the country reliant on the American Lend-Lease scheme to keep solvent.[30] When the Americans peremptorily stopped the scheme in August 1945, it forced Britain to move to fixed exchange rates and to make sterling fully convertible. The country faced an economic crisis forcing the Labour Government to cut government expenditure. Castle, with others on the left, thought it yet another attempt to enforce an economic orthodox doctrine which would, as it had in the 1930s, cause economic suffering to millions of the poorest. When the Bill to agree to the restrictive terms of the American loan was put forward in Parliament, Castle, along with Michael Foot and Jennie Lee, defied the party Whip and voted against.[31] In so doing, the three confirmed their standing as politicians willing to stand up for their principles, or as some believed, their status as left-wing over-emotional hotheads.

Unlike Bondfield and Wilkinson, Castle waited a few months before delivering her maiden speech. On Friday afternoon, November 16, 1945, with only three MPs present and a seemingly empty press gallery, Castle asked that skilled men in the armed forces be demobilised. She read letters from a coal miner and a bricklayer, both of whom had been trying to leave the armed forces yet had been unable to do so. The bricklayer had written that he would be better building houses than 'acting as a grease-monkey for Army lorries'.[32] It was an unexceptional first speech, quite short and very specific—but she had used the words of her constituents, reminding Parliament that it represented the people. Mrs Castle's first foray from the backbenches was reported in almost every newspaper, reinforcing her growing reputation as yet another red-headed female polemicist. Sadly, her father Frank Betts who had taken such pride in his daughter's achievement was not there to hear her: he had died aged 63 in August.

Barbara Castle, like Ellen Wilkinson and Margaret Bondfield, found it challenging to 'keep the attention of several hundred men who wolf-whistled and jeered and heckled'.[33] When Castle was drowned out by hundreds of Tory men, she resorted to shouting which made her seem 'shrill and vitriolic' rather than sounding reasonable.[34] In later life, she claimed that though there was a 'total male assumption that if there was a job in politics, it was natural for a man to fill it',[35] she had never consciously felt that she was breaking into a man's world. She was annoyed when people told her she had a 'masculine' mind, considering it a 'piece of male arrogance which assumes that anything which works at all efficiently must be of the male gender'.[36] Castle was a clever politician, navigating the gender politics of the masculine-dominated Westminster and the Labour Party by using her femininity in ways which would beguile her opponents, always making sure her hair and her clothes were stylishly elegant and often flirting outrageously. Protected by her polished appearance, she would then deliver a rousing socialist speech. The press, to both her chagrin and delight, often prefaced compliments about her politics with comments on her appearance, reporting that 'looking very much a slip of a girl with her bronze red hair set off against something green in her dress, Barbara is an effective debater'.[37] Years later the left-wing Paul Johnson observed—he thought sympathetically—that Barbara Castle's 'bright red hair is always in place. She is clean, scented, carefully made up. Her clothes are bandbox fresh. She spends a great deal of money on them and it is worth every penny'.[38]

Barbara Castle insisted that she was not a feminist, though she 'instinctively rejected the whole concept of dependence, which visualised most women as satellites of men'.[39] Throughout her career, Castle defended women's rights and promoted women's issues. She believed that it was 'grotesque' that there were so few women MPs, insisting that 'you can't have a balanced democracy when women are so desperately under-represented'.[40]

Fig. 6.1   Barbara Castle and Irene Ward with Equal Pay Petition, March 1954 (©
Dave Bagnall Collection/Alamy Stock Photo)

In her view, there should be a 'certain amount of positive discrimination' and asked that the Labour Party ensure that at least one woman should appear on every shortlist at selection meetings. At first, she disagreed with all-women shortlists, maintaining that women should be chosen on merit and only later was convinced of the necessity for them. Barbara Castle worked hard to make women economically independent, advocating retirement pensions for spinsters at 55 and arguing that married women be compelled to join the state insurance scheme rather than rely on their husbands' insurance to provide a pension. Her biggest commitment was to equal pay. In June 1947, the Labour Chancellor Hugh Dalton reneged on Labour's electoral promise, telling the House of Commons that the principle of equal pay for equal work could not be made law because the estimated cost would be too high. Barbara Castle was not convinced, replying 'that while women fully appreciated the country's economic difficulties they would be deeply disappointed at the suggestion that they alone should be expected to forego any satisfaction of just claims owing to inflationary pressure'.[41] She asked Dalton whether he would make a start in implementing the principle of equal pay in the civil service, only to be told 'No. The current economic situation does not admit even a start of the gradual implementation of equal pay for the Civil Service'[42] as it would cost too much. Castle was determined, and like a dog with a bone would not let the issue get buried. Women, she argued, wanted action on this and the only way 'women will get anything is not by sweet reasonableness ... but by making a terrible nuisance of themselves'.[43] In the early 1950s, as the above photograph shows, Castle and the Conservative MP Irene Ward 'worked very closely on this matter ... cutting across party lines, concerned not to score party points but to get positive action with regard to a principle in which we both believed' (Fig. 6.1).[44] Castle was criticised by other women Labour MPs, notably Alice Bacon and Elaine Burton for the 'iniquitous action of leading an all-party deputation to the Minister to demand equal pay'.[45] The acceptability of women working across party lines to achieve female equality had disappeared. Eventually the Chancellor gave an assurance that equal pay would be implemented. However, he was reluctant to fulfil his promise and so Castle pushed harder, insisting that if women did not obtain equal pay it 'will stand under the slur of political dishonesty'.[46] She had tried to drum up support outside Parliament. At a conference lunch of the National Council of Women, she told delegates to organise and 'make the Chancellor of the Exchequer and all the Ministers realise that women were not going to be satisfied with anything less than equal pay'.[47] In 1955, women civil servants were awarded equal pay, to be phased in over several years; the majority of women were obliged to wait longer.

Becoming Parliamentary Private Secretary

On August 10, 1945, Barbara Castle was appointed Parliamentary Private Secretary (PPS) to Sir Stafford Cripps, President of the Board of Trade, a department responsible for boosting British trade overseas, for controlling imports, directing raw materials and overseeing British industry. Castle knew she was 'the non-ministerial dogsbody who keeps the Minister in touch with backbenchers and the rank and file'.[48] The press assumed she would be at a disadvantage in this role because, as a woman, she would be unwelcome in the smoking room where the gossip took place. *The Telegraph* thought it an odd appointment for a woman which could only be explained by 'the fact that the Board of Trade is responsible for the rationing of women's clothes and for the production of those utility garments about which many women complain. Mrs Castle will be able to keep Sir Stafford Cripps informed of the views of women MPs on this subject'.[49] Success also aroused jealousy. Leah Manning said she herself had defended Barbara 'against the malice of Jean Mann ... More than once, I found the girl ... vulnerable and in tears in the Lady Members' Room'.[50] She was not, according to Manning, 'nearly as tough as she liked to make out'.[51]

Barbara Castle worked hard to advance her political career, sitting on the requisite standing committees particularly those concerned with allegedly 'masculine' topics such as finance and social insurance. In 1949 and 1950, she was a member of the British delegation to the UN, working on the Social and Humanitarian Affairs Committee. Clement Attlee did not promote Barbara above that of PPS. Michael Foot believed that this was 'sheer dammed prejudice' on his part because he preferred to stuff his government full of public school boy/s.[52] But, as Bondfield and Wilkinson had discovered, being a PPS was Castle's political apprenticeship for higher office. Here she learned about the art of government. The Board of Trade was a huge department with over a hundred divisions to manage. Cripps encouraged his young protégé to contribute to discussions, and until his civil servants objected, asked her to contribute to policy formation. Castle was undoubtedly competent in the job. Even so, she was not promoted further. When Stafford Cripps replaced Dalton as Chancellor of the Exchequer, Harold Wilson took over at the Board of Trade not Barbara Castle. Cripps humiliated Castle further by not appointing her his PPS at the Treasury, preferring her male co-PPS and fellow Blackburn MP as his Junior Minister.

Harold Wilson persuaded Barbara Castle to stay on as his PPS and the two quickly became friends, remaining so for forty years. They had lots in common. She was fond of Harold because like herself, he had been brought up in Yorkshire, had attended a grammar school rather than a public school and had been raised in a family with a modest income. She also felt affection for him because he did not come from a trade union background but had attended Oxford. Equally both shared a middle-class distaste for the upper-class clique of public school boy/s who tried to dominate the Labour Party. If Castle was disappointed and somewhat piqued when Wilson was promoted to Cabinet Minister she was even more displeased when Wilson took his male PPS Tom Cook rather than Castle on his trips abroad. She put her friend and boss under pressure about this and he eventually agreed to take Castle to Canada, before warning her that the country would not welcome a woman politician: indeed Castle was excluded from the evening dinners where business was discussed informally.

Castle liked and respected Wilson. Their personalities were similar in some respects as 'they were both driven, determined, competitive'.[53] However, there were also key contrasts in their temperaments, contrasts that would make a difference in a political career: Wilson was cool and detached, a consummate politician who could negotiate and compromise, good with statistics, an excellent speaker and able to make concessions. Castle by contrast was a passionate romantic with strong unwavering socialist values and beliefs and she was often unwilling to compromise. These personality differences helped by contemporary sexist attitudes would benefit Wilson rather than Castle in the climb to the upper echelons of politics.

Castle thought the Cabinet Ministers were tired old men—Ellen Wilkinson, the only female had died in 1947—and judged that new thinking and new people were needed to liven up the Labour Party. In spring 1947, Michael Foot and Ian Mikardo met at the Crossman's house in the Chilterns to put forward the left's thinking on Labour policy. *Keep Left* was born. Barbara Castle soon joined the group. She had had no time for the communists or the Communist Party and saw herself as part of a 'highly individualistic bunch to whom freedom of expression and democratic institutions were the breath of life'.[54] However, in the 1950s two powerful charismatic figures, Aneurin Bevan and Hugh Gaitskell, fought over the soul of the Labour Party: Bevan believed in the untrammelled goals of socialism whereas Gaitskell was willing to compromise in order to make the party electable. It was also a class issue with the party dividing between those like Bevan, a former miner who had impeccable working-class credentials and Gaitskell, a public school boy/s whose roots were patrician. Barbara Castle, though from a comfortable middle-class family, admired Bevan and his romantic idea of politics and at first disliked Gaitskell, commenting that 'the prim set of his mouth seemed to symbolize the primness of his political views – no adventurousness, no poetry'.[55] Later on, she warmed to him as she discovered 'an emotional man capable of great political passion and I have always admired passion in politics'.[56]

Tensions between the *Keep Left* group and the rest of the party emerged most strongly over foreign policy and public spending. The Labour Party had always had a strong anti-war element within its ranks, especially when a war was deemed imperialistic. In 1951, the Labour Party split over the Korean War and about the government's subservience to America. In March 1950 communist troops, backed by Russian armaments and tanks, had crossed the 38th parallel, the dividing line between North and South Korea. Almost immediately the Americans sent in forces demanding that Britain also help. Gaitskell, now Chancellor of the Exchequer, informed Cabinet that another £1.1 billion was needed to fund the war, and would be met by cuts to the health service. Immediately the *Keep Left* group criticised the Labour Government for its willingness to spend money on armaments while at the same time cutting the health budget and undermining the principles of the

National Health Service by charging for prescriptions, dental treatment and spectacles. After a long and acrimonious debate, the Labour Cabinet voted to introduce charges: Aneurin Bevan and Harold Wilson both resigned. The resignation of two young Cabinet members and the emergence of *Keep Left* led to a great surge of political activity in constituencies with people wanting to hear more about a left-wing alternative. The party leadership found the activities of *Keep Left* 'dangerous'; they disliked groups acting independently within the Labour Party and sought to repress it. [57]

THE DEFEAT OF LABOUR IN 1951 AND 1955

In September 1951, Attlee called a general election, Labour was defeated and Winston Churchill once more became Prime Minister. Until then Barbara Castle had been slowly climbing up the political ladder. In 1950, she was elected to the NEC in the women's section; in 1951, she was elected by the constituency parties, the first woman to be elected this way. However, she was less well-regarded by the parliamentary hierarchy, largely because of her forthright left-wing views, and her unwillingness to place party loyalty over her principles. One of the first clashes between Castle and the party hierarchy was over her criticism of the Conservative Government's arms budget. Churchill wanted to increase overall arms expenditure, an increase which required cross-party support. Labour MPs were told to abstain rather than vote against the Tory Government's defence programme. Barbara Castle, along with 56 other Labour MPs, defied a personal order from Clement Attlee by marching into the lobby against. It was, claimed the *Daily Mirror*, the biggest split in the Labour ranks since before the war,[58] exacerbating the breakdown in relationship between the different wings of the party, and leading to a row that 'helped keep the party out of office for thirteen years'.[59] It was a conflict between left and right that would continually bedevil the Labour Party, not helped by the right-wing press which stirred up this resentment. In October 1955, the unsympathetic *Daily Express* insisted that Barbara Castle and the left-wing had taken over the Labour Party. It claimed that 'the mutineers are on the bridge. The officers walk the plank. And the skull and crossbones fly from the battered hulk of British Socialism'.[60] Castle and *Keep Left* were condemned as 'comrades without a calling. The nearest most of them have ever come to manual work is in watching others do it. ... all graduates of Oxford'.[61] All were considered to be irresponsible and unrealistic socialists: *Keep Left* insisted they were merely principled.

In May 1955, Labour lost the general election once more; in December Clement Attlee resigned, forced out by the manoeuvring of the more right-wing Gaitskellites. In those days the party leader was chosen exclusively by Labour Party MPs, who favoured Gaitskell over anyone else. He never won the backing of the considerably more left-wing constituency parties leading Castle to remark 'how could the party be led by a man who could not win the support of the people in the constituencies who did the work?'[62] It was the beginning of a long internecine struggle to allocate greater power to the constituency parties at the expense of the Parliamentary Party and the trade unions.

Barbara Castle thought that Britain should divest itself of her colonies and joined the Movement for Colonial Freedom, a political civil rights group which campaigned against British colonial rule. In the 1950s, British rule in Kenya was threatened by a wave of nationalism and calls for independence. One liberation group, the Mau Mau, was accused of committing terrible atrocities, with hundreds of European farmers being hacked to death and women and even babies mutilated. The British response to these allegations was further repression, the incarceration of its leader Jomo Kenyatta and the imprisonment and maltreatment of thousands of other Africans. By 1954, there was evidence that the British handled the uprising in a brutal fashion. Rumours about torture circulated. These beliefs were given credence by the resignation of Colonel Young, a City of London police officer, who had been sent to advise the Kenyans on police strategy. Young's letter of resignation, which had been agreed with the government, was measured yet the sub-text hinted at serious misdemeanours by the British authorities. In his letter, Young condemned the lack of discipline in the Kenyan force which 'seriously jeopardised' public respect and led to abuses of power. Rumours that he had resigned because of horrendous abuses in the legal system were strengthened when the government refused to publish his full report. Castle sensed a massive cover-up. She contacted Colonel Young who confirmed that he had resigned because of police behaviour and promised to help Castle uncover the facts.

Castle began her quest. She noticed a mysterious death buried away in the press and searched for more details of the case: it revealed that the resident magistrate had criticised two white officers who had arrested the suspect, a man named Kamau Kichina. Barbara Castle, like Ellen Wilkinson before her, knew the importance of publicity if justice was to prevail. In November 1955, the *Daily Mirror* paid for the Blackburn MP to visit Kenya on a three-week fact-finding mission. Castle discovered from the court records that the coroner had changed his first certificate from 'death by beating' to 'unexplained' death. She wanted to know why? Soon Castle found out that police officers had 'flogged Kamau mercilessly, tied him up with his head between his knees, forced dirt down his throat, left him exposed in the open air at night and refused him food'.[63] The MP for Blackburn exposed the fact that Kamau Kichina had died in custody, still declaring his innocence. The perpetrators were given 18 months, later increased to three and a half years. During her visit, Castle exposed other cases of wrongful detention and maltreatment and wrote a series of articles in the *Daily Mirror* outlining the terror wreaked by the British on the Kenyans. Before long she gained a reputation for standing up for the rights of black Africans, becoming revered and reviled in equal measure. In English-speaking black Africa, Barbara Castle was a much-loved national treasure; in parts of Britain, she was condemned as a terrorist sympathiser.

In March 1959, news reached Castle of more brutality by the Kenyan authorities. Newspapers reported the death of eleven Africans in a camp at Hola who had been so malnourished that they suffered from scurvy before unexpectedly dying in police custody. The prison governor insisted the prisoners died because of drinking water from a contaminated source. D. N. Pritt, the lawyer who had been involved with Ellen Wilkinson in the Reichstag Mock Trial, informed Castle that it was 'a pack of lies' and that the men had been beaten to death.[64] Immediately, Barbara Castle sprang into action and asked for the court records. She discovered that 'the European officer in charge of the irrigation scheme at Hola, testified that he personally saw continuous beating of detainees, apparently for refusal to work and not for any disturbance'.[65] The Honourable Member for Blackburn brought this injustice to the attention of the House of Commons several times. She told the House about a young man who had had a rope tied to his wrists and was strung up to a crossbeam so that his feet were two or three feet above the floor and 'while so suspended he was severely beaten about the body and legs with strips of rubber cut from old motor car tyres. ... He died later of what was described as cerebral haemorrhage. Nobody was charged with murder because it was decided that the prisoner might have hit his head against a door'.[66] Her source, a British Second World War veteran, told her that the conditions were 'worse, far worse than anything I experienced in my four and a half years as a prisoner of the Japanese'.[67] She drew support from an unexpected source. Enoch Powell, later to be notorious for his racist comments, was 'equally outraged. His cold logic clinched our case'.[68] The Hola murders Castle insisted were 'an absolutely class piece of covering-up',[69] a 'classic case of misrule by a colonial government'.[70] The colonial government was not held accountable and changed the name of Hola to Galole in the hope that the massacre would be forgotten. Kenya became independent in 1963 with Jomo Kenyatta as its first Prime Minister; he changed the name of the town back to Hola. In 2018, after a four-year legal battle, the British Government agreed to pay an undisclosed sum to victims who were tortured, maimed or executed by British authorities.

Previously, in January 1958 *The Sunday Pictorial* paid for Mrs Castle to visit South Africa to cover a treason trial where 162 men and women were on trial for their lives. They were members of the African National Congress, an organisation which campaigned against the segregationist and racist policies of the white government. They were all acquitted. Here she met Nelson Mandela, also on trial and also released only to be re-arrested, retried and sentenced to life imprisonment. In 1959, the Anti-Apartheid Movement was founded and Castle set to work organising a boycott of South African goods and trying to expel South Africa from the Commonwealth. It was a vicious regime. On March 21, 1960, police fired on demonstrators at the township of Sharpeville. Sixty-nine people were killed, 289 were injured including 29 children. Many were shot in the back as they tried to leave. There was an international outcry. One of Barbara Castle's proudest moments, she said later, was when she helped organise a silent protest outside Lancaster House where the Commonwealth Conference was taking place. It was, 'a massive piece of organisation, hours I spent on it'.[71] In 1961, Castle became President of the Anti-Apartheid Movement.

Barbara Castle was equally committed to independence for Cyprus, a British Crown colony which the Conservative Prime Minister, Harold Macmillan, wanted to turn into a British military base. At the time Cyprus consisted of 80% Greek Christians or Greek Orthodox and 17% Turkish Muslims. The Turkish Cypriots wanted union with Turkey. The Greek Cypriots led by Archbishop Makarios demanded *enosis* that is union with Greece. Britain, they insisted, would play no role in its governance. On April 1, 1955, Colonel Grivas, a former army officer who led the National Organisation of Cypriot Fighters (EOKA), launched a guerrilla campaign targeted at cities and military bases.

Macmillan suggested partitioning the island into Greek and Turkish sections: Turkey was seen as a natural ally of the West, despite its deplorable record on human rights whereas the Greeks were seen as too-communist for comfort. Not surprisingly the Greek Cypriots rejected this proposal. It was against this background that Barbara Castle, now Vice-Chair of the Labour Party, made a speech at the 1957 party conference, outlining her commitment to 'complete this freedom operation for the people of Cyprus' by making it an independent country without partitioning it.[72] In the summer of 1958, Castle received a surprise telephone call from the Greeks inviting her to visit Athens and meet Archbishop Makarios. At the meeting, Castle told Makarios that 'if the unity of Cyprus was ever to be reborn ... the Greek-Cypriots must give up their idea of union with Greece'.[73] After careful negotiation, Makarios agreed to drop his long-cherished dream of union with Greece and accepted Castle's proposal for an independent Cyprus: no partition and no union with Greece. Barbara Castle returned to the UK ecstatic. She had achieved what no other diplomat had: the commitment of Makarios to abandon *enosis*. Unfortunately, the British Government declined Makarios's proposals and the matter was dropped.[74] In 1960, Cyprus was granted independence on the same terms negotiated by Barbara Castle two years earlier. Tensions between Greek and Turkish Cypriots continued: in 1963, fighting broke out between the two groups; in 1974, Greek Cypriot nationalists staged a coup d'etat to unite the island with Greece; five days later, the island was invaded by Turkish troops. In 1983, a separate Turkish Cypriot state was established in the north. Castle believed that if Macmillan had backed Makarios and 'built up his authority against the right-wing elements who were pressing for *enosis* and kept the Turks under control, the tragic partition of Cyprus need never have taken place'.[75] The island is still divided, despite efforts to unite it.

Barbara Castle's diplomatic success was overshadowed when she criticised the conduct of the British army in Cyprus. In an interview with the *Daily Mirror* she stated that 'troops were permitted and even encouraged to use unnecessarily rough measures' on the Cypriot rebels, a claim that generated widespread condemnation. She was attacked in the press, 'the Tories howled for her blood. And the Labour Party disowned her'.[76] In some quarters, she was denounced as a traitor who was guilty of treason and sedition for daring to criticise loyal British troops facing continuous sniping and ambushes from EOKA. It was thought that she was 'so furiously partisan a politician that her judgement is constantly warped. She would serve her country by maintaining silence on foreign affairs'.[77] Soon, Castle was regarded as something of a political liability to the Labour Party and her career was considered over. The leadership of the Labour Party—Gaitskell, Bevan and Callaghan—jointly and publicly attacked her for criticising British troops and accused Castle of endangering the Labour Party at the forthcoming election. At the party conference, several speakers 'expressed bitter resentment' at Castle's criticism of the British army, calling it an unjust and unwarrantable 'monstrous charge'. Even those sympathetic to Castle's view felt that if she had made her point differently and been circumspect in her language by 'saying that the troops, under great provocation and in extremely tense conditions, were using excessively tough measures' there would not have been the same uproar.[78]

Castle was unnerved by the media pressure which ensued. Even so she realised that negative press coverage was often short-lived and that if one can 'keep ones nerve and plug away at a reasoned argument, the natural fairness and common sense of the British people rally to one's side'.[79] A year later, when the furore had died down, the *Daily Herald* predicted that 'when a dispassionate history of Cyprus is written in a hundred years' time, I suspect she will appear in a more politic, wise and statesmanlike role than most .... She showed the strength of a woman of integrity and courage and compassion'.[80]

There were many other international flashpoints in the 1950s. One was Suez. On October 29, 1956, Israeli forces invaded Egypt and British and French troops launched air attacks to support them. The invaders aimed to regain Western control of the Suez Canal which President General Nasser had just nationalised and effect regime change by removing him from power. The combined force of the USA, the Soviet Union and the United Nations compelled Britain, France and Israel to withdraw. It was a deep humiliation for the Conservative Prime Minister, Anthony Eden. When Britain invaded Suez, the Labour Party 'erupted into a fury I had not seen since the war',[81] incandescent that the British Government had aligned itself with the Israelis in an act of aggression against Egypt. Gaitskell demanded Eden's resignation and the party moved a vote of censure on the government, unpopular moves because the country was surfing on a wave of jingoism. Castle was 'proud of the party's determination to stand by its principles regardless of the electoral consequences'.[82] Castle drew two lessons from the Suez debacle, firstly that Britain 'would never again be able to launch a military enterprise' without support from the UN and the USA and secondly that courage is the most important ingredient in politics for any 'government or politician unable to ride a burst of short-term unpopularity will not survive for very long'.[83]

In March 1954, when America exploded the first hydrogen bomb in the Pacific, the British Government decided to follow suit. At Easter 1957, five thousand demonstrators gathered in Trafalgar Square to protest at the British Government's willingness to make the H-bomb. From this the Campaign for Nuclear Disarmament (CND) grew, holding an annual march to Aldermaston. Castle joined CND believing that it was too expensive, a 'dangerous folly' and immoral to build a weapon which was capable of mass destruction. She and other left-wingers wanted the four nuclear powers—Russia, USA, Britain and France—to disarm.

THE DEFEAT OF LABOUR 1959

Labour lost the 1959 election—the third in a row—though Barbara Castle 'romped home' increasing her majority from 489 to 2866. In her view, it was a sign that the Blackburn electorate had been 'disgusted by the personal attacks made on me'.[84] However, the fact that the Conservative Party had won three successive elections led Castle to argue that Labour needed to modernise its approach to campaigning and improve its presentation if it was to win. In her view, 'the turgid verbosity' of the party's policy documents and the party's total indifference to appearances had helped Labour lose. Seemingly little had changed since Ellen Wilkinson complained about the sanctimonious loquaciousness of policy documents. 'There were' Castle commented 'of course members of the hair-shirt brigade who disapproved of all this razzmatazz'.[85] Castle, along with other left-wingers, also believed Labour lost because its socialist policies were not strong enough. The party leader Hugh Gaitskell, on the other hand, believed that it was because it was too socialist and sought to alter Clause IV with its demand for the 'common ownership of the means of production, distribution and exchange'.

In November 1959, Barbara chaired the Labour Party Conference at Blackpool, the eighth woman to do so.[86] 'Last year' she told conference 'we met in the bright hope of victory. This year we meet in the shadow of electoral defeat'.[87] Her role was to inspire the 3000 delegates to keep fighting against what seemed insuperable odds, and to keep on fighting for socialism. She told conference that nationalisation was not 'fusty and out of date' and that it was important to convince 'the people of this country - and not a few private interests – should control their economic lives'.[88] Aneurin Bevan said it was the best speech from the chair that he had ever heard; Richard Crossman believed 'she simply stole the show ... by making ... the most powerful speech of the conference. I should add that she is equal to men on their own ground'.[89] Barbara Castle thought it an 'overwhelming experience', telling conference that there was no 'higher honour' than to be the Chairman of the British Labour Party.[90]

Barbara Castle was a compelling speaker, loved by conference delegates. A year after she chaired the conference she gave a speech praising the decolonisation of much of Africa and insisting that Britain stop turning a blind eye to injustices perpetrated by countries where white people were in power. She criticised the British Government for not protesting about the Algerian war, for not objecting to the tyranny in Angola and Mozambique and by not compelling South Africa to end apartheid.[91] At the 1961 conference, she put forward a resolution calling for an end to Belgian violence in the Congo. This was the first time that all three future Cabinet Ministers spoke at the same conference: Barbara Castle condemning atrocities in the Congo; Judith Hart denouncing nuclear proliferation and Shirley Williams advocating closer ties with the European Union.[92]

By now Barbara Castle was attracting considerable attention. Norman Shrapnel, the *Guardian*'s political journalist, thought she had enormous stage presence. 'Some front-benchers' he commented, 'can be in their places for an hour before you even notice they are there. Mrs Castle's usual seat is far back, below the gangway, but you always know when she is there, pale, and vivid and watchful. ... In attack she provides one of the most awesome sights the House of Commons has to offer. She crouches forward, her glowing head lowered, gathering herself for the assault'.[93] She was certainly recognised as a key player in the Labour Party. Gaitskell appointed her as Shadow Minister of Works, a middle-ranking front bench position. Even so, Castle still did not regard Gaitskell highly and in late summer 1960 arranged a meeting of left-wing members to discuss removing Gaitskell as leader. Anthony Greenwood and Barbara Castle offered to challenge him. She wanted to establish the principle that women could be Leaders and Prime Ministers but to her mortification her male colleagues did not agree. Crossman recalls that 'she was nearly in tears insisting that she had the right, and later I went out into the kitchen and found Tony Greenwood with the uncomfortable job of deterring a termagant from suicide'.[94] It was clear that the left-wing men of the Labour Party were unwilling to let a woman stand: for them being leader of the party and being Prime Minister meant being a man. Harold Wilson was selected to challenge Gaitskell: he lost by 166 votes to 81.

In 1961, Harold Macmillan applied for Britain to join the EEC, a move that would exacerbate the already deep divisions within the Labour Party: George Brown and Roy Jenkins were in favour of joining; the left-wing and most of the Shadow Cabinet disagreed, fuelled by a concern over the Commonwealth. Castle had no doubts and launched an Anti-Common Market Committee with Douglas Jay and others. She wrote a piece for the *Daily Herald* entitled 'Why I say KEEP OUT!', arguing that the Common Market did not help international trade nor the development of more economically backward countries. In her view, rich countries protected their economies at the expense of other poorer ones; tariffs would be placed on Commonwealth countries whereas those in the Common Market were tariff free. Castle even pronounced that it would mean 'the end of Britain as an independent European state ... the end of a thousand years of history'.[95]

In January 1963, Barbara Castle was enjoying a sponsored trip to the Middle East when she heard that Hugh Gaitskell had died unexpectedly from a mysterious viral infection. The campaign to elect a new leader of the Labour Party was on. She did not stand, claiming later that at the time the 'idea never occurred to me – or to anyone else. For one thing, the Labour movement was still deeply imbued with the instinctive assumption that in the natural order of things you choose a man'.[96] In fact, she had a double handicap: she was an outspoken left-winger and she was a woman. Harold Wilson was elected leader and a new era of British politics was to begin.

Meanwhile, the Conservative Government was in trouble, beleaguered by a political scandal involving the Secretary of State for War, John Profumo and his alleged affair with 19-year-old Christine Keeler, who in turn was a lover of a Soviet naval officer. In March 1963, Barbara Castle helped bring the government down by asking whether it was 'true that the Minister of War was involved' with Keeler? Her question brought Profumo to the dispatch box the following day to declare that he 'had been on friendly terms with the girl, but denied any impropriety'.[97] Later Profumo confessed that he had lied, relinquished his Cabinet post and left Parliament. The affair severely damaged the Conservative Government and Macmillan resigned.

In the nineteen years that Barbara Castle had been MP for Blackburn she had created an image of herself as a strong principled left-wing socialist. She was a woman so there were regular comments about her appearance. The *Observer* spoke of her 'slim, smart good looks and her striking copper-coloured hair, pale skin and bright blue eyes mark her out from her dowdier, worthier and altogether less exciting rivals'.[98] Even so, Castle was regarded as a serious political figure who might 'come to feel that the satisfactions of being a peripatetic party rebel are ephemeral and limited' and if she chose to develop her political gifts in more constructive ways she had the 'ability and energy to follow in the steps of Ellen Wilkinson and to reach high Cabinet rank'.[99] Barbara Castle achieved this high rank and the next chapter will examine her role as Secretary of State in various Labour Governments.

NOTES

1. Barbara Castle, Report of the 44th Annual Conference, 1945, p. 98.
2. Quoted in Anne Perkins, *Red Queen: The Authorized Biography of Barbara Castle*, Macmillan, 2003, p. 7.
3. Interview with Barbara Castle, undated, Women's Library, 80DH/02/01/07 Box 1.
4. Ibid.
5. Barbara Castle, Interview with Richard Findlater, *Daily Herald*, March 10, 1961.
6. Ibid.
7. Vic Feather, quoted in Wilfred De'Ath, *Barbara Castle: A Portrait from Life*, Clifton Books, 1970, p. 27.
8. Ibid.

9. Barbara Castle, *Fighting All the Way*, Pan Books, 1993, p. 10.

10. Ibid., p. 24.

11. Ibid., p. 26.

12. Ibid., p. 43.

13. Ibid., p. 67.

14. Anne Perkins, *Red Queen: The Authorized Biography of Barbara Castle*, 2003, p. 13.

15. Barbara Castle, *Fighting All the Way*, 1993, p. 116.

16. Doodle-bug was the name given to a terrifying new flying pilot-less bomb, the 'Vengeance Weapon' developed in Germany during the war to target London.

17. Margaret McNamee, quoted in Wilfred De'Ath, *Barbara Castle: A Portrait from Life*, 1970, p. 83.

18. Barbara Castle, *Fighting All the Way*, 1993, p. 122.

19. Ibid., p. 131.

20. Barbara Castle, quoted in Wilfred De'Ath, *Barbara Castle: A Portrait from Life*, 1970, p. 16.

21. Ibid., p. 15.

22. *The Courier and Advertiser*, September 21, 1946, p. 3.

23. Walter Yeates, quoted in Wilfred De'Ath, *Barbara Castle: A Portrait from Life*, 1970, pp. 76–81.

24. Margaret McNamee, quoted in Wilfred De'Ath, *Barbara Castle: A Portrait from Life*, 1970, pp. 81–86

25. *The Lancashire Daily Post*, September 22, 1947, p. 1.

26. Ibid.

27. *The Lancashire Daily Post*, September 26, 1947, p. 1.

28. Barbara Castle, *Fighting All the Way*, 1993, p. 127.

29. *Daily Herald*, June 27, 1945, p. 2.

30. This was an American aid programme which distributed food, oil and other goods to the UK and other allies. Britain was the largest beneficiary, receiving over 31 million dollars.

31. The loan for $3.75 billion was made to support British overseas commitments and was not to be used for Labour's domestic welfare reforms. The loan was paid off in 2006, the total amount repaid was £7.5 billion.

32. *Daily Herald*, November 17, 1945, p. 1.

33. Anne Perkins, *Red Queen: The Authorized Biography of Barbara Castle*, 2003, p. 98.

34. Ibid., p. 99.

35. Interview with Barbara Castle, undated, Women's Library, 80DH/02/01/07 Box 1.

36. *Daily Herald*, March 10, 1961.

37. *The Sunderland Echo and Shipping Gazette*, March 13, 1946, p. 2.

38. Quoted in Melanie Phillips, *The Divided House*, Sidgwick and Jackson, 1980, p. 117.

39. Barbara Castle, *Fighting All the Way*, 1993, p. 135.

40. Interview with Barbara Castle, undated, Women's Library, 80DH/02/01/07 Box 1.

41. *Western Daily Press*, June 12, 1947, p. 1.

42. *The Northern Whig and Belfast Post*, February 25, 1949, p. 4.

43. Barbara Castle, Hansard, May 16, 1952, cc1834–1836.

44. Ibid.

45. Ibid.
46. Barbara Castle, Hansard, April 2, 1953, cc1347–1348.
47. *Hastings and St Leonard's Observer*, October 16, 1948.
48. Barbara Castle, *Fighting All the Way*, 1993, p. 135.
49. Quoted in Melanie Phillips, *The Divided House*, 1980, p. 110.
50. Leah Manning, *A Life for Education*, Victor Gollanz, 1970, p. 203.
51. Ibid.
52. Wilfred De'Ath, *Barbara Castle: A Portrait from Life*, 1970, p. 36.
53. Anne Perkins, *Red Queen: The Authorized Biography of Barbara Castle*, 2003, p. 86.
54. Barbara Castle, *Fighting All the Way*, 1993, p. 180.
55. Ibid., p. 192.
56. Ibid.
57. Ibid.
58. *Daily Mirror*, March 6, 1952, p. 1.
59. Barbara Castle, *Fighting All the Way*, 1993, p. 192. Barbara Castle, *Fighting All the Way*, 1993, p. 205.
60. *Daily Express*, October 1, 1955, p. 4.
61. Ibid.
62. Barbara Castle, *Fighting All the Way*, 1993, p. 192.
63. Barbara Castle, *Daily Mirror*, December 10, 1955, p. 2.
64. Barbara Castle, *Fighting All the Way*, Pan Books, 1993, p. 288.
65. Barbara Castle, Hansard, May 1959, cc1428–1433.
66. Barbara Castle, Hansard, June 16, 1959, cc299–312.
67. Ibid.
68. Barbara Castle, *Fighting All the Way*, 1993, p. 288. See Powell's speech, Hansard, July 27, 1959, cc232–238.
69. Barbara Castle, Hansard, June 16, 1959, cc299–312.
70. Barbara Castle, *Fighting All the Way*, 1993, p. 288.
71. Barbara Castle, quoted in Wilfred De'Ath, *Barbara Castle: A Portrait from Life*, 1970, p. 15.
72. *Birmingham Post*, October 5, 1957, p. 1.
73. Barbara Castle, *Daily Herald*, February 14, 1959, p. 4.
74. Ibid.
75. Barbara Castle, *Fighting All the Way*, p. 310.
76. *Daily Herald*, December 19, 1958.
77. *Birmingham Post*, September 24, 1958, p. 6.
78. *The Observer*, November 16, 1958.
79. Barbara Castle, *Fighting All the Way*, 1993, p. 306.
80. *Daily Herald*, December 19, 1958.
81. Barbara Castle, *Fighting All the Way*, 1993, p. 253.
82. Ibid.
83. Ibid., p. 254.
84. *Daily Herald*, October 9, 1959, p. 1.
85. Barbara Castle, *Fighting All the Way*, 1993, p. 313.
86. Susan Lawrence (1929–1930); Jennie Adamson (1935–1936); Barbara Gould (1939–1940); Ellen Wilkinson (1944–1945); Alice Bacon (1950–1951);

Edith Summerskill (1954–1955); and Margaret Herbison (1957–1957). Fifty-six men held this position during this period.

87. Labour Party Conference Report, 1959, p. 83.

88. *Evening Chronicle*, November 28, 1959, p. 9.

89. Quoted in Anne Perkins, *Red Queen: The Authorized Biography of Barbara Castle*, Macmillan, 2003, p. 164.

90. Labour Party Conference Report, 1959, p. 156.

91. Barbara Castle, Labour Party Annual Conference Report, 1960, pp. 115–118.

92. Labour Party Conference Report, 1961, pp. 179–180, 195–198 and 219 respectively.

93. *The Guardian*, November 23, 1959, p. 5.

94. Quoted in Anne Perkins, *Red Queen: The Authorized Biography of Barbara Castle*, 2003, p. 175.

95. Barbara Castle, *Fighting All the Way*, 1993, p. 329.

96. Ibid., p. 334.

97. *Coventry Evening Telegraph*, March 22, 1963, p. 1.

98. *The Observer*, November 16, 1958.

99. Ibid.

CHAPTER 7

In and Out of Cabinet, 1964–2002

At 9 a.m. on Saturday morning, October 17, 1964, Barbara Castle was still in her dressing gown when the telephone rang. It was Harold Wilson calling to tell her that he needed a 'keen and dedicated minister of Cabinet rank' to oversee his dream of a new international moral order. Aid was to be granted, 'not so much as a charity but as a real means to development, particularly within the Commonwealth'.[1] To her 'amazement', the 53-year-old Castle was asked to take on the newly created post of Minister of Overseas Development (Fig. 7.1). Wilson knew she was the right person to fulfil his goal: Castle was a leading figure in the Anti-Apartheid Movement and the Movement for Colonial Freedom and well known for her anti-imperialist credentials. Moreover in February 1964, eight months before Labour won the election she had passionately argued in the House of Commons for the creation of a World Development Agency to replace the previous inadequate, uncoordinated aid efforts of the British Government.[2]

As Prime Minister, Harold Wilson set the tone from No. 10 Downing Street and his government enjoyed the best record for promoting women to senior positions. In his first few years as Prime Minister, Wilson appointed eleven women to official posts, more than there had ever been, though there had been no increase in the number of female MPs. He also appointed women to a whole range of departments that had never had a female Minister such as the Foreign Office, Overseas Development, Transport, the Home Office and Paymaster General. Castle, who occupied four Cabinet posts in Wilson's government, told Shirley Williams that she was 'personally responsible for the installation of ladies' lavatories in more ministerial suites than anyone else'.[3]

Harold Wilson's motives in appointing Castle were not entirely altruistic. As with Attlee, he wanted a mixture of left and right in his Cabinet in order to achieve a stable government. He chose Castle as 'the public keeper of his conscience, guarantor of his principles, the outward symbol of his

© The Author(s) 2019

P. Bartley, *Labour Women in Power*,

https://doi.org/10.1007/978-3-030-14288-9_7

Fig. 7.1 Barbara Castle in Cabinet (©Keystone Pictures USA/Alamy Stock Photo)

government's embrace of the left wing'.[4] Castle fitted his bill completely: she was also clever, attractive and charming with impressive presentational skills, all of which was an added advantage. Furthermore, Wilson knew Castle would be a loyal ally and when politics got tough, could be relied on to give him support both personally and politically.

It was an exciting time for Labour: the country was ready for a change from the old school, grouse-shooting, upper-class ancien regime of the Tory party. Here was a—youngish—Prime Minister, from a modest background, educated at a grammar school and Oxford University promising that Britain would be forged in the 'white heat' of a scientific and technological revolution. Barbara Castle's appointment was welcome throughout the world, and she received hundreds of letters of congratulations from diverse groups such as the Afro-Asian Solidarity Association, the Anti-Apartheid Association, Left-socialist Zionists and the Rhodesian United National Independence Party. High-ranking individuals like the widow of Stafford Cripps and Bruce MacKenzie[5] congratulated her. Violent Bonham Carter wrote that she was the 'only woman Parliamentarian I have seen in action since Ellen Wilkinson'.[6] Even some of the press sent congratulations: a *Daily Mail* editor told her that she was his 'favourite woman politician'.[7]

At first, Castle was euphoric, thrilled to be part of a reforming Labour Government, delighted to be kissing hands with the Queen and dining at the

Guildhall. Soon she confronted the practicalities of building a new department, and coping with a huge workload, commenting that 'when you're in Cabinet, you can't get a free weekend of any kind, or free evening because of Cabinet boxes, I mean you would come wearily down, perhaps, to the cottage on a Friday night or a Saturday and the red boxes would be following you and there'd be 3 or 4 Cabinet boxes to read'.[8] Luckily, Ted Castle was a supportive husband. The couple had no children, and she was able to focus on her work without interruptions.

MINISTER OF OVERSEAS DEVELOPMENT, OCTOBER 1964–DECEMBER 1965

The title of the new organisation—Ministry of Overseas Development (ODM)—signalled a new approach to aid. It was responsible for all of Britain's overseas development programmes, and its purpose Mrs Castle announced in Parliament was to enable Britain 'to play a more effective part in the very great challenge affecting the whole world in the growing disparity between the rich and poor nations of the world'.[9] Her first task was to identify the aid programmes of various government departments, namely the Foreign Office, the Commonwealth Relations Office, the Colonial Office, the Board of Trade, the Department of Technical Co-operation and the Treasury, and bring them under the aegis of her new Department. Having done this, she set about developing an aid strategy which was independent of foreign policy, trade and the economy and which focussed on the needs of developing countries rather than the needs of the UK.

The ODM was a new department allowing Castle to shape it from scratch. She encountered a number of challenges after her initial euphoria had died away. Firstly, she had to tackle intransigent, conservative civil servants who seemed unwilling to implement her socialist policies. Certainly, a conflict seemed likely when Castle ignored the papers put forward by her civil servants and gave them copies of a Fabian pamphlet she had written on government aid as an outline of her departmental policy.[10] She notified her civil servants that it was their job to implement these policies. Tensions soon surfaced. Her Permanent Secretary, Sir Andrew Cohen, confessed to his wife that he would not work for a woman and—in a disgraceful break of protocol—made himself absent from London when Castle's appointment was announced. At first, relationships between the two were strained. Barbara Castle lost count of the number of times Cohen said 'Minister, while of course the decision is entirely yours, I would be failing in my duty not to tell you how unhappy it makes me'.[11] Fortunately, Cohen was a socialist and sympathetic to Castle's political direction and soon the two developed a mutual respect and a good working relationship. As he was a large man and his boss was physically tiny, the two became known as the 'Elephant and Castle'.

Secondly, the Minister of Overseas Development needed money—lots of it—in order to put her policies into practice. In its election manifesto,

Labour promised to increase spending on aid to 1% of GDP, but this was considered an unrealistic target in the economic crisis facing the new government. With Britain facing a predicted budget deficit of £800 million and the likely prospect of devaluation, import controls, spending cuts and borrowing, it was inconceivable that funds would be diverted to help other countries. Barbara Castle found herself in conflict with the Chancellor of the Exchequer James Callaghan, a man so determined to keep the price of sterling high that the very idea of borrowing money to fund unpopular policies was anathema to him. Castle was told that foreign bankers would not be happy to lend millions to Britain 'just to spend on soup kitchens for Africa'. Moreover, there seemed to be growing resentment by the electorate towards the Commonwealth where much of the aid went. Even so, Castle managed to gain £216 million from the Treasury, just 13.5% short of the £250 million she had initially proposed.

Thirdly Castle, like Margaret Bondfield and Ellen Wilkinson, would face challenges as the only woman in a Cabinet of 23. Chancellor James Callaghan, the Foreign Secretary Patrick Gordon Walker, the Defence Secretary Dennis Healey and the Secretary of State for Economic Affairs George Brown all grouped around the Prime Minister at the centre of the table. At first, Mrs Castle sat at the far end, well away from the centre of power and often out of earshot of the debate, side-lined by distance as well as by status: the ODM was not considered a significant department. It was, she confessed, extraordinarily difficult to make any impact. Even so, Castle was thought to fight above her station, leading one Minister to complain chauvinistically 'Look at her. She only has to waggle that bottom of hers and she gets it all her own way'.[12] In one of the first Cabinet meetings Castle attended, she was given a note claiming to be a Commons motion signed by four male Cabinet Ministers which stated 'That this House, noting the grace, charm, vitality and outstanding good looks of the Minister of Overseas Development, calls upon every Hon Member to show their appreciation of the unique qualities by all the means in their power'.[13] It was a male put-down of the only woman in Cabinet, a note that would not have been sent to Callaghan, Wilson or Healey. Castle was expected to respond humorously to sexist comments like these.

Fourthly, as Castle acknowledged, one of the problems she faced was the racism of sections of the British population which was far more widespread than politicians would admit. It was epitomised in the disgraceful cartoons published in the shockingly racist *Daily Express* which depicted her as 'a "n..... lover" who was squandering British tax-payers hard-earned money on feckless blacks'.[14] A toxic combination of sexism and racism merged when Castle, a white woman, mixed with black male leaders from former colonies on their visits to London to discuss development programmes. Generally, Castle was delighted to meet old friends from colonial countries, though her patience was tested when the totalitarian Dr Hastings Banda, Prime Minister of Malawi, came to visit her at her ODM office. Castle disliked him, disliked his dictatorial politics and disapproved of his friendliness with South Africa. Nonetheless, diplomacy prevailed and Mrs Castle agreed to meet Banda. She was infuriated when he turned her handshake into an embrace, a clasp which was caught on camera by the waiting press and published widely. As Castle noted 'it would have been an impertinence from any official visitor, but from him it was intolerable'.[15] This was clearly a chauvinistic gesture, but it was the ugly face of racist Britain which it triggered, not abhorrence at a sexist lapse of diplomatic protocol. Castle was shocked to receive the 'filthiest letters' she had ever received. One anonymous correspondent scrawled and underlined a message across the photograph saying 'Disgusting. Sooner these people are out of office the better for all decent white people. It makes you feel ashamed of been (sic) British'.[16] Another writer typed in red capital letters across the photograph 'IF A DIRTY ANIMAL IS ALLOWED TO DO THIS SORT OF THING IN FULL PUBLIC? (sic) WHAT GOES ON IN PRIVATE? ITS (sic) CHEAP COWS LIKE YOU THAT LET THE NATION DOWN'.[17] In 1968, the Race Relations Act was strengthened and gradually, until Brexit unleashed a further bout of repressed xenophobia, Britain seemed to transform itself into less overtly racially prejudiced country.

Castle undoubtedly loved her job and felt she was making an impact on international policy. She was thought to have 'managed to balance power and principle even more delicately than two angels on the head of a pin',[18] gaining admiration from all sides of the House. Under her guidance, the ODM funded development projects around the world with its annual budget of more than £200 million and a staff of about 2000. She may have been a woman, but she had a considerable amount of power, a power she used to forge 'a new identity for Britain in a world without empires'.[19] In January 1965, she visited India and Pakistan, and in April, she visited Tanzania, Zambia and Uganda to hold discussions on aid and development issues with the leaders of these countries personally.[20] She met and became on first name terms with Kenneth Kaunda, President of Zambia whom she thought 'informal but with great natural dignity', Seretse Khama, Prime Minister of Botswana who was 'charming and diffident' and Julius Nyerere, President of Tanzania.[21] On May 1, she met Dr Milton Obote, the Ugandan President. She spent ten days in Tanzania insisting that 'she had come as a friend to help Tanzania in its drive to prosperity'.[22] Britain's £7,500,000 aid budget, she stated, was to be spent improving facilities at the University and building new Houses of Parliament for the United Republic. Castle, however, warned the recipient countries that it would not be possible to 'dramatically increase' aid because of the financial crisis in Britain. Nevertheless, despite the economic climate Castle set out an ambitious agenda: in June 1965, she announced that all loans to the poorest developing countries would be interest free. She was appalled that in many countries as much as one-third of foreign aid was used to pay off the interest charges accrued when it had been given loans by Western countries. The only people who benefited from this, thought Castle, were the bankers.[23]

During her African visit, Mrs Castle was pressed about the Labour Government's attitude towards Southern Rhodesia. At the time, Southern Rhodesia was giving the Labour Government a crippling headache. In Castle's first few months of office, the Rhodesian leader Ian Smith threatened to declare a Unilateral Declaration of Independence (UDI) and the African leaders wanted to know what Harold Wilson planned to do, and whether he would use force to undermine the regime. Castle dodged the issue by arguing that the 'sign of success would be to achieve a peaceful settlement'.[24] When Smith declared UDI in November 1965, Castle advocated military intervention at Cabinet meetings, though she abided by the principle of Cabinet collective responsibility in public and defended the government when it decided not to invade. Just over a year later, Judith Hart would find herself immersed in the same Rhodesian problem.

Meanwhile, Labour followers expected their Government to tackle apartheid in South Africa and act against the white regime which was intensifying its repressive laws and eroding any black political rights remaining. In June 1964, Nelson Mandela was sentenced to life imprisonment for 'high treason' and spent the next 27 years in prison. There was worldwide condemnation over his imprisonment, and there were calls for sanctions. The Labour Government prevaricated. It agreed to honour a contract for 16 aircraft which had been signed by the previous Conservative Government, a move that Castle criticised though finally and somewhat reluctantly agreed to it. Less than a year later, the Labour Government wanted to veto a resolution put forward at the United Nations Security Council calling for economic sanctions against South Africa. Barbara Castle was in despair, arguing in Cabinet that if that happened she 'might as well pack up' her aid programme because she would no longer have any influence as Britain would have 'lost our moral standing'.[25] In the end, the UK abstained on the vote.

Castle spent time defending people who came to Britain from Commonwealth countries. When the Home Secretary Roy Jenkins pushed through a plan to cut down on Commonwealth immigration it led to a bitter row which split the Cabinet. The row was orchestrated by Mrs Castle whose outright hostility to curbing immigration seriously embarrassed the Prime Minister.[26] Harold Wilson became tired of Castle's forthright moral righteousness and her regular invectives against British foreign policy. Rather than confront her, he decided on a Cabinet reshuffle, one which would keep his friend busy, out of mischief and too far away to interfere in African politics. At least one other Cabinet Minister believed that Castle was moved because she had taken the black African point of view on too many issues and was overly critical of Rhodesia. She was redeployed, Richard Crossman believed, because Wilson did not 'want her formidable, old-fashioned, left-wing conscience' preventing him from achieving a settlement with Ian Smith in Rhodesia. Andrew Cohen and other senior officials were sad to see their Minister leave, saying that it was as if 'someone had switched off the current … it was like a morgue here'.[27] Castle had gained a reputation as one of the most effective Cabinet

Ministers of her generation, bringing in experts from outside Parliament and welding the 'regular civil servants and outsiders into a creative partnership'. Soon the ODM lost its status, its Minister no longer in the Cabinet. It remained outside the Cabinet for thirty years until Tony Blair appointed Clare Short as Secretary of State for Overseas Development.[28]

MINISTER OF TRANSPORT, DECEMBER 1965–APRIL 1968

On Tuesday, December 21, 1965, Harold Wilson invited the fifty-five-year-old Barbara Castle to be Minister for Transport. It was a surprise appointment. She was a woman—and she couldn't drive. At first, Castle was disappointed not to be offered a more prestigious Cabinet post—she had hoped to be offered the post of Home Secretary—and was hesitant about taking on this 'hot-seat of politics, littered with broken reputations'.[29] At the time, the Ministry of Transport was regarded as 'an open sesame to political unpopularity' and regarded as one of Britain's toughest jobs.[30] If Castle made a mess of it she might, as with the previous Transport Minister, be consigned to the political wilderness. Wilson persuaded her that he needed 'a tiger in my tank' to deliver the integrated transport policy he desired. Within a year of her appointment, the backwaters of the Ministry of Transport had been hit by the cyclone of Barbara Castle who stirred up enough water overturn the Department's customary tranquillity and bring it to the eye of the political storm. In the process, it did what Wilson hoped: she became so tied down by mammoth pieces of legislation that she had no time to get involved in other controversial issues.

Castle's new Ministry overlooked Southwark Street, a busy road with a constant traffic noise rumbling away, a constant physical reminder of the problems that needed resolving. But the new Minister was not going to get much help from her staff. Barbara Castle walked into a male misogynistic enclave. The place she noted 'seemed intimidatingly masculine'.[31] The office atmosphere was glacial, created by a large number of Scotsmen who were peeved that their beloved former and Scottish Minister had been replaced not just by someone who was English but by a woman. In addition, her department was staffed by male highway engineers whose interests lay in expanding the road programme for car drivers rather than improve public transport. Even the layout of the Ministry was unfavourable to women, there was, for instance, no women's lavatory on the ministerial floor, a physical reminder that women were not expected to be there. At first, Castle had to use the men's lavatory lined with urinals until a new one was constructed for her. On an individual level too, Castle faced antagonistic civil servants: her Permanent Secretary Sir Thomas Padmore was known to be apathetic, if not outright lazy. Castle tried—hard—to get rid of him and the fact that Padmore knew this did not help forge a good working relationship. In addition, Castle's Private Secretary Bill Scott was hostile to her and made no attempt to hide it. He would neglect to pass on Castle's instructions to the rest of the civil servants. 'I was in a man's world all right', she noted 'and I had to impose my will on it'.[32] After several months Castle managed to move Scott and appoint someone more congenial; Padmore remained.

At first, any idea put forward by a female Transport Minister who could not drive in a world of predominantly male car drivers, bus drivers and train drivers seemed doom to fail. Wilson commented that Castle's appointment 'received a predictable reaction from those commentators who felt that her inability to drive a vehicle was of more importance than her manifest ability to drive a ministry'.[33] Reporters were keen to interview Barbara Castle, certain of the humorous potential of a female Minister who had not passed her driving test. Rather than challenge the press's obsession with her appearance, Castle worked with it and used it to her advantage. At her first press conference Castle appeared in a red dress, well-styled hair and adorned with heavy gold costume jewellery, totally disarming all the reporters who became 'dazzled' by her appearance. Normally the press are sceptical about politicians, and sometimes scornful and judgemental but 'the scattered, embarrassed applause at the opening turned solid and unanimous when Mrs Castle left at the end'.[34] Her charm offensive had worked. Being chic and womanly, however, was a double-edged sword. On the one hand, it gained Barbara favourable publicity: she was often photographed opening a new road, a bridge or a motor-way interchange looking glamorous and politically appealing. On the other hand, her obvious attempts to look stylish led to sexual undertones and colleagues 'who wanted to undermine her, needed only to hint at her sex appeal to confirm suspicions that her success' was related to this.[35] Quentin Hogg, a Conservative backbencher, dubbed her 'the pussy galore of the Goldfinger government', a reference to a popular film which depicted a glamorous female (Pussy Galore aka Castle) being manipulated by a corrupt man (Goldfinger aka Wilson).

When Castle took over as Minister Britain's railway network was struggling with a mountain of debt and a reputation for inefficiency; bus services were in decline as private companies struggled to make a profit. The private car, it was believed, was the future. The former Conservative Minister of Transport Ernest Marples, a director of a road construction company, had been a strong advocate of road building and had encouraged the Chair of British Railways Richard Beeching to cut uneconomic and unprofitable railway lines. The new Minister of Transport on the other hand, was committed to making public transport reliable, efficient and affordable, bringing 'brave new thinking' to the post.[36] Castle set about a radical overhaul of the whole system, planning to reform it at every level, locally, regionally and nationally. Firstly, Castle aimed to reorganise public transport by creating a Passenger Transport Authority with the power to expand public transport, integrate road and rail services and re-nationalise private bus companies. An adequate rail network with subsidies for non-profit-making, socially necessary lines would be created. Castle reversed some of the Beeching cuts which had already closed more than 2000 stations and 8000 thousand miles of track, saving lines including those from York to Harrogate, and from Manchester to Buxton. In addition, Mrs Castle wanted to make bus services available and affordable to those who needed it. At the time, the bus services were rapidly declining as private companies could not afford to maintain loss-making routes. Under her aegis, more national bus companies came under the control of the nationalised National Bus Company, again subsidised by the government. Barbara Castle also saved the canal system. In 1967 when the Treasury planned to shut down the canals, Castle minimised the closures by re-classifying canals as leisure transport, arguing that she wanted 'new hope for those who love and use our canals, whether for cruising, angling or just walking on the towpath, or who want to see stretches of canal ... developed as centres of beauty or fun'.

Secondly, Barbara Castle wanted to reorganise the movement of freight by creating a new National Freight Authority to take over services from British Rail and British Road Services. It was given £200 million to buy up private road haulage firms. According to Castle, this would lead to an efficient integrated system, eliminating wasteful competition and promoting the transfer of freight from the roads to the railways. In addition, she aimed to improve the pay and conditions of lorry drivers, suggested a ten hour day and the use of a tachograph to ensure that drivers did not work over this time limit.

Thirdly, she aimed to reduce the growing numbers of deaths and injuries from road traffic accidents. Her Road Safety Bill brought in the breathalyser, extended the trial 70 mph speed limit and made it compulsory for all new cars to have seat belts. She also banned heavy goods traffic and all vehicles drawing trailers from the fast track of three-lane motorways. These policies set her on a collision course with the car-driving community. This time she was up against a substantially powerful—and again largely male—motoring lobby who regarded drink-driving, driving fast and driving without seat belts as an individual right. The state, they believed, had no mandate to intervene and impose its authority on the ordinary motorist. In their view, it was the action of a domineering, bureaucratic 'nanny' state, an infringement of their civil liberties and should be opposed. The famous racing driver and popular hero, Stirling Moss, declared that the speed limit was 'socialist hypocrisy'; and even one of her Labour colleagues, the Foreign Secretary George Brown, insisted that it was perfectly safe to drive at 100 mph down the motorways.

The breathalyser probably drew the strongest condemnation. When the Bill was being debated, the MP from Basingstoke, Mr Mitchell, complained that 'three small whiskies – three nips' would mean that anybody (i.e. a man) who goes 'to a civic function, a rugger club dinner, a working man's dinner or an NFU meeting and conducts normal social habits will find himself committing this offence'.[37] It was thought that it would damage the entertainment industry, hitting 'clubland where it hurts most – its pocket. ... she has devalued the social life of the country. Entertainment budgets have been cut and shows cancelled'.[38] No sooner was the breathalyser launched then Castle was inundated with mail, often containing many abusive and threatening letters, usually anonymous. One 'grubby epistle showed a dagger dripping with blood over the words: "We'll get you yet, you old cow"'.[39] Motorists burnt effigies of Barbara Castle. Thankfully, the threats remained verbal and Castle was never exposed to physical harm. The impact of the breathalyser on road accidents was staggering: at the end of the first five months 800 fewer people died from road deaths; in the first Christmas period deaths fell from 158 to 98. Barbara Castle had been vindicated and public opinion turned in her favour.

Castle faced a wall of antagonism when she advocated charging motorists to use roads in cities and large towns. It was, she believed, the answer to the growing road congestion, particularly in London. Critics felt otherwise, thought it would penalise drivers on low-incomes, and destroy the car industry as people would no longer be able to afford the price of driving in the cities. Her policy was ahead of its time: the London mayor Ken Livingstone introduced it in 2003, and Milan, Stockholm and Singapore followed suit. Castle received praise for her promotion of the 'Chunnel', the rail tunnel linking Folkestone and Calais. She visited Paris for talks with her French counterpart to resolve the legal and financial challenges to its completion: they predicted it would open in 1975. It eventually opened in 1994.

Castle's time managing the Ministry of Transport consolidated her reputation as a good administrator and inspiring politician. She was seen as hard-working, efficient, willing to listen to different points of view, undoctrinaire, consensual rather than argumentative, surprisingly informal and direct yet still willing to use 'feminine wiles' to get her way. Moreover, she remained firm in her convictions, once refusing a Treasury offer of an extra £20 million for her roads programme because the money came at the expense of overseas aid.[40]

Barbara Castle had put her own stamp on the Ministry of Transport, revolutionising the industry and making travel much safer. In 1968, she was at the top of her profession, feted by newspapers, riding high on a wave of popularity and seen to be operating well in a world which was still coming to terms with women being politicians. There seemed no limit, the press thought, 'to where her ambition might take her, perhaps to the office of Chancellor'.[41] By now, Castle was willing to compromise on socialist doctrine, lecturing Michael Foot and Richard Crossman on the need to be pragmatic, lecturing journalists on the responsibilities of office and her friends on 'the fact that there is more morality in responsibility than in agitation'.[42] At the same time as Barbara's popularity with the British population soared, her esteem among her left-wing colleagues diminished. Castle was not a clubbable woman, ill at ease in the bars, the tea rooms and the smoking rooms of the House of Commons, preferring to work in her room rather than socialise with a bunch of male colleagues who enjoyed a couple of drinks or more. Moreover, the House of Commons was not always a safe space for women: Barbara Castle once had to fight off a drunken George Brown who tried to unbutton her blouse in the division lobby.

SECRETARY OF STATE FOR EMPLOYMENT AND PRODUCTIVITY, APRIL 1968–JUNE 1970

On April 5, 1968, Harold Wilson asked Barbara Castle to be Minister of Labour, in charge of prices and incomes. Initially, Castle 'recoiled in horror' at being offered the job and told Harold Wilson that she was 'not prepared to become Margaret Bondfield, Mark II'.[43] 'I am under no illusions that I may be committing political suicide' she confided to her diary, fully aware of the fate of the previous female Minister. She had, as she noted in her diary, 'moved from the periphery of the whirlwind into its very heart',[44] and was now in charge of the most controversial of all Government policies, that of reforming the trade unions. This time she was swept up into the vortex of an inescapable hurricane that threatened to destroy her, or at the very least her reputation. This post, she predicted, would be her political reckoning, hurtling her towards a similar glass cliff as Bondfield's.[45]

In order to persuade her to take on the job, Wilson changed the name of the post from Minister of Labour to Secretary of State for Employment. At the same time, he offered her First Secretary of State, an honorary title which gave her seniority over all other Cabinet Ministers. It was too good to refuse: she was now the most powerful woman politician, sitting at the centre of the Cabinet table opposite Harold Wilson instead of on the outer fringes and being part of an inner Cabinet. Castle was viewed as 'the biggest personality in the Government today. Already she's a natural number two and if she weren't a woman she would be natural number one: she could conceivably be the first lady Prime Minister. ... She has the personality to control any Ministry not only by sheer will power but also by intellectual domination'.[46] In many ways, the industrial problem was a problem made for Castle. It called for a reassuring presence, it called for an ability to bargain behind the scenes with patience and judgement, it called for an ability to mix with and win the confidence of trade unionists and it called for someone with left-wing credentials. Castle fitted the job description perfectly.

Wilson wanted a strong Minister to reign in the trade unions that were thought to be out of control: in 1967 over 2.7 million working days had been lost through strike action, mainly called by shop stewards acting independently. The Prime Minister hoped that Castle would curtail the power of the trade unions and find a way to 'sell this policy as essentially socialist'.[47] Most of the left-wing press thought it was a 'big gamble' to put the 'flaming, dynamic Left-Winger in as poacher turned game-keeper' to sort out the trade unions.[48] Undoubtedly Barbara Castle was about to face the biggest political challenge of her life. There were early indications that Castle's job might be problematic. Ray Gunter, a powerful union leader and Cabinet Minister called her 'leather knickers', a demeaning chauvinist comment with sexual overtones that reflected his antagonism towards a female Minister with a tough reputation. Many other unionists were as bigoted as Gunter, disliking the idea of powerful woman telling them what to do. The TUC were thought to be 'anti-feminist to a man, so macho. ... They were really pretty dreadful'.[49]

When Labour first took office the trade unions had agreed to moderate their wage claims in return for the 'social contract', the government's continued provision of a range of social benefits like the Health Service, decent pensions and free education. This deal was not to last. Wages increased by 5%, far above the government-set recommendations of between 0 and 3.5%. Meanwhile, strikes continued with alarming alacrity and the press was full of reports of unofficial 'wildcat' strikes which allegedly undermined businesses and jeopardised jobs. The trade unions were accused of undermining the Labour Government and holding the country to ransom. In 1965, Harold Wilson and Ray Gunter set up a Royal Commission on Trade Unions and Employers' Associations chaired by Lord Justice Donovan to examine the ways to improve relationships between workers and employers so that strikes could be averted. Barbara Castle was to be responsible for the Government's response to the Donovan report when it was published three years later.

In November 1968, during a weekend at the civil service training college in Sunningdale, Barbara Castle thrashed out her programme for trade union reform. It was, she claimed in her diary, 'a fabulously successful weekend'.[50] Castle's proposals, based on the Donovan report, were eventually put forward in a white paper called *In Place of Strife*. She insisted that it was first and foremost a charter of rights: it gave workers the statutory right to belong to a trade union, legal protection against unfair dismissal, protection in relation to sympathetic strikes and the unions the right to operate a closed shop. However, her proposals also gave the government powers to order a pre-strike ballot if it judged the strike to be harmful to the economy, to order a 28-day conciliation pause before an unofficial strike, and to impose fines if these rules were broken.

Not surprisingly, the trade unions rejected the second part of Castle's proposals and threatened further industrial unrest. A bitter struggle was predicted as the political wing of the party, the government, was faced with curbing the power of its industrial wing, the trade unions. In Castle's view, there was a constitutional issue at state: if her proposal could not go forward because the TUC disapproved 'then the government could not govern'. Wilson agreed, arguing that the very essence of democracy was at stake. Here were the leaders of the trade unions threatening to make any trade union legislation unworkable and in direct defiance of the Labour Government. They were seen as above the law, challenging the right of an elected government to govern, an unacceptable breach of democratic values. Tensions were exacerbated because Castle's attitudes towards unions were shaped by the predominantly middle-class Labour intellectual left which 'regarded union barons as bullying autocrats'.[51] A leading trade unionist, Joe Gormley talking about politicians, commented that the 'higher ranks were filled by people – they call themselves intellectuals – who have little to do with the grass roots'.[52] Politicians like Castle were thought to be a different kind of socialist 'from the man who has spent his working life wondering where the next butty, or the next pair of shoes is coming from'.[53]

On January 3, 1969, the Cabinet met to discuss the policy. Barbara Castle showed guts, conviction and determination mixed with a dash of fire when she put forward her plans. It took a number of meetings, and heated and acrimonious discussions, before the Cabinet approved *In Place of Strife*. The bitter dispute was led by James Callaghan, a working-class former trade union official, who disliked and was jealous of Barbara Castle. He was not alone in his criticism: Castle's closest political allies like Dick Crossman and Judith Hart also opposed them. Later that day, Barbara wrote in her diary that she would succeed and that she wanted 'Dick and Judith to eat dirt. Their assumption of superior concern for rank and file feeling has been almost more than I could bear'.[54] Castle may have adopted a usual fearless façade but she was 'swept with doubt from time to time as to whether I have entirely misjudged reactions. If I have I shall have mortally damaged my political career'.[55] Initially, Wilson stood by Castle realising that not to do so would have meant that government was effectively the prisoner of the unions. Relationships with Wilson were more than cordial and the two used to write flirtatious notes to each other across the table at Cabinet meetings. One of their notes read '"What are you doing tonight, baby?" Me: "1. Meeting of IR Committee immediately after Cabinet; 2. Meeting with my officials to start drafting my speech, Daddy!!!!" Harold: "Don't be a spoilsport. I was wondering whether you'd like to come and see my etchings – with Vic Feather!"'[56]

On January 15, 1969, the draft Bill was eventually approved by Cabinet; on January 17, 1969, *In Place of Strife* was published. Press response was largely favourable. *The Guardian* was one of the few papers to criticise the penal clauses of the White Paper. The *Times* and the *Financial Times* liked the fact that trade unions might at last be controlled; the *Daily Mirror* gave unequivocal support to the government headlining Castle's proposals as 'BLOODY GOOD SENSE', grateful that it would bring law to the 'jungle of industrial relations' and arguing that she made a 'courageous and ingenious BEGINNING on this vital task'.[57] A *Daily Mirror* poll of 2000 male trade unionists showed overwhelming support for Castle's proposals.[58] The Prime Minister, the *Daily Mirror* urged, would commit electoral suicide by not implementing them. The majority of trade unions disagreed. On February 27, almost 3000 trade union delegates from all over Britain converged in a 'great Croydon Lobby' to protest against Castle's Bill, over 50,000 workers marched out of factories in Merseyside and over 40,000 Scottish miners went on strike.

By now all the various wings of the Labour Party had taken offence: the trade unions, MPs, the Cabinet, the NEC and the constituency parties all opposed Castle's White Paper. It is suggested that the Secretary of State for Employment had forgotten the debt that Labour MPs owed the trade unions: many had come up through the trade union ranks and were former trade union officials; many relied heavily on their union sponsors to provide help towards paying election expenses and the salaries of election agents.[59] In turn, it was expected that MPs would be loyal to the trade union movement: some unions, notably the AEF and the TGWU, held meetings with their sponsored MPs in order to make their opposition to Castle's White Paper known. Jack Jones, soon to be the leader of the TGWU reminded 'his union sponsored MPs of their obligations' to vote against *In Place of Strife*.[60]

In early June 1969, at a secret meeting at Chequers the leading trade unionists Vic Feather, Jack Jones and Hugh Scanlon met with Castle and Wilson to discuss how to resolve the conflict between the Government and the trade unions. The union leaders told Castle and Wilson that they would be opposed to any proposed legislation which eroded trade union rights. Vic Feather who was General Secretary of the TUC had personal as well as political reasons for his objections. He had known Barbara since childhood and was perhaps resentful of her privileged upbringing, perhaps jealous that she had gone to university and had risen to the top of the Labour Party. In his view, 'Barbara's knowledge and understanding of how trade unions work and function is nil'.[61] He once said 'I knew that girl when she had dirty knickers'.[62] It was misogyny dressed up as humour.[63]

In Place of Strife came closer to splitting the Labour movement than any event since 1931 and brought the government to the brink of catastrophe. The Government, Pimlott argues, entered a phase of near anarchy and Castle was driven 'into a corner by the ferocity of resistance to her measures and under almost intolerable strain'.[64] On June 18, 1969, Barbara Castle was forced to capitulate, undermined by Callaghan who plotted against her and finally scuppered her plans. A face-saving formula was agreed in which the TUC gave a 'solemn and binding undertaking' that it would do something about the irresponsible industrial unrest that was crippling the economy. The TUC put forward a *Programme for Action* which gave it power to intervene in strikes, a proposal which Barbara Castle dismissed it as a 'pious hope'. The government's capitulation 'confirmed that the Labour Party could not govern without the consent of the trade unions, which, for a Prime Minister seeking to establish that his party was that of the national interest, was a devastating conclusion … and laid bare the harsh reality of the balance of power inside the labour movement'.[65]

Labour was perceived as spineless, seen as a party of the trade unions not of the nation. Newspaper headlines condemned both the government and the unions. Even the sympathetic *Mirror* carried a leader with the heading 'There Exists in Britain a Power Outside Parliament as Great as That which Exists Within'.[66] The sovereignty of the British Parliament had been undermined, it was felt, by a non-elected, unrepresentative and browbeating body of stubborn men. Moreover, a 70% approval rate in the polls indicated that the general public backed Barbara Castle. The continuing industrial chaos and 'wild-cat' strikes were increasingly unpopular in the country. The trade unions, it was felt, needed to be controlled, and should be compelled to be responsible if they refused to act responsibly themselves. It was clear enough, insisted the *Illustrated London News* that 'that the bulk of the union members were on her side ... Most union members still think that legislation is needed to deal with unofficial strikes ... the legislation which their leaders forced the Government to drop'.[67]

The debacle destroyed Castle's career. From a rising star in the Labour Party, a darling of the left, the press and the public, her reputation plummeted to the depths. Her glitter had faded. Harold Wilson told Barbara 'I am the only friend you have and you are the only friend I have'. Trade unions turned on Barbara Castle: Jack Jones, the General Secretary of the Transport and General Workers' Union, proclaimed that she was 'totally politically discredited'. Castle commented in her diary on the 'bitterness and almost savage hostility' that was shown to her by the trade unions. By this time, Vic Feather made no attempt to hide his hostility telling Wilson in front of her that she was 'a liability'. And like Margaret Bondfield before her, the job of the newly named Minister of Labour was viewed as her political graveyard: Castle's chance of becoming Britain's first female Prime Minister was irretrievably destroyed. Moreover, her reputation as a left-winger was now in shreds. Barbara Castle titled the chapter in her autobiography that dealt with this period in office 'In Place of Popularity'. 'It was vanity' she later said 'to imagine that I could single-handedly turn a negative economic policy into a positive one'.[68]

Castle predicted that the TUC had 'done itself great harm and would pay the price under a Tory government'.[69] In her view, the left-wing and the trade unions 'will pave the way for an equally devastating right-wing swing in this country. I sometimes think a Labour Government cannot survive for the simple reason that the most idealistic of its own activists don't really want power'.[70] Her predictions proved accurate. Indeed some argue that if Castle had been successful in restraining the power of the trade unions a 'winter of discontent' under Callaghan's premiership could have been avoided, Labour could have won the next election and Margaret Thatcher stopped from becoming Prime Minister and introducing her much tougher anti-union laws. Shirley Williams certainly believed that it produced 'the situation in which Mrs Thatcher was able to come in'.[71] Others maintain that 'it might also have worked to prevent the subsequent rupture of British social democracy and formal split in the Labour Party after 1979 which led, indirectly at least, to eighteen years out of government'.[72] These theories of course contain only a partial truth: the massive inflation under Callaghan due to the oil price hike after the 1967 Arab-Israeli war and Thatcher's slick advertising campaign also contributed to Labour's defeat.

Like any consummate politician, Barbara Castle rescued herself from political oblivion by adopting another contentious issue: equal pay. In a bold new move, she pronounced that she was determined to force what she termed the 'macho male chauvinists'[73] in the Treasury to accept the principle of equal pay. 'It is a cause', *The Guardian* claimed 'which seems likely to attract wide

Labour support and could well restore some of the popularity Mrs Castle lost over the anti-strike legislation'.[74] Yet equal pay was not merely a quick fix to resuscitate a failing career since Barbara Castle was deeply committed to the principle: in 1954, as the last chapter has shown, she had supported a cross-party bill for equal pay.

A strike at the Dagenham Ford Factory provided the catalyst. In June 1968, women who made car seat covers at the factory came out on strike when their jobs were re-categorised as less skilled, paying 15% less than men doing an equivalent job. The women maintained they were being discriminated against 'because of their sex'. Car production came to a halt and Ford asked Castle to settle the dispute. Three weeks later, after tough negotiations with the women, the unions and the employers the women returned to work when Ford agreed to increase their pay to only 8% less than men.

In 1969, inspired by the Ford workers, the National Joint Action Campaign Committee for Women's Equal Rights was formed by women trade unionists. At the TUC women's conference that year, leaders of Britain's women workers warned that they would take strike action if equal pay was not granted. They accused Barbara Castle of betraying the cause by not promoting it as much as she should.[75] The Secretary of State rose to the challenge. In August 1969, still recovering from the aftermath of *In Place of Strife*, Castle took her proposed Bill to the Cabinet for approval. The discussion went 'much better than I had dared to hope',[76] with overwhelming support for her proposals in principle. On February 9, 1970, Barbara Castle put forward the second reading of her Equal Pay Bill to the House of Commons. There can be no doubt, she argued 'that this afternoon we are witnessing another historic advance in the struggle against discrimination'.[77] Castle reminded the House of how the struggle had begun 'as far back as 1888 ...when women who worked in industry were not considered respectable. ... Since then, the struggle ... has had a chequered course'.[78] Finally, after nearly a century of struggle, women achieved a modicum of equality. The Bill was widely and warmly welcomed in all parts of the House, drawing support from all sides. Margaret Thatcher congratulated Barbara Castle for introducing it but was saddened that 'not nearly enough hon. Members attended the debate' as only 60 or so MPs had bothered to turn up.[79] She went on to say that 'we should not delude ourselves by thinking that equal pay for women ... necessarily means equal opportunities. There is still a great deal of work to be done in that respect'.[80] Only a few MPs objected to Castle's Bill. One MP argued that men were stronger and were thus better workers; that equal pay would depress wages and lead to a demand for a massive increase in family allowances to compensate; that equal pay would lead to inflation; and that the state should not interfere in free markets.[81] Others argued that giving equal pay to women would cost too much to implement and damage the economy irreparably.

Feminists had fought for equal pay since the beginning of the century but the Equal Pay Act was definitely Barbara Castle's achievement. Without her commitment, equal pay might well have been postponed again. Yet Castle still did not consider herself a feminist and initially even rejected the term. When she visited America to talk to a meeting organised by the Women's Liberation Movement (WLM) she criticised them for being obsessed with trivia, insisting that she could not 'get excited about being called Chairman instead of Chairperson, or Ms instead of Mrs and Miss – If I'd bothered about being called Miz instead of Mrs and Miss, I would never have won the proud neuter title of Minister'.[82] In her opinion, the WLM was a little too keen on 'unhealthy introspection' with women too wrapped up in 'self-discovery in sexual terms'. She insisted that she had 'a mind as well as a vagina and I did not see why the latter should dominate'.[83] She was a late-convert to all-women short-lists and never actively sought to promote women in Parliament. However, on a personal level she encouraged Betty Boothroyd, Jo Richardson and Janet Anderson when they sought parliamentary seats and when Joan Lestor was short of electoral funds Castle wrote around to friends asking to contribute towards her expenses.[84]

Barbara Castle was a competent, clever Cabinet Minister well able to run a Department, yet even colleagues attributed her success to her sexuality. During this period there were constant rumours that Mrs Castle and Mr Wilson were more than just friends. Tom Driberg told the spy Peter Wright that he lent his flat to Harold Wilson so that he could meet his mistress, who he discovered was Barbara Castle.[85] This was the only reason, it was believed, why Castle had such power over Harold Wilson. Today, many remain curious about the relationship between Barbara Castle and Harold Wilson, but is it historically important? Perhaps it should remain significant because it illustrates how women were perceived. Some believed that women, especially successful ones, must have been promoted because they were willing to grant sexual favours. Women, even those as obviously competent as Castle, were thought to achieve their posts through sex rather than through evident ability.

In 1970, Labour lost the election and Ted Heath replaced Harold Wilson as Prime Minister. Many thought the election was lost because of the failure of Barbara Castle's paper *In Place of Strife* and the subsequent government's inability to curb the power of the unions. Castle was not surprised. She had a 'haunting feeling that there is a silent majority sitting behind its lace curtains waiting to come out and vote Tory', a majority who disliked Labour kowtowing to the trade unions. Castle was most annoyed by Labour's 'failure to proclaim our achievements, which were substantial despite the economic difficulties—the Equal Pay Act, the Open University, the legal aid scheme' and turning a deficit of £372 million into a surplus of £500 million.[86] Labour also abolished capital punishment, liberalised divorce laws, legalised abortion, decriminalised homosexuality, ended theatre censorship, reduced the voting age from 21 to 18, created new universities, passed a Race Relations Act, built more council houses, created a number of new towns, protected tenants from eviction, improved state education and upgraded working conditions.

The new Conservative Government was equally plagued by strikes: five states of emergency were declared during Heath's premiership. IS EVERYBODY GOING <u>BLOODY</u> MAD? asked a *Daily Mirror* headline when the Prime Minister declared a 'Three Day Week' because the country depended on coal and the miners were on strike.[87] In a desperate attempt to control galloping inflation, widespread strikes, a three-day industrial week, Heath called an election, asking 'Who Governs Britain?' The electorate showed its dissatisfaction for Heath by voting him out of office and in March 1974, the Labour Government returned to power with Harold Wilson as Prime Minister again.

SECRETARY OF STATE FOR SOCIAL SERVICES, MARCH 1974–APRIL 1976

Castle hoped to be given the post of Foreign Secretary, especially since she had had such a success as Minister of Overseas Development but as she noted, the idea of appointing a woman as Foreign Secretary was a step too far for Wilson's feminist sympathies. Wilson appointed her as Secretary of State for Social Services, even though she had been placed in a job well below her political capabilities. Wilson gave Michael Foot, one of the fiercer critics of Castle's prices and incomes policy, the job of being in charge of industrial disputes and wage restraint and appointed Shirley Williams to the Cabinet putting her in charge of prices. He was the first Prime Minister 'to risk' having two women in his Cabinet.[88]

It was Barbara Castle's fourth post as Cabinet Minister. One of her first jobs was to implement the Labour Party's manifesto promise to reform the pension system. Like Rodney Bickerstaffe, General Secretary of UNISON she believed that 'older people were entitled to dignity, respect and financial security in retirement'.[89] During her term of office, Castle put in place new occupational pensions through the State Earnings-Related Pension Scheme (SERPS) providing retired people with earnings-related pensions, thus taking them off demeaning mean-tested benefits. For the first time, the government gave all disabled people a mobility allowance, introduced a non-contributory pension for the disabled and a disability care allowance for carers. An Institute of Hearing Research was also set up. In addition, Castle reformed the way in which child benefit was paid by giving the allowance directly to the mother rather than as a tax break to fathers; and she helped bring the issue of battered wives to public notice.

The Secretary of State for Social Services also set out to improve the NHS. In an age of austerity, she managed to increase the budget of the NHS by 1.5% when all the other departments faced cuts. However, Castle encountered strong resistance when she tried to get rid of pay beds. At the time, NHS doctors were allowed to treat private patients in private rooms within an NHS hospital, and keep the money. Castle thought this inequitable, knowing that people who used pay beds jumped health queues. However, Castle soon found that nearly everyone, save the unions, was against her: the press, the doctors, her department, the civil servants, and several of her Cabinet colleagues all criticised her proposals.

In January 1975, the NHS faced its worst crisis when Britain's 52,000 doctors, consultants, junior hospital doctors and general practitioners threatened strike action. GPs demanded a pay rise, consultants demanded a new contract and junior doctors demanded that their working week be reduced from 80 to 40 hours a week. Consultants began a work-to-rule which closed hospital casualty departments, led to cancelled operations and longer waiting lists. To add fuel to an already raging fire, GPs threatened industrial action in support of pay claims. In March 3, 1975, all the doctors in Chippenham sent in their resignation letters in 'the smouldering battle' over pay.[90] In the end, Harold Wilson was forced to intervene and negotiate a compromise. It was a public gesture of no confidence in his Cabinet Minister.

By the mid-1970s Barbara's star was waning. She no longer had the ear of the Prime Minister, she sat at the end of the Cabinet table and her DHSS, the Department of Health and Social Security was dubbed the Ministry of Stealth and Total Obscurity. There were indications that her friendship and advice were no longer valued: Wilson changed his private telephone number and did not give his old friend his new one. The cosy intimacy she once enjoyed had disappeared. Early in 1976, Wilson told his former friend that he was tired of her endless capacity for causing a row. Her public image too went downhill. She was called the Red Queen, after the abhorred character in Alice in Wonderland, and came to be viewed as too doctrinaire and uncompromising for comfort. She had become old. Not old enough to be a national treasure, but old enough to be portrayed as a witch. In her younger days, attractive, sexy, flirtatious, Barbara Castle could wheedle her way out of trouble. Now at pensionable age, her sexual power had declined.

DISMISSED FROM CABINET, APRIL 1976

It got worse. On March 16, 1976, Wilson announced his resignation to the Cabinet and on April 5, 1976, Callaghan became Prime Minister. Three days later Callaghan summoned Barbara Castle to Downing Street. She was calm, not believing that 'Jim would sack me. I didn't deserve that'.[91] But Callaghan was about to take his revenge and asked her to resign. Castle was fired, partly for Callaghan's pleasure in getting rid of his adversary, partly to appease the trade unions by destroying the woman who had tried to curb them. He knew that he 'could sack her with impunity; his political position at that moment was impregnable, and she, although she had many personal and political friends, had no substantial body of people who could truthfully be called political allies'.[92] Castle was devastated, even though she knew it was likely. 'To be sacked from the Cabinet' Barbara Castle, 'is a humiliating experience at any time'.[93] She was deeply disturbed by 'Jim's cavalier discarding of me like so much old junk'.[94] She accused of him of being a bit of 'a male chauvinist' in contrast with Wilson who was 'more pro-woman than any other person I know'.[95] She told a Guardian journalist that she was very 'upset at being given the push. I felt I didn't deserve to be humiliated. ... It was all an emotional shock'.[96]

On April 27, 1976, Barbara Castle walked into the House of Commons 'self-consciously, looking for a seat on the back benches and feeling that all eyes were upon me, either sympathetically or patronisingly'.[97] The first day after you have been fired, she told a Guardian reporter, 'you go into the Chamber and find yourself walking to the Front Bench. Then you say to yourself, "Oh, no". Then you slink on to a seat three benches back. Everybody's eyes are on you. You feel naked. ... It took me four days ... to ask my first question as a backbencher'.[98] Undoubtedly, Castle felt the transition from power to powerlessness difficult to handle. It seemed as if the old cliché that all political careers end in failure was very apt.

It also seemed as if the cliché applied to government as well as individuals. Callaghan's Government faced seemingly intractable economic problems and was forced to clamp down on public spending and wage rises. In 1978, Callaghan fixed a norm for wage rises to a 5% ceiling. This was not welcome by trade unionists who had fought off Castle's attempt to curb their power and were more than ready to flex their industrial muscle. In January 1979, a nationwide strike of road hauliers and tanker drivers spread to other public services when refuse collectors, sewage staff, hospital porters, school caretakers and gravediggers all demanded an increase in wages. The newspapers and television were full of photographs of overflowing dustbins and striking gravediggers. Reports showed grieving families weeping because they could not bury their loved ones. It was dubbed the Winter of Discontent. By now, Callaghan's government was losing credibility. On March 28, 1979, it was eventually brought down by a vote of no confidence, the first time since 1924 that a government lost its authority by a parliamentary division. An election was scheduled for May 3. Labour's election manifesto was drafted by the party leadership and the NEC: Shirley Williams persuaded the Party to get rid of the more offensive anti-European sentiments and Callaghan used his veto to keep out proposals to abolish the House of Lords. It was not enough. Margaret Thatcher's election slogan 'Labour isn't working' struck a chord with the electorate; Callaghan, who had never contested an election as Prime Minister, lost.

On May 4, 1979, Margaret Thatcher became the first female Prime Minister. When Thatcher replaced Heath as leader of the Tory Party in 1975 Castle felt a 'sneaking feminine pleasure'. She could not 'help feeling a thrill' that Thatcher was elected as men had been 'been running the show as long as anyone can remember and they don't seem to have made much of a job of it. The excitement of switching to a woman might stir a lot people out of their lethargy. I think it will be a good thing for the Labour Party too. There's a male-dominated party for you – not least because the trade unions are male-dominated. ... The battle for cash wage increases is a masculine obsession. ... What matters to women is the social wage. ... to me socialism isn't just militant trade unionism'.[99] Her pleasure was short-lived.

Castle may have had a sneaking admiration for Thatcher's style but she loathed her monetarist policies and the way she governed the country. The Conservatives, she insisted, looked after themselves as shown by their cuts to the top rate of tax from 83 to 60% while at the same time increasing VAT from 8 to 15%, a policy which affected the poorest of society the most. Castle blamed the Conservatives for making inflation spiral to 22%, for increasing unemployment, for a balance of payments deficit which reached £4.4 billion, for 200 business failures a day and 300 daily home repossessions. Moreover, the government sold off British-owned assets like gas and electricity to companies which were often owned by other nation states.

Barbara Castle did not stand for Parliament in the 1979 election. Her decision to leave the Commons was thought to mark the end of an era, the last in a line of crusading women. By now Castle was tired and depressed, tired from working hard as a Cabinet Minister in challenging circumstances, depressed by the way she had been treated by the Labour Party. Moreover, she was full of self-doubt and gloom, blaming herself for the failures of Labour policy and for not fighting intensely enough. She could have spent her retirement looking after her, by now quite ill, husband, tending her garden, cooking meals. However, Barbara Castle was not about to take her pension, or abandon politics. Instead, she stood as a candidate for the newly elected European Parliament. She insisted that she would 'try to rise like a phoenix from the ashes and carry on my political fight in the new European scenario'.[100]

NEW DIRECTIONS 1979 ONWARDS

Her decision to stand for the European Parliament was surprising: Castle was known to be vehemently against the EU, then known as the Common Market. She had fought against Britain joining, arguing that membership of it would destroy Britain economically. In her opinion, Britain would lose its cheap food from the Commonwealth while at the same time expose herself to industrial competition from Germany with the removal of protective tariff barriers. Castle feared that the free-market philosophy of the Common Market 'would undermine a Labour government's power to plan our economy and help our own industries'.[101] She insisted that the Common Market was a group of rich nations 'insulating themselves against the rest of the world by a tariff wall. It was, in her view, "the supreme symbol of the rich countries" selfishness' because they pushed up the price of food by keeping out products from the Commonwealth.[102] In 1973 had Britain joined the Common Market but when Labour regained power Wilson was forced into holding a referendum on Europe. Castle had campaigned to leave.

In June 1979, Barbara Castle was elected Member of the European Parliament for Manchester North, a post which she held for ten years. For some, it was a *volte face*, a betrayal of her principles and of her anti-marketer colleagues. Castle defended her new role by saying that British membership of the EU was irrevocable, claiming that she wanted to fight inside the European Parliament against 'creeping federalism'. Barbara Castle was soon elected leader of the British Labour Group and vice-chair of the Parliament's Socialist Group. She was, after all, a politician with much experience, a rarity in the EU. Much of the work of the EU takes place in committees: Barbara Castle opted to join the Common Agricultural Committee because at that time two-thirds of EC money was spent on agriculture. At first, she was appalled at the economic flabbiness of the EU, the generous expenses allowance, the lavish receptions, the free language courses, the plush cars available to members. She was also critical of the turgid debates that took place in the European Parliament. When she was in full swing Castle, reported the *Telegraph* she was 'a truly awesome spectacle, her head tilted forward like an eagle about to swoop on a prey'.[103] Not surprisingly, her speeches were eagerly awaited by those unused to high-flying oratory from British politicians.

Castle agreed with Thatcher's proposal that Britain's net contribution to the EEC budget should be reduced. However, she disagreed with Thatcher's way of doing business, of the way she truculently banged the table and in raucous English demanded 'my money' back. Castle was also critical of Thatcher's signing of the Single Act which established the 'internal market'—a Europe without internal frontiers in which capital, goods and labour could move freely. It would be, Castle insisted, a catastrophe for Britain. 'No public authority faced with an EC bid' she argued 'would be allowed to allocate its contracts on any but commercial terms. In Britain, public contracts formed a considerable part of economic activity. In the North-West, with its high unemployment, it was a tradition among our Labour councils to attach certain conditions to their contract' such as a certain percentage of local labour had to be used.[104] In Thatcher's Britain, Castle maintained, it would become attractive—and easy—for continental firms to buy up any national asset, however essential, such as water or electricity. Britain would be up for sale.

In the 1980s under the Presidency of Jacques Delors, the EU began to change as did Barbara Castle's attitude to it. Barbara Castle approved of these changes, especially that of the social charter which guaranteed fair wages and hours of work, the right to a job, the provision of sick pay, paid holidays and redundancy pay, better health and safety provision at work, better care of the elderly, disabled; equal pay for women; full childcare including maternity and paternity leave. Margaret Thatcher refused to sign the charter.

By now Callaghan had resigned and Castle's good friend Michael Foot was leader of the Labour Party. It was no surprise to Barbara Castle that Labour lost the next election too: in 1983, Thatcher swept to power winning an overall majority of 144, partly due to the Falklands war, partly due to the ineptitude of the Labour Party. Thatcher's election campaign, according to Castle, its sheer professionalism, her Saatchi and Saatchi consultants, her ritzy rallies and extravagant press conferences with Thatcher appearing immaculately groomed contrasted with Foot who thought substance more important than image.

The difference between professional politician and amateur was, according to Castle, played out physically.

After Labour's disastrous election, Michael Foot resigned and Neil Kinnock took his place. Barbara Castle liked Neil Kinnock. She thought his acceptance speech 'one of the most moving and compelling I had ever heard. My spirits rose as he painted a picture of Britain he wanted to see: brave, realist and inspired'.[105] She campaigned for him in the 1992 general election, providing the fire and the passion that the newly polished Kinnock now lacked. Castle's appreciation of Kinnock, however, was not shared by the British public for despite being ahead in the polls, Labour suffered its fourth consecutive defeat with the Conservatives winning with a 102 seat majority. In 1992, John Smith replaced Neil Kinnock as leader of the Labour Party, only to die prematurely in 1994. Tony Blair was elected leader.

In 1989, Barbara Castle left the European Parliament; in 1990, she became Baroness Castle of Blackburn. Her elevation to the peerage caused astonishment too as people knew that she believed the House of Lords was 'a bit of an anachronism', and did not approve of political power being in the hands of a non-elected Assembly.[106] On November 14, she made her maiden speech in the House of Lords. It was political, partisan and contro-versial. And funny. She had, she stated, made three maiden speeches, once in the Commons, once in the European Parliament and once in the Lords. 'You may say' she commented 'Some maiden after 45 years of public life! Indeed a journalist said that politics must be the only profession in which one can be a maiden three times'. She had lost none of her political inten-sity either. She condemned the 'financiers, the big boys, the bankers, the City boys' for their emphasis on profits rather than people and criticised Margaret Thatcher's 'Boadicea chariot-style nationalism'.[107] After her speech, one Lord commented that Lady Castle had 'not lost her fire, her enthusiasm and her capacity for straight talking'. Baroness Castle was 80 years old.

In 1996, now aged 85, Barbara Castle was still fighting for justice. This time for pensioners, alongside the trade unionist Rodney Bickerstaffe.[108] Looking frail, she tottered up to the Labour Party Conference platform to deliver her speech. The same Barbara who had charmed delegates in the 1970s was still in evidence. According to the *Daily Express*, 'she wagged her finger, she flirted with the chairman, she charmed her audience'[109] and received two standing ovations, one at the beginning of her talk, the other when it ended. In her speech, Castle urged for the restoration of the link between pensions and average earnings. But in spite of her blistering ora-tory, conference voted against Castle's proposals. She had lost her final tussle with the Labour Party. But, as ever, she did not give up. Castle warned 'silly' Gordon Brown, the Shadow Chancellor, that she would not rest until the government had restored the link with earnings. And in 2000, a week before her 90 birthday, Castle joined forces with Bickerstaffe at the Labour Party Conference and insisted that a wealthy country like Britain could afford to give dignity to its pensioners. This time 60% of the delegates voted in favour of 'immediate and substantial rises in pensions'. It was seen as a damaging defeat for the new Prime Minister, Tony Blair.

In 1997, the gossip columnist William Hickey proclaimed Barbara Castle a 'National Treasure'. She remained, he argued, a 'furnace of strongly held opinions. More venerable than even Old Labour, she remains passionate, fiery and intellectually undimmed by the passing decades',[110] still enjoying a cigarette and a glass or two of gin before lunch. When she died in 2002, aged 91, she was viewed as an attractive figure from the idealistic past of the Labour Party, one of the few survivors of the great 1945 Parliament, one of the last great female British politicians, a feminist pioneer who wore her ideological heart on her sleeve.

CONCLUSION

For more than twenty years, Barbara Castle was Britain's best-known female Labour politician, one of the most recognisable and widely admired. She was a major figure in the Cabinet of the sixties and seventies, bewitching Harold Wilson with her radical views, a high-octane politician whose inspirational zeal fired up others. She had been forged in the heat of the 1945 Labour Government and was keen for Labour always to demonstrate such passion. She always had, according to Michael Foot, 'great powers of application ... once she got her teeth into a subject it was difficult to get them out again'. Barbara Castle, Foot believed, was 'absolutely born for executive jobs'.[111] Undoubtedly, for most of her political career she was a popular politician. People liked her because they saw her as an authentic North Country lass, someone who was approachable and friendly, and someone who was not grand or imperious. When she became Lady Castle she insisted that people called her Barbara, telling the interviewer on Desert Island Discs that she thought of herself as 'a commoner by heart, by history and by pride'.[112]

But what exactly was her legacy? In many ways, Castle provides a role model of what a strong and transformative Minister could do, regardless of gender. Like Ellen Wilkinson Castle was a conviction politician with a clarity of purpose. First elected at the height of the Labour Party's socialist ascendancy, Castle was formed by this optimistic era and kept to its underlying principles all her life. Her combination of high ideals with a grounded pragmatism allowed her to effect change, not just to talk about it. Her first Cabinet post in Overseas Development was 'a natural' for her and she maintained that she 'loved it because a) this is where I cut my ministerial teeth and b) because it was a great balm to your moral conscience'.[113] Few people, it was thought, could have been so successful in their first Cabinet post, particularly as the first-ever not just the first female Minister for Overseas Development. She made overseas aid a central issue, building the blocks that would allow the next woman Minister, Judith Hart to develop a socialist structure of the kind her mentor had envisaged.

One of Barbara Castle's lasting memorials was as Minister of Transport: she brought in the 70 mph speed limit, the breathalyser, the seat belt and the tachograph now part of the British way of life and yet once the cause of bitterness 'and the favourite topic of a million pub bores'.[114] As a consequence of her determination, innumerable lives were saved. Castle may not have succeeded in creating the coherent transport system she wished for but she managed to halt the closure of railway stations, protect the canal system and make public transport a viable option.

Less propitiously, Castle's brave yet forlorn bid to reform the trade unions almost ended her career. She was shattered by the experience, undermined by her colleagues in the Labour Party and destroyed by the 'concrete heads of the TUC, backed by Jim Callaghan, who refused her attempts to control the shop-floor chaos which once threatened to wreck the economy completely'.[115] Her popularity within the Labour Party plummeted and it took her a long time to regain the admiration of the conference crowd. This failure was thought to cost Castle the chance of becoming the first female Prime Minister. Later on, colleagues admitted it would have been better to introduce Castle's reforms rather than wait for the swingeing measures put forward by Margaret Thatcher. As mentioned earlier, Barbara Castle tried to regain her reputation by promoting equal pay, sponsoring an Act which established her reputation as a feminist icon.

In her final post as Secretary of State for Health and Social Security, she reformed the pension system, removed pay beds out of the NHS, made prescriptions free for children under 16 and for pensioners and brought in child benefits payable to mothers. In Castle's view, the latter policy had triumphed over instinctive male chauvinism and certainly over the wishes of James Callaghan who did not support it.

Barbara Castle stepped further up the political ladder than any other woman in the British Parliament—she was Deputy Prime Minister in all but name. The betting agency Ladbrokes regularly took bets on her becoming the first woman Prime Minister. Castle would have liked to be Prime Minister but believed that 'the Labour Party was not ready for a woman leader'.[116] The defeat of *In Place of Strife*, the press insinuated, meant that she could never lead the Labour Party, never become Prime Minister. In addition, it is alleged that Labour had an in-built resistance to women in positions of power: Bernard Ingram, Castle's press secretary, argued that the Labour Party and trade unionists were 'deeply dyed with male chauvinist piggery'[117] which prohibited women from reaching the very top. Ingram who later became press secretary to Margaret Thatcher is not the first to view trade unions as a homogenous group, or indeed to indulge in union bashing. The reasons why Barbara Castle did not become leader of the Labour Party are complex and cannot be reduced to simple male prejudice. In her later life, Castle morphed into the 'First Lady of Old Labour', a sentimental phrase that has little meaning and absolutely no power attached to it at all.

The next female Cabinet Minister, Judith Hart was also predicted to be the first Labour woman Prime Minister. Like Castle she was left-wing, university educated and married to a supportive husband; she was to become the first Cabinet Minister with children. The next chapter will examine Hart's early political life and her journey towards ministerial office.

NOTES

1. Harold Wilson, *The Labour Government, 1964–70*, Penguin, 1974.
2. See debate on International Development Association Bill, Hansard, February 3, 1964, Vol. 688, cc828–918.
3. Shirley Williams, *Climbing the Bookshelves*, Virago, 2009, p. 203.
4. Anne Perkins, *Red Queen: The Authorized Biography of Barbara Castle*, Macmillan, 2003, p. 188.
5. South African born Kenyan politician, Minister of Agriculture. He was later assassinated by Idi Amin's agents.
6. Violent Bonham Carter to Castle, November 19, 1964, MS Castle 260, Bodleian Library.
7. 'Tom', *Daily Mail*, October 18, 1964, MS Castle 260, Bodleian Library. She also received a letter from Paul Johnson, editor of the *New Statesman* who wrote that 'there is no-one in Britain who could do it better'and from the editor of the *Blackburn Times*.
8. Interview with Barbara Castle, undated, Women's Library, 80DH/02/01/07 Box 1.
9. Hansard, November 10, 1964, Vol. 701, cc840–845.
10. In 1940 the Fabian Society established the Fabian Colonial Bureau to research and plan left-wing approaches to the British Empire. It commissioned research, briefed Labour MPs and campaigned on issues. See Lydia Riley, '"The Winds of Change Are Blowing Economically": The Labour Party and British Overseas Development, 1940s–1960s', in Andrew W. M. Smith and Chris Jeppesen, *Britain, France and the Decolonisation of Africa*, UCL Press, 2017 for penetrating insights into the development of Labour Party thinking.
11. Anne Perkins, *Red Queen: The Authorized Biography of Barbara Castle*, 2003, p. 192.
12. Ibid., p. 205.
13. It was signed by Arthur Bottomley, Secretary of State for Commonwealth Relations; Fred Peart, Minister of Agriculture, Fisheries and Food; Ray Gunter, Cabinet Minister of Labour and Edward Short, Chief Whip and Parliamentary Secretary to the Treasury, MS Castle, Bodleian Libraries.
14. Barbara Castle, *Fighting All the Way*, 1993, p. 356.
15. Ibid., p. 357.
16. Anonymous annotated photograph, u/dated, MS Castle 260.
17. Ibid., p. 260.
18. Lydia Riley, '"The Winds of Change Are Blowing Economically": The Labour Party and British Overseas Development, 1940s–1960s', in Andrew W. M. Smith and Chris Jeppesen, *Britain, France and the Decolonisation of Africa*, UCL Press, 2017, p. 59.

19. Ibid.
20. Notes on Government Achievements, July 1965, MS Castle 260.
21. Undated notes, MS Castle 260, Bodleian Library.
22. *The Standard*, Tanzania, April 23, 1965.
23. Barbara Castle, *Fighting All the Way*, 1993, p. 344.
24. *The Standard*, Tanzania, April 23, 1965, p. 1.
25. Barbara Castle, *The Castle Diaries, 1964–1970*, March 23, 1965, Weidenfeld and Nicolson, 1984.
26. *Daily Express*, July 9, 1965, p. 11.
27. Anne Perkins, *Red Queen: The Authorized Biography of Barbara Castle*, 2003, p. 207.
28. The next two Ministers, Anthony Greenwood and Arthur Bottomley, served in the Cabinet but not as Ministers of Overseas Development.
29. *Daily Express*, December 23, 1965, p. 1.
30. *The Christian Science Monitor*, January 10, 1966, p. 4.
31. Barbara Castle, *The Castle Diaries, 1964–1970*, December 29, 1965, Weidenfeld and Nicolson, 1984, p. 82.
32. Barbara Castle, *Fighting All the Way*, 1993, p. 372.
33. Harold Wilson, *The Labour Government, 1964–1970*, Penguin, 1971, p. 249.
34. *The Christian Science Monitor*, January 10, 1966.
35. Anne Perkins, *Red Queen: The Authorized Biography of Barbara Castle*, 2003, p. 210.
36. *Daily Mirror*, January 7, 1966, p. 2.
37. Hansard, February 20, 1967, Vol. 742, cc1333.
38. *The Stage*, December 28, 1967, p. 5.
39. Barbara Castle, *Fighting All the Way*, 1993, p. 375.
40. *The Sunday Times*, July 2, 1967, p. 11.
41. Ibid., p. 11.
42. Quoted in Anne Perkins, *Red Queen: The Authorized Biography of Barbara Castle*, 2003, p. 233.
43. Barbara Castle, *Fighting All the Way*, 1993, p. 398.
44. Quoted in Barbara Castle, *Fighting All the Way*, p. 399.
45. Michelle K. Ryan and S. Alexander Haslam, 'The Glass Cliff: Exploring the Dynamics Surrounding the Appointment of Women to Precarious Leadership Positions', *Academy of Management Review*, Vol. 32, 2007, pp. 549–572 for a discussion on this.
46. Richard Crossman, *The Diaries of a Cabinet Minister*, Trinity Press, April 16, 1968.
47. Bernard Ingham, *The Sunday Express*, May 2002, p. 39.
48. *Daily Mirror*, April 11, 1968, p. 1.
49. Jo Haines, quoted in Lisa Martineau, *Barbara Castle*, Andre Deutsch, 2000, p. 218.
50. BC Diary, November 16, 1968.
51. Ben Pimlott, *Harold Wilson*, HarperCollins, 1992, p. 530.
52. *The Sunday Express*, April 4, 1982, p. 6.
53. Ibid.
54. Quoted in Anne Perkins, *Red Queen: The Authorized Biography of Barbara Castle*, 2003, p. 289.
55. Ibid., p. 289.

56. Barbara Castle, *Fighting All the Way*, 1993, p. 421.

57. *Daily Mirror*, January 18, 1969, p. 1.

58. Ibid.

59. Richard John Tyler, "*Victims of Our History*", *the Labour Party and in Place of Strife, 1968 to 1969*, PhD thesis, Queen Mary College, 2004, p. 117.

60. Eric Silver, *Victor Feather T.U.C.*, Victor Gollancz, 1973, p. 135.

61. Richard John Tyler, "*Victims of Our History*", *the Labour Party and in Place of Strife, 1968 to 1969*, Unpublished PhD thesis, Queen Mary College, 2004, p. 13.

62. Ibid.

63. These attitudes remain. In 2016, when Len McLuskey met Angela Eagle at the Labour Party Conference he told one activist 'you kiss her, I'll hit her'. He claimed, as with Feather, that it was a joke.

64. Ben Pimlott, *Harold Wilson*, HarperCollins, 1992, p. 533.

65. Richard John Tyler, "*Victims of Our History*", *the Labour Party and in Place of Strife*, 1968 to 1969, Unpublished PhD thesis, Queen Mary College, 2004, p. 272.

66. *Daily Mirror*, June 19, 1969, p. 3.

67. *The Illustrated London News*, September 6, 1969, p. 8.

68. Barbara Castle, *Fighting All the Way*, 1993, p. 402.

69. Ibid., p. 425.

70. Barbara Castle Diary, July 1, 1968.

71. Interview with Shirley Williams, Stephen Meredith, 'A "Brooding Oppressive Shadow?" The Labour Alliance, the "Trade Union Question" and the Trajectory of Revisionist Social Democracy, c1969–1975', *Labour History Review*, December 2017, p. 261.

72. Stephen Meredith, 'A "Brooding Oppressive Shadow?" The Labour Alliance, the "Trade Union Question" and the Trajectory of Revisionist Social Democracy, c1969–1975', *Labour History Review*, December 2017, p. 261.

73. Barbara Castle, *Fighting All the Way*, 1993, p. 409.

74. Quoted in Anne Perkins, *Red Queen: The Authorized Biography of Barbara Castle*, 2003, p. 325.

75. *Daily Mirror*, April 25, 1969, p. 4.

76. Barbara Castle Diary, September 4, 1969.

77. Barbara Castle, Hansard, February 9, 1970, Vol. 795, cc914.

78. Ibid.

79. Margaret Thatcher, MP for Finchley, Hansard, February 9, 1970, Vol. 795, cc1020.

80. Ibid., cc1026.

81. Ronald Bell, MP for Buckhampshire, Hansard, February 9, 1970, Vol. 795, cc914.

82. Interview with Barbara Castle, undated, Women's Library, 80DH/02/01/07 Box 1.

83. Anne Perkins, *Red Queen: The Authorized Biography of Barbara Castle*, 2003, p. 334.

84. Ibid., p. 325.

85. Tom Driberg was a Labour MP. He was said to be a double agent, employed by M15 but also receiving money from a Czech spy for providing information to the Soviets.

86. Barbara Castle, *Fighting All the Way*, 1993, p. 428.
87. *Daily Mirror*, January 29, 1974, p. 1.
88. *Daily Express*, March 5, 1974, p. 10.
89. Rodney Bickerstaffe, May 14, 2002, p. 5.
90. There were nine of them. *Daily Express*, March 3, 1975, p. 9.
91. Barbara Castle Diary, April 8, 1976.
92. Anthony King and Nicholas Allen, '"Off with Their Heads": British Prime Ministers and the Power to Dismiss', *British Journal of Political Science*, April 2010, p. 268.
93. Barbara Castle, *Fighting All the Way*, 1993, p. 490.
94. Barbara Castle Diary, April 11, 1976.
95. Barbara Castle, *Daily Mirror*, September 28, 1976, p. 5.
96. Interview with John Cunningham, *The Guardian*, March 1, 1977, p. 11.
97. Barbara Castle, *Fighting All the Way*, 1993, p. 490.
98. Barbara Castle, Interview with John Cunningham, *The Guardian*, March 1, 1977, p. 11.
99. Barbara Castle Diary, February 11, 1975.
100. Quoted in Anne Perkins, *Red Queen: The Authorized Biography of Barbara Castle*, 2003, p. 428.
101. Barbara Castle, *Fighting All the Way*, 1993, p. 445.
102. Ibid.
103. *The Telegraph*, May 4, 2002, p. 3. This quote echoed one made by Norman Shrapnel in *The Guardian*, November 1959.
104. Barbara Castle, *Fighting All the Way*, 1993, p. 542.
105. Ibid., p. 537.
106. Desert Island Discs, November 16, 1990.
107. HL Debate, November 14, 1990, Vol. 523, cc357.
108. Rodney Bickerstaffe (1945–2017) was General Secretary of the National Union of Public Employees and later of UNISON, at the time Britain's largest trade union.
109. *Daily Express*, December 3, 1996, p. 16.
110. *Daily Express*, September 13, 1997, p. 41.
111. Michael Foot, quoted in Wilfred De'Ath, *Barbara Castle: A Portrait from Life*, 1970, pp. 31–43.
112. Desert Island Discs, November 16, 1990.
113. Barbara Castle, quoted in Wilfred De'Ath, *Barbara Castle: A Portrait from Life*, 1970, pp. 9–22.
114. *Daily Express*, June 10, 1993, p. 44.
115. Ibid., p. 44.
116. Barbara Castle, *Fighting All the Way*, 1993, p. 604.
117. Bernard Ingham, *The Sunday Express*, May 2002, p. 39.

CHAPTER 8

From Burnley to Lanark:
Judith Hart, 1924–1968

1945 was a momentous year for socialists and feminists: Labour won a landslide victory, Ellen Wilkinson was appointed the first female Minister of Education, Barbara Castle was elected to Parliament and Judith, a bright young woman from Burnley, Lancashire gained a first-class degree in Sociology at the London School of Economics. Judith was 21 years old: she had come of age in a brave new world.

In 1959, Judith Hart was elected MP for Lanark, a Scottish constituency located in the Clyde Valley. She joined the newly elected Margaret Thatcher and twelve Labour women in the House of Commons, one of whom was Barbara Castle who had been in Parliament for 14 years. Castle warmed to her new colleague, viewing her as a kindred spirit, a woman who was 'dynamic, physically attractive, courageous and challenging'.[1] Castle helped Hart familiarise herself with the ways of the House of Commons and the two became friends. The women MPs shared a political philosophy, later agreeing on the great issues of the day such as whether or not Britain should stay in the EEC, how they could undermine the illegal Rhodesian regime, how to get rid of nuclear weapons and how to make Labour more left-wing. Their only serious disagreement was to be over *In Place of Strife* when Castle accused Judith Hart of 'conniving' with Dick Crossman to wreck her proposals.[2]

Hart and Castle may have developed similar beliefs, but Hart's background and her political journey were very much her own. Constance Mary, as she was named on her birth certificate, was born on September 18, 1924 at 51 Ennismore Street, Burnley, Lancashire, the daughter of Harry Ridehalgh, a lino-type printer and Lily a schoolteacher and Baptist lay preacher. In 1936, she was baptised and changed her name to Judith; she was later to change her accent from northern working class to an accent used by people with power, prestige and money.[3] The year 1936 was the year that she started noticing the poverty, the unemployment and the hardship around her. It was the year of

© The Author(s) 2019
P. Bartley, *Labour Women in Power*,
https://doi.org/10.1007/978-3-030-14288-9_8

Ellen Wilkinson's Jarrow Crusade. Judith became conscious of the 'groups of the unemployed standing at street corners and the rows of empty shops, closed down through lack of trade' in her hometown and began to question why this was so.[4] She went to her public library to find out, borrowed a copy of *Das Kapital* by Karl Marx and began to form her ideas about the causes of poverty. By the time, she was 16 she was 'political and extremely involved. … I was not thinking of a political career, but I was deeply interested and concerned'.[5] When she was 18, she joined the Labour Party and became converted to socialism by witnessing the effects of the Hungry Thirties in her home town.[6] Judith's emerging political beliefs were not derived from experience as were Ellen Wilkinson's, nor was she submerged in politics by her parents like Barbara Castle but they grew from her search for an explanation why poverty was tolerated in a civilised society. Judith's parents were 'liberals with a small "l"' who never engaged in formal political activity. However, her mother must have shaped her daughter's emerging civic conscience: a lay preacher, Mrs Ridehalgh was a woman aware of 'her own social responsibilities to the community, involved in a lot of activities and things non-political'.[7]

Judith was an academic high-flyer, winning a scholarship to Clitheroe Girls' Grammar School where she always came top of her class and eventually became head girl. This idyllic teenage life ended abruptly when her mother died. Judith was fourteen years old. She later confessed that she went a bit 'haywire' and 'did naughty things' at school like encouraging her classmates to climb on the desks and walk around the classroom without touching the floor.[8] This was considered unruly behaviour in the stricter world of the 1930s, and her relationship with the headmistress deteriorated. When Judith took a day off school to visit the Tate Gallery in London and refused to apologise for doing so, she was demoted from her position as head girl.

The death of her mother unsettled the teenage Judith considerably, but she suppressed her emotions and pretended to be tougher than she was. Years later, one newspaper reporter commented that 'a fountain of tears can bubble over when a tender spot is touched'.[9] The memory of her mother could 'discharge a flow of stopped emotion, an ineffable sense of loss, in her. … She is reckoned tough and able and a political realist – but the memory of her dead mother can turn her into a bereaved girl. Yet she would never, never cry to get her own way at the office'.[10] Generally, Judith held her emotions in check, a characteristic tendency which led people to assume that she was something of a 'cold fish'. It was apparent that her cool, quiet and thoughtful manner marked a contrast to the fiery, eloquent and passionate Barbara Castle. However, those who worked with her closely saw another side, especially when she was deeply involved in an issue, a person or a policy: they described a tearful, angry and passionate Judith, not at all composed and unruffled, not at all 'cold'.[11]

Judith may have been slightly rebellious at school but she studied hard, did well in her exams and won a scholarship to the London School of Economics, which had relocated to the safety of Cambridge during the

Blitz. Here she played an active role in Cambridge student politics, becoming secretary of the Labour Club and Chair of the Labour Party and then gained that first-class honours degree. When she left university, Judith found a job as lecturer at a teacher training college in Portsmouth. Here she met her future husband Dr Tony Hart at a trade union meeting; the two were engaged within a week and married six weeks later, in April 1946.[12] She was 21 and Tony five years older.[13] It seemed a curious act of passion from someone whose self-image was essentially rational. Undoubtedly Tony Hart, who was more politically experienced, clearly appealed to her intellect as well as her heart, somebody on her own wavelength who 'felt absolutely as I did about politics'.[14] She insisted that she could never ever have fallen in love with a Tory. The two remained together until she died—this was one of the great political love matches like that of Harold and Mary Wilson, Tony and Caroline Benn, Michael Foot and Jill Craigie; all couples who became friends of Mr and Mrs Hart.

In the 1940s and 1950s, men were considered the main breadwinners and women were expected to stay at home so when Tony Hart found a new job in Dorset it was assumed that Judith would give up her lecturing and move with him. However, Judith had no wish to be a housewife and soon found work as a researcher for the Ministry of Health. In 1949, the 25-year-old Mrs Hart made her political debut running for office on the municipal council; two years later she stood as a parliamentary candidate for Bournemouth West, a safe Conservative constituency. It was she later claimed 'merely a job one did for the party, for it was a hopeless seat'.[15] No one was surprised when Judith lost the election, but she was clearly destined for a political career. In her first speech to the 1951 Labour Party Conference, she suggested that it was a mistake for Labour merely to focus on food, housing and high prices when talking to women. 'Do not underestimate the womenfolk', she warned as 'every woman in this country wants, more than anything else in this world, the guarantee and the secure hope of peace in her children's lifetime'.[16] Hart was, of course, sending conference a clear message that her political ideas were broader than domestic programmes. Her speech was warmly received: she was making herself known on a wider Labour platform.

A couple of years later Tony Hart was appointed lecturer at the University of Strathclyde, and this time the whole family relocated to Scotland and found a council house to rent.[17] In 1955, Judith Hart made a second attempt at running for Parliament, contesting Aberdeen South, then held by the Tory Lady Priscilla Tweedsmuir. Mrs Hart ran a superb election campaign and reduced Tweedsmuir's majority significantly. Meanwhile, she took a part-time job as a researcher for East Kilbride New Town Development Corporation.[18] Little by little Hart was making a national name for herself: she broadcast on Woman's Hour and wrote articles for two left-wing papers, the *Clarion* and *The Tribune*. She was ambitious and not afraid to promote her career. In February 1957, she wrote to Michael Foot, offering to write for *Tribune* if he decided to print a Scottish edition. She told Foot that 'plenty of things are waiting to be written about – the closing of Clydebank's Royal Ordnance Factory (ROF), redundancy among building workers, New Towns, local authority fee-paying schools, local authority marriage bars, emigration, high rents, a socialist amateur film group, provision for handicapped children – all with a special Scots slant to them'.[19] Michael Foot replied that a Scottish edition of *Tribune* was unlikely; Judith Hart however was being noticed.

MP FOR LANARK, OCTOBER 1959–JUNE 1987[20]

In 1957, this talented young woman managed to get herself selected as parliamentary candidate for the constituency of Lanark, a huge constituency stretching from Beattock to East Kilbride and containing the mining areas of Lesmahagow, Douglas and Coalburn, the industrial areas of Carluke, Stonehouse and Larkhall as well as 100,000 hectares of countryside.[21] The Conservatives were in government; Harold Macmillan was Prime Minister; and Labour was led by Hugh Gaitskell. Hart's adoption speech was fluent, radical and persuasive. She told the selection committee that they needed someone to fight the election vigorously and effectively and that she was the person to do this. One of the things that attracted her to the constituency she stated was 'fighting the reactionary vicious kind of Toryism represented by Mr Patrick Maitland. If you are fighting a Tory, then let him be a real Tory, then you know where you are, you can roll your sleeves up. … There is going to be a tremendous amount to be done in our next term of office. There are all the measures which will have to be taken at once to wipe out the worst of the evil effects of Toryism upon the workers of this country and upon the oppressed people of the Commonwealth. … It is therefore all the more essential that we have a clear idea of our socialist purpose. … And that to me means public ownership in one form or another'.[22] The selection committee was convinced.

Many of the seats offered to women candidates were not safe seats—Lanark was no exception. Patrick Maitland, the Conservative sitting MP was popular and even though Judith Hart lived in East Kilbride, worked for the East Kilbride Corporation, had an efficient party machine behind her and the facts of her future constituency at her fingertips it would be a difficult seat to win. Neverthless, in the 1959 general election, bookmakers at East Kilbride gave Hart a 7–2 chance of overturning Maitland as MP.[23] The bookies were right and she beat Maitland by 540 votes.[24] Unlike Maitland, she lived and worked in Lanark and could draw on her local expertise to run her campaign. She was to fight—and win—seven more elections, remaining MP for the district for 28 years.[25] On October 21, the new MP for Lanark took her Oath of Allegiance in the House of Commons. At 5:27 p.m., November 3 she delivered her maiden speech, making a plea for Scotland and in particular for miners in her constituency facing pit closures. She told the House that in the mining villages of Lanark, 'there will be a threat of decay to the community' if the mines closed as the 'whole social fabric of community life' would be 'grievously disturbed. We must think in terms of communities and not just of individuals'. Hart asked for financial aid for her constituency and new industries based on science and modern technology to be brought in.[26] Less than a month later, she warned the Under-Secretary of State for Scotland that if he did not 'take action to promote alternative employment, he must accept responsibility for the decay in villages resulting from pit closures'.[27] The MP for Lanark was all too aware of the potential social dislocation when local industries shut down. 'When young people move because there are no prospects of employment for them, they leave behind older people and ... there are very serious effects ... to the people left behind'.[28] Later on, when Labour was in power Hart did everything in her power to bring industry and work to her constituency.

Judith Hart soon gained a reputation as a 'well-informed and hard-working member, with strong views of her own, on the Left-wing of the Labour Party'.[29] She joined the Tribune group and served as an Executive on the Victory for Socialism faction.[30] She was a fierce anti-imperialist. In the early hours of one July morning, Hart spoke in a debate in the House of Commons about the repression of the black majority in Southern Rhodesia. She asked the Conservative Government to inform the white settlers in Southern Rhodesia 'that they cannot hope to solve the problems of their part of Africa by reviving old-fashioned nineteenth century ideas that one can kill political ideas with a gun'.[31] She was referring to the repressive action of the Rhodesian authorities in Bulawayo which had occurred a few days earlier. Here, a demonstration of approximately 7000 Africans had been dispersed by force, 250 people had been arrested and beaten up by the police and nine protesters had died—merely for asking the government to grant them the vote. Hart continually fought against racial inequality, joining the Committee Against Racial Discrimination in Sport, the Anti-Apartheid Movement and urging Harold Macmillan the Conservative PM to expel South Africa from the Commonwealth.[32] All her political life she remained on the left-wing of the Labour Party, willing to speak out against injustice, often with scant regard for her parliamentary career.

In common with many on the left-wing, Hart wanted to abolish nuclear weapons. More particularly she condemned the positioning of the nuclear Polaris submarine at the Clyde naval base. In her view, the holding of nuclear weapons inflamed already provocative situations. She warned the House of Commons that submarines armed with nuclear weapons were 'capable of wreaking the most tremendous damage – it is a killer weapon on a massive scale ... likely to increase provocation. ... As soon as a weapon is developed by one side a counter weapon is developed by the other side ... the only way to defend the people of this country in a nuclear age is to prevent the outbreak of war. ... the whole policy on which Western defence is based ... that of providing deterrence in order to prevent the outbreak of war, is out of date and dangerous'.[33] At the 1961 Labour Party Conference, she assured delegates that her constituency party had 'expressed its complete and whole-hearted opposition to the establishment of a Polaris base' arguing that the construction of a base in the Holy Loch was 'an invitation to obliteration without representation'.[34] Hart was committed to unilateral nuclear disarmament, joined the Campaign for Nuclear Disarmament (CND) and walked on the first Aldermaston march with her husband and her two young sons. When Pat Arrowsmith, Secretary of the Direct Action Group of CND, went on hunger strike Judith Hart visited her in Gateside Prison, Greenock and persuaded her to stop.[35] However, in September 1963 Hart resigned from the Executive Committee of CND 'attributing her decision in part to an increasing burden of work in her marginal constituency'. She confessed to one reporter that 'I have always been a rather theoretical kind of person' and felt out of sympathy 'with many of the major activities of the Campaign' such as its various forms of civil disobedience.[36] Construction of the submarines went ahead: Polaris continued until 1996 when it was replaced by Trident.

On March 20, 1962 Hart introduced her first Bill, a private members' Bill to remove the property qualification for jury service.[37] At the time, people could only serve on juries if they were ratepayers or property owners which virtually excluded all married women and women and men who were less well off. 'It is ridiculous' protested Hart 'that in these days juries should be chosen only from the top layers of society'.[38] Even Lord Devlin, one of the top judges, expressed concern that British juries were predominantly male, middle-aged, middle-minded and middle-class. A Conservative MP Charles Doughty opposed Hart's Bill on the grounds that he was 'worried by the prospect that the majority of juries would contain more women than men. They were, he thought, undoubtedly more emotional in their thinking'.[39] Doughty's argument prevailed and Hart narrowly lost the vote by 178–167, just eleven votes short of victory. In 1974, the Labour Government amended the Act allowing those between the ages of 18 and 70 who were registered to vote in elections eligible for jury service.

Hart knew that a politician's life was precarious and realised that she would have to work hard to keep hold of Lanark for Labour. She was seen as a 'first-class' MP, ceaselessly spending her 'time and talents' helping her constituents and her local communities, becoming deeply involved in the lives of individuals who sought help. Here her compassion and kindness were at its strongest. People in Lanark knew that she listened. Indeed Hart received one of the heaviest posts of any MP at that time: in any one year, she helped solve well over 1000 problems, all of which added up 'to a lot of anxiety, distress, and sometimes downright despair'.[40] She knew that people's troubles were 'often urgent, desperate ... often they concern families and jobs, money and housing, all kinds of worries that can seem insoluble without a friend'. The help and advice she gave were never made public because each individual's circumstance was highly confidential.[41] Hart's surviving constituency papers are colossal, comprising 38 very big boxes piled high, mostly with letters from constituents: one of the boxes contained 3300 letters from constituents who wanted help, all of them categorised into name, electoral district and problem raised, marked as to what measures were taken and whether or not they were resolved.[42] She was an exemplary MP, helped by two loyal and hard-working individuals: Steven Small her constituency agent and later by Maggie Sidgreaves who became her political advisor.[43]

Hart's papers illustrate the range of individual problems MPs were presented with: hospital neglect, housing, pensions, benefit entitlement, capital gains tax, heating, tax issues, police victimisation, police arrests, gas and electricity supplies, industrial injuries, student grants, threatened eviction, poverty, naturalisation, visas, handicapped children, legal questions and planning permission. Some constituents asked Hart for advice on how to switch from an endowment to a repayment mortgage, how to find a relative who had disappeared, how to obtain a powered tricycle for a disabled constituent, how to stop being barred from a local pub and even how to help someone disturbed by the bee-keeping of a neighbour. Each individual was given advice.

Judith Hart never used the standard formulaic letter given to MPs to write to their constituents.[44] Each letter was personal, each problem dealt with promptly and sympathetically; no case was too small or insignificant. She was 'happy that her constituents feel they can bring their troubles to her and glad that she can often – though not always – help them'.[45] For one case involving a homeless schizophrenic Judith Hart wrote to fourteen different individuals and organisations trying to find a safe home and appropriate supervision for the vulnerable individual. Naturally, this generated a mountain of work as Hart and her office staff investigated each individual's case, checked facts, badgered officials and acted tough to get things done. Sometimes, she admitted that 'no matter the effort, a problem can defy solution—there's no magic wand that guarantees happiness'.[46] Years after her death, one of her former constituents wrote about Hart in an internet blog, saying how she had transformed his life by helping him gain a local authority grant to go to university.[47]

Hart tried to make her constituency a better place for all who lived in it. She successfully campaigned to supply mains electricity and mains water to the villages, to fight hospital closures, to set up maternity units in local hospitals, to improve ambulance services, to build new hospital extensions or to overcome school crises. In addition, she pressurised the government to provide better bus services and fought hard for an integrated road-and-rail system after the Beeching cuts threatened closure of the Glasgow line.

By the 1964 general election, Judith Hart had served Lanark for five years. Given her investment in the constituency, she was confident of victory, despite a scurrilous leaflet distributed by the Tory candidate which portrayed her as an unpatriotic crazy socialist under the control of Russia. In her view, it was the 'lowest and most degrading political conduct', full of inaccuracies and misquotations.[48] Hart's response was to attack the Conservative record, not the candidate's personality: she was far too principled to dirty her hands with character assassination. Instead, she denounced the thirteen wasted years of

Tory government, 'years to be remembered for the weakening of community service, the promotion of self-interest, rampant profiteering, recurring crises – and above all, the neglect of Scotland'.[49] She blamed the Tories for under-investment, for closing down the coal mines and not encouraging industry in areas with high unemployment. She promised that a Labour Government would site new industries in areas where jobs were needed.

The mining community was badly stricken. In 1950, there had been 60 mines in her constituency but each year more pits closed and more miners were thrown out of work. Judith Hart fought hard to keep the pits open, to attract new industry at Lesmahagow and Lanark and even to create new towns at Stonehouse and East Kilbride. In the House of Commons, she protested about the pit closures and asked for road improvements, better hospitals, community facilities in the new towns, the demolition of unfit houses, improved housing provision, more electric power stations and overall greater investment in Scotland. When Labour returned to power, it subsidised loss-making pits, and encouraged by Judith Hart, mounted a massive effort to protect workers' rights. The government introduced earnings-related unemployment pay, redundancy payments and a miners' pension scheme. It trebled industrial training and carried out a programme to cut industrial development in the south and to bring it to Scotland.[50] Nonetheless, by 1970 despite the efforts of Hart and her colleagues, only 3 pits remained in Lanarkshire.[51]

UNDER-SECRETARY OF STATE FOR SCOTLAND, OCTOBER 1964–APRIL 1966

In the 1964 election, Judith Hart increased her majority from 540 to 5320, a staggering increase. And Labour was back in power. Harold Wilson, the new Prime Minister, appointed Hart to her first ministerial job as Under-Secretary of State for Scotland. She had taken her first step on the political ladder. From October 1964 to the general election in March 1966, Judith Hart was at the Scottish Office under Willie Ross,[52] entirely concerned with home policy, and 'with restricted aspects even of that'.[53] It was a small office, a good training ground for an inexperienced newly appointed Minister, particularly when Ross gave Hart a 'pretty free run in her own field ... looking after health, education, children's services and the arts'[54] and expected her to deputise for him in the House of Commons. Suddenly Judith Hart was required to be an expert on the prevalence of rickets in Glasgow children, maternity units in West Fife, ambulance services, the construction of community centres in new towns, the shortage of teachers, school building programmes, pay and pensions of teachers, teaching Gaelic in schools and the supply of artificial limbs to patients—and be adept at defending these issues in the House of Commons. Hart was more than capable of mastering a brief and quickly learned the mechanics of government and of how to run a department. She soon gained a reputation as an accomplished and hard-working junior Minister.

In the 1960s, sexism was more rampant than sexual liberation. The *Daily Mirror's* comment that 'the male eye tends to follow admiringly when Judith Hart, smart and poised MP for Lanark, walks through the parliamentary lobbies'[55] was a typically chauvinist remark designed to flatter her. Hart ignored such comments. The Scottish Office was a very busy Ministry with Government Committees and meetings and debates and legislation in the House of Commons. She remained at the House until about 11 at night. She travelled up to St Andrew's House in Edinburgh 'for discussions, work with officials, public engagements and speeches and conferences, sometimes stretching into the weekend'.[56] On Friday evenings, she liked to be in Lanark or East Kilbride for her regular surgery and constituency engagements.[57]

Judith Hart made a significant impact in her ministerial post by encouraging her department to pioneer new approaches in social work and criminal justice.[58] Firstly, she took a 'long hard look at the reorganisation necessary in the social work services' to help the 'children in trouble' and coordinated the various Scottish social services which dealt with children and families at risk.[59] She instigated an integrated service which helped vulnerable families and in so doing cut down the rate of juvenile crime.

Secondly, the Scottish Health Service improved under her and Labour's watch. On September 16, 1965, Judith Hart opened an extension to Huntly Jubilee Hospital and witnessed the first phase of the extensions to Aberdeen Royal Infirmary which later provided 130 more beds, a large X-ray department and a four-theatre suite.[60] One year later, Hart opened a Maternity Unit in East Kilbride, something she had urged as the local member of parliament.[61] In addition, she initiated extended visiting hours for parents with children in Scottish hospitals, uneasy that in 45% of hospitals parents were allowed in for less than two hours a day. 'It is not much good' Hart insisted 'in removing a child's tonsils if you send him home with an emotional disturbance. ... I am convinced that if we dealt correctly with children we would eliminate a great deal of the mental disturbance in later life'.[62] In February 1966, inspired by Hart's local measures, the government compelled all hospitals to lengthen visiting hours for children in their wards. Thirdly, Judith Hart encouraged the Labour Government to invigorate the economy through the Scottish Plan, a scheme in which the government awarded £2000 million for new investment, thus creating 130,000 jobs. Scottish unemployment fell to its lowest for 10 years.

Judith Hart was the first of the five women Cabinet Ministers to be a mother as well as a politician. At 5:30 a.m. Thursday September 29, 1949, her son Richard was born in Ward 6 of the private ward at the Camelia Hospital, Poole. Like many a proud mother, Judith Hart recorded in a special notebook that he weighed 9 lb 3 oz and had a thatch of dark brown hair.[63] On Tuesday October 4, she noted that if it was near a feed, 'he cries when I hold him. Seems to recognise me by smell. Will gaze towards my face when I talk to him'.[64] In 1953, another boy, Stephen was born. When her sons were young, she declined trips abroad because she did not want to 'be missing from their environment or disturb their development'.[65] She stated that she had to fight against herself 'very hard' not to be a possessive mother. When they were older if the boys were late home, she worried; if they stayed out all night, she sat up waiting. As they grew up, her sons became politically active and at home were 'full of political advice', clearly proud and happy at their mother's achievements as she was of theirs.[66]

As a wife and mother, Judith Hart tried hard to balance the requirements of home and work. When she was a young MP without ministerial responsibility, she was able to stay in Lanark for some of the week and 'the long Parliamentary recesses gave her time to spend with her family'.[67] However, when she was appointed Under-Secretary of State life became difficult as she was forced to leave her husband and children in Scotland, live in a bedsit in London and dash home every weekend.[68] She told Melanie Philips that 'for the children, just the knowledge that you weren't sleeping in the same house at nights and never being able to see you in the morning and evenings wasn't fair to them'.[69] Tony Hart complained that he 'wasn't happy, she wasn't happy, the kids weren't happy'.[70] He was worried about his wife, writing that 'last night you sounded a little depressed. Anyway, you sounded as though you would have appreciated my company. I did so wish I was nearer, to give you some support, even if only to discuss the little irritating annoyances and fears. ... I do love you my dearest dearest, clever girl'.[71]

A woman MP, especially one with children, needs a strong supportive husband, one who is not daunted by his wife's success. Tony Hart was considerate enough to find a job in London and move the family down to the capital. He insisted that he did not have a 'slippers-and-hearth' approach to marriage, informing one reporter that 'in my world we don't wait for the women to pour out the coffee. We just cope with things like that ourselves'. Judith Hart was also fortunate in 'having an extremely good person who comes each morning to do all the housework. A sort of au-pair-plus – someone who is about 21 – does the cooking. ... If an absolute disaster occurs nowadays my sons can make themselves cheese on toast'.[72] Moreover, she had a sympathetic mother-in-law to help run the household and look after the children.[73] Hart recognised that bringing up children and holding down a full-time job required a 'certain amount of organisation. If you get the organisation right things look after themselves. We occasionally have a crisis, but not often'.[74]

MINISTER OF STATE FOR COMMONWEALTH AFFAIRS, APRIL 1966–JULY 1967

When Labour was re-elected in 1966 Judith Hart was 41 years old. She now enjoyed a comfortable majority of 7740. She had nursed her constituency carefully and ran a good election campaign. Humour helped: heart-shaped stickers and heart-shaped beer mats were distributed to the electorate in an attempt to gain votes. Harold Wilson recognised her achievements and promoted her to Minister of State at the Commonwealth Relations Office under Herbert Bowden, Secretary of State for Commonwealth Affairs.[75] Hart had proved to be a competent and innovative Minister in the Scottish Office and had a well-known interest in Commonwealth: she was a former vice-chair of the Movement for Colonial Freedom and had been particularly concerned with the problems of Commonwealth immigrants and would-be immigrants to Britain.[76] It was one step up the ministerial ladder from Under-Secretary and a job which would require travel. Fortunately, her sons were now teenagers and no longer needed constant maternal supervision. Judith Hart, now unencumbered by very young children, was at liberty to concentrate on her political career.

The member for Lanark quickly switched her focus from Scottish domestic politics to international affairs, answering questions in the House of Commons on the Commonwealth rather than Scotland. The *Scottish Miner* judged that she immediately 'felt at home' in the Commonwealth Office because she was a 'profound believer in what she sees as a new and increasingly radical multi-racial Commonwealth of Nations'.[77] One newspaper described her work in a less flattering and rather sexist manner. The reporter stated that 'Herbert Bowden was still bed-ridden yesterday, so Judith Hart a mere woman, did the Commonwealth chores. A morning Cabinet on Malta, Malta again in the House with criticism coming in barrages: Zambia's £14 million support plan; the end of the West Indies statehood crisis; plus an interview with the Governor of Gibraltar. A dizzy round she completed to high praise from all sides'.[78] Even the female literary editor of the *Tribune* felt compelled to ask whether her husband and children had suffered any neglect, a question which irritated Mrs Hart who nevertheless felt obliged to explain at great length how her domestic life was structured.[79] The reporter was told that Hart's son Richard had just won an open scholarship in mathematics to Cambridge providing 'a spectacular answer to those who still complain that the children of professional women were neglected, backward, delinquent and worse'.[80]

Predictably, some newspapers seemed more interested in the new Minister's looks than her brain. 'The quick click of high heels yesterday sounded down the corridors of power, as one of Britain's rulers headed home to help with dinner. Scots MP Mrs Judith Hart is the most glamorous woman ever to rule over a Government department as well as a home'.[81] Judith Hart retaliated, pointing out that 'women have to triumph over prejudice by sheer ability'.[82] Indeed, Hart's new appointment would make full use of a brain which was more piercing than any stiletto. Tensions in Rhodesia, issues in Ghana, Zambia, Sarawak, a new constitution in Bermuda, the situation in St Kitts, Nevis and Anguilla, a Malawi Republic Bill, Singaporean independence and British emigration to Australia and Canada represent a sample of the issues she and her department would have to resolve.

THE RHODESIAN CRISIS

Judith Hart's political acuity was harshly tested when Harold Wilson gave her specific responsibility for developing and overseeing Labour policy on Rhodesia.[83] She agreed to the mission even though she had 'no power, responsibility without power, that's me at present'.[84] As a Minister of State, Hart had no independent authority, only that which was delegated by the Secretary of State Herbert Bowden, and no departmental responsibilities. She could advise, write papers, make suggestions but did not have the right to frame policy. Ministers of State are generally experienced politicians who are expected to handle complex and awkward issues: Rhodesia was both immensely complex and operationally awkward.

In 1961, a new Rhodesian constitution had effectively excluded black people from power by limiting the vote to property owners.[85] At the time, the country was self-governing, under British jurisdiction. However, Rhodesians wanted full independence, a demand backed by the Labour Government as long as the principle of one person, one vote was honoured. The majority of white Rhodesians disagreed with this ruling, wishing to exclude the black majority from the democratic process. At 11 am on November 11 (Armistice Day), 1965, after a series of increasingly fraught meetings with Harold Wilson, Ian Smith the Prime Minister of Rhodesia had declared a Unilateral Declaration of Independence, illegally severing links with Britain and announcing that Rhodesia was now an independent sovereign state.

The Cabinet was in session when the Reuters report came through. Harold Wilson instructed his Cabinet that public speeches on Rhodesia should be 'sombre and responsible' reminding them that it could be the 'start of 3rd world war – between white and black: but avoid saying so'.[86] The last time a colony was so defiant was in 1776 when the USA broke away from Britain. Rhodesia was different: this was not merely a bid for independence; it was a declaration of bigotry. Ian Smith was a well-known white supremacist whose instigation of a racist constitution effectively prohibited the majority of people—that is the indigenous black community—from voting. Under Smith the 220,000 white Rhodesians dominated—politically as well as economically—approximately four million black Rhodesians.[87]

On the day that Smith declared UDI, Harold Wilson and the Labour Government were clinging on to power with a majority of just one in the Commons. Even so, they were expected to take action against this illegally racist regime: Labour after all believed in self-determination for everyone in the former colonies and declared its commitment to No Independence Before Majority African Rule (NIBMAR).[88] The seizure of power by a white colonial power was condemned internationally; the UN Security Council denounced the UDI as an illegitimate 'usurpation of power by a racist settler minority' and called on all countries to boycott the regime. In December 1965, the Foreign Ministers of the Organisation for African Unity urged the Labour Government to remove Ian Smith by force. However, Wilson very publicly rejected a military invasion, saying that he preferred to use sanctions, including stopping all British aid, banning the export of oil to Rhodesia, prohibiting the import of Rhodesian goods to Britain and recalling the British High Commissioner.[89]

Judith Hart's appointment coincided with ever-increasing political tension between the Commonwealth and Britain over the latter's compromising stance on Rhodesia. Hart was given responsibility for the Rhodesia X Committee: here she was expected to advise Wilson on how to deal with Rhodesia and how to persuade the African states to remain in the Commonwealth. It was to be her first ministerial ordeal, trying to balance her personal idealism with the demands of collective responsibility and the imperative to construct a workable policy.

In May 1966, just a few months after Ian Smith had declared UDI and the situation in Rhodesia was reaching a climax, Hart was sent to Africa on a mission to lower the political temperature and to convince the Zambian Government that Britain was not 'double-crossing' and was 'quite determined to break the illegal Smith regime'.[90] It was hoped that she could persuade Zambia not to take impetuous action against Rhodesia or—as it threatened to do—cut off copper supplies to Britain.[91] Judith Hart was the 'only Minister Wilson dared send out to Lusaka … correctly judging that Kaunda would not be willing to insult a woman'.[92] Barbara Castle, who was now Minister of Transport, noted that he was again 'entrusting a woman with a responsible job'.[93] It was an unenviable task. Dr Kenneth Kaunda was threatening to call for Britain's expulsion from the Commonwealth at the forthcoming Commonwealth Conference,[94] disappointed that Labour's promises in opposition were jettisoned as soon as it was in government. Certainly, Kaunda was in no mood to listen to the pleas of a junior emissary, commenting icily 'of what is the use of sending this poor girl to us?'

When Mrs Hart arrived at the airport, she was given a 'frosty reception', met only by two minor officials rather than Ministers, an act considered to be a gross discourtesy.[95] In addition, a few hours after her arrival, Dr Kaunda criticised Britain in a radio broadcast and insisted that British 'policy has been evasive and the shiftiest'[96] and that Zambia was 'utterly contemptuous of the way Britain was handling the Rhodesian question'.[97] After two days, Dr Kaunda changed his mind about this 'poor girl' and acknowledged that Judith Hart was a formidable politician. It helped that Judith Hart was an MP for a Scottish constituency. Dr Kaunda felt a warm affection towards the Scottish people: his father had been a Minister in the Church of Scotland, he had been educated at a Presbyterian school and had attended Edinburgh University. With great presence of mind, Hart had brought a present from one of her constituents, Kaunda's former landlady whom he regarded affectionately.[98] Barbara Castle thought Hart had also broken through the initial frosty reception 'by two moves which only someone on the Left could make: 1) she had issued a warm message on Africa Freedom Day, and 2) she had written a personal letter to Kaunda which ended: "Eighteen months ago I was chairman of the Movement for Colonial Freedom and nothing that happened since has changed my views." She therefore got a friendly talk with Kaunda'.[99]

On June 19, 1966, Judith Hart returned for an 11-day round of talks to discuss more intensive sanctions by Britain and Zambia against Rhodesia and to try to cement the relationship between the two governments'.[100] This was a delicate and difficult negotiation as the Zambian Government continued to insist that force could still be used to end the crisis. The second round of talks ended on an unexpectedly icy note: Judith Hart was not senior enough to promise much and the talks were adjourned.[101] Basically, the Zambian Government claimed that Britain's offer of financial help was too inadequate to mitigate the money lost by its severance of trade with Rhodesia.[102] Moreover, President Kaunda called for a total economic blockade against Rhodesia, alleged that the British Government was guilty of selling-out and insisted that he had reached a stage of 'total disillusion with the Labour Party'.[103] Zambia, commented the government-owned newspaper, 'is fed up to the teeth with Britain's timid attempts to bring down the Smith rebellion'.[104] Certainly, there was a growing belief that Judith Hart was in Zambia merely to keep its government quiet while the British-Rhodesian talks continued in Salisbury. It was feared that 'far from being determined to topple Smith by sanctions, Britain is now desperately searching for an acceptable compromise'.[105] Harold Wilson was thought to be more 'motivated by greater tenderness towards his "kith and kin" in Rhodesia than by solicitude for the Commonwealth'.[106]

Wilson wanted a negotiated settlement, rather than continued conflict and asked his Minister for advice. In August 1966, Judith Hart sent a confidential memo to Harold Wilson outlining the advantages and disadvantages of negotiating a settlement with Ian Smith. Privately, she thought Smith a 'raw, uncouth racist'.[107] She warned Wilson that a 'soft settlement' with Smith would totally alienate African opinion, would be a disastrous blow to the prestige of the Prime Minister and would probably mean loss of investments in black Africa. There could, Hart cautioned, even be a break-up of the Commonwealth 'for though a departure of Zambia and Tanzania could be survived there is a real danger of a chain reaction'.[108] She advised her boss that most African countries would maintain that the British Government should have used force.[109] Britain, she told Wilson, was at risk of losing both the fight with Smith and much of the Commonwealth. She advised the Prime Minister that 'if we are doubtful about the final outcome re Smith, are we better to nail our colours to the mast and at least keep Commonwealth trust?'[110] In Hart's opinion, the only advantage to a deal with Smith was that the issue would be resolved and the drain on Britain's balance of payments would stop. The disadvantages, Hart argued, outweighed a settlement. Privately, she was worried that Wilson might concede to Ian Smith's demands. Instead of this, Hart wanted the government to present a robust challenge to the racist policies of the new illegal Rhodesian government.

On August 2, 1966, Judith Hart was invited to a Cabinet meeting to discuss her memorandum. She was nervous at presenting her proposals, aware
that some Cabinet Ministers like her boss Herbert Bowden favoured compromise with the Rhodesian regime. Barbara Castle—now Minister of
Transport—offered support. A couple of weeks earlier Hart had discussed
her view of Rhodesia with Castle, and both 'agreed Harold had put himself
in a weak position by ruling out force so categorically'.[111] In her presentation to the Cabinet, Judith Hart insisted on more punitive sanctions against
Rhodesia, arguing that such a policy 'would also help to restore Zambian
confidence in the United Kingdom and might prevent a decision by Zambia
at the Commonwealth Prime Ministers' meeting in September to leave the
Commonwealth or sever relations with us, either of which courses could lead
to a break-up of the Commonwealth'.[112] She asked Cabinet to approve a further £7 million on top of the £6.85 million already promised to the Zambian
Government to help offset the situation.[113] Hart 'fought like a tigress'[114]
to get the Cabinet to increase the aid budget to Zambia. Fortunately, the
Chancellor of the Exchequer Jim Callaghan supported her, arguing that a
'break-up of the Commonwealth, would be so serious, both politically and
economically, that it would be worth paying the £7 million if this avoided
such an outcome'.[115] Judith Hart had proved herself to be an able, intelligent
and persuasive Minister.

Harold Wilson's anxiety about Rhodesia increased, particularly after his
experience at the Commonwealth Conference held a month later. Wilson
thought it a 'nightmare conference, by common consent the worst ever'.[116]
In his conference speech, Wilson reiterated his government's determination
to bring the illegal regime in Rhodesia to an end and confirmed his commitment to a government which represented all races in Rhodesia.[117] However,
the African leaders were not placated and had no wish to 'tone down their
demands for British action against Smith'.[118] Kenneth Kaunda refused
to attend the conference and sent two Ministers in his place; the Zambian
Foreign Minister stormed out, describing Wilson as a 'racialist supporting a
fascist government'.[119] The conference ended on a sombre note. All of the
22 delegations recognised that 'the possibility of Zambia's resignation from
the Commonwealth still lay like a shadow across the conference table'.[120]
Harold Wilson feared the imminent dissolution of the Commonwealth.[121]
Fortunately, behind the scenes, Judith Hart helped to secure a £21 mil-
lion Commonwealth aid package for Zambia, which combined with Harold
Wilson's later public commitment to NIBMAR[122] averted the threat of the
Commonwealth breaking up.

Judith Hart warned Harold Wilson that mandatory sanctions would not
succeed.[123] Certainly, Rhodesia was able to circumvent sanctions by using
South Africa as a transit country for buying and selling their goods. Hart
offered Wilson two strategies to resolve the continuing crisis. Firstly, she suggested implementing sanctions against South Africa in order to stop Rhodesia
side-stepping trade restrictions; secondly, Hart argued for a targeted bombing

of economic targets in Rhodesia.[124] Wilson was unwilling to take her advice, though she was proved correct in her analysis. Sanctions in Rhodesia were all too easily evaded and were seen as classic British duplicity by the newly independent black African countries. Moreover, Harold Wilson continued to meet Ian Smith and his delegates to try to resolve the conflict. Despite Wilson's efforts, these meetings not only proved fruitless but the political cost was inestimable since any dealings with the racist Smith were regarded as morally reprehensible by many in the Labour Party. Nine African states, including two members of the Commonwealth, Tanzania and Ghana broke off diplomatic relations in protest against British prevarication.

Once more, on November 21, 1966, Judith Hart flew to Kenya for further talks with President Kenyatta of Kenya and President Obote of Uganda to discuss sanctions against Rhodesia (Fig. 8.1). Britain's talks with Rhodesia had just broken down again because Smith refused to commit to majority rule, and the British Government wanted to consult Commonwealth leaders before seeking United Nations approval for mandatory sanctions. It was felt that Mrs Hart would not 'undertake such a mission unless it was to put forward a policy and a strategy that she believed in firmly. This suggests that there is a fairly detailed plan for mandatory economic sanctions ready for submission by Britain to the Security Council' of the United Nations.[125]

Hart spent a few days in Kenya before visiting Uganda. In theory, it was a social good-will tour as the above photograph tries to indicate: the Minister visited Jinja on the shore of Lake Victoria, had lunch with the Chair of the Ugandan Electricity Board at the Owen Falls and then visited the Bujagali Falls and a textile factory. She met the Minister of Foreign Affairs, went on the requisite tour of the parliamentary building accompanied by the Deputy High Commissioner and the Head of the East African Commonwealth Department. More crucially, she met Dr Milton Obote, the President to discuss 'matters of mutual interest' including that of Rhodesia. In reality it was soft diplomacy, giving Judith Hart the opportunity to reinforce her friendly relationships with various Commonwealth politicians.

In a television interview in Kampala, Judith Hart defended British policy on Rhodesia despite her reservations. When she was asked whether the Rhodesian crisis could have been prevented if there had been a prompt use of force, she hid her own views and replied that it had been impossible to do so since 'Britain had no military units in Rhodesia – unlike other colonial countries where force had been used'.[126] She insisted that sanctions had hit the Rhodesian economy very hard and that 'Britain was not surrendering her responsibility for Rhodesia' and was determined to end the illegal regime.[127] Moreover, she strongly denied that Britain was duplicitous and 'trying to please both South Africa and the rest of Africa in its handling of the crisis'.[128] But she dodged the allegation that Wilson's premature assurances that no force would be used against Rhodesia had encouraged UDI, saying that this was 'now academic discussion and we should now look ahead'.[129] As we know from her memos to Wilson, Judith Hart had criticised the use of

Fig. 8.1   Judith Hart visiting Uganda (Courtesy of Peoples History Museum)

sanctions and had recommended the use of force but her ministerial position committed her to defend government policy whether she agreed with it or not. At this stage in her political life, she was willing to accept the collective responsibility that came with her ministerial post even though she disagreed with the government policy she was required to defend.

Privately, Judith Hart feared that some colleagues and even her chief Herbert Bowden would make concessions which would be unacceptable to the Africans. In a Secret Memo to Cabinet, Judith Hart maintained that Britain was 'caught in an acute dilemma. Put in a nutshell, this is that we cannot retreat from the Rhodesian situation – without dishonour, and without immense loss of prestige, and without grave offence to the Commonwealth. … Yet the only policy we have, that of mandatory sanctions, will not succeed; and we reject the other three possibilities – the use of force, confrontation with South Africa and turning the problem over to the United Nations'.[130] Harold Wilson, aware of Judith Hart's position on Rhodesia, began to exclude her from the meetings of the Rhodesia X committee. Judith Hart, according to Barbara Castle 'was boiling', asking her friend '"Why have they kept me out? Why won't anyone tell me what is happening?" … Judith and I agreed that it looked as though Harold had developed cold feet when it came to the point of decision on sanctions. Our resignations were on the cards'.[131]

Judith Hart felt compromised. Undoubtedly her sympathies lay with the Kenyans, the Ugandans and the Zambians rather than with the British Government in which she served and whose reluctance to invade Rhodesia so frustrated her. By this time, she was not enjoying life or work. Earlier she had written in her diary that she found the work 'so depressing and at the same time frustrating that it saps all my mental and emotional energies, and leaves me none to enjoy any other aspect of living. I feel I want to retreat into myself – not to talk at home, or to others. Everyone is an irritation, so to deal with them I must put on an artificial cloak, be another person. The frustration is as bad as the anxiety'.[132] On November 29, 1966, Judith Hart wrote a resignation letter to Harold Wilson. She had written the letter 'after much thought and anxiety', arguing that 'one is worth nothing to the Party and to a Labour Government if one compromises with principle in a field in which one carries some responsibilities'.[133] She discussed her resignation letter with friends such as Jenny Lee, but the letter was torn in two and never sent.[134] For a while, she was prepared to compromise.

On December 2, 1966, Wilson met Smith met off the coast of Gibraltar aboard HMS Tiger, a British naval cruiser. Judith Hart publicly defended the Prime Minister. She had little choice: she was a member of the government, albeit in a junior position, and would have to abide by Cabinet decisions or else resign. The party's anti-racist lobby was shocked when she defended the Tiger deal with Ian Smith.[135] She even had to placate her son who had written to his father to 'ask mum to tell me what the hell is happening on board TIGER. Seems everybody has forsaken their principles'.[136] Privately, Hart loathed Smith and continued to argue the importance of standing by the principles embodied in NIMBAR. She again threatened to resign if the Tiger agreement with Smith went through.[137] In addition, she met secretly with Barbara Castle to discuss the issue: both women, along with the recently elected Shirley Williams, agreed to resign in unison if there was a deal without NIMBAR.[138] The press too thought that Judith Hart would not be able to swallow her misgivings as she was 'deeply committed politically and personally to many of the African leaders'.[139] The Tiger talks failed, sanctions were introduced and all previous offers to Smith were scrapped in favour of withholding independence for Rhodesia unless there was African majority rule.[140] Harold Wilson had tried hard to resolve an intractable problem, but the intransigence of the white Rhodesians defeated him.

As Minister responsible for Rhodesian policies, she was forced to defend Wilson and the breakdown of the *Tiger* talks in Parliament. She was more comfortable in criticising Rhodesian politics, criticisms that provide important clues to her real standpoint and beliefs. In several moving speeches in a parliamentary debate lasting six hours, Hart put forward a motion firstly deploring the rejection by 'the illegal regime in Rhodesia' of a constitutional settlement which would grant majority rule and secondly asking Parliament to implement oil sanctions. She ended her speech with a rousing plea, arguing that 'Tonight, we shall be voting for our belief in non-racialism, for the future of the Commonwealth ... for Britain's honour and integrity in the world, and for our belief in democracy and in the human rights of men and women. ... We shall be voting, also, for the simple proposition that principles should determine politics and that moral issues demand moral decisions'.[141]

In January 1967, Judith Hart was upgraded in ministerial rank. Wilson moved her away from her former responsibilities for African affairs and placed her in charge of the Caribbean and the remaining colonies.[142] The press suggested that in fact she was 'surreptitiously demoted' even though her new job was graded senior to her previous. Moreover, it was thought that Judith Hart's Commonwealth promotion away from African affairs meant that Harold Wilson was keeping his Rhodesian options open.[143] She was seen to identify too much with African aspirations, particularly Zambian ones and her friendliness with Dr Kenneth Kaunda was 'something of an embarrassment to Mr Wilson and Mr Bowden while they were trying to do a deal with Mr Smith. She could be moved now without its being thought that any change in British policy is implied. When the next round in the Rhodesian crisis begins, she will be safely occupied with the Bahamas and St Vincent'.[144] Certainly, for the next year Judith Hart's time was taken up with issues such as the establishment of domestic security forces in the Bahamas, whether or not there would be constitutional changes in Pitcairn Island, changes in the constitution of the Seychelles, and the working hours of young people and women in Hong Kong.[145] It was thought to be a 'particularly neat redeployment because it moves Mrs Hart and her troubled radical conscience right out of the Rhodesian sphere'.[146]

However, Harold Wilson sought advice from Judith Hart on an informal basis. At a weekend meeting at Chequers held to discuss Castle's *In Place of Strife*, he placed Judith Hart and Barbara Castle on either side of him at dinner 'because he wanted to sound us out about Rhodesia'. Wilson wanted to know whether he should resume talks with Ian Smith or whether he should set up a Royal Commission. 'Jumping in together, Judith and I left him in no doubt that we preferred neither'.[147] Harold Wilson ignored their advice, the Smith regime survived and 'became a testament to British impotence and fallen status'.[148] It was seen to do 'our standing in the world, — and most of all our self-respect, incalculable damage'.[149] Indeed, Britain's response 'came close to destroying the Commonwealth' as nine African states broke off diplomatic relations.[150] For fifteen years, Ian Smith and his white Rhodesian regime held 'international diplomacy and British domestic politics to ransom'.[151] Eventually after resistance by black Rhodesians, the regime collapsed in 1979. A year later, the country achieved legal and internationally recognised independence: Robert Mugabe became the first Prime Minister of the Independent Republic of Zimbabwe.

MINISTER OF SOCIAL SECURITY, JULY 1967–NOVEMBER 1968

Eventually, Harold Wilson moved Judith Hart well away from Commonwealth affairs. On July 25, 1967, she answered questions on Hong Kong; on July 27, she had switched to family allowances in Britain: Mrs Hart had been promoted again, this time to become Minister of Social Security. She took the place of a popular Minister, Margaret (Peggy) Herbison, who had resigned office out of principle when the government refused to raise the family allowance to her recommended level of 10 shillings a week (50p). Richard Crossman thought Hart would struggle in her new post firstly because she would need to surrender her left-wing ideals and secondly because she took over from a respected Minister who was well liked by the civil service. He warned her 'don't for heaven's sake be crazy enough to take her place'.[152] The Permanent Secretary, Sir Clifford Jarrett let Hart know 'how much they'd all loved Peggy and how they were giving a dinner for the most wonderful Minister they'd had. He said all this without inviting poor Judith to attend'.[153]

Judith Hart was ready for the challenge, maybe more ready to compromise one or two of her political principles to achieve results. Her salary was raised from £5625 to £8500 a year plus parliamentary allowances of £1250, making her one of the top female salary earners in Britain. The promotion was seen as her big break; she was now just a very short step away from Cabinet. By now, her eldest son Richard was just finishing his first year at Cambridge and her younger son Stephen had just taken his 'O' levels.

The newly appointed Minister was seen as a new broom, sweeping everything before her, changing everything, even changing the decoration of her new office. Newspapers reported that Mrs Hart's style differed from Mrs Herbison's because the former Minister's 'home-spun taste does not co-incide with that of 42 year old Mrs Hart'.[154] The new incumbent admitted that 'although the office is not ready for redecoration, I felt it needed cheering up … Now the ceiling has been painted sunshine yellow. Elaborate curtains and pelmet have been swept away in favour of simple white-painted wood and net'.[155] Judith Hart even instituted different coloured stickers for letters coming into the Ministry. A green sticker meant a letter needing an urgent reply; a red sticker meant immediate and a purple sticker meant it was a letter from a constituent. The latter letters were answered quickly and were known around the Ministry as 'Judith's Purple Hearts' a reference to a popular drug in circulation at the time.[156]

At 7:45 a.m., October 31, Judith Hart made her first broadcast as Minister of Social Security. She had chosen to speak to Radio 2, a middle-of-the-road channel which had just started up a month previously and which was beginning to attract millions of listeners. She told her audience that the government had helped 'our people' by giving higher pensions to six-and-a-half-million individuals.[157] Her Ministry, she promised, would do a 'great deal to protect the more vulnerable women – women deserted by their husbands, unmarried mothers and other minority groups'. Hart went on to say that she was very much concerned about the plight of these particular women remarking that 'someone once said the problem of Social Security is a problem of women'.[158] She assured her listeners that the government would put up family allowances, maintaining that 'it cost a lot to do this. We believe it is the right thing to do'.[159] On April 2, 1968, Judith Hart introduced the Family Allowances and National Insurance (2) Bill which proposed increasing family allowance by 7 shillings a week, well short of the 10s recommended by Peggy Herbison. Margaret Herbison who had promised Harold Wilson not to embarrass her new colleague, 'was as good as her word' and said nothing.[160]

Soon Judith Hart was forced to compromise her left-wing ideals. She was criticised by the left when she brought in two new checks to prevent so-called abuses of unemployment benefits. First, all newly unemployed people under the age of 45 had to endure a 'searching and detailed' interview to discover why they were still unemployed. Hart insisted that 'if it appears that a man is not genuinely seeking work, he will be told very frankly that he must do so'.[161] Second, people who retired after the age of 58 with a work pension would no longer be eligible for unemployment benefits.

Her left-wing credentials were further undermined when she claimed that 'scroungers', 'layabouts' and 'lead-swingers' preferred unemployment benefits to an honest day's work.[162] She warned that the government was planning to beat these social security 'fiddlers' who illegally claimed social security benefits.[163] Even the *Telegraph* felt she was 'very much in the Victorian Lady Bountiful tradition; benefits for the deserving poor were her constant concern. For scroungers and loafers she showed a fierce contempt'.[164] This type of rhetoric fed into and encouraged public prejudice against welfare payments to the very poor. The Child Poverty Action group insisted that most of those regarded as 'workshy' were found to be severely physically or mentally handicapped.[165] Moreover, the government was also divided over the issue: Hart's labelling of the unemployed as 'scroungers', 'lead-swingers' and 'layabouts' caused 'a minor political stir'[166] in that it contradicted Richard Crossman's defence of the voluntary unemployed. In his view, people who received benefits and 'turned down jobs while they waited for something better were "sitting fully on their rights"'.[167] In response, Hart argued that social security benefits were too generous and had 'overtaken the wages of our lower-paid workers. It is now the case that the poorest in Britain are not the sick, or the unemployed or the old but those earning very low wages'.[168] It was seen as a forthright speech designed to leave people in no doubt where Hart stood over welfare benefits. She made it abundantly clear that she parted ways with Crossman, arguing that the tiny minority who abused the system had to be tackled because those who paid taxes would not have confidence in the Welfare State if they knew people were 'scrounging' a living.[169] Political compromise is essential if there is to be workable policy, but Hart was condemned for moving too far to the right. Some accused her of submerging her left-wing principles to maintain office. She was thought 'charming and amusing. But I think everybody knows there is steel underneath'.[170] Judith Hart defended her decisions by arguing that government was 'all about power. There comes a time yes when you might feel you have to resign over an issue, but what is more important is supporting a Government that is working towards that broad direction that you believe in. That is a fairly hard statement of practical politics'.[171] Certainly, in this ministerial post Hart was learning to balance her idealism with political realism, willing to adopt a more pragmatic stance, willing to conform to the status quo rather than shake-up her department and undermine government policy. It seemed to some in the Labour Party that she had abandoned her moral principles.

Judith Hart did not last long in the post. In a government reshuffle, Harold Wilson merged the Ministries of Health and the Ministry of Social Security into the Department of Health and Social Security. He appointed Richard Crossman as secretary of state; Judith Hart's job disappeared. Dutifully, she publicly expressed regret at leaving the department; privately, she was delighted as she never really liked working there, much preferring her job in the Commonwealth office.[172] Moreover, Judith Hart was a visionary comfortable with big ideas such as colonial freedom; she was not as comfortable as an enforcement officer dealing with so-called abuses of social security. Certainly, Hart's work during the Rhodesian crisis had developed her deep commitment to the Commonwealth and particularly to the independent African countries that were its members. It was while she was a junior Minister at the Commonwealth Relations Office that she seemed most fulfilled and her achievements in helping to hold the Commonwealth together at this time undoubtedly gave her a great deal of pride and satisfaction.

Judith Hart was destined to play a larger role in government: the next chapter will examine her promotion to Cabinet Minister and her subsequent success as Minister for Overseas Development. Here, her political idealism would be further tested by a Prime Minister determined to show that political dissent did not pay.

Notes

1. Barbara Castle, obituary of Judith Hart, *The Guardian*, December 9, 1991, p. 33.
2. Ibid.
3. Allan Hall, *The Sun*, October 23, 1968, p. 3.
4. Interview with *Clitheroe Advertiser and Times*, February 9, 1968, HART/13/70.
5. Ibid.
6. Ibid.
7. Ibid.
8. Interview with Mary Kenny, *Liverpool Daily Press*, November 27, 1968.
9. Ibid.
10. Ibid.

11. I am grateful to Peter Freeman, who worked closely with Judith Hart, for this insight.
12. Thanks to the youngest son of Judith and Tony Hart, Steve Hart for this information.
13. Anthony Bernard Hart was born on July 7, 1919 and died in 2009.
14. Interview with Mary Kenny, *Liverpool Daily Press*, November 27, 1968.
15. Interview with *Clitheroe Advertiser and Times*, February 9, 1968, HART/13/70.
16. Labour Party Annual Report, 1951, p. 111.
17. I am grateful to Steve Hart for this information.
18. *The Tribune*, 1966, HART/10/03.
19. Judith Hart to Michael Foot, February 2, 1957, HART/1/1-6.
20. Lanark was a county constituency from 1918 to 1983. It was replaced by Clydesdale after boundary changes.
21. Interview with *Clitheroe Advertiser and Times*, February 9, 1968, HART/13/70.
22. Speech to Selection Committee, 1957, HART/1/1-6.
23. *The Guardian*, October 6, 1959, p. 2.
24. Judith Hart won 25,171 votes; Patrick Maitland won 24,631.
25. 1959, 1964, 1966, 1970, 1974 (twice), 1979, 1983.
26. Hansard, November 3, 1959, Vol. 612, cc860–985.
27. Hansard, December 1, 1959, Vol. 614, cc992–993.
28. Hansard, December 2, 1959, Vol. 614, cc1303–1306.
29. *The Tribune*, 1966, HART/10/03.
30. *The Guardian*, October 26, 1959, p. 4.
31. Hansard, July 26, 1960, Vol. 627, cc1533–1563.
32. *The Guardian*, March 12, 1961, p. 1.
33. Hansard, March 2, 1961, Vol. 635, cc1807–1919.
34. Labour Party Conference Report, 1961, p. 179.
35. Arrowsmith had been on hunger strike for 11 days, was forcibly fed and was close to being a martyr for the cause. *The Guardian*, October 17, 1961, p. 2.
36. *The Observer*, September 22, 1963, p. 1.
37. Hansard, March 20, 1962, Vol. 656, cc210–220.
38. *Daily Mirror*, May 28, 1962, p. 10.
39. *The Guardian*, March 21, 1962, p. 2.
40. *Lanark Post*, October 1964, p. 1.
41. Ibid.
42. These are held in Glasgow City Archives.
43. Maggie Sidgreaves was a former civil servant, working as a highly regarded diary secretary in various ministerial offices. She became Hart's political advisor in 1977.
44. Interview with Maggie Sidgreaves, November 13, 2018.
45. Press release, October 7, 1969, Constituency Papers, Glasgow.
46. *Lanark and East Kilbridge Post*, 1970, HART/9/2.
47. James M. Gordon, Internet blog, December 19, 2010.
48. Leaflet produced by Judith Hart repudiating the leaflet, HART/9/1.
49. Election newsletter, 1964, HART/9/1.
50. Election news bulletin, 1970, HART/9/1.

51. Northern Mines Research Society, Internet source.
52. Ross was a strong unionist, calling the SNP the 'tartan Tories'.
53. Notebook, undated, HART/2/40-46.
54. *The Tribune*, 1966, HART/10/03.
55. *Daily Mirror*, October 2, 1964, p. 2.
56. Judith Hart, *Lanark and East Kilbride Post*, Election Special, March 1966, p. 1.
57. Ibid.
58. The Conservative government had set up a working party under the chairmanship of Lord Kilbrandon to examine the way in which 'children in trouble' were treated by the legal system. The report was published in 1964.
59. Judith Hart's notebook, undated, HART/2/40-46.
60. *Glasgow Herald*, September 16, 1965.
61. Press release, February 4, 1966, HART/10/03.
62. *Daily Herald*, November 8, 1965.
63. Judith Hart, notebook, HART/1/1-6. She had previously given birth to a still-born baby.
64. Ibid.
65. Judith Hart, informal notes on a visit to Israel, HART/13/76.
66. Steve Hart was Chair of the Hornsey and Wood Green Labour Party, the political director of Unite and vice-chair of Stand Up to Racism.
67. *The Tribune*, 1966, HART/10/03.
68. The comedian Spike Milligan lived in the same corridor opposite her and once composed a poem. 'Judith Hart once made for me, An early morning cup of tea, It isn't every day that we, Are waited on by an MP'. Thanks to Steve Hart for this information.
69. Interview with Judith Hart, Melanie Phillips, *The Guardian*, May 13, 1980, p. 8.
70. Anthony Hart, *Daily Express*, September 16, 1968, p. 2.
71. Letter from Anthony Hart to Judith, Wednesday 30, probably 1964, HART/9/1.
72. *The Daily Telegraph*, March 4, 1970, HART/10/5.
73. Interview with *Clitheroe Advertiser and Times*, February 9, 1968, HART/13/70.
74. Interview with Judith Hart, South East Television, July 27, 1967, HART/13/76.
75. This position was created in August 1966. In 1968, the department merged with the Foreign Office and its Minister became the Secretary of State for Foreign and Commonwealth Affairs. Herbert Bowden later joined the SDP.
76. *British News*, Kampala, November 19, 1966, p. 1.
77. *Scottish Miner*, June 1966, HART/10/03.
78. Unnamed newspaper, February 5, 1965, HART/10/03.
79. Elizabeth Thomas, *The Tribune*, 1966, HART/10/03.
80. *The Tribune*, 1966, HART/10/03.
81. Unnamed newspaper, April 12, 1966, HART/10/03.
82. Ibid.
83. Rhodesia was named after the arch-imperialist Cecil Rhodes, a British colonialist who expanded the Empire by violently annexing African land.

84. Judith Hart, unpublished notes, October 11, circa 1966.
85. Rhodesia was a democracy but a very limited one based on property qualifications: only those owning property with a minimum value of £150 or had an annual income of over £100 qualified and this meant that white settlers had an overwhelming majority.
86. Harold Wilson, November 11, 1965, CAB/195/15.
87. See Richard Coggins, 'Wilson and Rhodesia: UDI and British Policy Towards Africa', *Contemporary British History*, Vol. 20, No. 3, September 2006, pp. 363–381 for an excellent summary of British policy.
88. The Labour Government was committed to five principles: unimpeded progress towards majority rule, guarantees against retrogressive amendment of the Constitution, immediate improvement in the political status of the African population, progress towards ending racial discrimination and evidence that any proposal for independence was acceptable to the people of Rhodesia as a whole.
89. In November 1965, all Rhodesian ministers were dismissed, the British High Commissioner was withdrawn, a ban declared on the export of arms and spares, the export of UK capital to Rhodesia was banned, the import of Rhodesian tobacco and sugar was banned, Rhodesia was removed from the sterling area, currency restrictions were introduced on residents travelling to Rhodesia, aid was stopped. In December 1965, there were further bans including limited travel facilities to Rhodesia, a ban on oil imports and exports. In 1966, there was a prohibition of all trade between the UK and Rhodesia, ban on export of iron ore, chromium, sugar, chrome, asbestos and pig iron.
90. Unnamed and undated newspaper, HART/2/39.
91. Britain depended on Zambia for its copper supplies; Wilson thought that two million British workers would be laid off if Kaunda stopped supplies. Zambia was in a difficult position, utterly dependent on Rhodesia for coal, electricity, food supplies and consumer goods; in addition the landlocked country relied on Rhodesian rail transport for its imports and exports to the coast.
92. *The Guardian*, March 20, 1983, p. 7.
93. Barbara Castle Diary, May 23, 1966.
94. *The Guardian*, May 23, 1966, p. 1.
95. Cyril Osborne, House of Commons, quoted in *Times of Zambia*, June 15, 1966, HART/2/39.
96. *The Guardian*, May 25, 1966, p. 1.
97. *The Guardian*, June 3, 1966, p. 13.
98. Kaunda had a warm relationship with his former landlady, and the two remained friends after he returned to Zambia. Thanks to Maggie Sidgreaves for this information.
99. Barbara Castle Diary, May 31, 1966.
100. *The Observer*, June 19, 1966, HART/2/45.
101. *The Guardian*, July 1, 1966, p. 13.
102. Ibid.
103. *The Guardian*, November 5, 1967, p. 3.
104. Quoted in *The Sun*, June 25, 1966, HART/2/39.
105. *The Daily Telegraph*, June 20, 1966, HART/2/39.

106. *The Daily Telegraph*, August 11, 1966, HART/2/39.
107. Judith Hart's notebook, undated, HART/02/40.
108. Secret Memo, Judith Hart to Wilson, August 1966, HART/2/46.
109. Ibid.
110. Ibid.
111. Barbara Castle Diary, July 22, 1966.
112. Judith Hart, Cabinet Meeting, August 2, 1966, CAB/128/41.
113. Ibid.
114. *The Economist*, October 27, 1966, p. 2.
115. James Callaghan, Cabinet Meeting, August 2, 1966, CAB/128/41.
116. The Conference was held in September 1966. Harold Wilson, *The Labour Government 1964–1970*, Pelican, 1974, p. 358.
117. Harold Wilson's speech, HART/2/45.
118. *The Economist*, October 27, 1966, p. 3.
119. Quoted in Philip Alexander, 'A Tale of Two Smiths: The Transformation of Commonwealth Policy, 1964–70', *Contemporary British History*, Vol. 20, September 2006, pp. 303–321.
120. *The Guardian*, September 16, 1966, p. 2.
121. Harold Wilson, *The Labour Government 1964–1970*, Pelican, 1974, p. 364.
122. Britain contributed £14 million and Canada £7 million to the fund.
123. Judith Hart, Secret Memorandum, *Future Policy: A Possible New Approach to Sanctions*, R(X) Committee, November 15, 1966, HART/2/28.
124. Ibid.
125. *The Guardian*, November 17, 1966, p. 11.
126. *The People*, November 29, 1966, HART/2/40-46.
127. *Uganda Argus*, November 26, 1966, HART/2/40-46.
128. *The People*, November 29, 1966, HART/2/40-46.
129. Ibid.
130. Memo from Judith Hart, undated, HART/2/40-46.
131. Barbara Castle Diary, November 28, 1966.
132. Judith Hart's private notebook, October 21, 1966.
133. Letter to Harold Wilson from Judith Hart, November 29, 1966, HART/2/40-46. In her letter, she stated that Wilson should insist on '(1) the establishment of a broad-based government; (2) the entrenchment of Chapter 37; (3) the release of detainees and the lifting of censorship; (4) a military presence to provide more than paper guarantees after independence'.
134. The original torn-up letter is in the People's History Museum.
135. Nora Beloff, *The Observer*, October 20, 1968.
136. Stephen Hart to 'Dad', October 14, 1966, HART/2/45.
137. No Independence Before Majority African Rule. *The Guardian*, July 27, 1967, p. 6.
138. Barbara Castle Diary, December 5, 1966.
139. *The Guardian*, December 5, 1966, p. 1.
140. *The Observer*, December 11, 1966, p. 3.
141. Judith Hart, Hansard, December 8, 1966, Vol. 737, cc1587–1714.
142. *The Scotsman*, January 12, 1967, HART/10/33.
143. *The Guardian*, January 13, 1967, HART/10/03.
144. *Glasgow Herald*, January 12, 1967, HART/10/03.

145. See Hansard, 1967.
146. *The Guardian*, January 12, 1967, p. 8.
147. Barbara Castle Diary, July 22, 1967.
148. Lord Thompson, former Cabinet Minister, Ben Pimlott, *Harold Wilson*, HarperCollins, 1992, p. 381.
149. Ben Pimlott, *Harold Wilson*, HarperCollins, 1992, p. 381.
150. Philip Alexander, 'A Tale of Two Smiths: The Transformation of Commonwealth Policy, 1964–70', *Contemporary British History*, Vol. 20, No. 3, September 2006, pp. 303–321.
151. *The Independent*, November 22, 2007, p. 5.
152. Richard Crossman, June 14, 1967; *The Diaries of a Cabinet Minister, 1966–1968*, Trinity Press, 1975.
153. Ibid., August 1, 1967.
154. *The Sunday Express*, September 10, 1967, p. 4.
155. Ibid.
156. *The Guardian*, March 27, 1968, p. 8.
157. Broadcast by Minister of Social Security on Radio 2, October 31, 1967.
158. Interview with *Clitheroe Advertiser and Times*, February 9, 1968, HART/13/70.
159. Broadcast by Minister of Social Security on Radio 2, October 31, 1967.
160. Harold Wilson, *The Labour Government, 1964–70*, Penguin, 1971, p. 538.
161. Judith Hart, quoted in *The Guardian*, July 26, 1968, p. 2.
162. *Daily Mirror*, September 10, 1968, HART/10/03.
163. *The Guardian*, June 12, 1968, p. 1.
164. *The Sunday Telegraph*, HART/13/76
165. *The Guardian*, January 4, 1969, p. 16.
166. *The Times*, September 10, 1978, HART/10/03.
167. *Daily Sketch*, September 10, 1968, HART/10/03.
168. *Daily Mail*, September 10, 1968, HART/10/03.
169. *The Sun*, September 10, 1968, HART/10/03.
170. Allan Hall, *The Sun*, October 23, 1968, p. 3.
171. Ibid.
172. Interview with Maggie Sidgreaves, April 13, 2018.

CHAPTER 9

The First Woman Paymaster General and Beyond, 1968–1991

In October 1968, Judith Hart lost her job as Minister of Social Security. Almost immediately Harold Wilson promoted her to Secretary of State as Paymaster General. It appeared that her willingness to rein in her idealism, her willingness to adopt a pragmatic approach to social welfare, her willingness to compromise and her willingness to make unpopular decisions made her a safer pair of hands. She was now in the Cabinet, one of the senior politicians in Britain sitting alongside household names such as Richard Crossman, Jim Callaghan, George Brown, Dennis Healey and Barbara Castle and helping to govern the country. It was a double first: the first time in history that two women simultaneously served in the same Cabinet; and the first time that a woman held the post of Paymaster General. Hart, like Bondfield, Wilkinson and Castle before her, was now addressed as Rt Honourable (Fig. 9.1).

It was the fiftieth anniversary for votes for women and 'what could be neater' the press commented, than to have two women sitting at the government top table. Prime Ministers 'should always have a sense of history, as well as a sharp instinct for novelty. When the two combine, the effect is quite irresistible'.[1] Lady Falkender, Wilson's secretary, maintained that her boss had an impressive record of promoting women even though there was 'a great deal of hostility towards women politicians among men in the House. ... Harold could have put more in the Cabinet ... but he had to stop because he thought he had reached a point beyond which he would have been accused of overdoing it a bit'.[2] Some did think this anyway: even the allegedly sympathetic *Guardian* thought he 'overdid it' claiming that Mr Wilson had a fondness 'for giving ministerial posts to anything vaguely articulate in skirts',[3] pointing out that nine of the 19 women elected in 1966 had been given jobs.

The year 1968 was an auspicious year for British women: a new Abortion Act was passed, legalising abortion; women strikers at the Ford Factory at Dagenham won their fight for equal pay hastening the Equal Pay Act and encouraging the rise of the Women's Liberation Movement; and Virginia

© The Author(s) 2019
P. Bartley, *Labour Women in Power*,
https://doi.org/10.1007/978-3-030-14288-9_9

Fig. 9.1 Judith Hart in the Cabinet (©Keystone Pictures USA/Alamy Stock Photo)

Wade beat Billie Jean King to win the US Open tennis competition. It may have been a new dawn for women's equality but most of the press remained in the dark. Hart came to be regarded as Wilson's 'glamour girl'. One female reporter wrote that her 'first impression of Judith Hart is that she looks far too young, pretty and feminine to be Paymaster General'. Some newspapers were malicious, insinuating 'that Mrs C is wildly jealous of Mrs H because Judith is some years younger than Barbara and good-looking to boot'.[4] The *Sunday Express* published perhaps the most repugnant comments, claiming (inaccurately) that Judith Hart's appointment was 'most distasteful' for Barbara Castle because 'Mrs Hart is cleverer than she is. She is good-looking. She has just as much Left-wing glamour. And while Mrs Castle is 57, Mrs Hart is a mere lass of 44. … Henceforth, compared with Judith, Barbara is going to seem old hat. It is up-and-coming young Judith who will increasingly collect the admiring headlines. Judith, who will be replacing Barbara in the front-page pictures'.[5] A few newspapers poured scorn on these kind of comparisons: the *Sun*, a left-wing newspaper at the time, declared that 'to see any competition between two utterly serious working Ministers like them is pathetically searching for the non-existent sensational'.[6]

Judith Hart was certainly contemptuous of such comparisons, especially since she got 'along marvellously' with Barbara Castle. The two women were friends; they saw each other socially and the Harts and the Castles met regularly for dinner with other left-wing couples.[7] Contrary to most press reports, Castle gave Hart a very warm welcome to the Cabinet, pleased to have another woman appointed to a leading position, pleased to have a female colleague as an ally in a predominantly male Cabinet.

PAYMASTER GENERAL, NOVEMBER 1968–OCTOBER 1969

Judith Hart's new job of Paymaster General was an odd one. She was not given a department to manage but had a 'rag-bag of responsibilities': to oversee government policy; to bridge the ever-widening gap between Parliament and the electorate by making politics attractive; to supervise the devolution of powers to Scotland and Wales; to be a 'mini-Minister of Youth' by appealing to young people; and lastly, to promote the equality of women. The new Paymaster General was warned that if she took even half of her workload seriously she risked having a nervous breakdown as 'Mrs Hart's responsibilities cover the philosophy of the whole of modern politics, with the Chelsea pensioners added'.[8] It was suggested that even the ablest Cabinet Minister would find it 'difficult to do more than shovel smoke'.[9]

It was assumed that Harold Wilson was grooming Hart for even more important roles in government, especially when he allocated her an office in 10 Downing Street, at the topographical centre of the politics of power rather than side-lined away in a far-off office of her own.[10] Some believed that she would become a very formidable figure in the senior ranks of government, the most powerful woman in British politics and perhaps the country's first woman Prime Minister.

The first part of Hart's job included monitoring the speeches of other Ministers to make sure that they adhered to government policy.[11] Inevitably her role made the new Paymaster General unpopular with her peers in Cabinet as she was 'regarded as a henchman of the Prime Minister'.[12] Judith Hart insisted that she was no 'ticker-off of people, and I certainly shan't be ticking-off Ministers in my new job. … but … I hope to help avoid situations where two Ministers make speeches on the same day in different directions'. She thought it helped being a woman because she had an innate ability 'to identify with the other person's point of view more easily than a man can, so she tends to be more tactful and understanding'.[13] However, Ministers feared that Judith Hart was Harold Wilson's spy and were wary of her.

The second part of Judith Hart's role was less contentious: her responsibility was to 'win the hearts and minds' of the 2,500,000 under-21s who would be eligible to vote at the next general election.[14] As the mother of two teenage sons, Mrs Hart was thought well-placed to give a 'youthful look to Labour policy',[15] particularly as she knew something of the generation gap as she had it at home.[16] Both her sons were 'very articulate and involved politically. They worry about racialism and social injustices. They study current affairs. I like to think there is no generation gap between us. But there is. I have to make a conscious effort to understand their point of view'.[17]

The *Daily Sketch* asked a few young people for their response to Hart's appointment. One of them was Richard Branson, then aged 18 and editor of *Student* magazine who said that students would be 'be quite prepared to listen to what she has to say. If it sounds like sense I don't think her age will matter'.[18]

The third part of Judith Hart's brief was to prepare for Scottish devolution and to stop the electoral drift towards the Scottish National Party. Wilson made a wise choice: Hart was known as an ardent devolutionist, a firm advocate for Scotland and well respected as a Scottish MP.[19] She had empathy for Scotland, all too aware that Scottish people saw Westminster as a remote centre of power 'where "they" decide what "they" are going to do for or to "us"'.[20] Political disillusion, she recognised, was reinforced by an increasing sense of a Scottish national identity, and of a people who resented the domination of England. Wilson shared her concern. In 1969 he set up a Royal Commission, under the chair of first Lord Crowther and then Lord Kilbrandon, to examine changes to the constitution of the UK. In 1973, the Report was published and recommended that directly elected Scottish and Welsh Assemblies be set up.[21]

The final part of Hart's jobs was to oversee Labour's policy on women's rights. On July 21, 1969, Judith Hart was appointed co-chair of the Women's National Commission, an independent body sponsored and financed by the government to promote female equality. Hart was a self-confessed feminist keen to advance the rights of women, and who knew that there was much to change and improve. There were gross inequalities at work, in marriage and in general life: women were not allowed to become clerics or stockbrokers; many medical schools put a cap on women entrants, restricting them to between 10 and 15% of students; only 7% of girls were released on day courses compared to 30% of boys; only 12% of local government councillors were women; only six women were bank managers; only one woman was trained in government centres for every 1000 men. More egregiously when a woman was appointed to a post she was paid considerably less than a man for doing the same job. Marriage laws favoured men: a child's nationality was decided by their father's nationality; husbands were able to claim damages for their wives' adultery whereas women could not claim against 'the other woman'; single men could claim a tax allowance for a housekeeper but single women could not; husbands received their wives' tax rebate; wives were not allowed to take out a mortgage or sign a hire-purchase agreement without the consent of their husband. Expectations around sexual behaviour differed too. Sex before marriage was unacceptable for women whereas it was assumed that men needed an outlet for their 'natural' sex-drive. Even here, the law protected men rather than women: a prostitute who solicited on the streets could be prosecuted, fined and imprisoned whereas a man who accosted women was never charged.[22] The Commission lobbied Ministers 'on every question from health, education, women in society, to even general problems like race relations'.[23] It investigated divorce law reform, the problem of single parents, equal pay and the overall status of women in British society.[24] The Women's Commission worked hard to reverse this inequality but it was Barbara Castle who achieved equal pay in 1970; and the Women's Liberation Movement which led the campaign for abortion rights.[25]

Judith Hart continued to remain alert to the problems of her constituents, always willing to help people in need. During one week alone, she obtained a refund of school travelling expenses; helped an old couple living in 'deplorable conditions' to have their home repaired; persuaded the tax authorities to cancel the tax owed by an impoverished constituent; and sorted out the postal difficulties of another. She even compiled a reading list for a constituent interested in socialism, recommending R. H. Tawney's *Equality* and *The Acquisitive Society* and Max Beer's *History of Socialism* as a start. On one occasion, she persuaded the East Kilbride Development Corporation to pay part of the electricity bill of tenants living in a damp fungus-permeated, beetle-infested flat. As ever, Judith Hart was attentive to the most vulnerable local people, believing that individual lives could be transformed given the right circumstances and opportunities. Her constituency work reflects a deep compassion for those defenceless individuals who few cared about and even fewer were willing to help. It was behind-the-scenes work, without glory, publicity or political advantage.

On one occasion, the MP for Lanark worked assiduously to move Mr G, a 29-year-old special needs constituent incarcerated in a state mental hospital, to another more congenial one. Judith Hart's notes document in detail how Mr G's case was a typical case of neglect: his mother died when he was 11 and his father when he was 13. In July 1953, aged 12, he was convicted of theft and because of his limited mental ability was detained. He became a very angry young man who 'assaulted other patients and in 1959 knocked another patient unconscious,' and was generally 'noisy, insolent, truculent and impulsive'.[26] Hart's appeal was refused on the grounds that Mr G's emotional instability and aggression made him unsuitable for an ordinary 'mentally deficient hospital and quite unsuitable for discharge'.[27] Judith Hart was undeterred, arguing that 'all boys pinch things around the 9-12 age group – any shopkeeper will vouch for that. But once they get a conviction they are doomed. The younger they are, the more statistically inevitable it is that they will be in and out of jail for the rest of their lives. And Mr G was convicted at the age of 12. I'd like to think we could give him some reason for hope – without which his behaviour pattern isn't likely to improve'.[28] Her appeal was not granted and Mr G remained in the state hospital. Cases such as Mr G's were typical of the hundreds and hundreds of constituency problems that Judith Hart tried to resolve.

Within a year, Judith Hart had fallen out of favour at Westminster. The first rumblings of discontent emerged when Harold Wilson declined to appoint Judith Hart to the election campaign committee despite the fact that her job had direct relevance to fighting an election campaign, and 'especially as someone will have to woo the newly enfranchised 18-21 year olds'.[29]

Hart's disloyalty rather than her competence was seen to be at fault: she had after all done a good job as Cabinet Minister. Hart was a high-octane emotional politician who was passionate about her beliefs and willing to shout and bellow to get her point across. The breaking point occurred over Castle's *In Place of Strife*. In Cabinet meetings, Hart's tone was 'distinctly confrontational and she took a leading part in the opposition to the Prime Minister and to Barbara Castle'.[30] Harold Wilson confided to Barbara Castle that he was going to dismiss Hart and others who had opposed their joint policy. He was determined to show that disloyalty did not pay and he reshuffled his Cabinet, 'determined to punish his enemies'.[31] On October 6, 1969, Judith Hart was dismissed from the Cabinet. She had been in post for less than one year.

MINISTER OF OVERSEAS DEVELOPMENT OCTOBER 1969–JUNE 1970[32]

Shortly after the reshuffle, Hart was appointed Minister of Overseas Development (ODM) when its incumbent Reg Prentice resigned. She was well known as a 'passionate advocate of increased aid to the underdeveloped world',[33] already familiar with development policies from her days as Minister at the Commonwealth Office. The new Minister was an active member of the Movement for Colonial Freedom, Chair of the Mediterranean and Middle East Committee, supportive of the West African struggles against Portuguese colonialism, and enjoyed cordial relationships with the Commonwealth leaders.[34] She was too good a politician to be left on the backbenches. At ODM, she would have the opportunity to put her ideals to work in alleviating some of the world's poverty and be able to put her principles into effect without compromising her values or beliefs. More importantly, Hart was in charge of her own budget and her own policies even though the ODM was no longer a Cabinet post.

As soon as she took office, Judith Hart was faced with defending the aid programme from drastic governmental cuts. The country was suffering an economic crisis with a huge trade deficit, a recent devaluation in the pound, growing inflation and a wave of unofficial strikes. All departments, including the ODM, were asked to save money. The new Minister was not, pronounced Norman Shrapnel, in 'danger of being elected Miss World Aid'.[35] Even as Britain faced economic turmoil she persuaded Cabinet to increase the level of aid from £227 to £300 million and tried to convince her colleagues to implement the Pearson proposals.[36] In August 1968, the President of the World Bank had asked Lester Pearson, the former Canadian Prime Minister, to investigate world poverty and ways to overcome it. In his report *Partners in Development*, he and his Commission recommended that richer developed nations should contribute 0.7% of their gross national product (GNP) to their aid programme and aim to contribute 1% as soon as economically viable. Judith Hart agreed with this principle, maintaining that it was 'a dangerous coincidence' that the world was divided economically by race, 'the better-off peoples were mostly white, and the poorer were mostly in Africa, Asia, the

Pacific and the Caribbean'.[37] If this division was maintained, she insisted, world peace would be under threat. Hart proved to be a tough and clever negotiator but it took her until 1974 to win government approval and only 'in principle' to her 0.7% target.[38]

One of Hart's departmental roles was to respond to catastrophes caused by war. In May 1967, fighting had broken out between the Nigerian government and the secessionist state of Biafra, home of the Ibo people. Between half a million and 2 million Biafrans died of starvation. Images of malnourished and starving children in the press led to a swell of sympathy for the Biafrans and a humanitarian campaign was organised by a number of key charities to help them. One of Judith Hart's challenges was to supply aid: she set up an emergency action group and provided £5 million to help the crisis. On January 14, 1970, the Biafrans surrendered to General Gowon, the Nigerian leader.

Judith Hart was a formidable character, a senior Minister in charge of her own department, but she was a woman working in a predominantly male world, and open to sexual harassment. Her Principal Private Secretary, a senior civil servant in charge of her office, was so infatuated with Hart that he placed love poems at the top of her ministerial box just before it closed and sent her many expressions of his feelings for her. During a ministerial visit to India, the Private Secretary clearly overstepped the mark, was sent home, and dismissed from his post. He wrote to his Minister a couple of times, first of all asking that a false cover be provided for his sudden return and secondly excusing his behaviour by saying that 'the silly song "you always hurt the one you love" has, sadly much in it'.[39] He continued to pester Hart even after his dismissal, begging to be reinstated, claiming that his 'feeling for you has got to a stage when I am quite confident that because I am fond of you without any expectations, illusions or pedestalling, I can become quite reasonably phlegmatic, 'cos this is what you need. ... Specifically, I won't crowd you or try to be possessive'.[40] He maintained that he felt a 'very real deep affection and admiration for yourself, and a horrid feeling of bereftness at not being allowed to ever be with you'.[41] Fortunately, Judith Hart was his boss not his underling—she had the power to remove him from her office rather than put up with his unwelcome attentions. She did not ask for him to be dismissed from the civil service but agreed that he should be transferred to Science and Technology. He ended his days as a vicar in the Church of England.

Judith Hart's new job was time-consuming but she remained alert to the challenges in Lanark, fully aware of the need to nurse her constituency, fully aware of the singular needs of her constituents. In October 1969, she helped the 800 members of the Amalgamated Union of Engineering and Foundry Workers at the British Sound Reproduction Factory in East Kilbride in their fight for union recognition. In November 1969, after a 12-year struggle to attract industry to the area, Judith Hart opened two new factories in Douglas, giving work to 230 miners who had been made redundant when the pits closed.[42] She also set up a branch of the Overseas Aid Ministry in East Kilbride where it remains today employing over 600 people.

On the Opposition Benches

In June 1970, Labour lost the election and Judith Hart returned to the opposition benches as Shadow Minister for Overseas Development, a post she held throughout Labour's opposition years. After her electoral victory, she received a number of nasty abusive letters, often semi-literate, often in capital letters, often racist and generally misogynistic. One anonymous undated letter from 'a Tory' berated Hart for being 'an overbearing, aggressive, self-important, heartless and hard nasty piece of work. ... All the adjectives apply equally to your fellow _ex_-minister, Mrs Castle – and a great many people think of you as a pair of first class Sour battleaxes'.[43] Another from 'A Willesden Worker' complained that 'you and Mrs Castle are back in Parliament, two skid-row backbenchers but as your lousy government has been thrown out you and she are now only! And old Jennie Lee has gone completely. So you three gaggle of old Labour geese are now chopped! Oh lovely! Oh Joy! ... How we hate and loathe you n.....-loving old Labour whores'.[44] In 1968, Enoch Powell's hateful 'Rivers of Blood' speech encouraged such attitudes but despite her strong aversion to Powell's racism, she gave him a lift in her ministerial car when they were both on 'Any Questions', her kindness overriding political differences.[45]

Fortunately, Judith Hart remained popular in her constituency, always committed to solving the often intractable problems of her constituents. One typical case, involved 'Mr M' who had been dismissed for embezzlement. He wrote to Hart asking for help, telling her that he had five children, an ill wife and was in deep financial trouble: his electricity had been cut off, his rent was in arrears, and he owed money to a furniture store and a money lender. The family had no heating and had to use candles for light. Judith Hart tackled the problem with exemplary professional skill, writing to the East Kilbride Welfare Department, the Department of Health and Social Security[46] and the Electricity Board to arrange a pre-payment meter.[47] She even wrote to a number of firms requesting that Mr M be given a job. Eventually, the Co-op agreed to employ him. However, in April 1973, the Co-op wrote to Judith Hart saying that 'our "do good" exercise ... has had an unhappy and costly ending' because Mr M had failed to throw off certain bad habits.[48] Once again, he had embezzled the firm's money. Judith Hart told the Co-op that she was 'deeply distressed that your wonderful efforts have ended in this way. You could not have done more, and I shall always be grateful to you. I suppose the real difficulty one has to face is that some people are problem people and that at the end of the day very difficult to help'.[49] Judith Hart was disappointed rather than embittered; in general, her irritation was with an unfair economic system rather than the failures of any particular individual.

Judith Hart enjoyed many successes: helping the development of a new town at Stonehouse, fighting to save the Rolls-Royce factory in East Kilbride,[50] saving and improving the village of Lesmahagow,[51] and keeping the Kennox Colliery open.[52] Now, with more time at her disposal, she had the freedom to write a book on international aid, *Aid and Liberation*. Aid policy, she argued, should be directed to improve the lives of the poorest, often the peasant population. If this meant nationalisation and the 'expropriation' of foreign assets then this was justifiable since development should be 'for the people, rather than benefiting elites'. It was—critics complained and supporters welcomed—pure socialism.

Opposing the Chilean Regime

In 1973, Judith Hart became deeply immersed in opposing the Chilean regime. On September 11 that year, the democratically elected socialist government of Chile was overthrown in an American CIA-backed violent coup d'etat. General Pinochet deposed Dr Salvador Allende, ending 160 years of democracy and beginning seventeen years of a murderous military dictatorship. The military junta immediately banned all left-wing parties, outlawed trade unions, imposed a strict censorship of the press, abolished the Congress and the Constitution and replaced public officials such as Ministers, provincial governors, university heads, town mayors and head teachers with military officers of their own political persuasion. University departments, especially sociology and politics, were closed and degree courses ended. The new regime burned books. *The Times* believed 'that a country so recently a model of democracy and moderation should be reduced to this situation is deeply depressing'.[53]

From the outset, the Pinochet regime committed flagrant human rights violations. Planes bought from Britain bombed the Presidential Palace, Allende was murdered, and those opposed to the new regime were herded into the national stadium, military bases and even naval ships, often to be tortured and murdered. Over 3000 were left dead or missing; tens of thousands were tortured; approximately 200,000 fled their country. A special army task force known as the 'Caravan of Death' toured the country killing prisoners. Jeremy Corbyn informed the House of Commons that many 'died a painful and slow death; their bodies were mutilated, their eyes carved up with knives, their limbs torn apart'.[54] One of Pinochet's methods was to drop pregnant women known to oppose his regime out of aeroplanes, saying 'If you kill the bitch, you kill off the offspring'.[55]

For Judith Hart and the Labour Party, it was a re-enactment of the Spanish Civil War. It was also highly personal. Some of those killed, tortured or imprisoned were people she knew well through the Socialist International. At once, Hart sprang into action. On September 19, two days after the coup, she wrote a *Guardian* article calling for the non-recognition of the Chilean state because it was the 'most vicious fascism we have seen for generations'.[56] Her advice was ignored. On September 23, the Conservative Government recognised Chile's military regime: Judith Hart described it as a 'squalid act' and protested that Britain 'stood with some of the world's most reactionary regimes in being among the first to recognise the military coup. What the

Government has recognised', she insisted 'is a regime of terror. This hasty act will only encourage the junta to believe they can continue to violate human rights with impunity'.[57]

Judith Hart called for the imposition of sanctions, including measures to 'prevent any sale of arms from Great Britain to the Junta'. She was a key figure for the Chile Solidarity Campaign (CSC) and the Chile Campaign for Human Rights (CCHR) established to campaign for human rights. Both used traditional middle-class methods of organising: lobbying government, organising letter campaigns, petitions, delegations and demonstrations. Imaginative new methods of propaganda were developed: Chilean women sewed scraps of fabric together to create tapestries depicting Chilean life. These rag pictures were sold internationally; the Chilean Junta labelled them 'Tapestries of Defamation'. Judith Hart also campaigned in support of Chilean political refugees fleeing from persecution and put many of them, including the widow of Salvador Allende up in her home.[58] The Conservative Government was unimpressed and Judith Hart had to fight for each person to be accepted into Britain which took up an inordinate amount of her time as she organised petitions, demonstrations and letter-writing to help further each case.

Meanwhile, in large capital letters, the front page of the *Daily Mirror* asked its readers IS EVERYBODY GOING BLOODY MAD?[59] On January 24, 1974, the coal miners had voted to strike. Less than a fortnight later the miners withdrew their labour, resulting in a three day working week for large swathes of the country. Judith Hart accused the Tory Government for wreaking economic havoc by not settling the miner's strike. 'Let us be clear', she insisted 'It is not the miner's fault. ... It is directly due to the appalling economic management' of the Conservative Government.[60] She appreciated 'what mining is about – the long crawl to the coalface, risking injury and disease, and bringing home less than one's young daughter earns as a secretary in Glasgow'.[61] Mr Heath, she insisted, was 'utterly determined not to negotiate, stubbornly resisting every TUC initiative, arrogantly insistent on his terms, and only his terms'.[62] Rocketing prices, soaring rents, frightening mortgage rates, the obscene profits of the land and property speculators and what she called the 'greatest single capitalist scandal of the Conservative Government – the foreign exploitation of North Sea oil at fantastic profit to the multinational companies'[63] had led to an economic meltdown. Judith Hart knew only too well that the three day week hit her Lanark constituents harder than most. 'This crisis' she insisted 'will not go away even if a stubborn and irrational Prime Minister abandons confrontational politics and settles with the miners'.[64]

In February 1974, Edward Heath called for a general election, asking the country 'Who Governs Britain?' By now, Judith Hart's constituency was a marginal one, due to boundary changes that hived off the huge Labour-dominated new town of East Kilbride. Judith Hart was very aware of her political vulnerability and campaigned forcefully, asking well-known MPs to visit Lanark to give her support.[65] Elections are won on local issues as much as national ones so Judith Hart's election leaflets focussed on improvements she had initiated in the constituency. 'Without Judith Hart's involvement and hard fighting', they stated 'Abington might not have its public toilets scheduled. Leadhills would not have kept its ambulance service … It would not now have a new sewage … Woodford would still be without coal. … Rigside would not have had its sub-post office restored'.[66]

Experts forecast that Hart would be defeated. They were proved wrong: Judith Hart was re-elected for Lanark with a majority of 2100. The electoral turnout was high: 83% overall and an astonishingly high 97% in the area of Rigside. However, the election produced the first hung Parliament since 1929 and Labour returned to power as a minority government. On his second day in office, Harold Wilson settled the miner's strike; on the third day, he announced that Britain could return to a five-day week. Wilson opted not to go into a coalition with the other minority parties and a few months later called for new elections. In the October election, Hart's majority dwindled to 698; Labour won by a majority of three. The SNP candidate came second, foreshadowing future elections.

MINISTER OF OVERSEAS DEVELOPMENT II, MARCH 1974–JUNE 1975

When Labour returned to government Judith Hart was given another chance to make her mark as ODM. Under the previous Conservative Government, the department had been in the Foreign Office and was renamed the Overseas Development Administration (ODA).[67] Judith Hart wanted it to be independent, free to determine its own policy, free to spend its own budget, 'an independent voice exercised on behalf of the Third World'.[68] There was a struggle between Hart, Harold Wilson and the Foreign Secretary, Jim Callaghan who wanted jurisdiction over overseas aid.[69] Judith Hart, who had no desire to be a Junior Minister under Callaghan, won. The Ministry's name was restored to Ministry of Overseas Development (ODM) and she became the only Minister who headed a department outside of Cabinet, in charge of its own policy and its own budget.[70]

At first, MI5 refused to give Mrs Hart security clearance, citing that they held evidence that she was a communist. Harold Wilson told Hart that she could not appoint her to the post. Barbara Castle, who had a dinner engagement with Judith Hart and her husband, commented that 'Judith came in late, obviously upset. … Harold had sent for her and told her she was being positively vetted. … She poured her heart out to me. The very idea that anyone could consider her a Communist!'[71] Wilson was convinced by Judith Hart's rebuttal and asked MI5 to provide proof of her communism. The head of MI5 secretly visited Wilson at No 10 to show him photographic evidence of Judith Hart at a communist meeting. Unfortunately for MI5, they had confused the MP for Lanark with someone of a similar name, a Mrs J. Tudor

Hart. Judith Hart was given clearance, much to the chagrin of Foreign Office officials who probably disapproved of her leftish leanings and her solidarity with Chile.[72] It was not surprising that by this time she was smoking around 60 a day—Senior Service untipped. The cigarette packets were useful: she used the back of them to jot down policy ideas.[73]

On the first day of her appointment, she arrived at the office straight from seeing Harold Wilson and pulled out a priority list—written on the back of her cigarette packet—from her handbag. Item No 1 was to cut aid to Chile. It was to be her first clash with the civil service, many of whom disapproved of Hart politicising the aid programme and especially disliked the cancellation of the existing large and effective programme of aid which they were administering in Chile.[74] There were fierce arguments between very upset civil servants and a determined Hart over aid to Chile, not helped when the new Minister went beyond her brief by demanding a ban on the sale of arms and a more sympathetic attitude towards refugees fleeing from the Junta.[75]

There was certainly a divided response in the civil service to Hart's reappointment. Some were delighted that Judith Hart had returned, welcoming her commitment to end world poverty; others were less keen. Her allies regarded Hart's high profile, high energy and highly emotional personality as assets whereas her adversaries thought that Ministers should be 'cold and remote and intellectually driven and didn't like the idea of someone who was so emotional'.[76] All the staff knew that their returning Minister had a strong ideological vision and that she would be an intense, fierce, hard-working Minister who expected unreserved dedication from her civil servants.

In the spring and early summer, Hart set about helping the drought and famine in the Sahel, on giving aid to developing countries who had been hardest hit by the rise in oil prices and on trying to secure a good deal for Commonwealth and developing countries in the European Community.[77] Under Hart's aegis three priorities were established for foreign aid: first it should be used as a political tool to support left-wing governments and undermine right-wing ones; secondly that it should be aimed predominantly at the poorest people in the very poorest countries; and thirdly that it should focus on rural as opposed to industrial development. Her concern was to 'do everything we can to help the developing countries increase their own production of food, and to distribute it in such a way that the poorest people are able to eat better'.[78]

In her short time in office, Judith Hart revolutionised the way in which aid was granted. In her view, too much emphasis was placed on industrial development at the expense of agriculture. This she feared had resulted in a drift to the towns which had impoverished the villages even more.[79] As Chase and Wilkinson point out, malnutrition was rampant, infant mortality was high, life expectancy was low, illiteracy widespread and unemployment and underemployment growing in the rural areas of developing countries.[80] She put forward policies suggested by the President of the World Bank, Robert MacNamara, which aimed to transform poor rural areas into cohesive self-sufficient communities. This came to be known as 'integrated rural development'. Hart duly prioritised land reform, water management, electric power, fertilisers, co-operatives, and the provision of farm machinery in ODM's distribution of aid. As a result roads, small-scale dams and investment in health centres—all which might improve the lives of people in small villages—were included in the aid package.[81] Unfortunately, it proved to be an over-ambitious very expensive failure, often in areas like Sub-Sahara Africa where progress was needed the most.[82]

Hart was keen to award money to governments carrying out social change to help the poorest, regardless of whether or not they were friendly to Britain. In 1965, aid to Tanzania had been stopped when President Julius Nyerere broke off diplomatic relations over Britain's failure to end UDI in Rhodesia. Judith Hart was well-disposed to Nyerere's politics and wanted to renew aid to Tanzania because of the President's promise to help the poorest people in his nation. The big unresolved question was that several British farmers had had their properties nationalised by the Tanzanian Government and the owners of that land demanded compensation. Nyerere refused. He was committed to *Ujamaa* (a word meaning extended family in Swahili) a programme of creating collective settlements from previously small independently owned farms. It sounded like the peasant socialism of which Judith Hart approved. This, in fact, was an example of her naivety. Rural people were moved compulsorily into villages and expected to work collectively; there was little investment, and agricultural production fell steeply. Moreover both Wilson and Callaghan were being pestered by friends of British land-owners and refused ODM's proposal to resume aid until the farmers were compensated. For a while, there was a political impasse but Judith Hart was undeterred and resolute. She flew out to Tanzania to restore diplomatic relations and negotiate a deal on farm compensation, the key to an aid package being awarded. In June 1974, aid was resumed: ten million pounds of aid was promised consisting of £4 and a half million in grants, the rest interest-free loans payable over 25 years. At the same time, money was found by the Tanzanian Government to compensate a very limited group of elderly expatriates whose farms and industries had been nationalised.[83] Once more Hart had proved to be a skilled negotiator, persuading both the Cabinet and Tanzania to compromise.

The ODM was aware that women were often the poorest in poor countries. In 1975, in a talk at the International Women's Year Seminar, Hart argued that everything was stacked against women who made a meagre living from the land, 'lucky if she can manage to supply two or three reasonable meals a week for her family'. Women, she told her audience, often lived in often dry, unirrigated countryside, without proper roads, 'a countryside which produces food sparsely – and only with a struggle. If there is a drought or a flood next year's food supplies have gone. Picture in your minds the woman working on the ground, tilling the soil, helping the family cultivation of their own little plot, with probably five, six, seven children and maybe another one on the way'. Her department's focus on rural development she argued helped 'the woman trying to keep her family alive'.[84]

Judith Hart was an instinctive moderniser. In March 1975, she set up a 'Disaster Unit' to provide a flying squad of people, supplies and transport which could act immediately in response to natural disasters. In August, Hart's new approach was tested when floods hit Bangladesh: British aircraft carrying 20 tons of anti-cholera vaccine and other medical supplies were swiftly despatched to help.[85] The Ministry also helped when a hurricane hit Honduras, a famine occurred in Somalia, cholera broke out in Kenya, an earthquake shook Pakistan and a cyclone damaged parts of Mauritius.[86]

One of Hart's lasting achievements in office was helping to change the EEC's relationship with developing countries. At the time, EEC aid and trade focussed on countries with which its six founding members (Belgium, France, Italy, Luxembourg, the Netherlands and West Germany) enjoyed special bonds in the Yaounde Convention: France and Belgium, for example, had had colonies in Africa and were keen to foster good relationships via an aid programme. Initially, Judith Hart's inclination was to have very little to do with the aid programme—she was after all vehemently anti-EEC. However, she changed her mind when she realised that the EEC could be a force for good internationally. Furthermore, she came under strong pressure from both her civil servants who wanted her to take a lead in allocating European aid and from the Foreign Office who wanted her to make sure that Commonwealth countries benefited.

Judith Hart joined other European Ministers on the left such as Jan Pronk, the socialist Dutch Minister for Development Cooperation, who shared her commitment for a more equitable distribution of power and wealth worldwide to fight against injustice. Soon Hart helped persuade the EEC to develop a more coherent and generous policy towards the rest of the world, in particular extending EEC aid to former colonies such as India, Pakistan, Sri Lanka and Bangladesh. She also helped convince members of the EEC to sign the Lomé Convention which gave aid and trade preferences from Europe to 46 of the world's poorest countries. Harold Wilson congratulated his Minister publicly. 'A great tribute is due here' he maintained 'to the Minister for Overseas Development' for the 'transformation of a paternalistic arrangement ... into a relationship based on cooperation with 46 countries in Africa, the Caribbean and Pacific', twenty-two of which were from the Commonwealth.[87] The UK had secured a commitment during the accession negotiations for the poorest developing countries to have similar access so Judith Hart did not have to push very hard for these policy changes.

Judith Hart's greatest achievement and lasting impact were committing British overseas aid to a percentage of its GDP. It was not easy. Under her influence, the 1974 Labour manifesto promised that the United Nations target of 0.7% of a country's GDP would be designated for overseas aid but the new Chancellor Dennis Healey refused to allocate any increase in the aid budget, arguing that the British economy was much too weak to do so. Judith Hart fought back and in the first few months of the new government, there were heated exchanges between the ODM and the Chancellor over the aid budget. Mrs Hart won, the aid budget was increased and she secured, in principle, the first-ever government commitment to a 0.7% target, a target finally reached in 2013.[88] For a while, it was thought that Judith Hart would be returned to Cabinet.

TENSIONS BETWEEN HART AND WILSON

However, relationships between Wilson and Hart soured. In November 1974, a big row flared up when Judith Hart, Tony Benn and Joan Lestor voted in favour of an NEC resolution condemning a forthcoming Royal Navy exercise with the South African navy. Harold Wilson 'blew his top' and sent letters of rebuke to the guilty Ministers.[89] Harold Wilson told his Ministers either to stand by the collective decisions of the government or resign.[90] In a terse letter to Hart personally, Wilson demanded that she write 'an unqualified assurance that you accept the principle of collective responsibility and that you will from now on comply with its requirements and the rules that flow from it, in the NEC and in all other circumstances. I must warn you that I should have to regard your failure to give such an assurance, or any subsequent breach of it, as a decision on your part that you did not wish to continue as a member of this administration. I should of course much regret such a decision; but I should accept it'.[91] At first, Judith Hart prevaricated and refused to agree to the Prime Minister's demands. However, when Wilson replied that 'if you want to be free ... to criticise or differ from the Government, then you can enjoy that freedom only outside the Government', Hart gave her boss the assurances he demanded.[92] This was a big climbdown by the Minister for Overseas Development.

The relationship between Wilson and his Minister was further strained when Judith Hart wrote a paper on the Steel Industry for the Industrial Policy Sub-Committee of the NEC. Her paper was regarded as a 'stab in the back' to Wilson and as blatant and unacceptable interference in the affairs of another department, a department led by Tony Benn.[93] Once again, Harold Wilson wrote to his ODM asking for an explanation.[94] He told Hart that Ministers 'may not in their non-ministerial capacity, initiate or propose policy proposals', particularly those against government policy.[95] Again, rather than resign, Judith Hart apologised.

Her final disloyalty towards Wilson was over the European Economic Community which Britain had now joined. Hart had strong reservations about the free movement of capital, the loss of sovereignty and the balance of payments. In particular, she was concerned about the effects on the Clydeside market-garden industry of cheaper continental imports sold by countries which had a lower standard of living and paid their workers considerably less.

More importantly perhaps, Hart had a strong personal attachment to the Commonwealth and feared that relationships between Britain and its former colonies would deteriorate as new trading partners in Europe replaced old alliances.

In 1973, Edward Heath had managed to take Britain into the European Union. But when Labour was re-elected in 1974, there was a clamour by left-wingers like Judith Hart to honour the party's manifesto which had pledged to renegotiate the terms of accession and which had promised a referendum on the outcome. In order to pacify his party, Wilson agreed to a referendum and temporarily suspended the doctrine of collective responsibility allowing his Cabinet and Ministers to argue their case in public. By now, Harold Wilson was publicly committed to Europe, expecting the Labour Party to follow his lead. He was taken aback when a tidal wave of opposition threatened to submerge the party and its leader. Judith Hart campaigned vigorously to withdraw from the EEC 'warning that it would lead to a federal Europe, and threatened parliamentary sovereignty'.[96] In the end, Britain voted to Remain and the matter was again thought settled.

Harold Wilson was obviously annoyed by Hart's perceived disloyalty. She was now politically vulnerable, an 'irritant to the so-called moderates of the Party'[97] who disliked her insistence on driving the Labour Party leftwards and an irritant to the Foreign Office who regarded her views as 'incompatible with HMG's interests' when she refused to grant aid to certain countries because of their political stance.[98] Judith Hart was dispensable. When the results of the EEC referendum came through Harold Wilson used the occasion to reshuffle his Cabinet and his Ministers, get rid of the anti-marketers and resolve a conflict between Government and the Foreign Office. Judith Hart was the sacrificial lamb. Wilson offered to transfer her to Transport but Hart refused to leave a department to which she was fully committed, especially when she was in the middle of drafting an important White Paper on overseas aid.

Judith Hart was replaced by Reg Prentice. The ODM lost its independence, was relabelled the ODA and came once again under the Foreign Office, a change Judith Hart thought was 'a casualty' and 'betrayal of a firm and fulfilled Labour commitment'.[99] Another top civil servant noted that 'ODM had ceased to exist; Prentice was Minister; we were again part of the Foreign Office. The era of Judith Hart and Overseas Development was over'.[100] Barbara Castle, Michael Foot and Tony Benn all went to Wilson's office to try to persuade him to reinstate their friend. They 'repeatedly said it was a terrible injustice to drop Judith',[101] and even threatened mass resignation. Wilson remained unmoved. The next day Judith Hart made a personal and emotional statement to the House of Commons. 'I say at once that it is a real sadness to me that I can no longer continue my work at the Ministry of Overseas Development.... I had a White Paper in draft. ... Frankly', she avowed, 'I can see no reason for the Prime Minister to sack me from my Ministry'.[102] Hart's political career seemed over. She was now a backbencher, free to criticise the government, no longer bound by collective ministerial responsibility. Barbara Castle observed that her friend was 'throwing her weight about as a freebooting left-winger'.[103]

Judith Hart's 'free-booting' was limited. At times she was willing to sacrifice her beliefs if they threatened her electoral prospects: in 1976, she voted for the Glasgow MP James White's Private Member's Abortion Bill, a Bill which aimed to curtail women's access to abortion, largely because 'of the strong views held in my constituency'.[104] Privately, she supported women's right to choose though was more circumspect in public because she had to 'tread a tightrope very discreetly and carefully. I sit on a majority of 698 with a totally unscrupulous SNP opponent. I always do the right thing, but I feel always that I must be discreet and non public on these matters'.[105] In 1977, she abstained on—rather than vote for—a Bill put forward by the Tory MP William Benyon which would have slashed women's right to abortion to 20 weeks. She was not courageous enough to vote against it, all too aware that a 500-strong meeting of the Motherwell Lay Apostolate Council had made it clear that if the principle of abortion on demand became Labour Party policy then Roman Catholics would not vote for its candidates.[106] Moreover, Hart was regularly lobbied by local anti-abortionists, once receiving a petition signed by 1750 of her constituents who were opposed to abortion. Judith Hart had no wish to be cast into political oblivion and so kept her opinions on abortion to herself, her family and close friends.

Minister for Overseas Development III, February 1977–May 1979

In April 1976, Callaghan replaced Wilson. In a reshuffle following the death of Anthony Crosland, Judith Hart was returned for the third and last time to her old stamping ground. She was recalled, the press believed 'because of her sway inside the national executive committee and in Labour politics generally'.[107] However, Callaghan was as circumspect as Wilson: Hart was not given a Cabinet post and the ODA remained under the Foreign Office. In the past, Judith Hart had fought for ministerial independence, though she now claimed that this was no longer a problem: the Foreign Secretary David Owen 'didn't interfere' and she was able to 'put in a paper and come to the Cabinet meeting'.[108]

When Judith Hart was appointed her department administered aid to about 113 countries of which the Commonwealth countries 'tend to take first place because of its historical relationship'.[109] In her third spell at the post, Judith Hart was determined to increase the level of funding and change the way overseas aid was delivered. The British, she complained 'spend about as much on foreign aid as they do on processed pet food' which amounted to about a quarter of what Britain spent on tobacco and a fifth of what it spent on alcohol.[110] In October 1977, she persuaded the Cabinet to increase the aid budget by £20 million, bringing it to £683 million in total, still at

0.4% well below the UN target of 0.7%. David Owen was unhappy about the money allocated to ODA. On one occasion, when Hart was in Tanzania she was telephoned by a friendly Cabinet Minister who warned her that Owen proposed to cut the aid budget while she was out of the country.[111] Owen had underestimated Judith Hart. She caught the next aeroplane to London, paying her own fare, and walked unannounced into the Cabinet meeting. The Cabinet, surprised by her attendance, did not cut ODA's budget.[112] In July 1978, at a conference of seven leading industrial nations, Hart urged the cancellation of debts, debts totalling £1.1 billion. Britain led the way. In August 1978, Judith Hart announced that 17 of the poorest countries would have their outstanding loans written off by the British Government. It would remove the burden of past aid loans from Afghanistan, Bangladesh, Botswana, Egypt, the Gambia, India, Indonesia, Kenya, Lesotho, Malawi, Nepal, Pakistan, Sierra Leone, Sri Lanka, Sudan, Tanzania and Western Samoa, countries which had loan repayments outstanding to the value of about £1000 million. Not all countries benefited. Aid, she insisted, would not be extended to governments which had seriously violated human rights such as Idi Amin's regime in Uganda,[113] or to Chile, Kampuchea, Equatorial Guinea and the Central African Empire.[114]

Not everyone shared Hart's commitment to politicising aid. In 1977, she was reproached for giving aid and support to an undemocratic Marxist Government accused of murdering its people.[115] She had just paid a visit to Mozambique, a country which had recently won its independence from Portugal and had offered a further loan of £5 million on top of a previous loan of £10 million. Judith Hart's personal political beliefs were felt to have paid too much of a part: she was a well-known member of the Movement for Colonial Freedom and had campaigned for freedom for the Portuguese colonies. She had supported the Front for the Liberation of Mozambique (FRELIMO) which fought a guerrilla campaign against Portuguese rule and became friendly with the new President Samora Michel and his wife Graça who later married Nelson Mandela. Once in power Samora Michel established a one-party state based on Marxist principles, nationalising land and industries and imprisoning those who opposed them. Judith Hart insisted that there was no evidence to suggest any fundamental abuse of human rights in Mozambique. Many did not believe her.

Even so, Judith Hart's international standing was impressive. She was called 'the African Queen'. In Botswana, she was given a personal reception party by the President, an 'unusual honour' for a visiting politician. The British High Commissioner believed 'that it was because Mrs Hart demonstrated her deep and sincere sympathy based on a lively perception of the problems; ... After the visit my diplomatic colleagues expressed envy that I had been so fortunate to have a Ministerial visitor who in so short a time had done so much for our relations with Botswana'.[116] Not all agreed with Hart's policies. In September 1978, a conference of leading figures from a number of developing countries joined those from donor countries to discuss world aid. Here, Hart's policy of distributing aid to countries with decent human rights record was criticised by a number of delegates who felt that the concept of human rights was too narrowly defined in terms of civil liberties such as free speech and freedom of expression.[117] In their view, human rights should encompass the basic need for food and shelter. Human rights, they argued, 'started in the stomach'.[118] Mrs Hart defended her position, arguing that 'gross violations of basic human freedoms could not be overlooked. … crimes like wholesale murder, torture and imprisonment without trial'. Mr Abdul Latif Al Hamad, Director General, Kuwait Fund for Arab Development, stated that his country 'tried to keep out of human rights questions'.[119]

In 1979, Judith Hart fought her eighth election. She viewed it as the most critical election for generations. The country, she insisted, could not risk the extremist policies of the Conservative Party under the leadership of Margaret Thatcher.[120] In her election campaign, Hart warned that Scottish 'enterprise would be under threat of death or decay from Tory policies. The National Enterprise Board, which saved Ferranti, Rolls-Royce and 8000 Rolls-Royce jobs in Scotland; the Scottish development Agency; Shipbuilding assistance; our programme of assistance to industry to create jobs—all would be emasculated if we do not win this election. And prices? Well! Thatcher conservatism, the most reactionary since the thirties, would cut taxes on the rich, increase spending on arms, cut other public expenditure. That includes housing subsidies. … There is no crock of gold at the end of a Tory rainbow'.[121] Her words were prophetic as Scottish devolution was abandoned, Scotland entered a period of economic decline and the independence movement grew.

THE DEFEAT OF LABOUR

On May 3, 1979, Judith Hart celebrated 20 years as MP for Lanark with a 5000 majority. However, the Labour Government was defeated and Hart returned to the opposition benches, still in charge of Labour's overseas development policy. She was given one last chance to be part of the political decision-making process from a surprising source. In June 1979, the new Prime Minister Margaret Thatcher gave a 'friendly and non-party political Yes' to Hart representing the UK at an international conference on agricultural development and rural reform.[122] The two were first elected at the same time, had shared an office when they were young MPs and Hart had often helped Thatcher 'into her finery'.[123] Even so, this was a generous gesture since Judith Hart was no longer part of government and therefore no longer a properly accredited representative. It was to be the last time the MP for Lanark represented the British Government.[124] Under Margaret Thatcher, ODA's budget was reduced dramatically, a cut Hart believed was a 'savage and foolish and short-sighted … arbitrary act of inconceivable Tory blindness'.[125]

In 1980, Judith Hart resigned from being opposition spokesperson on overseas development, citing the cause as not being 'free on the front bench' to speak her mind.[126] Increasingly, she felt restrained from holding forth on issues such as defence and industrial affairs and told friends that her 'efforts from the backbenches will I hope, be as formidable as in the past – in fact more so! I will not be restricted to the front-bench convention of not taking part in subjects not relevant to my own post'.[127] Judith Hart received a large number of sympathetic letters from embassies. The letter from the High Commission in Guyana was typical, stating that 'you had become more than a household name in Third World circles for your understanding and empathy with our problems and aspirations. I do speak on behalf of my Government when I say that we would miss hearing your voice from the front-bench'.[128] However, now she was no longer in office Hart's international authority was limited. For instance, Robert Mugabe ignored her letter when a few days after his election she offered to 'gladly come for a week or two to talk with your Ministers and officials, and give any advice I can, at no expense to your Government'.[129] A month later, two weeks after the independence of Zimbabwe Hart wrote again, this time to the Minister of Manpower and Planning and sent it via the British High Commission. She stated that she had written to 'Prime Minister Mugabe a month ago, but I do not know whether he received my letter, in all the pre-independence activities'. Again she offered help. The Minister agreed to accept a paper from her, outlining her proposals but nothing came of it.[130] This really showed her naivety. It was unthinkable that a former British Minister, whatever her reputation, could ever be a politically acceptable advisor to a newly independent government.

In 1979, Judith Hart was made a Dame Commander of the British Empire in James Callaghan's retiring Honours List. She claimed that 'she was accepting it on behalf of the Third World and not for herself; implying that there were celebrations all over Africa' when her honour was announced.[131] Not surprisingly, she was ridiculed for accepting such an honour both because of her politics and because there was no longer a British Empire.

The defeat of Labour in 1979 meant a change of lifestyle. Judith Hart ceased to enjoy spacious parliamentary office space, a chauffeur driven car, a large personal staff and a department to supply her with information and statistics. Red dispatch boxes were no longer delivered daily. Judith Hart moved her office from Whitehall to her home in Kew.[132] She continued to help her constituents. On June 2, 1980, she wrote to a teenager who was having a difficult time at school and advised him to keep going, praised him for his high IQ and encouraged him 'to use it, and work hard at basic subjects to get really high marks'. Judith Hart was so anxious about his progress that she let him stay in her London home until he was settled. Nothing was too trivial for her: she even wrote a congratulatory letter to a local couple celebrating their golden wedding anniversary when asked to do so by their family.

After its defeat by Margaret Thatcher, the Labour Party hurled itself into yet another of its intense internal battles, boosted by Trotskyist revolutionary groups who were organising unchecked within the Labour Party. It was difficult, Kenneth Morgan writes, 'to find a more dismal and depressing time in the history of the Labour Party'.[133] Once again it developed the conviction that it lost the election because it had not been socialist enough. Judith Hart was at the centre of a group which aimed to shape Labour policy towards a more left-wing agenda. Even out of office, she remained an influential figure in the Labour Party, able to influence policy through her role on the NEC between 1969 and 1983 and especially as Party Chair between 1981 and 1982.

A few years earlier the NEC had revoked the party's list of proscribed organisations and this led to the re-emergence of Militant, which with its own structure, publications and programmes, aimed to capture control of the Labour Party. In 1975 Reg Underhill, the party's National Agent, had published his report warning of Trotskyist infiltration into the Labour Party, called on party moderates to speak up for what they believed in and advised them to detach themselves from the 'sillier forms of militancy' and those 'who seemed hell bent on nationalising everything'.[134] In effect, the party had to decide 'whether Labour eventually re-emerges as a natural governing party or disappears up its own ideological black hole'.[135] However, when Underhill's report was discussed by the NEC, Hart was among those who voted not to publish it or take any action against the growing threat of Militant. Tensions escalated, especially when Militant campaigned to deselect MPs who were not considered left-wing enough. In July 1975, Reg Prentice had been deselected from his seat, the victim of a concerted campaign by Militant to get rid of him. Prentice appealed for the decision to be overturned but the NEC refused to do so. Judith Hart, possibly still angry about Reg Prentice taking her job at ODM, had earlier launched her own attack and was soon regarded as 'one of the most active snipers in the weekend war of words'.[136]

Now in opposition, the Labour Party shifted leftwards. In 1980, the Labour Party Conference was opened with a speech by Tony Benn in which he advocated renationalising Britain's leading industries, withdrawal from the EEC, unilateral disarmament and the abolition of the House of Lords. Benn's speech received an instant roar of approval. Conference also voted to abolish private education, introduce a wealth tax and a 35 hours week, to leave Europe, remove all American missile bases, reselect MPs and support unilateral disarmament. Michael Foot was elected Leader.

At the time, the Labour leader was elected by MPs but the left wanted trade unions and the constituency parties as well as MPs to vote. On Saturday, January 24, 1981, at a special Conference in Wembley delegates took away the power of MPs to choose their parliamentary leader: leaders would now be elected by 30% of MPs, 30% by the constituency parties and 40% by the trade unions. It was apparently 'a dreadful occasion in every respect, with vitriolic bitterness among many delegates towards the party right. Figures like David Owen … were jeered at'.[137] Peter Shore blamed the

NEC—on which Judith Hart was a leading figure—for giving encouragement to people 'whose faith in democratic and parliamentary socialism is virtually non-existent'.[138] On the day after the conference, Shirley Williams, Roy Jenkins, David Owen and Bill Rogers issued their Limehouse Declaration; within three weeks, a major Labour split took place. Judith Hart later accused Shirley Williams of 'being cynical and power hungry'.[139]

In September 1981, Judith Hart chaired the annual Labour Party Conference. Under her chairmanship, the conference descended into chaos and she had to ban television cameras and reporters from the floor when things got too heated. She had to 'learn to run the world's longest democratic riot on the job. ... yesterday the Comrade Dame seemed torn stylistically between trying to be Penelope Keith opening a fete and Rosa Luxembourg in a tight corner'.[140] The conflict arose for two main reasons. Firstly, delegates were asked to vote for Labour to take control of the 'commanding heights of industry', to nationalise the banks, insurance companies and building societies and to renationalise other industries. Judith Hart made an impassioned plea for conference to produce 'a considered report' on nationalisation rather than take hurried decisions. What was needed, she advised were 'concrete, explicit and practical policies to deal with such a situation, not to extend Clause Four in this absolutely desperate way'.[141] However, Judith Hart did endorse what she called the three policy imperatives: Labour's alternative economic strategy, withdrawal from the Common Market and an end to nuclear weapons and nuclear bases sited in the UK.

Secondly, it got even more fractious when Tony Benn insisted on running for the Deputy Leadership, then held by Denis Healey. By this time, Judith Hart was worried about the escalating tensions within the Labour Party and had earlier written a 'cutting open letter'[142] urging Benn, as a friend, not to continue because 'the effects will be divisive and damaging, at the very point in time when our comrades are sweating their guts out in the local elections; ... and when our people and our supporters long for us to concentrate all our energies on the fight against the Thatcher Government without yet more internal party division'.[143] Tony Benn took little notice and campaigned against Healey. When the elections were held Judith Hart abstained from the vote and Dennis Healey won by a tiny margin. The upshot of Labour's disarray, according to *The Times*, was 'now such that it not only no longer qualifies as the natural party of government ... it no longer qualifies as the natural party of opposition'.[144]

As respect for Labour's policies deteriorated among the electorate, Michael Foot was pressurised to take action against Militant to prevent the 'hard left' taking over the constituency parties.[145] There was it was claimed 'a widespread revulsion against the intimidation and authoritarian tendencies of the hard left'.[146] Judith Hart was not convinced and continued to defend Militant candidates. When the far-left Peter Tatchell was chosen by Bermondsey to represent them Michael Foot, in desperation, persuaded the NEC not to endorse him. Judith Hart disagreed and voted in support of

Tatchell's candidature.[147] She even voted in favour of Tariq Ali, a well-known revolutionary and leader of the International Marxist Group to be accepted as a member of the Labour Party.[148]

The battles for control of the party meant that Margaret Thatcher faced no real opposition even though unemployment was rising, manufacturing industries collapsing and interest rates escalating. Denis Healey argued that the 'unrepresentative clique' that was 'temporarily entrenched in positions of power' meant that Labour was unable to fight against the 'most unpopular government in its history' and was heading for 'electoral disaster'.[149] In an attempt to make Labour electable, Judith Hart wrote a series of articles in *The Times* outlining Labour's political framework. Can people, she argued 'any longer tolerate a government which for another two years will go bull-headed into intensifying depression, threatening our very social fabric?'[150] However, despite Hart's arguments, it was generally felt that Labour was too busy fighting internal battles to take action against the increasingly confident Conservative Government.

On April 2, 1982, Argentinian forces invaded a tiny group of islands in the South Atlantic and the Falkland War broke out. It was an avoidable war: the Argentinians believed that Britain was not interested in its colony because Thatcher had scrapped a Royal Naval vessel that protected the islands and had taken away the islanders' British passports. Judith Hart, still Chair of the Labour Party, warned of the consequences of a 'shoot first maxim' rather than a negotiated settlement. In her view, it was essential to ensure peaceful solutions to international disputes.[151] In May 1982, Hart tabled a House of Commons motion urging an immediate truce in the Falklands dispute before further lives were lost. The motion asked 'that this House, deeply concerned at the escalation of conflict and loss of life in the region of the Falkland Islands, fearing that there are grave dangers of further escala-tion involving other countries' wanted the UN to help negotiate a peace.[152] Judith Hart thought that extra-parliamentary activity might help shift public opinion and quickly convened an Ad Hoc Falkland Islands Peace Committee which demanded an unconditional ceasefire. She warned that we are 'at the very edge of a war whose end we cannot foresee. Nobody knows whether tactical nuclear weapons could be used and what the consequences might be'.[153] Denis Healey and Michael Foot were concerned about the damage such remarks could do to the party because her calls for an immediate truce were out of line with NEC policy.[154] Peter Shore made a scathing attack, arguing that Hart's views could cost Labour the next election. 'By what right' he argued 'does the chairman of the Labour Party go around saying that she is speaking on behalf of the party and then produce a whole serious of policy statements on the Falklands crisis which are directly opposed to statements and viewpoints put forward by Michael Foot and Denis Healey'.[155] Labour, once more, was divided. According to *The Times*, the Labour Party's 'rift over the Falklands crisis exploded' when Judith Hart and Tony Benn led 31 other MPs to defy the Shadow Cabinet's recommendations and voted against the government when it sought Commons approval for the continuation of the war.[156] Most Labour MPs were angry at this disloyalty: Foot called it a 'stab in the back for those who had been sent into battle'.[157] In June 1932, ten weeks after it began the Falklands War ended with a British victory, and a newly upbeat Tory Party buoyed up by victory and Labour's disarray prepared for an election.

Labour entered the 1983 general election with Michael Foot as leader and a manifesto which promised withdrawal from the EEC, the removal of American bases, getting rid of nuclear weapons and the renationalisation of a number of industries. Gerald Kaufman, a Labour MP, famously called it 'the longest suicide note in history'. Margaret Thatcher strengthened by the jingoistic spirit prevalent in the UK, was re-elected in a landslide victory. Labour lost sixty seats with its share of the vote (28.3%) worse than that of the electoral disaster of 1931 (30.8%). Some blamed the manifesto and divisions within Labour; others blamed Margaret Thatcher's success in the Falkland war. Michael Foot stood down and Tony Benn lost his seat. Judith Hart had made her seat safe, mainly through the care she took of her constituents: her majority was 4866, only a small and insignificant decrease. Neil Kinnock was elected leader of the Labour Party, arguing that it was more important 'to put principles into effect than to enjoy powerless perfection in opposition' reshaped the Labour Party, abandoned its commitment to withdraw from the EEC and to renationalise industry and freshened up the party's image by adopting the red rose as its symbol. More significantly, it promised not to raise taxation. Kinnock's new focus was endorsed by the party. In the NEC elections, only 9 left-wingers out of 29 were elected: Judith Hart who had sat on the NEC since 1969 lost her place. Neil Kinnock now had the commanding control of the NEC; Judith Hart's power base had vanished.

In 1987, Judith Hart, now aged 60, retired as MP. She was the 'Mother of the House', the longest-serving female MP; she had been an MP for 28 years and had fought eight elections.[158] 'I leave you' she wrote to her constituents 'all with very mixed feelings. I look forward to having time of my own—to write, and to do more on third world issues. I can truly say that my constituency work on so many of your personal and community problems through three decades has been the most deeply rewarding part of the job of being your member of parliament'.[159] These were the customary words of a retiring MP but Judith Hart had lost none of her radical spirits. In her letter, she also spoke of how Thatcherism had destroyed the best of Britain. In Clydesdale, she maintained, the effects were devastating. Was this, she insisted, a thriving economy? Thriving for whom? 'Unemployment' she wrote 'has trebled here. A quarter of our men are without work, and our young people face a hopeless future. The jobs which do emerge are so often at scandalously low wages: to be paid only £50 or £60 a week is not unusual. Yet in the South the "yuppies" of the money markets are taking home £2000 a week, buying their Porsches and their country homes. And here I see the 80s – the housing lists which have grown long again ... rates by poll tax, social security cuts, Health

Service constraints and all the rest'.[160] It was the last cry of a now-powerless backbench MP who free from governmental constraints could say what she liked.

In 1988, Judith Hart was elevated to the Lords as Baroness Hart of South Lanark. By now, she was too ill for much political involvement and her name disappears from newspapers. She died from bone cancer on December 8, 1991, aged 67 at Queen Mary's University Hospital, Roehampton. Her son Steve suggests that her cancer might have been the result of a few days visit to Sellafield (Windscale), Cumbria after the worst nuclear accident in Great Britain's history.[161]

CONCLUSION

Judith Hart's legacy in Lanark was huge. She was an assiduous MP, always willing to help with the problems of her constituents, always trying to make her constituency a better place to live and work. Her lasting achievement finds physical expression in the hospitals, schools and even new towns that she encouraged government to finance and build. And it is thanks to Judith Hart that the joint headquarters of the Department for International Development is located in East Kilbride, still providing around 600 jobs and administering half of DfID's international aid programme. It was, according to Douglas Alexander at the time 'a unique arrangement in Whitehall reflecting the imagination and vision of a unique woman. Not for her the idea that all things Westminster had to be in London'.[162] Between 2007 and 2013, a Judith Hart Memorial Lecture was held bi-annually to commemorate the life of the former Lanark MP: in 2009, Harriet Harman gave the oration.

Hart was only in the Cabinet for a short time, thus unable to make a solid contribution to British politics as Secretary of State. It is safe to say that Judith Hart's most important legacy lies in her international work. As a junior Minister, she helped avert a Commonwealth disaster by steering Wilson's Rhodesian policy and visiting the countries threatening to leave. Undeniably, her major success was as Minister for Overseas Development, a post she held three times. Here, she built on the work of her colleague Barbara Castle, going further than any of the two imagined. She cancelled third world debt, focussed aid on rural development, set up a Disaster Unit, persuaded the EEC to ratify the Lomé Agreement and more importantly set the government on track to allocate 0.7% of its GDP to overseas aid.

In April 1992, the Chilean Government awarded the decoration 'Orden Al Merito de Chile', the Order of Merit to two British citizens—Harold Pinter and Judith Hart—for offering their 'moral support, raising their strong voices of protest to back the efforts of the Chilean people ... to put an end to dictatorship and start the difficult path back to freedom'.[163] In February 2001, Jeremy Corbyn paid tribute to the 'wonderful work by Dame Judith Hart' in supporting the Chilean people.[164] Earlier Neil Kinnock had remarked that she was a woman 'of high abilities who will long be admired for her distinguished work to advance human rights and her tireless courage campaigning for the defeat of world poverty'.[165] But perhaps the last words should be from Harriet Harman who spoke of Judith Hart 'as a woman ahead of her time in combining her commitment to politics with her commitment to her family; a formidable fighter for socialism; a great champion of Scotland for democracy; and for International Development'.[166]

As a Minister and as Secretary of State, Judith Hart helped shape Labour policy and was fortunate to see that policy enacted. For a while, Labour seemed a natural party to govern, a party with high ideals, an intellectual coherence and a proven ability to put its principles and beliefs into effect. After 1979, it collapsed into a period of acrimonious bickering which reduced its electoral attractiveness and obliged the next and the last of our Cabinet Ministers to leave the party she had joined as a young woman.

NOTES

1. David Wood, *The Times*, October 21, 1968, HART/13/76.
2. Quoted Melanie Phillips, *The Divided House*, Sidgwick and Jackson, 1980, p. 170.
3. *The Guardian*, November 2, 1972, p. 11.
4. Majorie Proops, *Daily Mirror*, 1968, HART/10/03.
5. *The Sunday Express*, undated, HART/13/76.
6. *The Sun*, October 23, 1968, p. 3.
7. These regular meetings were known as the Husbands' and Wives Club.
8. David Wood, *The Times*, October 21, 1968, HART/13/76.
9. Ibid.
10. *Thames Valley Times*, October 22, 1968, p. 1.
11. *Daily Mail*, October 29, 1968, HART/10/03.
12. Richard Crossman, *The Diaries of a Cabinet Minister, 1966–1968*, February 8, 1968, Trinity Press, 1975.
13. Judith Hart Interview with Rhona Churchill, *Daily Mail*, HART/13/76.
14. In 1969 the Representation of the People Bill lowered the voting age from 21 to 18.
15. *Newcastle Journal*, October 18, 1968, HART/10/3.
16. *Express & Star*, October 21, 1968, HART/10/03.
17. Judith Hart, Interview with the *Daily Mail*, October 29, 1968, HART/10/03.
18. *Daily Sketch*, 1968, HART/10/03.
19. *Glasgow Herald*, October 18, 1968, p. 1.
20. Press release, December 1, 1968, HART/10/03.
21. This was shelved by Margaret Thatcher and only resuscitated in 1997 when Labour returned to power. On May 12, 1999, the Scottish Parliament met for the first time.
22. *Liverpool Daily Post*, August 13, 1969, HART/10/5.
23. *The Telegraph*, August 13, 1969, HART/13/76.
24. *The Guardian*, July 22, 1969, p. 4.

25. In 1970, the first WLM conference was held at Ruskin College, Oxford. Over 600 delegates attended. They discussed the first four demands: equal pay, equal educational and job opportunities; free contraception and abortion on demand; free 24 hours nurseries.
26. Willie Ross, Scottish Office to Judith Hart, May 6, 1970, Hart's constituency papers.
27. Ibid.
28. Judith Hart to Willie Ross, May 24, 1970, Hart's constituency papers.
29. *The Guardian*, August 5, 1969, HART/10/5.
30. *Sunday Mirror*, July 20, 1969, HART/10/5.
31. *The Guardian*, October 31, 1969, p. 15.
32. See Barrie Ireton's, *Britain's International Development Policies: A History of DFID and Overseas Aid*, Palgrave Macmillan, 2013 for an analysis of the history of Britain's international development policies.
33. *The Guardian*, October 21, 1969, p. 20.
34. *West Africa*, October 25, 1969, p. 1269.
35. *The Guardian*, November 29, 1969, p. 16.
36. Barbara Castle Diary, November 25, 1969.
37. *The Guardian*, December 9, 1969, p. 6.
38. It took Clare Short to make it happen in practice and George Osborne to achieve it for the first time in 2013.
39. Letter to Hart, Madras, January 31, 1970, HART/7/21; letter to Hart, New Delhi undated but would have been written in January 1970, HART/7/21. I have not named the individual concerned as members of his family may still be alive.
40. Letter to Hart, Madras, January 31, 1970, HART/7/21.
41. Ibid.
42. *Hamilton Advertiser*, November 21, 1969, p. 3.
43. Anonymous letter, July 1970, HART/4/4.
44. A Willesden worker, June 1970, HART/4/4.
45. Maggie Sidgreaves, April 17, 2017.
46. Judith Hart to Ministry of Social Security, December 16, 1970.
47. Judith Hart to Electricity Board, January 7, 1971.
48. Rutherglen Co-operative Society to Judith Hart, April 6, 1973.
49. Judith Hart to Rutherglen Co-operative Society, April 17, 1973.
50. *East Kilbride News*, February 12, 1971, p. 12.
51. *Hamilton Advertiser*, March 22, 1970, p. 8.
52. *Hamilton Advertiser*, January 23, 1970, p. 12.
53. *The Times*, September 29, 1973, HART/4/4.
54. Jeremy Corbyn, Hansard, February 6, 2001, Col 194.
55. According to a later (1991) National Commission on Truth and Reconciliation Report (known as the Rettig Report), there were three stages of violent repression. The first stage occurred between September and December 1973 with massive arrests, prisoners interned in concentration camps and political prisoners executed after a mock trial. Corpses were hidden, thrown into the sea or dynamited. In the second phase, between 1974 and 1975, the regime built up a 'systematic policy of repression in order to exterminate those whom it deemed a political threat. ... The goal was to kill

and hide the bodies of the dead in order to destroy the supposed enemy'. These years produced the greatest number of disappearances. The third and final stage from 1977 to 1989 there was a lull in repression, largely due to international pressure. Even so, opposition was squashed, prominent opponents of the regime were murdered and when people protested they were killed by police bullets.

56. *The Guardian*, September 19, 1973, p. 21.
57. *Labour Weekly*, September 28, 1973, HART/4/4.
58. *The Sunday Times*, November 18, 1973, HART/4/4.
59. *Daily Mirror*, January 29, 1974, p. 1.
60. New Year Message from Judith Hart, 1974, HART/9/1.
61. Election broadsheet, 1974, HART/9/1.
62. Ibid.
63. Judith Hart, *Stonehouse News*, February 22, 1974, p. 9.
64. Judith Hart, *Hamilton Advertiser*, January 25, 1974, p. 8, HART/9/2.
65. Letter to MPs, January 28, 1974, HART/9/1.
66. Election leaflet, 1974, HART/9/2.
67. Barrie Ireton, *Britain's International Development Policies*, 2013, p. 60.
68. Judith Hart, *Administering an Aid Programme in a Year of Change—A Personal Diary*, Address to the Royal Commonwealth Society, February 1975, p. 2, HART/10/11.
69. I am grateful to Peter Freeman for this information.
70. I am grateful to Peter Freeman for this information.
71. Several left-wing couples: Barbara and Ted Castle, Tony and Caroline Benn, Michael Foot and Jill Craigie, John and Rosamund Silkin, Tom and Penelope Balogh and Judith and Tony Hart met regularly and informally for dinner. They naturally discussed politics. It could sometimes be 'a tetchy affair' (BC Diary, October 17, 1974).
72. Annie Machon, *'Spies, Lies and Whistleblowers'—Subversion Chapter*. Internet site for a review of British intelligence gathering. I am grateful to Peter Freeman for this reference.
73. I am grateful to Maggie Sidgreaves for this information.
74. Interview with Peter Freeman, October 4, 2017.
75. *The Times*, March 28, 1974, p. 1. In 1979, when Margaret Thatcher came to power, she restored diplomatic relations and resumed arms sales.
76. Interview with Peter Freeman, October 2017.
77. Judith Hart, *Administering an Aid Programme in a Year of Change—A Personal Diary*, Address to the Royal Commonwealth Society, February 1975, p. 2, HART/10/11.
78. Ibid., p. 9.
79. *The Guardian*, March 13, 1975, p. 4.
80. See Susan Chase and Elisa Wilkinson, 'What Happened to Integrated Rural Development?', *The Hunger Project*, August 11, 2015 for an analysis of IRD.
81. Interview with Peter Freeman, October 4, 2017.
82. IRD failed for a number of reasons which include the fact that rural communities were not consulted in projects that affected them; most projects were organised by central government; projects were often too complex and with too many agencies involved; the rural poor were often too inarticulate and ill-educated to make decisions which were then taken by the urban elite.

See Susan Chase and Elisa Wilkinson, 'What Happened to Integrated Rural Development?', *The Hunger Project*, August 11, 2015.

83. I am indebted to Peter Freeman for much of this information.
84. Judith Hart's speech to International Women's Year Seminar, March 19, 1975.
85. *The Times*, August 13, 1974, p. 1.
86. Judith Hart, *Administering an Aid Programme in a Year of Change—A Personal Diary*, Address to the Royal Commonwealth Society, February 1975, p. 4, HART/10/11.
87. Harold Wilson, *The Guardian*, March 19, 1975, p. 10.
88. In 2013, Britain became the first G7 country to meet this UN target; in 2015, a Private Members' Bill sponsored by a Lib-Dem MP made the 0.7% target legally binding.
89. *The Sun*, November 7, 1974, HART/10/8.
90. *The Guardian*, November 1, 1974, p. 1.
91. Harold Wilson to Judith Hart, November 1974, HART/13/30.
92. Judith Hart to Harold Wilson, November 5, 1974, HART/13/30.
93. *The Guardian*, June 15, 1975, p. 10.
94. Harold Wilson to Judith Hart, May 13, 1975, HART/13/30.
95. Harold Wilson to Judith Hart, May 21, 1975, HART/13/30.
96. Duncan Sutherland, 'Hart, Judith, Baroness of South Lanark (1924–1991)', in *Oxford Dictionary of National Biography*, Oxford University Press, 2004, Online Edition, May 2008, accessed April 11, 2016.
97. Unpublished manuscript of events between June 5 and June 11, 1975 by a former high-ranking civil servant.
98. Ibid.
99. Judith Hart, World Development Movement meeting, Bloomsbury Baptist Church, June 14, 1975, HART/10/12.
100. Private memo. Reg Prentice was thought to have been a good Minister but he was no longer interested in overseas development and left the running of the department to his civil servants. Furthermore, he was already having secret negotiations with the Conservative Party which he later joined.
101. Bernard Donaghue, June 10, 1975, p. 411 and *Downing Street Diary*, Jonathan Cape, 2005.
102. Hansard, June 11, 1975, Vol. 893, cc418–420.
103. Barbara Castle Diary, November 10, 1975.
104. Judith Hart to Ms B, December 14, 1976.
105. Judith Hart, marked Confidential, April 9, 1976.
106. *Glasgow Herald*, January 7, 1978, p. 3.
107. *The Times*, February 22, 1977, p. 1.
108. Judith Hart Interview with Christopher Erswell, January 8, 1991, quoted in Christopher C. Erswell, *UK Aid Policy and Practice, 1975–90*, PhD dissertation, University of Liverpool, 1994, p. 60.
109. Judith Hart Interview with Aggrey-Orleans, Ghana Radio Programme, January 1979, HART/ 2/10.
110. *The Guardian*, May 6, 1978, p. 7.
111. The Cabinet Minister was John Silkin, Minister of Agriculture, Fisheries and Food.
112. Interview with Maggie Sidgreaves, April 13, 2018.

113. *The Guardian*, August 1, 1978, p. 19.
114. The Government Record, 1974–79, HART/2/34.
115. Lord Orr-Ewing, House of Lords Debates, December 8, 1977, Vol. 387, cc1742–1745.
116. Wilfred Turner, British High Commissioner to David Owen, August 18, 1978, HART/2/3.
117. Judith Hart, Confidential Notes for UK eyes only, October 1978, HART/8/8.
118. Ibid.
119. Ibid.
120. *Hamilton Advertiser*, April 13, 1979, HART/5/55.
121. Judith Hart, Gazette, March 23, 1979, HART/5/55.
122. *The Guardian*, June 15, 1979, p. 23.
123. Interview with Maggie Sidgreaves, April 13, 2018.
124. *The Guardian*, February 19, 1980, p. 10.
125. Judith Hart notebook, HART/8/13.
126. Judith Hart, July 31, 1980, HART/8/9.
127. Judith Hart, August 21, 1980, HART/8/9.
128. Guyana High Commission, September 18, 1980, HART/8/9.
129. Judith Hart to Robert Mugabe, March 10, 1980, HART/2/4.
130. Hart to Tekere, May 1, 1980, HART/2/4.
131. *The Guardian*, March 18, 1984, p. 18.
132. Interview with Tom Gill, 1979.
133. Kenneth O. Morgan, *Michael Foot: A Life*, Harper Perennial, 2007, p. 370.
134. *The Guardian*, September 26, 1973, p. 1.
135. *The Guardian*, November 6, 1982, p. 8.
136. *The Guardian*, September 27, 1973, p. 1.
137. Kenneth O. Morgan, *Michael Foot: A Life*, p. 393.
138. Peter Shore, *Labour Solidarity*, March 1981, p. 1.
139. *The Guardian*, October 6, 1981, p. 4.
140. *The Guardian*, September 28, 1982, p. 26.
141. *The Guardian*, September 29, 1981, p. 4.
142. *The Times*, April 3, 1981, p. 1.
143. Judith Hart, letter to Benn published in *The Guardian*, April 3, 1981, p. 2.
144. *The Times*, September 21, 1981, p. 9.
145. *The Guardian*, September 4, 1984, p. 7.
146. *The Times*, October 3, p. 16.
147. Eventually, after a lot of debate Tatchell's candidacy was endorsed: in 1983, he lost the seat in the erstwhile Labour stronghold to Simon Hughes, the Liberal candidate.
148. NEC decision, HART/12/27.
149. *Labour Solidarity*, March 1981, p. 8.
150. *The Times*, August 30, 1982, p. 6.
151. *The Times*, April 14, 1982, p. 6.
152. *The Times*, May 6, 1982, p. 2.
153. *The Times*, May 10, 1982, p. 4.
154. *The Times*, May 13, 1982, p. 6.
155. *The Times*, May 18, 1982, p. 28.
156. *The Times*, May 21, 1982, p. 1.

157. *The Times*, May 22, 1982, p. 3.
158. **Lanark**—1959: 540 majority; 1964: 5320 majority; 1966: 7740 majority; 1970: 2473 majority; 1974 (February): 2100 majority; 1974 (October): 698 majority; 1979: 5139 majority. **Clydesdale**—1983: 4866 majority.
159. Judith Hart's resignation address, May 3, 1987, HART/5/5.
160. Ibid.
161. Thanks to Steve Hart for this information. Bone marrow is thought to be the most susceptible to radiation damage, damage that impairs the immune system by not replacing white blood cells.
162. Douglas Alexander, Judith Hart Memorial Lecture, May 13, 2013.
163. Speech delivered by the Ambassador of Chile, Senor German Riesco, April 14, 1992.
164. Hansard, February 6, 2001, Col 194WH.
165. *The Guardian*, December 9, 1991, p. 4.
166. Harriet Harman, Judith Hart Memorial Lecture, *Daily Record*, May 14, 2009.

CHAPTER 10

Climbing the Parliamentary Ladder: Shirley Williams, 1930–1974

Shirley Vivian Teresa Brittain-Catlin was the most privileged of all the Cabinet Ministers. She was born on July 27, 1930, at 19 Glebe Place, just off the Kings Road in Chelsea; her father George Catlin was a political scientist; her mother was the famous novelist Vera Brittain, author of the best-selling *Testament of Youth*. The family was rich enough to employ a house-keeper, butler, parlour maid, secretary and governess. Amy and Charlie Burnett who were employed as housekeeper and butler at the time did so much of the caring for Shirley that she came to regard them as her surro-gate parents. Indeed, when Amy died Shirley wrote 'To my other mother' on her wreath. Certainly, her birth mother Vera Brittain was often too engrossed in work to pay much attention to her young children, a fact that Shirley resented. At one time, Vera wrote to her husband that Shirley had been complaining about the 'importance of mothers bringing up their children themselves. … Sometimes I think she genuinely would have preferred Amy as her mother rather than myself'.[1] Vera Britain was impeccably dressed, had an 'iron self-discipline and liked an ordered routine'.[2] Shirley was the oppo-site: untidy and unpunctual. Her lack of ability to be on time is legendary. It seemed as if this girl did not want to be like her mother.

Little Shirley was adventurous. Her mother commented that 'As she grew out of infancy she became a dynamo of energy; she never walked when she could run, and she climbed everything. At three she climbed her father's bookcase, which stretched from floor to ceiling; at thirteen she climbed the perilous roof of a hotel in Estoril; at fifteen she climbed Helvellyn; at nineteen Cader Idris; at twenty-one Snowden; and at twenty-two the Dolomites'.[3] At the age of two when on holiday with her parents, she climbed right over the rails of her cot and 'fell with a terrific bump on the floor; I heard it in my room and dashed in to find her already at the door, roaring but apparently unhurt. She will now have to be strapped (in); where she gets all this adven-turous rashness from I cannot imagine'.[4] A couple of days later, she 'fell and

P. Bartley, *Labour Women in Power*,
https://doi.org/10.1007/978-3-030-14288-9_10

grazed one eye – on the pavement – about her fifth mishap since we came'.[5] On one windy and rainy day, on returning from a visit to their grandmother, Shirley and John 'dashed out of the bus ... and escaped from me ... and lost themselves in wild roaring wet, so that when I got in they were not there. ... When they came in I was really angry and packed them off to bed without supper. Went up later and found Shirley quite uncrushed, bobbing about in her bed, but poor John very subdued'.[6] Shirley was seven years old. All her life she remained indomitable, high-spirited and energetic.

She was a clever girl. At the age of two and a half years old she had mastered all the Montessori apparatus at her nursery school and would have moved up to an older group but was thought 'too tiny'.[7] At the age of four, she wrote her first letter to her parents when they were campaigning for her father. It began 'Dear Mummie and Daddy. I hope you will get into Parliament'.[8] Her school reports were excellent, 'only 6 marks lost on a total of 250, and full marks for many subjects'.[9] Her first school was Christ Church Elementary before she moved, aged 8, to a boarding school at Swanage, away from potential war-time air-raids. From then on, her schooling was nomadic as she shifted from one school to another, from one country to another. In 1940, as bombs fell on London, Shirley and her brother were sent to Minnesota, America to stay with family friends. Her parents feared a German invasion and believed 'that if the war went badly for Britain we should both be "for it". We also realised that the children of political victims were likely to suffer'.[10] This American experience shaped the precocious ten-year old. Here, without parental influence, she discovered the joys of independence. The lack of formality and pomposity in America affected the young girl, as did the 'incorrigible optimism' and 'can do' mentality of Americans in general. 'I lived' she wrote 'in a classless society, whose members all shared the same accent and the same values', an assessment she later realised was not as strictly accurate as she wished.[11] Here too, her love of the countryside and outside activities was shaped as she explored old Indian trails, built rafts and tree houses, camped in pinewoods, learned to sail and canoe and learned to ski on the winter snow.[12] She always liked adventurous holidays, riding, canoeing and hill walking as well as the more familiar cultural visits to art galleries, museums and historic Catholic churches. She even learned to rock climb.

In August 1943, now aged 13, Shirley travelled home alone on a Portuguese liner, and experienced cyclones, an attempted gang rape and being stranded in Lisbon. When she eventually arrived safely back in England, Shirley had been three years without her parents, three years with strangers, three years of autonomy and self-sufficiency in which she had drawn upon—and learnt from—her own reserves of independence and courage. Now she was expected to resume being her parents' loving daughter. She told her mother that 'you weren't real to me at all. You seemed more like a person in a book'.[13] It took her several years, she later admitted, to learn to love her mother again, and even then 'it was to love her as an adult ... rather than as a child loves its mother'.[14]

Shirley was now a teenager. She would answer questions in monosyllables and become obstinate and argumentative. Both Shirley and her brother loved verbal combat which made their mother furious, especially when Shirley, with 'her logical mind ... frequently triumphed'.[15] Her mother believed her young daughter was unconsciously 'practising, at her brother's expense, for the political speeches in which she was to prove so effective a few years later'.[16] Now back in Britain, the young Miss Catlin refused to go to boarding school so was enrolled at St Paul's Girls' School, an elite girls' day school, the *alma mater* of a number of politicians.[17] It was a shock to the American-educated teenager used to an informal, freer system to attend a school which was focussed on academic excellence, decorum, obedience and a strict adherence to the dress code of a navy-blue uniform, white shirt and felt hat. Not surprisingly, this boisterous, rebellious 'swashbuckling extrovert'[18] rebelled and was threatened with expulsion for her combative behaviour. For a time, she felt she neither belonged to her family nor to the school.

Religion was a formative influence on a lot of Labour politicians and so it was with Shirley. Her mother was an Anglican but Shirley's father was a Catholic convert, advising his daughter to 'Keep to the Socialism of the Right and the Catholicism of the Left'. Unquestionably, her Catholicism was influenced by the Sermon on the Mount—blessed are the poor for yours is the Kingdom of God; blessed are those who hunger now, for you shall be satisfied—Christian ideals based on love and compassion rather than sin and retribution. In later life, she was sympathetic to the liberation theology of South America, a Catholic theology which focussed on helping the poor and oppressed. But it was perhaps her adoptive parents, as much as her father, who shaped much of the young Shirley's Catholicism, particularly her more sentimental and passionate side. Shirley Catlin was an emotional Catholic as much as a spiritual one. Until she was nine, Amy Burnett took her to the Holy Redeemer each Sunday, setting down the principles and beliefs that Shirley would carry all her life. Sunday mass was a stirring experience: she enjoyed the 'grandeur of the traditional Mass, recited in Latin by a priest whose beautifully robed back was turned to the congregation .... The insistent rise and fall of Gregorian chant and the smell of incense infused by being, and became the sensual context of the Sabbath'.[19] As a teenager, Shirley sampled a number of religions 'from the Quakers to Spiritualism, and also tried doing without religion altogether'.[20] After a couple of years, Shirley decided that she belonged in the Catholic Church. She had not been baptised because her parents preferred to leave her free to decide on her own religion when she became an adult; in October 1948, when she was at Oxford University, Shirley organised her own baptism.

Shirley was now officially a Roman Catholic and remained so all her life. It was not always a 'comfortable Church ... partly because it's full of inconvenient rules. ... It's a Church of sinners, which I like a lot'.[21] She held the traditional Catholic views on abortion, thinking that 'one has to be terribly careful about protecting the sacredness of human life'.[22] She also disapproved of divorce. However, Shirley was not an uncritical Catholic: she maintained that the Church never really came to terms with women and was disappointed that it seemed to treat them either as Madonnas or Mary Magdalens rather than unique individuals. She joined a Catholic feminist organisation and the Catholic Agency for Overseas Development (CAFOD).

Shirley grew up among 'the intellectual establishment of the Left as friends round the tea table'.[23] These included Cabinet Ministers, world-famous writers and visitors from India, Africa and China. She sat on Nehrus's knee. At the age of six 'Poppy' as the young Shirley was called, handed out lemonade to George Lansbury when he visited their home.[24] Her mother was a feminist and a pacifist; her father a socialist who stood twice as a Labour candidate. Both parents were friends of Ellen Wilkinson; her father George Catlin had even walked with the Jarrow marchers. Her parents brought her up to be equal to men, to be ambitious, to want to make the world a better place.

Shirley was keen on politics, keen even to be the youngest MP. At 16, she joined the Labour Party; at 17, she attended the 1946 Labour Conference with her father, meeting more of the Labour Party elite. Herbert Morrison, in particular, encouraged her to enter politics. Between school and university, Shirley chose to work on a co-operative farm near Colchester that had been founded for conscientious objectors and which was partially financed by her mother. It seemed an odd choice for a budding politician. However, according to her mother, Shirley had 'made a preliminary chart of her course through life; for a would-be Parliamentary candidate, the experience of everyday work among ordinary people would be more useful than three terms in the top form at St Paul's'.[25] She worked at the farm for six months as assistant cowman to a herd of Ayrshire dairy cows, getting up at 4:30 a.m. to be at the milking parlour by 5 a.m. to attach the milking machine to each cow, then to finish off the milking by hand.[26] She missed the Labour Conference at Scarborough as a result. Her father was annoyed but her mother commented that Herbert Morrison would be impressed by her daughter's choice.

When she left St Paul's Vera Brittain was eager for her daughter to go to her old college and wrote to the Principal of Somerville, a former contemporary, to say that her daughter had 'always been extremely interested in politics and hopes to enter the House of Commons at an early age. This is not a wild ambition, two Cabinet Ministers are keenly encouraging her'.[27] She won a scholarship and went up to take the degree much favoured by budding politicians: philosophy, politics and economics.

Oxford was, and still is, a training ground for ambitious public figures. Certainly, Miss Catlin met Emmanuel Shinwell, Dick Crossman and Jim Callaghan who came to speak to the Labour Club; her fellow students included the Labour politician Tony Crosland, the television presenter Robin Day, the philosopher Bernard Williams, the Olympic athlete Roger Bannister and the future Archbishop of Canterbury, Robert Runcie. Her tutors, the economist Margaret Hall among them, were some of the sharpest brains of the period and provided robust role models for young undergraduates like Shirley. There may have been students who felt overwhelmed and intimidated when confronted by such high achievers but Shirley Catlin was not one of them.

Soon she became immersed in student politics, campaigning to get women elected to the male-only Oxford Union. On one occasion she imitated the suffragettes by chaining herself to railings outside its premises in a protest against its 'institutional sexism'. When the Oxford Union members proved inflexible Shirley joined the Oxford University Labour Club (OULC). In 1950, she was appointed the first female President and chaired meetings addressed by the leading ministers of Attlee's government. Like the other Oxford debating societies, the OULC encouraged its members to be politically involved: many who had once been on its executive committee—Tony Benn, Barbara Castle, Roy Jenkins, Michael Foot, Peter Mandelson, Rushanara Ali and Ed Miliband—became politicians. Shirley was a natural performer. She had learnt her stage-craft from Sybil Thorndike, an old family friend who taught her how to use her voice to the greatest effect. In the 1940s, she had auditioned for the lead in *National Velvet* but was beaten to it by Elizabeth Taylor. *The Observer* thought it was a pity because she has a 'far huskier, more actressy voice than Elizabeth Taylor ever managed'.[28] Her dramatic potential was reinvigorated at Oxford: she became a member of the Union Dramatic Society and the Experimental Theatre Club. Her father disapproved: he thought acting a frivolous pastime and would distract his daughter from higher intellectual pursuits. She ignored his advice. Undaunted, she went on a summer tour of the USA acting as Cordelia to her boyfriend's King Lear, visiting nine states, playing at 15 venues and giving 22 performances in six weeks in the blistering heat of an American summer. George Catlin was wrong to object to his daughter's acting because Shirley's theatrical experience added a new dimension to her personality, providing her with an ability to relate to audiences, and charm them. Moreover, her setback in not getting the lead role in National Velvet was thought to steel 'Miss Catlin for reverses which were to come when she moved her career in a different direction'.[29] Shirley also became features editor for *Isis*, one of the university's high-profile journals, seen as a launch pad for glittering careers in literature and the arts: Graham Greene, Sylvia Plath and George Osborne were previous contributors. Unlike many students, Shirley was comfortable in this cerebral world, familiar with the leading figures of the Labour Party and intellectually confident enough to discuss politics authoritatively. Not surprisingly, she was 'the most celebrated female undergraduate of her time'.[30]

In July 17, 1951, Shirley left Oxford and returned home. A few days later Herbert Morrison invited her to lunch and asked her to be his private secretary. Most recent graduates would accept such an offer without hesitation but Shirley, who wanted to enter Parliament on her own terms, turned him down to continue her studies and revisit her 'American childhood paradise'.[31] She had just won a Fulbright Scholarship to Columbia University,

New York to study economics and the political action programmes of American trade unions. She arrived in the USA just as McCarthyism was at its strongest.[32] The American enemy of this period was thought to be communism and Senator McCarthy was determined to root it out: Shirley was one of its victims, denied entry to the USA because of her political activities. Fortunately, her influential friends persuaded the American Ambassador to intervene on her behalf and she was eventually given a visa to enter the country to begin her studies. She was lucky in other ways. Herbert Morrison had provided her with a letter of introduction which meant that she was invited to staff seminars on labour, the first ever student to be asked to do so. She was, according to contemporaries, a rising star in British politics.

TOWARDS PARLIAMENT

In November 1952, Shirley Catlin abandoned her thesis and left America before her yearly scholarship ended. She had been lured back to Britain by a telegram asking her to stand for selection as Labour parliamentary candidate for Harwich. Unlike most Labour politicians 'she never had to beat her way into politics through the ranks of a trade union. She never had to find her political bearings out of anger, struggle or oppression. She was born and raised to them and that piece of good fortune may explain, partly at least, the absence of visible scar tissue, the grace with which she appears to take her politics'.[33] Bitterness, envy or spite was not to be found in this charming young politician.

A *Daily Mirror* journalist was waiting for her ship to arrive at Southampton, ready to offer her a job on the newspaper. Again, Shirley displayed that same single-mindedness and independence she had shown Morrison. It was not, she maintained 'the type of job I had in mind'.[34] She was focussed on a parliamentary career. However, the young Miss Catlin was still waiting for an election to be called so that she could stand as Labour candidate for the Harwich constituency. She was unable to find another job and in January 1953 she reluctantly joined the *Daily Mirror*.[35] Here, apart from one report on the Duke of Edinburgh which hit the headlines, Miss Catlin attended weddings, wrote up stories about house fires and interviewed men to find out whether or not they carried a man-bag. Shirley disliked her job, disliked the long periods of boredom and disliked trying to find a story to report. Eight months later in October 1953, she was asked to resign. In November, Herbert Morrison offered to find her a safe Labour seat and help her become a junior whip—if she 'adhered to his political line and gave him an occasional smile'.[36] She was independent and confident enough to decline his offer, reminding him that she had already been adopted for Harwich, at the time held by a Conservative. Shirley Caitlin was 23 years old.

In January 1954, Shirley was in Paris when her mother telephoned her to say that the MP for Harwich had been elevated to the peerage and an election would take place. It was a safe Conservative seat with a majority of 7925. The Harwich division at the time consisted of Harwich, Clacton-on-Sea, Frinton-on-Sea and Jaywick, a cluster of beach huts and bungalows which today is one of the most poverty-stricken places in Britain. Shirley's indefatigable energy was evident in the election campaign. It was icy and exceedingly cold with full blasts of wind from the North Sea but Miss Catlin worked hard, speaking at over a hundred meetings, sometimes three or four a night 'ploughing through snow, mud and the darkness of the countryside'.[37] Her campaign, largely focussed on rising prices and farming issues, awakened 'curiosity in the villages ... by her spirited advocacy of Labour's agricultural policies'.[38] She lost the by-election, though decreased the Conservative majority a little.[39] However, she claimed that she had won 'priceless assets', gaining experience in campaigning and becoming recognised nationally.[40] Both national and local papers reported the result: at only 23 years old, Shirley Catlin was good copy. Edith Summerskill, a family friend, wrote to the *Daily Herald* that 'we have heard so often in the past that women make bad candidates. I think it only just that attention should be drawn to the result achieved by 23 year old Shirley Catlin ... the result compares favourably with all the recent by-elections, and proves once more what we women have always known, that women like a woman candidate'.[41]

In April 7, 1955, Churchill resigned and Anthony Eden became Prime Minister. Immediately, he called for new elections and the young enthusiastic Shirley Catlin had another chance. Once again she was not elected: the sitting Tory increased his majority to 9464. However, she learned a lot about campaigning with little money and 'learned how to make a few hundred pounds go a long way in producing leaflets and stickers. ... I learned how to rally volunteers by taking out canvassing teams with a couple of experienced people'.[42] Miss Catlin's days working at the *Daily Mirror* had helped as she knew how to attract publicity, knew how to write up stories about Labour Party meetings and knew strategies to get them published in the local press.

On July 2, 1955, in the same church at which her parents had wed, Shirley married Bernard Williams at St James' Catholic Church, London. Before the ceremony, the couple agreed that neither would stand in the way of the others' career. In January 1958, Bernard Williams was offered a job in Ghana, teaching philosophy at the University College. Shirley dutifully accompanied her husband but she was not and never would be a stay-at-home wife. She found work teaching economic theory and international trade to various groups and used her Ghanaian experience to write an article for *The Times* in which she urged foreign capital to invest in the newly independent country and warned that the proposed establishment of the European Economic Community (EEC) would have a deleterious effect on the cocoa trade which was the basis of the Ghanaian economy.[43] In January 11, 1959, while her husband remained in Ghana to finish his contractual term, Shirley returned to Britain to find a constituency to represent before the next general election.

It was difficult to find a safe seat: Shirley Williams was not a trade unionist but a privileged intellectual from a middle-class family. She tried and failed to be selected for Epping before being adopted for Southampton Test, a marginal seat with a large Catholic population. In a hard-fought campaign, Shirley toured the constituency either riding on the pillion of her agent's motorbike or in her husband's green sports car. The Tories led by Macmillan and campaigning under the slogan 'Life's Better with the Conservatives. Don't let Labour ruin it', were once more returned, this time with over a 100 parliamentary majority; it was Labour's worst result since 1935. Shirley Williams increased the Labour vote marginally—by nearly 1000—but the Tory incumbent was safe.

Shirley Williams was more of a pragmatist than idealist. She agreed with the Labour leader Hugh Gaitskell that Labour needed to modernise if it wanted to be elected and both recognised that the traditional working-class Labour voter was disappearing as greater affluence made the attractions of nationalised industry and socialism less appealing. Williams wrote a letter to the *Sunday Times* entitled 'Labour and Radical' in which she argued that Labour needed to transform itself to appeal to the newly emerging middle class. In her opinion, industrial disputes, nationalisation and bureaucracy had damaged Labour's credibility and she warned against the disruptive effects of unofficial strikes, demarcation disputes and the allegedly increasing power of the shop steward. On November 28, the Labour Party met at Blackpool for its annual conference, this time chaired by Barbara Castle. The Labour leader Hugh Gaitskell without consulting the NEC or the Shadow Cabinet advocated amending Clause 4—considered to be an untouchable tenet of British socialism—by getting rid of Labour's commitment to nationalisation because it was thought unpopular. Shirley Williams approved. In her view, getting elected was a priority and urged delegates to stop bickering as 'every time we cut each other's throats we give the Conservatives a chance to get in, time and time again'.[44]

In May 20, 1961, Shirley gave birth to her daughter Rebecca Clare, the only one of her 'four potential children to survive to full term'.[45] Rebeca was thought a miracle, 'a tiny human being with every finger and toe perfect'. Shirley was back at work within a couple of weeks, taking her baby daughter to her office and letting her sleep in a carrycot under her desk. Two years later with a small baby in tow, Shirley Williams was adopted for Hitchin, Hertfordshire another constituency safely held by the Conservatives. It was a fortuitous time. Macmillan's government was racked by the Profumo scandal whereas the new leader of the Labour Party Harold Wilson appeared dynamic and in touch with the mood of the country. Williams who was President of the Fabian Society resigned her job to concentrate on nursing her new constituency, as well as her baby.

MP FOR HITCHIN 1964–1974

In October 16, 1964, Shirley Williams, now aged 34, was elected MP for Hitchin with a majority of 3385. The Labour Party under the leadership of Harold Wilson had only narrowly won the election, with an overall majority of four. It had been out of office for thirteen years. Now at last she was an MP, one of six new Labour women in the House of Commons. Shirley Williams MP was excited catching her breath as she first climbed the stone stairs and walked 'into eight hundred years of history'.[46] She was also baffled. There was no help for a newly elected MP, no welcoming ceremonies, no introduction to the procedures of the House of Commons, and even no tour of the very complicated building. MPs were expected to fend for themselves. This led to unexpected embarrassments as when Mrs Williams, exploring the House of Commons, pushed open a door marked 'Members Only' to discover that it contained a row of urinals (though as she commented the phrase 'male members' might have been more amusing).

Shirley Williams was fortunate that, unlike earlier female MPs, she did not feel 'isolated or alone'.[47] The House of Commons, she thought was 'an unusually friendly place'.[48] She knew many of the MPs from her Oxford days, and 'everyone of note appears to have been in love with her'.[49] Moreover, women like Jennie Lee, Barbara Castle, the redoubtable Bessie Braddock and 25 other MPs were in Parliament, making it much more welcoming and agreeable than women had found it previously. Moreover, when she was younger Williams had met a number of the older women MPs: Edith Summerskill, a junior Minister in Attlee's government, was a friend of her mother's and had been something of a role model for the younger Miss Catlin. The new MP for Hitchin experienced 'camaraderie among the women MPs, which even extended beyond party. We wanted to see one another do well. We knew what we were up against, the unstated but pervasive view that women weren't up to the hard choices of politics, that they at best might contribute to 'soft' subjects like health, pensions and education'. Even Margaret Thatcher, not known for her feminism or support for women, gave encouragement. Once, when Shirley Williams had faced a gruelling hour of hostile questioning, Thatcher told her 'You did well. After all, we can't let them get the better of us'.[50]

Initially, Williams was not impressed with the behaviour of her colleagues in the Chamber. She 'was staggered by the baying sound they make sometimes as though they were at a foxhunt kill – it's to say the least an unfeminine sound'.[51] The women MPs may have been friendly; large numbers of men were not. The House of Commons remained dominated by nearly 600 men who swamped the twenty-nine women. Mrs Williams, like other female MPs before her, suffered the exclusive masculine atmosphere of the Smoking Room, the anachronistic all-night sittings, 'the barrack room camaraderie and the raw tribalism of the party battle'. The House of Commons she said 'is like a minor boys' public school'.[52] The final hours of major debates, she insisted 'are like football matches, full of heckling and abuse'.[53] It was certainly like a male-only club. When the MP for Hitchin entered the Smoking Room, she was told that her presence was 'obscene'. Labour MPs in particular treated the bars of the House of Commons like a working man's club with its heavy beer drinking culture and masculine atmosphere.[54] Williams knew, as had Ellen Wilkinson, that access to these venues mattered because they 'were where networks were established, networks that were important for selection, promotion, exchange of opinion and information'.[55] The bars, smoking rooms and clubs were places where male MPs networked, discussed parliamentary business, talked about other MPs, deliberated over who was in line for promotion and so on. It also made it hard to find a political mentor, someone who could provide information, guidance and motivation and help the new MP through the often impenetrable systems of the House of Commons. Fortunately, Williams was helped by one of Labour's senior politicians, Herbert Morrison. More importantly, as more and more women were elected, these bars became more woman-friendly.

Women MPs not only faced disapproval but they had to put up with sexual harassment and sexist comments. When a number of women became fed up with having their bottoms pinched in the division lobby by one particular miscreant, Shirley encouraged them to take collective action by wearing high stiletto heels to stamp on his feet. He never pinched a bottom again. They had less success with the press. Newspapers felt they had the right, indeed the responsibility to report on Mrs Williams looks. In December 1970, the *Daily Mirror* remarked that 'Shirley is solid, half girl, half matron; she has clothes that keep her warm, a hair-do that sometimes looks like a home perm and an adorable waddling walk like that of a barefoot goose-girl'.[56] Shirley Williams was exasperated, later commenting that 'people don't judge a man on whether his suit has recently been pleated or pressed. The obsessive interest of the Press with my hair – it's just gone on for years. It doesn't have the effect of making me have my hair done, except very occasionally, it just makes me cross'.[57]

For the first three months, Mrs Williams did not have a desk or a telephone and had to spend much unnecessary time searching for an available place to work. In this particular session of Parliament, Labour MPs had to stay in or very close to the Commons because the government had such a small majority and each vote counted. Politics, Williams maintained, was a 'hell of a profession to combine with motherhood'.[58] At the time, she was a married woman with a young child, forced to balance her family responsibilities with parliamentary duties. Each evening, Mrs Williams would try to go home to give her daughter supper, read her a bedtime story and dash back to the house for the 10 p.m. vote. Many children, she realised, saw little of their MP parent so their lives tended to become 'a series of small tugs on the heart-strings, another disappointment, another unintentionally broken promise'.[59] Fortunately for Shirley Williams her husband and the people with whom she shared the house all helped.

At 5:30 p.m., November 10, 1964, Shirley Williams made her maiden speech. It was a short seven-minute talk which conformed to parliamentary tradition in that it was somewhat anodyne and ingratiating. Williams complimented the Speaker on his 'dedication, deep feeling and judgment in public service', paid tribute to her Conservative predecessor and eulogised her constituency.[60] She went on to argue that 'we will not get economic progress unless we can revolutionise the status of the industrial worker', but did not say how.[61] It was an example of Shirley Williams' 'niceness' and good behaviour: throughout her parliamentary life, Williams would be nothing less than polite. Unlike the street-fighting 'hooligan' that was Ellen Wilkinson, Williams would always be the 'prefect', always aspiring to engage in adult, reasonable discussions, disquieted by too much acrimonious debate.[62] The *Daily Mail* asked 'could she be Britain's first Prime Minister?'

CLIMBING THE POLITICAL LADDER

Climbing the political ladder is a lot harder than climbing a bookshelf yet Williams quickly moved up the parliamentary hierarchy. In her first few days as MP, she was appointed Parliamentary Private Secretary to the Minister of Health, Kenneth Robinson. It was, as in Ellen Wilkinson's day, an unpaid position, but one which was viewed as the first step on the way to the top of the political tree. Her new boss believed in female equality and discussed policy with his protégé, took her to departmental meetings and, much to the astonishment of the civil servants, encouraged Williams to express her opinions.[63] Under Robinson's aegis, new hospitals were built and administrative reforms implemented in the NHS, thereby placating GPs who were threatening mass resignation. In 1966, the department addressed most doctors' medical concerns by providing well-equipped premises, a basic pay structure, pension provision and greater autonomy. All the time, the young MP for Hitchin was learning how government worked and how to negotiate complex issues with various conflicting parties.

In 1966, two years after she was first elected, she was appointed to her first ministerial role as Parliamentary Secretary to the Ministry of Labour, the third level of government minister below Minister of State and Secretary of State. Her new boss Ray Gunter a working-class trade unionist from South Wales, called it a 'bed of nails'.[64] It was a time of continuing industrial crisis as trade unions battled with a hard-pressed Labour Government to increase the pay of their members. In order to placate its heartland and to curb inflation Labour introduced a prices-and-incomes policy in which unions were expected to limit pay rises in exchange for price controls. This agreement often broke down. In May 16, 1966, just six weeks after the election of a Labour Government, the National Union of Seamen, a closed-shop union that Williams maintained was run by the hard left, called a strike. They demanded a reduction in hours from 56 to 46 hours a week and higher wages, the equivalent of a 17% pay rise thus undermining Labour's attempts to restrain wages. The ensuing strike was solid and by the end of May 651 ships were stranded in the docks. Stocks of food and fuel ran low causing massive disruption and damage to the economy. On May 23 Harold Wilson, who believed the strike to be a strike against the nation which was instigated by communists, called a national emergency: the government put a cap on food prices and brought in the Royal Navy to clear the ports.

In the middle of the crisis the Minister of Labour, Ray Gunter collapsed from a heart attack. Harold Wilson stepped in, insisting that he would be personally responsible for handling the strike.[65] However, with her boss incapacitated Shirley Williams was in overall control of the Ministry of Labour, attending Cabinet to report on the progress of the strike, answering questions in the Commons and dealing with the senior civil servants. Unfortunately, the civil servant in charge of her department opposed Williams' appointment, largely ignored her and did not help her prepare her case, all of which made it doubly difficult for Williams.[66] In the end, Harold Wilson set up an independent court of enquiry under Lord Pearson which offered a compromise solution, recommending substantial cuts in the working week though no increase in pay. John Prescott, former seaman, Hull student and future Labour Party Deputy Leader, co-wrote a pamphlet *Not Wanted on Voyage*[67] which denounced the Labour Government and the employers for not agreeing with the seamen's demands. Initially, Williams was supportive of the seamen's cause but their initial refusal to accept Pearson's compromise made her less sympathetic. In July 1, 47 days after its start, the seaman's strike was settled at a percentage well above inflation, allegedly damaging the already fragile economy.

Voluntary wage restraint was clearly not working and *In Place of Strife* had failed. As a consequence, the government brought in a new Prices and Incomes Bill which proposed a six-month wage freeze followed by another six months of restraint. In spite of the fact that both the trade unions and employers disliked the policy, the Labour Government pressed on. Shirley Williams and her colleague Bill Rogers were responsible for guiding the Bill through Parliament, first at Committee stage then in the Commons. This again was to prove a fruitless endeavour as neither prices nor incomes were held down.

One issue Williams faced was a demand to cut down immigration, said to cause unemployment among the native population. The Conservative Duncan Sandys pleaded for immigration cuts, 'convinced that blacks and whites could never live in harmony' and cautioned that rising unemployment would lead to racial strife.[68] Sandys' views did not go unchallenged. Shirley Williams condemned his views and urged 'public acceptance of the fact that all men and women were equal, no matter what the colour of their skin' and that 'equality must be achieved for the immigrant population ... equality of opportunity, equality of employment and equality of promotion'.[69]

MINISTER OF STATE FOR EDUCATION
AND SCIENCE, AUGUST 1967–OCTOBER 1969

In January 1967, Shirley Williams was promoted again, this time to be a Minister of State at the Department of Education and Science, at first under Tony Crosland, then under Patrick Gordon Walker and finally under Ted Short (Fig. 10.1). Mrs Williams' political world changed from concerns about industry, industrial workers, unemployment, metal foundries, occupational hazards and antioxidants in Japanese cars to concerns about school building programmes, school books, dyslexia, thalidomide children and married women teachers. Education was an issue about which she felt particularly passionate. Her first boss, Tony Crosland, was a man who 'relished intellectual argument'[70] and who patently respected his young Minister, regularly inviting her to his informal think-tank at home. Here, the group would 'discuss comprehensive schools, tertiary and sixth-form colleges, how to integrate the state system and the public schools'.

Shirley Williams, like her boss, wanted to reverse the policy of Ellen Wilkinson and the first Labour Government. By now, grammar schools were seen as elitist middle-class institutions with working-class pupils largely confined to the less-well funded secondary moderns. Williams believed that abolition of the 11+ system and the replacement of grammar schools by comprehensives was the key to a fairer, worthier, more egalitarian system. Comprehensive schools based in the local community would, Williams believed, make for an 'inclusive, cohesive society' and eliminate the 'privileges, patronage and preferment' that characterised so much of Britain.[71] Public and private schools, whereby richer parents paid for an exclusive education and which undermined the idea of educational equality, were never endangered. In October 1963, Tony Crosland had issued Circular 10/65 requesting every local authority to submit its plans for local schools to turn comprehensive. According to Williams, most authorities were willing to comply as education committees disliked selection and parents disliked it when their children failed the 11+ examination and were forced into less well-endowed secondary moderns. In 1965, only 8.5% of pupils attended comprehensive schools; in 1975, the number rose to 85%.

In August 1967, Crosland was replaced by Patrick Gordon Walker and he immediately appointed Alice Bacon to join Jennie Lee and Shirley Williams as his ministerial staff. Leading newspapers commented on the lack of governmental balance. 'One woman Minister in a Government department' the *Daily Mirror* argued 'is ideal. Two is fine for the feminist cause. Three is perhaps over-egging the pudding'.[72] Alice Bacon persuaded the new Secretary of State to move Shirley Williams from the schools portfolio to that of higher education so that she could take her job. Shirley Williams stepped into her new ministerial role at a time when there was widespread student unrest across the university sector. When Williams visited Birmingham, she was barricaded in the Vice-Chancellor's room and only escaped through a

Fig. 10.1 Shirley Williams as Minister of Education, 1967 (©Trinity Mirror/Mirrorpix/Alamy Stock Photo)

central-heating duct. The student revolution gradually disintegrated. In April 1968, Gordon Walker was forced to resign and was replaced by Ted Short. Williams helped her new boss draft an Education Act which gave students representation on university tribunals and academic boards and provided autonomy for student unions.[73] The Act also required polytechnics and further education colleges to appoint governing bodies consisting of representatives from both staff and students. Shirley Williams claimed she learned three things from this experience. Firstly that leadership 'must be a blend of toughness and compromise'; secondly that academics should not be too involved in educational reform because they disappeared when under attack; thirdly the media cared only about getting a good story and would engineer one if they could not.

Undoubtedly, her first few years in Parliament were a success. MPs from all sides of the House thought her one of the nicest MPs, largely because she always treated people courteously. She was liked and respected, reckoned to be a dedicated, efficient and approachable Minister who was always on top of her brief. Perhaps more importantly, most of the Cabinet Ministers rated her highly: Callaghan told her directly that she would hold high office in any future Labour Government. One friend spoke of her 'infectious warmth, fierce intelligence and generosity of spirit' as well as an abiding optimism and an upbeat personality.[74] She was liked because she treated everyone equally regardless of their background, tended to see the best in individuals, did not speak ill of anyone and was always willing to make light of the defects of others. Her husband thought she wanted to be liked by everyone, even those she disliked.[75] Of course, there are negative sides in being so popular: some thought her too quixotic, too flexible, too given to political manoeuvring, too inconsistent, too prone to say what people wanted to hear. Others felt she was too unmethodical, too immersed in detail at the expense of the wider picture and often found it difficult to delegate. The fact that she could never say no meant that her generosity was sometimes exploited.

MINISTER OF STATE FOR HOME AFFAIRS, OCTOBER 1969–JUNE 1970

In November 1969, Harold Wilson transferred Williams to the Home Office under Jim Callaghan. Here, she found herself in a highly charged political world. And instantaneously she switched her focus to her new department, dealing with issues ranging from overcrowding in prisons, parking penalties and illegal betting to the putative 'danger of increased Arab terrorist activities'.[76] Wilson moved Williams to the Home Office in an attempt to win over the Catholics in Northern Ireland: Callaghan was a Protestant; Williams a known Catholic. At the time, Northern Ireland was administered by a devolved Parliament, itself under the control of the Home Office. Shirley William's tenure at the Home Office coincided with the decision to send British troops to Northern Ireland to help keep the peace between the Catholics and the Protestants, a decision which was welcomed at first but that later proved to be an unmitigated disaster. Shirley Williams believed that more money needed to be pumped into Northern Ireland, arguing that it should mirror Roosevelt's New Deal which had helped alleviate poverty and had given people hope that their government cared about the vulnerable.

As well as assisting Callaghan with Northern Ireland, Shirley Williams had responsibility for what she termed the three Ps: prisons, probation and pornography. Each week she had to look at pornographic material to see whether it should be banned. She 'found the endless pages of huge breasts and naked women straddling chairs numbingly boring. ... I began to feel a bit sorry for the men who were turned on by pornographic pictures. They seemed such pathetic counterfeits'.[77] She was particularly concerned about sadism and found herself banning pictures of women being whipped while being dressed as school-girls. After a time of viewing these images, Shirley Williams concluded that some men held an intense hatred towards women.[78]

As Minister with responsibility for prisons, Shirley Williams decided she would find out what they were like—as an inmate rather than as a visitor. She persuaded the prison authorities not to divulge her identity to either the prison officers or the inmates. Of course, it is hard to believe that the officers and the prisoners did not realise who their famous inmate was: she was a high-profile politician, regularly appearing in the newspapers and on television. Masquerading as a convicted prostitute, Williams went through the admission process, 'stripped and searched, given prison clothes … and put in a stained and grubby cell'.[79] She experienced the slopping out system whereby inmates were forced to use a bucket as a lavatory, throw out the contents each morning and clean the bucket. Prisons, she wrote, had a smell of disinfectant, urine and decay. These experiences compelled Shirley Williams to try to provide adequate lavatory facilities in prisons.

She wanted to reform the prison system in other ways. At the time, the prison population was increasing at the rate of 1000 a month. The poor state of the prisons and the high rate of recidivism led Williams to believe that parole rather than imprisonment was the way forward. In her view, there should be more non-custodial sentences and greater use of the probationary service as a 'path back to citizenship and self-respect'.[80] Respect for human life was also paramount and the Catholic Shirley Williams disapproved of the death penalty. In 1965, capital punishment was suspended for five years; it was due to expire in 1970 and the government decided to settle the matter. The Shadow Home Secretary Quintin Hogg wanted to delay the vote to abolish the death penalty but Williams demolished his arguments and ended her speech by declaring: 'I hope that the decision will be to remove once and for all the shadow of the gallows from this humane land'.[81] The next day the abolition of the death penalty was passed by a huge majority.

Williams' Catholicism may have encouraged her to disapprove of abortion. In April 27, 1968, David Steel's Private Members' Bill, backed up by the government, to legalise abortion for the first 24 weeks of pregnancy became law. Before this Act, women who tried to end a pregnancy could be imprisoned for life under the 1861 Offences Against the Person Act, an Act amended in 1929 so that an abortion carried out if the mother's life was in danger would not be an offence. These laws, of course, did not stop unwanted pregnancies or the need for abortions: women resorted to back-street abortionists or to abortifacients advertised in newspapers as cures for 'menstrual blockage'. Thousands of women died or else became poisoned by semi-legal medicines. The new Bill was passed overwhelmingly: 223 to 29. Shirley Williams did not speak in the Debate but voted against the Bill.[82] However, she refused to bow to pressure from SPUC (the Society for the Unborn Child), a fiercely anti-abortion Catholic pressure group when they tried to engage her support. But Williams was no unthinking Catholic: she believed that birth control should be free and easily accessible, a belief which contravened the policy of the Church.

Shirley Williams worked well with Jim Callaghan over Ireland and Home Affairs but the two disagreed strongly over the plight of East African Asians. In 1963, when Kenya won its independence the Conservative Commonwealth Secretary promised the 185,000 Asians who held British passports that they would have a right of entry to Britain should the Kenyan government discriminate against them. In 1968, the Kenyan Asians were threatened with expulsion. When 13,000 came to Britain, Enoch Powell and other Conservative figures demanded that the right be revoked. The Labour Government caved in to public and newspaper pressure and restricted the number of immigrants to 1500 a year, arguing that Britain could not absorb such a large number of Kenyan Asians. Members of parliament on both sides of the House objected, arguing that immigrants and in particular those fleeing persecution, contributed to the country more than they took from it. Shirley Williams was appalled at the treatment of Kenyan Asians and wrote a letter of resignation to Harold Wilson, only to be persuaded by the Chair of the Race Relations Board not to send it. The Hitchin Labour Party most of whom favoured immigration control quizzed her but she told them that no one could be proud of the fact that the government had limited the number of British citizens of Asian origin from coming to their country.

At the time, Shirley Williams was one of the most popular politicians in Britain. In a flattering editorial, the usually Conservative *Times* urged readers to vote for Shirley Williams in the forthcoming general election. 'If one had to pick a single Labour MP in whose social conscience one would trust it would be Mrs Shirley Williams. ... It is also not easy to be a successful woman politician. The pressures are very intense and they are pressures which can make a woman unattractively aggressive ... Shirley Williams is not a bit like that, she is one of those very rare women who could become Prime Minister (and perhaps should) without losing a scrap of her good nature and charm'.[83]

In Opposition

In 1970, Labour was defeated by Edward Heath's Conservatives. Labour, which liked to see itself as the party of women's rights, was humiliated because only 10 Labour women were elected whereas 15 Conservative women had won seats. It was the smallest number of Labour women since 1935. Shirley Williams believed that Labour was out of office partly because of its perceived inefficiency at managing the economy, partly because of a growing trade deficit, partly because the unions and not the government were seen to be running the country. Shirley Williams won her seat but found herself on the opposition benches, trying to cope with her husband leaving, the death of her mother (March 29, 1970) and living with her daughter in Hertfordshire, a long way from Parliament. There was no need, it was claimed 'to speculate about the misery she went through when, possibly for the first time, her life went badly wrong. It was written all over her face. She looked dreadful and was clearly in no mood to disguise her state of mind by putting on a front as many other public figures would have done'.[84] Her inability to dissemble was seen as a dangerous display of vulnerability for a career-minded politician, rather than a positive attribute for a human being.

Shirley Williams was able to survive on a few hours sleep in a life consumed by politics: the concept of work/life balance was unthinkable in her frenzied over-worked world. Inevitably late, she was always trying to cram yet another meeting into an already crowded schedule. The material things of life never really interested her, her home was quite austere with cardboard boxes and filing cabinets in the sitting room, she rarely spent money on clothes and always used public transport to the House of Commons. The problem was that Shirley and her husband led separate lifestyles and Bernard, who had had numerous affairs and who felt neglected by his politically engaged wife, found comfort elsewhere. Shirley Williams loved Bernard: she had endured four miscarriages, put up with his various affairs and believed that marriage was forever. However, Bernard wanted to leave. In August 1974, the two were officially divorced—Shirley Williams stated that she had not divorced her husband but had 'consented to him divorcing her on grounds of two years separation'. By this time, Shirley had a new partner, Professor Anthony King but maintained that she could not live with a man to whom she was not married. However, as a practising Roman Catholic she did not feel free to marry until July 1980 when her marriage to Bernard was eventually annulled. Meanwhile, Anthony King had married someone else.

At times public life seemed 'unendurable ... the eyes and ears of the media are everywhere; there are few hiding places'.[85] The public are all too often unsympathetic when politicians experience difficulties, often forgetting that MPs have feelings, can be hurt, depressed, unhappy and vulnerable. Shirley Williams learned to keep her emotions in check, maintaining that 'one learns composure, to keep hand and eye steady, to never let go except with the most trusted friends. That discipline helps, acts as a life-line when the foundations themselves crumble away'.[86] As she emerged from her 'own cocoon of wretchedness' she began to enjoy Opposition'.[87]

Williams decided to move back to London. She bought a house in Hammersmith from her former sister-in-law and made a choice that would haunt her in the future: she chose to send her daughter Rebecca to an all-girls direct-grant school after she had passed the 11+. As a junior Minister, Mrs Williams had criticised grammar schools for their elitism, their consolidation of privilege, their exclusivity and was proud of her contribution to the growth of comprehensive schools. Yet, seemingly what was good for the majority of children in the country was not good enough for her daughter: it was not just seen as a mixed message but a duplicitous one. Her popularity in some quarters diminished.

Shirley Williams' private life may have crumpled but her political career was blossoming. Harold Wilson appointed the 40-year-old Williams, first as Shadow Secretary of State for Health and Social Services (June 1970–October 1971), then as Shadow Home Secretary (October 1971–May 1973). She was the youngest member of his Shadow Cabinet. These promotions indicated that she would be one of the big players when Labour returned to office.

However, her first job was short-lived. Williams was shunted out of the Home Office to make way for Roy Jenkins and demoted to Shadow Secretary of State for Prices and Consumer Protection (May 1973–March 1974). Wilson knew he could treat Shirley Williams in a way he would not treat Jenkins. She was known to be consensual and co-operative—she disliked dissension and certainly would not be ruthless enough to jockey for position. One Labour MP thought that she represented 'everything that is most agreeable, most civilised about English life. She's liberal, rational, intelligent, concerned'.[88] It was thought she might be altogether too nice to be a leader.

Meanwhile, the Conservative Government was selling off the profitable part of the nationalised industries such as telecommunications and airline routes. Shirley Williams objected to the sale of assets owned by the nation. In her view, it represented harmful 'redistribution of power from the state to private individuals', because power was transferred from nationalised companies under parliamentary control to another which was not. A transfer of this kind, she argued was 'a transfer to a hierarchical private power structure. It does nothing to increase the economic and political power of the ordinary citizen'.[89] Williams believed that publicly run services were essential: better schools, better roads and better hospitals improved our individual as well as collective lives. [90]

Edward Heath came to office with a majority of thirty, a strong enough majority to put his policies in place. He had one objective in mind: to join the European Union, then known as the EEC, or the Common Market, in order to construct a new Europe, free of conflict. The decision to join the EEC caused dissension among the political parties, not between them. Many Labour MPs were against joining, thinking the EEC a capitalist club and preferring to do business with the Commonwealth. Certainly, opposition to the EEC became a rallying cry for left-wing MPs like Barbara Castle, Judith Hart, Michael Foot and Tony Benn. In contrast, Shirley Williams was pro-Europe, believing that the social model of Europe, with its superior public services, social benefits and greater economic egalitarianism, was what Britain needed. British people, she believed, needed to realise that the world had changed. There was a 'profound nostalgia' afflicting the country and a misguided belief that Britain was still one of the great powers and could 'get food from Commonwealth countries grateful to dispose of it to us more cheaply'. It is difficult, she thought, to 'fight a dream' but the country needed to realise that it was in a fiercely competitive world and being in Europe gave us protection. Once tariff barriers were re-instated, she argued, there would be less trade with Europe and firms might decide to relocate to mainland Europe to take advantage of the less restricted market.[91]

In July 17, 1971, it all came to a head at a special conference on Europe where Labour Party delegates voted overwhelmingly to oppose Britain's entry to Europe. This decision was later endorsed by the NEC and the Shadow Cabinet. Opposition to the EEC was now official Labour Policy and

MPs, especially those in the Shadow Cabinet, were expected to tow the party line. It was a sad moment for Shirley Williams. A couple of weeks later she made 'an impassioned plea' for Labour 'not to turn its back on Socialism in Europe by taking a tragic decision that would lack credibility'.[92] She lost. The Labour Party made a decision to oppose entry to the Common Market and expected all its MPs to vote accordingly. In contrast Edward Heath took a more democratic decision and offered his MPs a free vote on entry to the EEC. In October 1971, when MPs debated the Treaty of Accession, Shirley Williams along with 68 other Labour MPs, refused the party whip and voted in favour of British entry. The government won with a 112 majority; Shirley Williams was reprimanded for voting against Labour policy.

In January 22, 1972, Edward Heath signed the Treaty in Brussels and returned to Britain to receive parliamentary assent. In February 17, 1972, when the second reading of the Bill took place, Labours pro-Europeans, including Williams, voted against. She was voting against a principle she dearly believed in: European unity. Shirley Williams wrote to Harold Wilson warning him that she would find it impossible to continue in the Shadow Cabinet if it 'refused to adopt a more constructive approach towards British entry'.[93] Her threatened resignation never materialised. In January 1, 1973, Britain along with Denmark and Ireland joined the EEC; in 1992, the Treaty of Maastricht created the European Union.

By now the Labour Party was seen to be damagingly fragmented. *The Times* blamed rival power bases in the Labour Party—the trade unions, the party conference, the NEC, and the constituencies—each of which sought to control MPs.[94] In its opinion, the debate over the Common Market propelled a 'predictable return to the old division between those who see their duty primarily to satisfy the party activists and those who interpret it as the need to act in the wider interest of the electorate on which they depend'.[95] In addition, there was too wide a gap between the reformists—like Gaitskell—who wanted to improve the existing system and the revolutionaries—like Benn—who wanted to recast society. As a consequence, the poor British voter 'might be forgiven for feeling more than ordinarily confused about the Labour Party just now' because it was much too divided and inchoate.[96]

Meanwhile, the UK not just the Labour Party was falling apart. In January 30, 1972, thirteen civil rights demonstrators were shot on the streets of Londonderry; the IRA retaliated by detonating a bomb at a British Army base in Aldershot, killing seven civilian staff, mostly cleaners. It was the first attack in England. The British Government responded by introducing internment and tightening up security. As Shadow Home Secretary, Williams maintained that the government 'can never find a military solution to political problems' and feared that legislation 'could all too easily be misinterpreted and misunderstood and become another dangerous factor in the Northern Ireland situation'.[97]

In January 1, 1974, Edward Heath announced a three day week in response to a miners' strike that threatened to derail the economy. Williams wrote to her father saying 'I think myself if the miners' strike isn't settled next week we'll have an election on a "Who Governs Britain?" basis'.[98] The election took place as she predicted, Labour won and Shirley Williams was catapulted into high office. The following chapter will examine her role as Cabinet Minister and chart her growing disillusion with Labour.

NOTES

1. Vera Brittain to George Caitlin, October 1946 quoted in Mark Peel, *Shirley Williams: The Biography*, Biteback, 2013, p. 54.
2. Mark Peel, *Shirley Williams: The Biography*, 2013, p. 8.
3. Vera Brittain, *Testament of Experience*, 1957, Victor Gollancz, p. 62.
4. Vera Britain, *Chronicle of Friendship: Diary of the Thirties*, Victor Gollancz, July 28, 1932.
5. Ibid.
6. Ibid., January 15, 1939.
7. Ibid., December 21, 1932.
8. Ibid., November 13, 1935.
9. Ibid., March 31, 1939.
10. Vera Brittain, *Testament of Experience*, 1957, p. 193.
11. Shirley Williams, *Climbing the Bookshelves*, Virago, 2009, p. 35.
12. Ibid., p. 36.
13. Vera Brittain, *Testament of Experience*, 1957, p. 323.
14. Shirley Williams, *Climbing the Bookshelves*, 2009, p. 51.
15. Vera Brittain, *Testament of Experience*, 1957, p. 350.
16. Ibid.
17. For example, Jane Bonham Carter, Vicky Ford, Harriet Harman, Susan Kramer, Mavis Tate, Anne-Marie Trevelyan, Jo Valentine, and Eirene White were all educated at St Paul's.
18. Mark Peel, *Shirley Williams: The Biography*, 2013, p. 16.
19. Shirley Williams, *Climbing the Bookshelves*, 2009, p. 23.
20. Shirley Williams interview, *The Guardian*, March 22, 1981, p. 15.
21. Ibid.
22. Ibid.
23. Liz Forgan, *The Guardian*, November 4, 1978, p. 7.
24. George Catlin, *For God's Sake, Go*, Colin Smythe, 1972, p. 286.
25. Vera Brittain, *Testament of Experience*, 1957, p. 440.
26. Shirley Williams, *God and Caesar*, 2003, Continuum, p. 57.
27. Vera Brittain to Janet Vaughan quoted in Mark Peel, *Shirley Williams: The Biography*, 2013, p. 57.
28. *The Observer*, October 23, 1977, p. 25.
29. *The Times*, February 18, 1981, p. 13.
30. Mark Peel, *Shirley Williams: The Biography*, 2013, p. 65.
31. Shirley Williams, *Climbing the Bookshelves*, 2009, p. 90.

270 P. BARTLEY

P. BARTLEY

270

P. BARTLEY

270 P. BARTLEY

270 P. BARTLEY

270

270

270
270

270

270
270
270

270

270

270 P. BARTLEY

32. An American senator, Joseph McCarthy, targeted government employees, academics, trade unionists and those employed in the entertainment industry and forced those suspected of communist sympathies to be questioned by the House Un-American Activities Committee (HUAC). Otto Katz was in Hollywood at this time.
33. Liz Forgan, *The Guardian,* November 4, 1978, p. 7.
34. Shirley Williams, *Climbing the Bookshelves,* 2009, p. 90.
35. Ibid., p. 104.
36. Mark Peel, *Shirley Williams: The Biography,* 2013, p. 96.
37. Shirley Williams, *Climbing the Bookshelves,* 2009, p. 104.
38. *The Times,* February 5, 1954, p. 2.
39. Shirley Catlin won 13,535 votes; the Conservative Julian Ridsdale won 19,532, a majority of 5007. At the previous election the Conservative candidate enjoyed a majority of 7925.
40. Shirley Williams, *Climbing the Bookshelves,* 2009, p. 112.
41. Edith Summerskill, *Daily Herald,* February 17, 1954, p. 4.
42. Shirley Williams, *Climbing the Bookshelves,* 2009, p. 113.
43. *The Times,* November 9, 1959, p. 3.
44. Shirley Williams, Labour Party Conference Report, 1959, p. 144.
45. Shirley Williams, *Climbing the Bookshelves,* 2009, p. 140.
46. Ibid., p. 145.
47. Ibid., p. 148.
48. *The Guardian,* November 4, 1978, p. 7.
49. Ibid.
50. Shirley Williams, *Climbing the Bookshelves,* 2009, p. 148.
51. *The Illustrated London News,* June 12, 1965, p. 21.
52. Mark Peel, *Shirley Williams: The Biography,* 2013, p. 134.
53. Shirley Williams, *The Guardian,* December 15, 1997, p. 4.
54. Shirley Williams, *Climbing the Bookshelves,* 2009, p. 149.
55. Ibid., p. 150.
56. Quoted in Melanie Phillips, *The Divided House,* Sidgwick and Jackson, 1980, p. 117.
57. *The Observer,* March 22, 1981, p. 15.
58. Shirley Williams, *Climbing the Bookshelves,* 2009, p. 153.
59. Ibid., p. 154.
60. Hansard, November 10, 1964, cc880–882.
61. *The Times,* November 11, 1964, p. 16.
62. Clare Short suggests that female MPs can be divided into 'hooligans' and 'prefects'.
63. Shirley Williams, *Climbing the Bookshelves,* 2009, p. 163.
64. Ibid., p. 164.
65. *The Times,* June 29, 1966, p. 1.
66. Shirley Williams, *Climbing the Bookshelves,* 2009, p. 167.
67. John Prescott and Charlie Hodgins, *Not Wanted on Voyage,* NUS Hull Dispute Committee, June 1966.
68. Duncan Sandys, *The Times,* November 9, 1966, p. 1.
69. Shirley Williams, *The Times,* November 9, 1966, p. 1.
70. Shirley Williams, *Climbing the Bookshelves,* 2009, p. 169.

71. Ibid., p. 175.
72. *Daily Mirror*, February 16, 1968, p. 13.
73. Shirley Williams, *Climbing the Bookshelves*, 2009, p. 182.
74. Quoted in Mark Peel, *Shirley Williams: The Biography*, 2013, p. 161.
75. Quoted in Mark Peel, *Shirley Williams: The Biography*, 2013, p. 161.
76. Hansard, November 20, 1969, Vol. 791, c1487.
77. Shirley Williams, *Climbing the Bookshelves*, 2009, p. 189.
78. Ibid.
79. Ibid., p. 191.
80. Ibid., p. 192.
81. Hansard, December 15, 1969, Vol. 793, cc939–1062.
82. Hansard, July 22, 1966, Vol. 732, cc1067–1165. Many women spoke in this debate.
83. *The Times*, June 4, 1970, p. 11.
84. Liz Forgan, *The Guardian*, November 4, 1978, p. 7.
85. Shirley Williams, *Climbing the Bookshelves*, 2009, p. 213.
86. Ibid.
87. Ibid.
88. *The Observer*, September 16, 1973, quoted in Mark Peel, *Shirley Williams: The Biography*, 2013, p. 197.
89. *The Times*, September 26, 1970, p. 18.
90. *The Times*, September 26, 1970, p. 18.
91. Shirley Williams, *The Guardian*, May 17, 1975, p. 6.
92. *The Birmingham Post*, July 29, 1971, p. 1.
93. *The Times*, April 11, 1972, p. 1.
94. *The Times*, November 9, 1972, p. 19.
95. Ibid.
96. *The Times*, November 16, 1972, p. 18.
97. Hansard, February 23, 1972, Vol. 831, cc1363–1422.
98. Quoted in Mark Peel, *Shirley Williams: The Biography*, 2013, p. 197.

CHAPTER 11

In the Cabinet
and Out of Labour, 1974–2018

In February 1974, Labour won the general election and once more Harold Wilson became Prime Minister, this time with a majority of only three. He appointed Shirley Williams, now aged 43 as Secretary of State for Prices and Consumer Protection, a new department largely created to give Williams a place in Cabinet (Fig. 11.1). Once again, there were two women in the top tier of government 'not because they're women. It's just that they can run rings round most men in the Commons'.[1] As with other female Cabinet Ministers, Shirley Williams received equal pay, earning £16,000 a year (£13,000 from her Cabinet position and £3000 parliamentary allowance) making her a top earner.[2] And like Castle and Hart before her, she was tipped to become Britain's first woman Prime Minister.[3] The American *Time* magazine thought her 'the most brilliant woman in British politics' and predicted that she would become one of the world's future leaders.[4] It was never to be. Just after she was appointed to her first Cabinet post Shirley Williams confessed that 'the thing she really dislikes is feeling herself disliked', a character trait that ill-suits a politician, especially one who aims for the top government position.[5]

Secretary of State for Prices and Incomes, March 1974–September 1976

For nearly two and a half years, Shirley Williams took on 'the awesome task of damming a river in spate'.[6] Her main role was to control prices, a job at which she could fail firstly because she was a new Secretary of State, in charge of a new department and secondly because she was in charge of 'prices – over which she had no control, at a moment of unprecedented inflation'.[7] Most of the nationalised industries, including coal, electricity and the railways, wanted to increase prices as the cost of oil was escalating daily, and they needed to

© The Author(s) 2019
P. Bartley, *Labour Women in Power*,
https://doi.org/10.1007/978-3-030-14288-9_11

Fig. 11.1 Shirley Williams on the Front Bench (©Keystone Pictures USA/Alamy Stock Photo)

absorb the costs. In addition, world food prices were predicted to rise by 30% which would inevitably hit the British consumer.[8] The *Financial Times* commented that it 'is a pity that male Prime Ministers tend to think of women in terms of the shopping basket and it is particularly a pity for Mrs Williams to have been handed a booby-trapped shopping basket'.[9] 'I do not deny', Williams told the Commons 'that I have a daunting job at a daunting time'.[10]

Williams was very aware that low-income families spent a higher proportion of their incomes on food than the rich and wanted to make the price of food her priority. As soon as she took office, Shirley Williams promised to protect the weak, 'those who are ravaged, terrified and worried by inflation … we shall do all we conceivably can to control these disastrous inflationary pressures upon ordinary men and women'.[11] On March 12, 1974, she asked the Cabinet to approve 'stricter price controls, to make selective use of subsidies for items which are significant in the family budget, to improve price marking and to require unit pricing'.[12] Williams 'had in mind payment of subsidies on a short list of selected foodstuffs' such as milk, butter, cheese, sugar and bread.[13] The Cabinet agreed and the Labour Government subsidised six basic foods, namely milk, butter, bread, cheese, flour and tea 'because of their importance to the budgets of low-income families and not least pensioners'.[14]

In addition, Williams proposed cutting the profit margins of shopkeepers. In June 1974, her well-known negotiation skills became evident when she persuaded the Retail Consortium to offer a list of essential foods and household supplies—potatoes, beef, lamb, chicken, baby milk, bread, butter and cheese—at special reduced prices.[15] In addition, Williams stopped all rent increases for a year and pegged the interest rate for mortgages. She also negotiated a 50% price reduction with Roche for Librium and Valium: the pharmaceutical company had been grossly over-charging the NHS for use of its drugs. Wilson praised her publicly; *The Guardian* reported that she possessed 'an admirable reputation for integrity, personal and public. Seen by many as thoroughly decent, honest and honourable, the ideal of what a politician should be'.[16]

Most people enjoyed working with Shirley Williams since 'she was always very appreciative, avoided apportioning blame and could express herself candidly without causing offence'.[17] A few disagreed: one Conservative MP called her the Mary Poppins of the present administration; Tony Benn maintained that she was the most reactionary person he knew. 'She gives the impression of being so nice' Benn stated and she 'is now being built up as the great heroine. "Shirley keeps our food prices down. Shirley protects our shopping baskets" and so on when she is, in fact, doing nothing beyond doling out money to industry'.[18] Tony Benn's comments were vindictive rather than accurate. Shirley Williams had earlier attacked Benn's industrial strategy in Cabinet, an attack viewed 'as the mostly closely argued and fully backed with evidence. ... Benn sat there looking very pale, first rocking back and forwards in his chair and later scribbling furiously, no doubt for his diary'.[19] Benn's industrial strategy was completely defeated and 'everyone went away very happy – except Benn'.[20]

Shirley Williams was popular with the civil servants in her department because she held regular briefing sessions and took them out to lunch.[21] Wilson's head of policy research felt that her weakness was being a little disorganised, rarely punctual, and seeming rather befuddled. In fact, he argued 'she is not particularly muddled on politics or policies, but she gives that impression. ... If she could get herself 'organised' with all the trappings of efficiency, she would have to be taken very seriously indeed'.[22]

Certainly, Williams tried to keep a grip on prices. But she couldn't keep a grip on wages. Michael Foot, who had replaced Barbara Castle, favoured free collective bargaining rather than wage restraint and wages ineluctably rose. This could have caused personal conflict, but luckily for Cabinet harmony, both parties were collegiate, polite and charming—Shirley Williams penned notes to Foot in Cabinet which began 'Michael Honeybunch'.[23] Nevertheless, it was an unmanageable situation: no government could hope to hold down prices without controlling wages. In 1975, inflation was running at 26%, fuelled as much by wage increases as by price rises. Wage demands, sometimes of 30%, were seen to be crippling the economy.

The left-wingers in the Labour Party thought the economy would improve if Britain left the Common Market, citing high food prices as a reason for leaving. Shirley Williams thought otherwise. At the September Labour Party Conference, she announced she would resign if a Labour Government tried to take Britain out of the Common Market.[24] Wilson, now with a tiny majority after the October 1974 election, decided to hold a referendum, basically to placate some of his fractious backbenchers and party activists and to keep his carefully cemented Cabinet from cracking. He was seen as taking a risk with the country's future for the sake of keeping his party more-or-less united.

Harold Wilson, like Edward Heath before him, broke the constitutional convention of collective Cabinet responsibility and allowed his Ministers to put forward their own beliefs and campaign against each other. Harold Wilson, Shirley Williams, Roy Jenkins and Roy Hattersley led the campaign to stay in Europe; Barbara Castle, Michael Foot and Tony Benn led the campaign against. Williams was chair of the Labour Campaign for Europe. She warned that leaving the EU would be a 'stupendous act of folly' and would lead to greater unemployment. People did not realise, she insisted, 'how sharply retaliatory other countries would be to Britain if we left the Market. ...It is nicer to believe Britain is still one of the great powers ... and can get food from Commonwealth countries grateful to dispose of it to us more cheaply ... in spite of the fact that Commonwealth leaders have said they want us to remain in the Market'.[25] Moreover, Williams maintained that firms with a potential selling market of 250 million would be more likely to invest in Britain if we stayed in. And leave Britain if we were no longer in the EEC. She criticised those who saw Europe as a 'rich man's club' arguing that the European Commission had put forward minimum working conditions, redundancy rights, pension provisions and other welfare rights.

In an article for *The Guardian*, Williams insisted that the world was too interdependent for Britain to go it alone. Many of the world's pressing problems, she argued, were 'multinational or international: how to control nuclear weapons ... how to cope with environmental pollution which respects no boundaries; ... how to feed the fast-rising population ... how to curb multi-national companies; how to distribute the wealth and resources of the globe more fairly; ... how to keep the peace'.[26] The British electorate agreed with her. The remainers won by over 60%: 17.3 to 8.4 million voted in favour of staying in the EEC. The matter was thought settled.

On March 16, 1976, Harold Wilson resigned. He had been leader of the Labour Party for 13 years, Prime Minister for over seven. There was a struggle over who should succeed: Shirley Williams was considered a candidate. She was one of the country's favourite politicians 'coming over as concerned, sincere, highly intelligent and human'.[27] A month earlier Margaret Thatcher's election as leader of the Conservative Party prompted one political analyst to comment that a short time ago 'the odds against Britain's major political parties being led by two women would have been as astronomical as those on lightning hitting the same place twice. But if Mrs Margaret Thatcher wins the next general election, it is possible that the Labour Party too might swallow its male chauvinist pride and turn to a woman'.[28] In reality, Williams' chances of securing the leadership were seriously damaged by the election of Margaret Thatcher as it 'would look too much like a gimmick'.[29]

Michael Foot, Tony Crosland, Roy Jenkins, Tony Benn and Denis Healey all entered the leadership contest; Shirley Williams did not. In her own view, she was too inexperienced and at the age of 46, too young. She had never coveted the top job, confessing to one reporter that she did not think she was good enough and that there were several people in the Labour Party who were better than her.[30] It seemed as if she was frightened of success, perhaps she had genuinely thought she had come far enough. Moreover, analysists have suggested that a woman will only apply for a job if she is certain she can do it well, and if she thinks she does not have *all* the necessary attributes she will not even put herself forward. Certainly, some believed that Shirley Williams was not tough enough to rule Labour and was sometimes too woolly and uncertain in her judgements.

Jim Callaghan won. Callaghan dismissed Castle, kept Williams at the DPCP and put her as chair of several fractious Cabinet committees knowing that her amenable and collaborative nature would ensure results. Shirley Williams was now the only woman in the Cabinet. The Chief Secretary to the Treasury Jack Diamond, a powerful figure, urged an end to food subsidies. Shirley Williams disagreed because any increase in the price of basic commodities would hit the most vulnerable sections of the community hardest such as 'pensioners, those on low incomes, and those with large families. We subsidised the cheaper sources of nourishment to help the poor; hence, sharp price increases in subsidised foods must discriminate against them'.[31] She won the argument in Cabinet, but by now, the Labour Government had lost a series of by-elections and was dependent on Liberal support to remain in office.

Secretary of State for Education and Paymaster General, September 1976–May 1979

In September 1976, Callaghan moved Williams to Secretary of State for Education and Paymaster General posts which she held concurrently. Here, she was pushed to the limit of her endurance, trying to balance parliamentary business with that of parenting. 'You get your sleep down to 5 and half hours a night'. She confided to Melanie Phillips that 'the basic question is how you fit everything in. … After I get home with my red box it's half past eleven at night. I manage it because I'm physically strong, and I live nearby and I dash to and fro'.[32]

Just after her appointment, Tony Crosland became ill and resigned as Foreign Secretary. Rumours were rife. Newspapers expected the Chancellor Denis Healey to replace him and discussed who should follow Healey: Shirley

Williams was a favoured candidate, largely because she had a good intellectual grasp of economics. In addition, the appointment of Williams would appeal to the electorate 'counter-balancing to some extent the loyalty many women voters feel for Mrs Thatcher'.[33] It would claimed *The Observer* 'bring into the key post ... one of the most original and sensible minds in British politics'.[34] However, Callaghan left Healey as Chancellor and appointed David Owen as Foreign Secretary. Shirley Williams remained in Education.

Shirley Williams had already shifted her parliamentary focus from prices to education. From now on, all her parliamentary contributions, from comprehensive education, teachers' salaries, school meals and parental choice focussed on education. Williams was appointed because she was likeable and thought to have enough personal authority to convince teachers and the general public of the need to reform. James Callaghan, who had not attended university, believed in the power of education to transform society. In October 1976, he gave a speech at Ruskin College, Oxford in which he spoke of the unease felt by parents about the current informal methods of teaching. In his speech, he argued for a 'basic curriculum with universal standards' and for all pupils to have 'basic literacy, basic numeracy'.[35] Shirley Williams was invited to write a consultation document, known as a Green Paper, on curriculum reform. A series of eight regional conferences—known as the Great Educational Debate—were held in which Williams listened to all the various pressure groups: teachers, unions and parents. Not surprisingly the Green Paper was a compromise document, seen to be too conciliatory and too unwieldy. The Cabinet rejected it and Williams was forced to re-write it six times.

On July 4, 1977, Shirley Williams introduced her final draft. In the 54 page document, she argued that the government must complete the process of making secondary schools comprehensive and that schools 'should be accountable for their performance'. Williams advocated a core curriculum of fundamental subjects which every pupil in UK schools should study and which would take up half the school day. She insisted that as 'our society is a multicultural, multiracial one, the curriculum should reflect a sympathetic understanding of the different cultures and races that now make up our society'.[36] Her proposals were not enacted, but her idea of a national curriculum was taken up by Margaret Thatcher who authorised 'a much more draconian' one.[37]

In addition, the Secretary of State for Education aimed to raise standards by making the teaching profession a graduate profession and by setting up a General Teaching Council which would be consulted about entry levels to the profession, standards of professional behaviour and requirements for in-service training. Williams succeeded in making teaching a graduate profession but failed to set up the Council. The next Labour Government introduced this: the dynamic feminist Carol Adams became its first chief executive and steered its development in a way Williams would have favoured.[38]

In January 1977, Williams announced the closure of 30 teacher training colleges because a dramatic decline in the birth rate had led to fewer pupils and thus a need for fewer teachers. In fact, the government could have chosen to decrease class size and make state schools more like public and private schools with their generous staff-pupil ratios. Williams defended her decision by arguing that to do otherwise meant 'leaving our kids a legacy of £9,000 million debt by the year 2005. ... we have to live in the real world, we have to be realistic Socialists, and we have to decide what our priorities are'.[39] She was all too aware that government debt was increasing and that there was pressure from the International Monetary Fund to cut public expenditure. As she pointed out, the Labour Government 'was believed by the financial markets to lack financial discipline, to be unwilling to grasp economic realities, and to be profligate with public spending'.[40] Consequently, Williams felt she needed to cut back on teacher training. At the time of these cuts, large reserves of gas and oil were discovered in the North Sea, though unfortunately royalties from the oil would not be received until the late 1970s.

Shirley Williams is best remembered for her championing of comprehensive schools. The 1976 Education Act required local authorities to re-organise their secondary schools into comprehensives, but a number of local authorities remained vague about their plans, hoping that if they delayed until the next general election, the policy might be overturned if Labour lost. Shirley Williams took these reluctant authorities to court: the High Court ruled that the 1976 Act required local authorities to do the government's bidding. In 1978, Williams informed the House that comprehensive schools provided for over 80% of secondary schools compared with 62% in 1974 'but I shall not be satisfied until all schools are reorganised'.[41]

Williams faced opposition from both sides of the political spectrum: the Labour left felt she was not putting her words into deeds quickly enough. Caroline Benn, Tony Benn's wife, accused Williams of being reluctant to push forward comprehensive education. In contrast, the Conservatives called her a 'tyrannical bully girl' for overriding local authorities. At the 1977 Tory Party Conference, Margaret Thatcher deplored the destruction of grammar schools in the name of equality. People from her background, she claimed, 'needed grammar schools to compete with children from privileged homes like Shirley Williams'.[42] Moreover, Williams was accused of hypocrisy because she had sent her daughter Rebecca to Godolphin and Latymer, a voluntary aided girls' grammar school and then to Camden High School for Girls.

Shirley Williams' appointment as Minister of Education had been greeted positively, but two and a half years later, her popularity had slipped. There were 'damaging criticisms (emanating from the Civil Service) of her abilities as an administrator. Everyone loved her but she had the place in chaos and dithered badly'.[43] Tony Crosland thought she spent too much time worrying about detail which should have been handled by her civil servants rather than directing overall policy. She also found it hard to make a decision independently and constantly needed the re-assurance of Cabinet. Moreover, Shirley Williams found that her negotiating skills were not strong enough to convince the teaching profession of the need to curb their pay claims. Her final weeks in office were marked by an acrimonious dispute with the teaching profession: in March 1978, she was forced to settle two educational disputes by awarding a 10% pay increase to teachers and a 9.8% increase for university lecturers.

OUT OF OFFICE AND OUT OF LABOUR

Shirley Williams went into the May 1979 election confident that she would return to Parliament as MP for Hertford and Stevenage; she had after all enjoyed a 9000 majority at the last election. She lost, her majority swept away by an 8.1% swing to the Tories. Labour lost 50 seats overall, Callaghan resigned and Margaret Thatcher became the first-ever female Prime Minister of a party that historically had opposed women's equality. Undoubtedly, Williams was affected by a general dissatisfaction with Labour, but she had forgotten an important rule in politics: the need to look after her local elec- torate. During the campaign, she was largely absent from Hertford because she was 'constantly used at Labour Press conferences to present the accept- able face of socialism, thus neglecting her constituency'.[44] In contrast, the Conservative candidate, Petrie Bowen Wells, knew the importance of nursing a district and focussed his campaign on popular policies like offering the sale of council houses at reduced prices. At the count, Williams stood tired and red-eyed as the returning officer read out the news of her defeat. It was the defining moment of the 1979 election—she was the only Cabinet member to lose her seat. It was seen as a shattering psychological blow to Labour. Callaghan stated 'she is one of the most distinguished Parliamentarians, a woman with great heart and intellect and sympathy to match'.[45] She had once been tipped as the first female Prime Minister. Now it was the end of an era. A different type of women—Maggie Thatcher—was set to dominate.

Shirley Williams was 49 years old. There was a widespread assumption that her political life was dead. Williams was out of Parliament, though not without influence and used her new found freedom from Parliament to write regularly in newspapers and appear frequently on television. She also remained on the NEC, battling to keep the Labour Party in the middle ground of politics. When the position of Deputy Leader fell vacant, Shirley Williams reluctantly agreed to put her name forward. Fearing unwelcome publicity, she did not campaign or garner support for herself: Michael Foot won by 166 to 128.

After its defeat, the Labour Party became embroiled in another of its familiar battles, emerging with a conviction that it lost because it was not 'socialist' enough. In contrast, Williams thought it was too socialist. She and others hoped that the Labour Party might show a willingness to admit past errors and be more sensitive to the concerns of the electorate rather than

Labour Party members or trade unionists. Shirley Williams was a moderate who feared that Labour's radical agenda would scare off voters, particularly as the Militant tendency seemed to be growing within the Labour Party. Earlier, Williams had been outraged by the dismissal of Reg Underhill's report on Militant, a report which warned that representative democracy was at stake if the group was allowed to continue. She insisted that 'the tactics of the hard left, dragging the meetings out, moving resolutions when most people had gone home, upbraiding and sometimes intimidating their opponents, wearied local members'.[46] When Reg Prentice was de-selected from East Ham North, Williams argued that the Revolutionary Socialist Party and the Militant Tendency were trying to take over the Labour Party. She criticised its idea of a monolithic political system with a monolithic economic ownership and control which meant a one-party state and the nationalisation of all industry and commerce.[47] 'Modern Trotskyism' she insisted 'holds liberty and democracy in total contempt. Its version of socialism has nothing to do with the British Labour Party's version'.[48] In her view, the Labour Party was devoted to the 'method of democracy – progress by persuasion rather than by compulsion – as to the objectives of socialism'.[49] Moreover, Williams believed Labour needed to match party policy to the demands of the electorate, maintaining that there was a 'troubling divergence between the priorities of Labour activists and those of the electorate'.[50]

The Labour Party, despite the attempts of Williams, moved leftwards. At the October 1979, Conference Callaghan and the Parliamentary Party were criticised for selling out socialism. Conference called for the mandatory reselection of MPs, for the party manifesto to be written jointly by Ministers and the National Executive and for leaders to be elected by an electoral college consisting of trade unions, party members and MPs. Conference voted overwhelmingly for the first two proposals, but the last was deferred for a special meeting to decide. Nonetheless, the vote marked the tolling of the 'Passing Bell', warning of the impending death of the independence of MPs, the parliamentary representatives of the Labour Party. It wasn't too little socialism, Williams insisted, that lost Labour the election but too much trade union power. Shirley Williams appealed to conference 'for God's sake stand up and start fighting for yourselves. The Parliamentary Labour Party has a right to be heard before it agrees to its own castration'.[51]

Shirley Williams was still loyal to Labour, still trying to heal the wounds inflicted by its electoral loss. Her initial desire to fight the battle within the Labour Party, according to *The Guardian*, was clear evidence that she had 'every intention of carrying on in the party and none at all of sliding off into the centre ground'.[52] On May 31, 1980 at a special Labour conference, she began to change her mind, largely because of the fierce fighting over proposals to change the way the leader of the Labour Party was elected. At the time, the Labour leader was elected by MPs, but in the name of greater democracy, the left wanted trade unions and the constituency parties to have an equal vote. In Williams' opinion, this meant compromising the integrity of the Parliamentary Party, which had been elected by millions of voters. Once again, the Labour Party was in turmoil, the main difference being that this was a constitutional wrangle rather a debate about policy.

Shirley Williams complained that the conference 'indulged in an orgy of condemnation' when both Callaghan and Healey were heckled and booed throughout their speeches and David Owen was jeered all the way through his. 'The intolerance and savagery of the conference delegates' drove Williams towards breaking away from the party.[53] She insisted that the NEC was 'acting like crewmen of the Titanic who've decided to have a punch-up in the engine room'.[54] 'What a bloody mess' she wrote in her diary.[55]

On August 1, 1980, three of Labour's leading moderates, Shirley Williams, David Owen and Bill Rogers issued an 'uncompromising call to fellow members of the party to join them in a last-ditch battle to save the party and the Labour movement for democratic socialism'.[56] Voters, they insisted, 'would undoubtedly refuse to back a far-left party'.[57] They published a 3000-word statement in the *Guardian* and the *Daily Mirror*. Its opening sentence read 'The Labour Party is facing the gravest crisis in its history – graver even than the crisis of 1931... If the Labour Party abandons its democratic and internationalist principles ... the argument may grow for a new democratic socialist party'.[58] They called for a mixed economy, British membership of the EEC and NATO and included a thinly veiled threat that if the Labour Party abandoned its democratic principles, a new social democratic party (SDP) might be created. In a direct attack on Tony Benn, the three condemned the 'willingness of some leading members of the party to flirt with extremists who openly regard democracy as a sham'.[59]

In September 1980, at the Labour Party Conference in Blackpool chaired by Judith Hart, another nail was hammered into the moderate Labour coffin. The conference opened with a speech by Tony Benn in which he advocated re-nationalising Britain's leading industries, withdrawing from the EEC, disarming unilaterally and abolishing the House of Lords when Labour was next elected. Benn's speech received an instant roar of approval; Shirley Williams commented 'I wonder why Tony was so unambitious? After all, it took God only six days to make the world'.[60] There were appalled reactions from a number of moderate delegates who were 'undeniably angry that through his demagoguery he had nullified the party's earnest attempts ... to get itself taken seriously'.[61] Conference also voted to abolish private education, to introduce a wealth tax and a 35-hour week, to leave Europe, to remove all American missile bases, to ratify the reselection of MPs and to support unilateral disarmament.

At an evening meeting organised by the Campaign for Labour Victory, Shirley was shouted down and even spat at. The hall 'seethed with hatred' of her, especially when she condemned the NEC for agreeing to allow the Leader of the Parliamentary Labour Party to be elected by party members rather than MPs, calling it a 'travesty of democracy'. Shirley Williams was at her best: clear, direct, combative with a political ruthlessness that she had never shown before. Perhaps for the first time in her life, Shirley Williams was up for a fight. She believed that her Labour Party, the party she had joined at 16, a party to which her parents, family and friends belonged, a party she had been involved with all her life was under threat. She was fighting for her political life, trapped in a corner by the left and their acolytes, witnessing the party she had loved and nourished, self-destruct. Williams was most probably personally wounded by this antagonism. She liked being popular and was certainly unused to the level of abuse hurled at her by so-called colleagues, members of her party. Not surprisingly, she threatened that if she found 'the party moving away from the values of political democracy, then I would find it impossible to stay'.[62] She urged the silent majority in the party to mobilise, warning that 'too many good men and women have remained silent – keeping their heads down. The time has come for them to stick their heads up over the parapet and start fighting, because if they don't they won't have a Labour Party any longer that is worth its name'.[63] A significant number of delegates agreed and she was re-elected to the NEC, though she slipped down to second place behind the more radical Judith Hart.

It got worse for Mrs Williams. On October 15, 1980, Callaghan resigned and elections were held for a new leader. Shirley Williams remained one of the most popular personalities in the party and could possibly have won the leadership contest. However, because she was no longer an MP, she was debarred from standing: Michael Foot beat Denis Healey to the leadership by ten votes. Shirley Williams congratulated Foot on his win though warned him that he needed to control the far left. She was worried that the new Labour Party leader 'seemed to accept blithely the erosion of democratic forces within the party and was unable to fathom the gravity of Labour's plight'.[64] It was to be the last time a leader was chosen by MPs.

According to the *Liverpool Echo*, Shirley Williams gave one of her finest performances at the conference. She knew the 'gap between reformers, revolutionaries and utopians in the Labour movement had always been wide' and believed that the present Labour crisis 'was a conflict about its character – whether the party was to be a protest movement or a prospective government of the country'.[65] In an open letter to Eric Heffer, Shirley Williams warned of the danger of imposing party control on elected representatives, using the words of Clement Attlee to shore up her argument. Attlee, Williams stated, had insisted that the Prime Minister must always remember that he is more than a party leader. 'His Government' Attlee stated 'is responsible to Parliament, and through Parliament to the nation. If you begin to consider yourself solely responsible to a political party, you're halfway to a dictatorship'.[66] Williams maintained that the party 'has just thrown away any chance of defeating Mrs Thatcher in the next election'.[67] She was to be proved right. In November 1980, Shirley Williams declared that she would not run again as a Labour candidate if the party carried on with its current policies.

In January 1981 at a special conference delegates voted for a change in the way it elected its leader. In future, the party leader would be elected at the party conference in which 40% of the votes would be held by trade unions, 30% by constituency parties and only 30% by the Parliamentary Party. It was viewed as a 'savage slap in the face' for Labour MPs, a 'disaster for the Labour moderates. A shattering triumph for the Left'.[68] Shirley Williams believed that a secret ballot of MPs was the only democratic way to choose a leader. In her view, to describe the new voting system as being 'more democratic than a secret ballot by individual MPs who are members of the PLP and elected by millions of Labour voters is a travesty of language'.[69] It was hard to see, she insisted, how it could be 'compatible with parliamentary democracy' when MPs and Labour leaders were more accountable to the party than the electorate.[70]

By this time, Williams was fed up with the way the Trotskyist Militant tendency tried to manipulate parliamentary politics, unhappy with what she saw as 'the calamitous outcome'[71] of the Labour Party Conference, repelled by the current direction of Labour policy and hurt by the bitter personal recriminations against her. She was set to leave. The conference decision propelled the march out of the party by what was known as the 'Gang of Four': Shirley Williams, David Owen, Roy Jenkins and Bill Rogers. On January 18, 1981, the four met at David Owen's house in Limehouse, wrote and read out a joint declaration (the Limehouse Declaration) to the reporters gathered outside, a declaration which was published in *The Guardian* a week later. The 'Gang of Four' complained that 'a handful of trade union leaders can now dictate the choice of a future Prime Minister. The conference disaster is the culmination of a long process by which the Labour Party has moved steadily away from its roots'.[72] Their policy was targeted to appeal to the middle ground: they sought to reverse Britain's economic decline with a healthy public and private sector, to create an open, classless and more equal society, to improve the quality of public services, to correct 'ugly prejudices based upon sex, race or religion', to encourage public enterprise, co-operative ventures and profit-sharing, to de-centralise decision making in industry and government and to keep Britain in the European Community, in NATO, the UN and the Commonwealth. An official split had been declared. Shirley Williams likened the experience to taking a raft down the Colorado River—full of rapids and unknown rocks that could capsize the newly built raft of social democracy.[73]

On February 9, Williams resigned from the NEC and from the Labour Party. The party, she argued, was 'not the democratic socialist party I joined but a party intent on controlling those of its members who are elected to public office by the people of Britain. I believe that to be incompatible with the accountability of MPs to their electors which lies at the heart of parliamentary democracy'.[74] Michael Foot, the newly elected leader tried to persuade Williams to stay in the party on the grounds of loyalty, predicting that she and her allies would destroy the party or at least keep it out of office. Foot regarded Williams highly: she was a decent human being, a good Cabinet colleague and a popular politician who could appeal to the general public.[75] His appeals were to little avail.

Founding the Social Democratic Party, March 1981

On March 26 at the Connaught Rooms, Covent Garden, Shirley Williams and the group launched their new party, the SDP the first political party to be formed since Labour in 1900. It was thought to be a huge success: 500 reporters from newspapers and journals came to the launch and 43,000 new members were recruited. At first, Williams had been reluctant to form a new party, fearing that a centre party would have 'no roots, no principles, no philosophy and no values'.[76] It was not an easy decision to leave the Labour Party and she compared it with 'pulling out my own teeth'.[77] In her letter to the NEC, she wrote that she was resigning from the executive 'only because I believe the party I loved and worked for over so many years no longer exists'.[78] She was accused of deserting Labour because she had too genteel an upbringing and had not been 'able to stand the rough and tumble like those of us who are used to scrapping in working-class organisations'.[79]

Most thought Williams was a great loss to the Labour Party; it had lost one of its most popular figures and one of its most successful campaigners. Those on the left-wing of the party disagreed. Tony Benn was unsympathetic, claiming that 'some left to establish a political party more worthy of their own personal ambitions. Others because they resented the challenge from Labour's rank-and-file to hold them accountable for their actions. Some because they should never have been in the Labour Party in the first place and the rest because they were too stupid or corrupt to be able to survive. Whoever ends up in partnership with such a motley crew of careerists, elitists and deadbeats will need all the media support they can get'.[80] As mentioned earlier, Judith Hart accused Shirley Williams of 'being cynical and power hungry'.[81] The upshot was that it split the Labour Party, transformed the political landscape and weakened the left, thus helping to keep Margaret Thatcher in power.

Shirley Williams wanted the new party to be democratic and 'socialist, committed to greater equality, redistribution of income and wealth, comprehensive schools and the National Health Service'.[82] The Social Democrats believed in collective leadership: Shirley Williams, David Owen, Roy Jenkins and Bill Rogers jointly headed the new team. It was agreed that Jenkins would be in charge of co-ordinating policy; Rodgers would look after party organisation; Owen would lead the parliamentary group; and Williams would be in charge of communications and publicity. A Steering Committee, which became the National Committee, was set up, chaired in rotation by one of the Gang of Four. It was a new form of democracy. In Williams' view, 'collective leadership spelled friendship and a common objective, by contrast to the civil war in the Labour Party and the growing strains in the Conservative government'.[83] At the launch, the group showed its commitment to a collective approach by answering questions in rotation.

Shirley Williams was still out of Parliament and needed to find a seat to contest. Unfortunately, she found it difficult to make hard decisions. When a Labour seat in Warrington became vacant, she resisted, despite fierce persuasive tactics by her colleagues and a headline in *The Sun* shouting 'You Can Do It, Shirl' and declined to run for Parliament. The response to her turning down the offer was far from what she expected: newspapers turned on her. She was thought to lack political guts and accused of abandoning the parliamentary ship. Journalists asked whether her indecisiveness was the whole pattern of her career because 'she likes being liked and making decisions makes enemies'.[84] Her good common sense and instinctive caution allowed her not to crash, Robin Oakley commented, but it meant that she could not fly either. David Owen believed it to be the worst decision Williams had ever made, the most damaging decision for the future of the SDP and put paid to her chances of leading the new organisation.

However, it was not caution that led her to decline the candidacy but something far more pragmatic: Shirley Williams had a young daughter, a dependent stepmother and no substantial financial resources; if she gave up her job and failed to win a seat, she would be economically challenged. Her 'daughter was doing her university finals and she has a hard enough time without my adding to it. Sometimes you have to not do something in politics if you want to keep your family in one piece. It is true for men, but especially true for women. But the media never believe that there really can be a personal reason and I was portrayed as a coward. I don't regret it in the sense that my daughter's wellbeing would always have to come first, but politically it was a big mistake'.[85] In the end, Roy Jenkins ran for Warrington and lost.

In 1981, a seat became vacant in the Conservative stronghold of Crosby, and this time Williams was persuaded to fight it, knowing that if she refused the media would regard her as a coward. She felt 'like someone on the edge of a cliff that was crumbling beneath me'.[86] The Liberal candidate gallantly withdrew and campaigned for Williams instead. Shirley Williams started from scratch with no party base in a constituency that was quintessentially Conservative. It was the height of the Thatcher government's unpopularity: interest rates and unemployment were both high, and there was a lot of unrest in the cities. Yet Crosby was no sinecure and Williams had to fight hard for the seat. She was criticised for her support of comprehensives, her dislike of independent private schools and by the anti-abortionist Society for the Protection of the Unborn Child for not opposing abortion vigorously enough. But Williams knew how to campaign: she was a seasoned politician. She visited schools, knocked on doors and held countless meetings. Once she went on a six-hour tour of the constituency in an open Land Rover in the pouring rain, confirming her total dedication to win the by-election. *The Times*, which could never pass up an opportunity to make comments on her appearance, said she looked 'like a furry little creature of field and woodland' because she refused to wear any head-covering.[87]

SOCIAL DEMOCRATIC PARTY MP FOR CROSBY, NOVEMBER 1981–JUNE 1983

On November 22, 1981, Williams 'pulled off the most dramatic success'[88] when she overturned a Conservative majority of 19,272 into an SDP one of 5289, an unprecedented 25% swing. It was seen the biggest upheaval in a by-election and as 'convincing confirmation' that the Alliance was going to be successful, as 'if the present disarray in the Labour Party continues the SDP may even find itself becoming the main opposition'.[89] She was seen as the woman politician that both men and women liked and trusted, 'the only candidate with an established national reputation'.[90] Immediately after the result was declared, Shirley Williams claimed that her victory was a 'new beginning for Britain'.[91] There was not she claimed 'a single safe seat left in the country' and predicted that the Social Democratic and Liberal Alliance would win the next general election.[92] There were, claimed *The Guardian*, 'few sights more cheerfully disgusting than a victorious election team at breakfast' when at 4 a.m. Shirley Williams celebrated on an early breakfast of champagne, bacon and eggs.[93] When she met her campaign team, Shirley Williams 'unzipped a great soppy grin of pure delight, and the roaring crowd fell even more deeply in love'.[94] The next day she did what Margaret Bondfield and others had done before her: she toured her new constituency. As she stepped out of her hotel, she was spontaneously hugged by a local woman.[95] It was, one commentator noted, as if people felt liberated, hanging out of bedroom windows to see her pass by and blowing car horns when they spotted her. She was borne 'in triumph through the sweaty mass, symbolically and precariously perched on the shoulders of Mr Tony Hill, the Liberal candidate who stood down' in her favour.[96] *Newsweek* claimed that 'the rules of British politics suddenly changed last week. In a remarkable changing of the guard, the Tories lost their Crosby bastion to Shirley Williams ... and to her eight-month-old party, the Social Democrats'.[97]

Shirley Williams was the first elected SDP Member of Parliament. In what she called her 're-tread' maiden speech, Williams spoke of her 'great delight' in returning to the House, 'a particular delight to be elected the first Social Democrat Member of Parliament'.[98] In marked contrast to her first maiden speech, Williams was confident enough to criticise, confident enough to dissent, confident enough to be unpopular. She attacked Thatcher's government, claiming that 'in the two and a half years that I have been out of the House, we have seen nothing but deterioration in the prospects of the British economy.

Today, the British people are being sacrificed on the altar of monetarism ... perhaps the epitaph written on the coffin of the British economy will read "Rest in peace. You died for the cause of a lower public sector borrowing requirement"'. All that might have been acceptable, she insisted 'if there were any evidence that the Government was building for the future, but sadly, there is none. ... the Government are at present operating just as fierce an economic and financial constraint against investment and capital expenditure as against any other sort of expenditure', a situation which disadvantaged us in Europe and the wider world.[99] She said she was returning to 'an old man's club. ... It's terribly out-dated: there's too much spare time boozing and too many old men. We could do with more women to put it into shape with regular hours of 9 to 8'.[100] *The Times*, which could not resist the opportunity to comment on her appearance, said 'She was looking very smart. This meant she had sacked Oxfam as her couturier'.[101]

The SDP needed a leader and Shirley Williams was a significant contender. However, Roy Jenkins was hungry for the job and briefed against her, making continuous derogatory remarks about her disorganised lifestyle. David Owen wanted her to run for the leadership as she had a higher profile and was more popular than Jenkins. 'What he failed to recognise', she noted, 'was my lack of self-confidence. ... I was also concerned about making enemies'. Shirley Williams did not run for SDP leader. On July 2, 1982, Jenkins became leader of the SDP; in September, Shirley Williams was elected President. Her role was to lead the party in the country while Roy Jenkins led the SDP in Parliament.

This time Shirley Williams nursed her constituency in Crosby. She read every letter, signed each one personally and held regular surgeries. She would travel up from London every fortnight to meet her constituents. Don't turn anyone away, she told her liaison officer. She listened to their problems and helped solve them. She visited schools, colleges and hospitals. But it wasn't enough. She had won her seat in a by-election, at a time when the Conservatives were at a political low. General elections are different: Williams recognised she had a 'Herculean task on her hands' if she was to win the next election.

The next election took place against the background of the Falklands War, a war that ended with a British victory and a huge wave of support for Margaret Thatcher and the Conservatives. The electorate had forgotten that the war had been avoidable. Williams realised that 'as the Conservatives rose, the Alliance sank'.[102] In the 1983 general election with a newly upbeat Conservative Party buoyed up by victory over Argentina, Shirley Williams lost her Crosby seat by 3405 votes.[103] She was never to sit in the House of Commons again.

On June 21, 1983, David Owen replaced Roy Jenkins as leader of the SDP. Unfortunately, according to Williams, David Owen preferred to lead by personal command rather than democratic means, preferred to use his charm and evangelical gift for attracting publicity rather than build a party. Williams warned him that 'democratic governments aren't formed by one, or even two, people'.[104] He ignored her advice. The SDP became a one-man band rather than the well-rehearsed orchestra Shirley Williams had envisaged.

In the 1987 general election, Shirley Williams ran as SDP candidate for Cambridge, thought to be 'a nice, reasonable, Shirley Williamsish sort of place full of thoughtful, moderate people'.[105] It was to be the last seat she would fight. Thatcher's government was unpopular in the university town because of its cuts in the higher education budget: Cambridge's Conservative MP Robert Rhodes James looked vulnerable. However, Rhodes James was an outstandingly good local MP who had opposed the education cuts and supported grammar schools. The Cambridge electorate valued its grammar schools and remembering Williams' commitment to comprehensive educa-tion voted for the sitting candidate. She lost the election by 5000 votes. It was a disappointing result overall for the SDP which only won five seats; the Conservatives won an overall majority of 101 and Labour, now under the leadership of Neil Kinnock, was regaining its strength. Shirley Williams, Roy Jenkins and Bill Rodgers, three of the founders of the SDP all lost their seats.

The SDP was now too weak to go it alone: it merged with the Liberal Party. At first, the combined party called itself the Social and Liberal Democrats, then the Liberal Democrats under the leadership of Paddy Ashdown. It was a troubled period for the new party, largely calmed down by the re-assuring presence of Shirley Williams. Charles Kennedy maintained that in the time 'leading up to the merger, Shirley was a tower of strength where others wavered. And in the aftermath, as the infant Liberal Democrats struggled to be recognised as a new force in British politics, she was in some respects the guarantor of our credibility'.[106] David Owen refused to join them, despite the pleas of Williams.

On December 20, 1987, now safely divorced in the approved Catholic way by having her first marriage annulled, Shirley Williams married an American academic and political advisor Richard Neudstadt. In June 1988, she became Public Service Professor of Electoral Politics at Harvard. Meanwhile, the Liberal Democrats were in decline. The great breakthrough and transforma-tion of British politics never came. The SDP had emerged during a period of turbulence in the Labour Party. By 1990, the situation was very different. Under the leadership of Neil Kinnock, the Labour Party fought to restore its credibility and electability making the Liberal Democrats almost a redun-dant force. In a final irony, *The Times* argued 'they merely became party to Labour's reawakening'.[107]

Shirley Williams may have left Parliament but she was not finished with politics. In 1989, she became immersed in the aftermath of the fall of the Berlin Wall and the collapse of communism, launching Project Liberty an organisation which offered advice to the newly created democratic countries. She wanted to stop the 'cowboy capitalists' who were taking over the for-mer Soviet Republic and 'snapping up state assets for a song'.[108] She called it 'jungle capitalism, the capitalism of unrestrained greed'[109] and warned that the winners in the short term would be the 'spivs and wide boys' not the long-suffering people of Eastern Europe.[110]

A LIFE PEER, 1983

In 1993, she was created a life peer—Baroness Williams of Crosby—and for the next three years, she commuted between the House of Lords and Harvard until she moved back to Britain. It was perhaps in the House of Lords that Williams found her true voice. She was known for being organisationally haphazard but brilliant at speaking. She was ever a collegiate person, never a leader, always willing to compromise, always willing to see the other person's point of view, always willing to listen and always reluctant to take unpopular decisions. She never enjoyed having to fight her corner, to reprimand those who did not tow the party line or do her bidding. In the House of Lords, Williams had no department to run, no civil servants to organise, no constituents to nurse and no elections to fight. She was free to speak her mind, to be herself.

In her maiden speech, Williams focussed on the situation in the former Yugoslavia. In 1980, President Tito of Yugoslavia had died, followed by the collapse eleven years later of the Soviet Union. Yugoslavia was a multi-ethnic country which had been kept together by the force of communism and the magnetic personality of its President. It soon fell apart. First of all Slovenia seceded, then Croatia, followed in April 1992 by Bosnia–Herzegovina—each of these moves was opposed by the Serbian leader of Yugoslavia, Slobodan Milosevic whose primary wish was to keep the country united. Soon, encouraged by Milosevic, Bosnian Serbs took over large parts of (mainly Muslim) Bosnia and laid siege to Sarajevo, its capital. In her speech, Williams specifically and prophetically mentioned the vulnerability of approximately 700,000 men, women and children, mostly Bosnian Muslims (Bosniaks), trapped by the Bosnian Serbs. In Sarajevo, she had seen 'children dodging down the streets – many of them marked by snipers from the hills surrounding Sarajevo – in a desperate attempt to get water, bread and other supplies for their families'.[111] She asked for peace monitors to be placed on the Bosnian-Serbian border. Every subsequent peer who spoke paid tribute to her. Baroness Chalker commented that she would bring an 'incisiveness, clear-thinking and forward-looking mind for which she is so well known' to the House of Lords.[112]

During the break-up of Yugoslavia, Shirley Williams went with Paddy Ashdown and members of the UN High Commission to report on the situation. They found villages that had been pillaged, torched and abandoned. During a visit to one village, she left the group because she had noticed that only men from the village turned out to meet them. Williams knew that Kosovar Muslim women would be unlikely to talk freely with male visitors and went to seek them out. She found women hidden at the back of farms, out of sight, and discovered that many of the women had been systematically raped and abused as a weapon of war. This was nothing less than a form of genocide because no traditional Muslim man would marry a woman who had been raped.[113] Williams appealed to the Conservative Government for safe havens and safe passages for the civilians fleeing from the conflict and for the British Government and the UN to protect civilians from the 'Bosnian Serbs who have never proved themselves willing to accept any of the norms or understanding of civilised conduct'.[114] Her words carried little weight. Not until July 1995 with the massacre of approximately 8000 Muslims at Srebrenica did the world take notice. In 1997, a Labour Government returned. It supported NATO's decision to intervene; in early 1999, the Serbs withdrew from Kosovo leaving the area under NATO protection.

In 1997, Labour won a landslide victory with a manifesto which closely resembled the manifesto produced by the SDP—more closely, Williams pointed out 'than co-incidence alone could explain'.[115] She was not tempted to join New Labour, possibly because she thought Blair lacked a clear set of principles. According to Paddy Ashdown, Williams did not have a high opinion of Tony Blair, thinking him to be a fixer who did not know what he stood for.[116] She considered that Labour was now 'efficient, modern, centralised and managerial. … It was just that the values of liberal democracy and of social democracy got lost somewhere along the line'.[117]

In 1998, Williams became the Lib-Dem spokesperson for Foreign Affairs and its Deputy Leader in the House of Lords; in 2001, now aged 71 she was elected Lib-Dem leader in the Upper Chamber. Here, she helped shape the Lib-Dems response to the Iraq war. After the September 2001 attacks on America, George Bush sought revenge and accused Iraq of holding 'weapons of mass destruction'. The United Nations pleaded for restraint. Both the Americans and the British Government ignored the United Nations and in March 2003 declared war on Saddam Hussein. All the Lib-Dems voted against the Iraq war, with Shirley Williams warning that the war would create 'a human catastrophe on a scale that we cannot imagine'.[118] Saddam Hussein was deposed, and when no weapons of mass destruction were found, Williams questioned the way in which the government had taken Britain to war. Iraq, she claimed, was a mess as the country slid into chaos. She asked Tony Blair 'was it for this outcome that so many lives have been sacrificed? Was it for this outcome that so much destruction was permitted? Was it for this that we have now brought about an even more difficult situation vis-à-vis the terrorist threat?'[119] Earlier Shirley Williams had warned that 'there is always a danger that, far from suppressing terrorism, we will encourage a new wave of terrorism'.[120]

Shirley Williams wanted to combat terrorism by transforming the world's global economic institutions. She believed that military power alone would not eradicate terrorism, arguing that three things were essential 'first, the belief that the constitutional and peaceful path can lead to results that will not be achieved by violence alone; secondly, that the world is ready to address some of the issues that are the causes of terrorism; and thirdly that the world recognises the level of resentment towards the global injustice that still exists so powerfully in our world and that seems so far to have been little lessened by the forces of globalisation'.[121] Williams had been brought up by a pacifist mother and throughout her life was opposed to nuclear proliferation. She was a leading member of several anti-nuclear organisations and served as Commissioner of the International Commission on Nuclear Non-proliferation and Disarmament. In 2007, she accepted a Labour Party position, in a group consisting of former senior Ministers in foreign affairs, as an independent advisor on nuclear proliferation; in 2009, she joined a cross-party group—the Top Level Group of UK Parliamentarians—for the advancement of nuclear disarmament and non-proliferation.

In the 2010 general election, the Labour Party was led by a vacillating Gordon Brown, the Conservative campaign lacked focus and the Liberal Democrats were buoyed up by the charming personality of their leader Nick Clegg. It looked as if the Liberal Democrats might be on course for a huge gain in seats. This was not to happen: the party in fact lost four seats. It was, once again, the first-past-the-post system which failed them. However, the Conservatives did not win a majority and went into coalition with the Liberal Democrats. Shirley Williams hoped that the Liberal Democrats would make a pact with Labour but its leader Nick Clegg thought otherwise and agreed to join the Conservatives with devastating results for the party she had helped create.

In 2016, Williams retired from the House of Lords; in 2017, she received the Order of the Companion of Honour in recognition of her services to political and public life.

CONCLUSION

Shirley Williams achieved much in her life. At times, the press depicted her as prime ministerial material: in 1974, she was *The Sun*'s Woman of the Year, a natural performer at ease in the spotlight. Her popularity with the public made her a likely choice as leader who would win elections. But whereas Thatcher became leader of her party then Prime Minister, Shirley Williams never became *primus inter pares*, that first among equals. Instead, she is viewed as a great 'might-have-been' in political history.[122]

There were a number of reasons why she did not become leader of the Labour Party. Some believed Williams' refusal to look the part hindered her in reaching the top. It is argued that her unkempt image, her disregard for how she looked seemed to hint at a disorganisation in her life which made her unsuitable for high office. Bernard Donoughue argues that the 'the fact that she dresses, stands, walks and sits like an over-full sack of cabbages does not help'.[123] This is pure sexism: Michael Foot faced all sorts of adverse and negative comments about his appearance yet still became leader. Others explain her lack of advancement to deeper and at times more misogynistic causes: she was a woman in a predominantly male party. The *Guardian* later alleged that the Labour Party 'has been led by a long procession of straight male Wasps ... women find it hard to advance beyond the Blair Babe cheerleader stage: namely its appetite for jargon and boys-toys technospeak, its domination by pompous, lecherous, seat-sniffers, the tourniquet-tight Boy's Town inner circle of spinners and bullies'.[124] This is ironic given that these were often the same reporters who regularly dismissed or undermined women politicians by referring to their looks rather than their capabilities. In fact, the Labour Party has always been committed to women's equality: it was the first political party to support votes for women, had championed equal pay and put in place all-women shortlists which gave a huge boost to the numbers of women MPs elected in 1997.

More crucially, Shirley Williams was thought to be too amiable to preside over Labour's bouts of internecine warfare. She disliked 'ousting rivals, disciplining colleagues or taking unpopular decisions'[125] and liked being liked too much, a personality trait that did not lend itself to the role of party leader. In order to reach the top, Shirley Williams would have needed to accept that being unpopular was part of the package of power. She also needed to be more ambitious, more ruthless and cunning: she certainly lacked the killer instinct of Tony Blair or Ed Miliband who were willing to jeopardise friendship and family to gain the top position. 'Like many women of my generation and of the generation before mine' she confessed, 'I thought of myself not quite good enough for the very highest positions in politics. I ran for Deputy Leader of the Labour Party in 1976 against Michael Foot, but never for leader. I was President of the SDP and the first SDP MP to be elected, but I conceded the party leadership to Roy Jenkins without a fight'.[126] Without the hunger or the adversarial skill to get to the top, Williams seemed destined to underachieve.

Significantly, neither Wilson nor Callaghan promoted her to Home Secretary, Foreign Secretary or Chancellor of the Exchequer, high offices which are considered stepping stones to becoming Prime Minister. Her lack of promotion may have been due to sexism though it was more likely to have been because Williams was not considered a good manager. Tony Crosland had doubts about her effectiveness in government. 'She was seen as a brilliant performer ... but taking charge and managing a team and taking a risk and being unpopular was another matter'.[127] According to Callaghan, Williams failed to make a distinct and positive mark in education. She may have re-organised secondary education by closing grammar schools and supporting comprehensives, but this was not policy formation. In fact, it was Williams' greatest characteristic—her willingness to listen, to compromise and to understand—that was her downfall. She saw, like the intellectual she is, both sides of the question and was thus considered indecisive. However, running a department is not the same as running the country. She was one of the government's best spokeswomen, 'an undoubted vote-winner, coming over as concerned, sincere, highly intelligent and human'.[128] As a figurehead, Shirley Williams would have been a popular choice among voters and may well have changed the nature of the prime ministerial role by being more collegiate than others before or since.

While Shirley Williams was a distinguished politician for over 45 years with many achievements to her credit, it is perhaps her character and her personality that are her most remarkable features: she is seen as one of the few honest open and authentic faces in a political world often regarded as mendacious and insincere. David Steel considers her 'a rare being in the world of politics: she is regarded as a national treasure'.[129] People believed that Shirley Williams was in politics to make a difference to the world, not make a difference to her personal life.

One of Williams' legacies was setting up the SDP which at one time was predicted to replace Labour as the official opposition. Those on the left still see her as betraying Labour by not sticking with the party in times of stress and consequently allowing Margaret Thatcher to reign supreme for over a decade; others see the SDP as a catalyst, forcing Labour to scrutinise its electoral failures and return to a more moderate stance. Ultimately, of course, the SDP failed to capture the middle ground. When Tony Blair moved the Labour Party to the centre of politics, the SDP joined the 'elephant's graveyard of breakaway parties, its tomb alongside those of the New Party, National Labour, the National Liberals and even the once-proud ILP'.[130] In the 1990 Bootle by-election, the SDP candidate won fewer votes than Screaming Lord Sutch's party: Shirley Williams' dream of restructuring British politics was ended.

NOTES

1. *Daily Mirror*, September 24, 1974, p. 9.
2. The average wage in 1974 was £2020.
3. *Daily Mirror*, March 6, 1974, p. 4.
4. Ibid.
5. *Daily Mirror*, August 2, 1974, p. 10.
6. *The Guardian*, March 4, 1974, p. 14.
7. *The Times*, November 22, 1976, p. 8.
8. *The Guardian*, March 6, 1974, p. 6.
9. *The Times*, March 6, 1974, p. 13.
10. Hansard, March 14, 1974, cc499–511.
11. Ibid.
12. CAB 129/175/5 March 12, 1974.
13. Ibid.
14. Hansard, January 30, 1975, Vol. 885, cc636–757.
15. *The Times*, September 6, 1974, p. 4.
16. *The Guardian*, March 19, 1976, p. 14.

17. Mark Peel, *Shirley Williams: The Biography*, 2013, Biteback, p. 204.
18. Ibid., p. 212
19. Bernard Donoughue, *Downing Street Diary*, June 28, 1974, Jonathan Cape, 2005.
20. Ibid., August 2, 1974, 2005.
21. Ibid., June 26, 1975, 2005.
22. Ibid., June 26, 1975, 2005.
23. *The Guardian*, March 22, 1994, p. 12.
24. *Birmingham Post*, September 26, 1974, p. 1.
25. Shirley Williams, *The Guardian*, May 17, 1975, p. 6.
26. Shirley Williams, *The Guardian*, May 18, 1975, p. 11.
27. *The Guardian*, March 19, 1976, p. 14.
28. Milton Shulman, *Newcastle Evening Chronicle*, August 8, 1975, p. 4.
29. Shirley Williams, *The Guardian*, March 17, 1976, p. 1.
30. *Newcastle Evening Chronicle*, August 8, 1975, p. 4.
31. Shirley Williams, Memorandum CAB/129/190/23, July 12, 1976.
32. Shirley Williams, quoted in *The Guardian*, May 13, 1980, p. 8.
33. *The Times*, February 17, 1977, p. 15.
34. *The Observer*, February 20, 1977, p. 12.
35. James Callaghan, Ruskin College, October 18, 1976. Callaghan sent his daughter to a fee-paying school.
36. Shirley Williams, *Education in Schools: A Consultative Document*, CAB 129/197/4, July 4, 1977.
37. Shirley Williams, *Climbing the Bookshelves*, Virago, 2009, p. 235.
38. Carol Adams began her career teaching History at an inner London school. She then taught at the Tower of London before managing the History and Social Science Centre. In the 1980s, she became the country's first inspector for equal opportunities. In 1990, she became Chief Education Officer for Wolverhampton, moving from Shropshire four years later. She resigned from the GTC in 2006 because of ill health and died on January 11, 2007. David Cameron abolished the organisation she had helped create.
39. *The Guardian*, October 1, 1976, p. 7.
40. Shirley Williams, *Climbing the Bookshelves*, 2009, p. 241.
41. Hansard, May 16, 1978, Vol. 950, cc90.
42. Margaret Thatcher, quoted in *The Guardian*, October 15, 1977, p. 3.
43. *The Guardian*, November 4, 1978, p. 7.
44. *The Birmingham Post*, May 5, 1979, p. 5.
45. *The Birmingham Post*, May 5, 1979, p. 1.
46. Shirley Williams, *Climbing the Bookshelves*, 2009, p. 267.
47. Shirley Williams, *The Times*, October 30, 1980, p. 12.
48. Simon Hoggart, *The Guardian*, January 22, 1977, p. 1.
49. Ibid., p. 6.
50. *The Guardian*, October 3, 1973, p. 5.
51. Williams, quoted in Mark Peel, *Shirley Williams: The Biography*, 2013, p. 284.
52. Simon Hoggart, *The Guardian*, January 22, 1977, p. 1.
53. Shirley Williams, *Climbing the Bookshelves*, 2009, p. 267.
54. *The Guardian*, December 30, 1979, p. 22.

55. Shirley Williams Diary, June 4, 1980, quoted in Mark Peel, *Shirley Williams: The Biography*, 2013, p. 286.
56. *The Guardian*, August 1, 1980, p. 1.
57. *The Liverpool Echo*, August 1, 1980, p. 7.
58. Shirley Williams, *Climbing the Bookshelves*, 2009, p. 275.
59. *The Guardian*, August 1, 1980, p. 1.
60. *The Times*, September 30, 1980, p. 1.
61. Ibid.
62. *The Journal*, September 29, 1980, p. 1.
63. *The Journal*, September 30 1980, p. 1.
64. Mark Peel, *Shirley Williams: The Biography*, 2013, p. 294.
65. Shirley Williams, *The Times*, October 30, 1980, p. 12.
66. *The Times*, September 30, 1980, p. 12.
67. Shirley Williams, *The Times*, October 2, 1980, p. 1.
68. *Sunday Express*, January 25, 1981, p. 1.
69. Shirley Williams, *The Times*, October 30, 1980, p. 12.
70. Shirley Williams, *The Times*, January 24, 1981, p. 12.
71. Statement by Shirley Williams, David Owen and Roy Jenkins, *The Guardian*, January 26, 1981, p. 2.
72. *The Illustrated London News*, March 1981, p. 15.
73. Shirley Williams, *Climbing the Bookshelves*, 2009, p. 282.
74. Shirley Williams, letter of resignation to the NEC, *The Times*, February 10, 1981, p. 1.
75. Kenneth O. Morgan, *Michael Foot: A Life*, Harper Perennial, 2007, p. 394.
76. Phillip Whitehead, *Dictionary of Labour Biography*, Palgrave Macmillan, 2001.
77. Shirley Williams, *Climbing the Bookshelves*, 2009, p. 278.
78. Shirley Williams, *The Guardian*, February 10, 1981, p. 1.
79. John Golding, quoted in *The Guardian*, July 14, 1983, p. 15.
80. Tony Benn, *London Labour Review*, December 1981, p. 17.
81. *The Guardian*, October 6, 1981, p. 4.
82. Shirley Williams, *Climbing the Bookshelves*, 2009, p. 280.
83. Ibid., p. 285.
84. Robin Oakley, *Daily Mail*, quoted in Mark Peel, *Shirley Williams: The Biography*, 2013, p. 314.
85. Shirley Williams, *The Times*, December 30, 2003, p. 8.
86. Shirley Williams, *Climbing the Bookshelves*, 2009, p. 291.
87. *The Times*, November 23, 1981, p. 3.
88. *The Guardian*, November 27, 1981, p. 1.
89. *Illustrated London News*, January 1982, p. 5.
90. *The Times*, November 23, 1981, p. 9.
91. *Liverpool Echo*, November 27, 1981, p. 6.
92. *The Guardian*, November 27, 1981, p. 1.
93. *The Times*, November 28, 1981, p. 2.
94. *The Guardian*, November 28, 1981, p. 1.
95. *Liverpool Echo*, November 30, 1981, p. 8.
96. *The Guardian*, November 28, 1981, p. 1.
97. Charles Kennedy, 'A New Politics, 1981 and 2010', in Andrew Duff (editor), *Making the Difference: Essays in Honour of Shirley Williams*, 2010, Biteback, p. 67.

98. Hansard, December 8, 1981, Vol. 14, cc725–818.

99. Ibid.

100. Shirley Williams, *The Times*, December 2, 1981, p. 1.

101. *The Times*, December 2, 1981, p. 26.

102. Shirley Williams, *Climbing the Bookshelves*, 2009, p. 301.

103. In the 1983 general election, the SDP and Liberal Alliance gained 25.4% of the votes, only 2.2% less than Labour's 28% though the iniquities of the first-past-the post system meant that the SDP gained 23 seats and Labour 209.

104. Shirley Williams to David Steel, quoted in Mark Peel, *Shirley Williams: The Biography*, 2013, p. 324.

105. *The Guardian*, June 4, 1987, p. 6.

106. Charles Kennedy, 'A New Politics, 1981 and 2010', in Andrew Duff (editor), *Making the Difference: Essays in Honour of Shirley Williams*, 2010, p. 75.

107. *The Times*, June 4, 1990, p. 11.

108. Shirley Williams, *Climbing the Bookshelves*, 2009, p. 341.

109. Ibid., p. 344.

110. Shirley Williams, *The Guardian*, July 6, 1990, p. 23.

111. Hansard, HL Deb, May 27, 1993, Vol. 546, cc502–538.

112. Baroness Chalker, Hansard, HL Deb, May 27, 1993, Vol. 546, cc502–538.

113. Shirley Williams, *Climbing the Bookshelves*, 2009, p. 374.

114. Hansard, HL Deb, July 12, 1995, Vol. 565, cc1717–1728.

115. Shirley Williams, *Climbing the Bookshelves*, 2009, p. 322.

116. Paddy Ashdown, *The Times*, October 23, 2000, p. 3.

117. Shirley Williams, *Climbing the Bookshelves*, 2009, p. 322.

118. Mark Peel, *Shirley Williams: The Biography*, 2013, p. 387.

119. Shirley Williams, Hansard HL Deb, September 7, 2004, Vol. 664, cc448–556.

120. Shirley Williams, Hansard HL Deb, November 28, 2002, Vol. 641, cc860–898.

121. Shirley Williams, Hansard HL Deb, May 14, 2003, Vol. 648, cc245–293.

122. Roger Liddle, 'Is the Progressive Alliance Dead? A Personal Reflection', in Andrew Duff (editor), *Making the Difference: Essays in Honour of Shirley Williams*, 2010, p. 90.

123. Mark Peel, *Shirley Williams: The Biography*, 2013, p. 224.

124. *The Guardian*, February 16, 2002, p. 7.

125. Mark Peel, *Shirley Williams: The Biography*, 2013, p. 225.

126. Shirley Williams, *Climbing the Bookshelves*, 2009, p. 395.

127. Bill Rodgers, quoted in Mark Peel, *Shirley Williams: The Biography*, 2013, p. 420.

128. *The Guardian*, March 19, 1976, p. 14.

129. David Steel, 'The Liberal View', in Andrew Duff (editor), *Making the Difference: Essays in Honour of Shirley Williams*, 2010, p. 67.

130. *The Times*, January 16, 2001, p. 7.

CHAPTER 12

Conclusion: From 1997 Onwards

'Watch out, boys – they're coming. From now on, the House of Commons will no longer be a men-only club'.[1] One hundred and one Labour women won seats as MPs in the 1997 general election.[2] There had never been so many women in Parliament, let alone from one political party. Inevitably, the press could not resist a bit of sexism and the women MPs soon came to be dubbed 'Blair's Babes'. Blair himself did not escape scot-free: newspapers referred to him as 'Bambi' for quite some time. Neither Labour nor women were seen as natural rulers by the largely Conservative press.

Tony Blair can claim little credit for the dramatic increase in the number of women MPs in the 1997 election. Exasperated by the overwhelming male Parliament, women took action. In 1980, Lesley Abdela set up the 300 Group, a cross-party organisation dedicated to getting women into Parliament. The group put on staged debates in the House of Commons and ran courses around the country to help train women in the art of presenting themselves. In 1987, the number of women MPs increased to 41 (21 Labour) and in 1992 to 60 (37 Labour). It was still not enough—women remained grossly under-represented in the House of Commons. The Labour Party, historically committed to women's equality, decided it 'must give immediate attention to developing a strategy' for encouraging women to enter Parliament.[3] It recommended a five-point programme: to make the party aware of the disproportionately small number of women in public life; to have a discussion on the problems women faced in getting elected; to promote an intensive education and training programme; and to encourage constituency labour parties to include women on selection lists.[4] At the 1982 party conference, female delegates proposed that every constituency be compelled to include at least one woman on their shortlist for the selection of its parliamentary candidate: the larger trade unions voted against and the motion failed.

© The Author(s) 2019
P. Bartley, *Labour Women in Power*,
https://doi.org/10.1007/978-3-030-14288-9_12

After yet another defeat in 1987, Clare Short initiated 'a quiet revolution ... inspired by the need for Labour to win more women's votes, the need to regenerate the party and to improve women's representation in public life'.[5] The Labour leadership set about introducing quota systems to select women at local party and executive levels. In 1992, following another electoral defeat, the Women's Committee recommended that all-women shortlists be adopted, a resolution which was passed a year later at the Labour Party Conference. 'It is clear' Short argued in her *Briefing for MPs* 'that the selection process so far has excluded women, especially in the most winnable seats. Increasing women's representation in parliament is essential if we are to build a House of Commons which more truly represents the whole population. As more women come into the Commons, the culture will change, the agenda of politics will broaden, and the institution itself will be transformed'.[6] There was strong opposition to all-women shortlists: in 1995, Tony Blair announced he would abandon the policy after the 1997 election; in 1996, an industrial tribunal found that all-women shortlists contravened the 1975 Sex Discrimination Act by precluding men. Both Blair and the tribunal were thwarted. In 2002, Labour now the party of government introduced the Sex Discrimination Act which permitted positive discrimination in the selection of candidates.

In 1997, Tony Blair appointed five women to his first Cabinet. Margaret Beckett,[7] Harriet Harman,[8] Mo Mowlam,[9] Clare Short[10] and Ann Taylor[11] were all experienced politicians, all elected to Parliament before Blair took office and most importantly all members of the Shadow Cabinet. A few years earlier, encouraged by the then Labour leader Neil Kinnock, women MPs had pressed for a minimum of 4 women to be elected by the Parliamentary Labour Party to serve in the Shadow Cabinet. Critics within the party called their proposal a 'tart's charter', a 'skirt too far' and fiercely opposed it. In 1993, the policy was adopted and MPs were required to vote for at least four women to the Shadow Cabinet. In July 1996, just one year before the general election, expectations were surpassed when five women were elected: Margaret Beckett, Ann Taylor and Clare Short came top of the polls, beating all the men on a list which included Robin Cook, Gordon Brown and David Blunkett. Mo Mowlam and Harriet Harman were also elected. Tony Blair, his freedom of action circumscribed by party expectations, dutifully promoted all five women. Never before had so many women served together as Cabinet Ministers; not all of them continued in the post.

Women's political participation had certainly improved since the beginning of the twentieth century: in 1900, women could not vote, let alone become MPs or Cabinet Ministers. In 1929, when Margaret Bondfield became the first-ever female Cabinet Minister, it was only 11 years after women over 30 gained the vote, only 10 years after the first woman took her seat in Parliament and only one year after women could vote on the same terms as men. Many hoped, and some feared, for an upward trajectory, but after

Bondfield resigned, it took 14 years for a second woman—Ellen Wilkinson—to be appointed to Cabinet. When Wilkinson died in 1947, women had to wait even longer—17 years—to hold high office in a Labour Government. In 1964, when Harold Wilson became Prime Minister, the country was on the brink of a sexual revolution which in turn generated a new awareness of gender inequality. Three women—Barbara Castle, Judith Hart and Shirley Williams—served as Labour Cabinet Ministers in the 1960s and 1970s. After Callaghan's defeat in 1979 and Thatcher's election, it took 18 years for the Conservative political hegemony to be overturned and thus for Labour women to occupy Cabinet posts. By the time, Blair became Prime Minister in 1997 women's place in the political workforce was established, helped by the fact that the Labour Party had taken action to improve women's electoral opportunities. Naturally, the story of women Cabinet Ministers is inextricably related to the fortunes of their party: in the twentieth century, Labour was in government for 23 years, during which time 11 women were appointed to Cabinet posts. Labour had a significantly better record of promoting women than the Conservatives: during the same period, Conservative Prime Ministers—who were in government for far longer—appointed only five women.[12] Six Conservative Prime Ministers—Andrew Bonar Law, Stanley Baldwin, Neville Chamberlain, Anthony Eden, Harold Macmillan and Alec Douglas-Hume—appointed no women at all. Margaret Thatcher appointed one in her first Cabinet, but none in her later ones.[13]

The election of 101 Labour women and the promotion of five of them to the Cabinet was some sort of progress to be sure. But is the job done merely because a number of women are elected to Parliament and chosen for leading positions? Obviously, the answer is no. Labour women are needed, not just because they make the House of Commons more representative of the country at large, but because they bring a different perspective to politics. As we know, the Labour Party was formed as a party to represent the interests of the working class. Both male and female Labour MPs had a class consciousness: they fought for better pay and working conditions, for health services, for education, better housing and other social and economic developments which benefitted the majority of the British population not just the wealthy. In addition, the Labour Party was—and is—committed to equal rights for women, though it has often been women who have set the agenda and who have fought for women's needs to be taken into account.

The first five Labour women Cabinet Ministers made a mark out of all proportion to their numbers. These Cabinet Ministers were strong, determined and effective women—socialist women—who in various ways helped improve the lives of their own sex: for example Margaret Bondfield's work as a trade unionist improved the lives of working-class women[14]; Ellen Wilkinson's outspoken commitment to equal suffrage helped gain women the vote on the same terms as men; Barbara Castle's dedicated advocacy of equal pay resulted in the Equal Pay Act; Judith Hart's focus on rural development helped women in British colonies and protectorates overseas, often the poorest in poor societies; and Shirley Williams' efforts to keep down prices in the turbulent 1970s made a significant difference to working-class women trying to balance their household budgets.

In 1997, for the first time in parliamentary history, there were more than two women in the Cabinet. This is not the place to discuss the achievements of these women—another book is needed here—but all broke through the political glass ceiling. Margaret Beckett was the first woman appointed President of the Board of Trade, then to Leader of the House of Commons; Harriet Harman became Secretary of State for Social Security and the first-ever Secretary of State for Women; Mo Mowlam became the first woman to hold the post of Secretary of State for Northern Ireland; Clare Short was the first Secretary of State for International Development; and Ann Taylor was the first woman to serve as Leader of the House of Commons, the first to serve as Lord President of the Privy Council and the first to serve as Chief Whip. In 1998, Margaret Jay, daughter of Jim Callaghan, was appointed the first woman Leader of the House of Lords.[15] Most of these women considered themselves feminists, two of them well known for campaigning for women's rights.[16]

With greater numbers of women both in Parliament and in Cabinet, there was renewed hope for women's equality. In her first major speech after the election, Harriet Harman announced that a turning point for women had now been reached, claiming that the government was committed to 'building and sustaining a new habit of governance that has women's voices and women's interest at its very heart'.[17] Jesse Phillips, elected in 2015 as MP for Birmingham Yardley, was 16 years old in 1997. She spoke of how she grew up in a Labour world where there were free nursery places, Sure Start, tax credits, children's savings accounts, maternity leave, paternity leave, attendance allowances, improved hospitals, better educational facilities and improved health care.[18] All these policies had a major impact on the lives of women. Phillips said that 'the list of things those women rose to their feet from the green benches to demand for girls like me meant everything'.[19] Labour also brought in the minimum wage, a policy advanced by Clare Short and the leading trade unionist Rodney Bickerstaffe.[20] Certainly, many of the newly elected women MPs spoke of putting forward a new political agenda that focussed on women's issues such as childcare, education, equal opportunities, violence against women, women's health and family law.[21]

However, it was not at all 'bread and roses', a term used in a speech by a friend of Margaret Bondfield in which she urged that 'the worker must have bread, but she must have roses too'. In reality, the newly elected female MPs had an 'immediate effect of introducing an inexperienced group of women to an intensely competitive masculine environment'.[22] It also, according to Germaine Greer, produced a 'biddable House of Commons' full of naïve women who could be manipulated more easily than seasoned politicians like the women Cabinet Ministers.[23] This new intake of Labour women was regarded, as numbers of trade union-sponsored MPs had been before them, as lobby fodder who could be relied upon to vote for the government, especially one which demanded strong party discipline. When Harriet Harman proposed to cut benefits to some single parents, a cut which would largely affect the poorest women in society, Donna Covey, a union official in the GMB, criticised Labour women MPs who supported the cuts arguing that 'they had no right to get elected on the back of women-only shortlists and then vote for anti-women policies'.[24] The policy proved to be hugely unpopular: it remained in force, but Harriet Harman left the Cabinet.

Despite these setbacks, it was hoped that the election of so many women would herald an irreversible advance of women into politics which in turn would change the nature of parliamentary politics. Senior Labour women prophesied that the culture of the House of Commons would undergo a radical overhaul because the number of women MPs had more than doubled. 'Any male institution' it was predicted 'can survive more or else unchanged as long as the proportion of women within it remains small. But there comes a point at which the minority becomes large enough to influence the majority, and, through them, the institution itself, in much more effective ways. ... They will rewrite the agenda and the language of politics'.[25]

These newly appointed women Cabinet Ministers were all too aware that their political forbears had worked in an overwhelmingly male environment not just within the Cabinet but within Parliament the civil service and the wider world. Four of them—Margaret Bondfield, Ellen Wilkinson, Barbara Castle and Shirley Williams—experienced being the only woman in the Cabinet; Ellen Wilkinson twice faced being the only woman on the opposition benches. All were subjected to sexist behaviour of one form or another, ranging from comments about their appearance to unwanted sexual advances from colleagues and equals. Moreover, all were expected to respond amicably to such conduct or be classified as sour, grim and humourless.

Journalists had often noted the 'extreme school-boyishness of the House of Commons with its public-school rules, gangs, drinking and shouting'.[26] Jo Richardson, at one time Labour's spokesperson on women, complained that when 'it's a special debate to do with women, yahoos tend to come into take the mickey. It makes me so angry. It's so juvenile'.[27] In 1997, there was real hope that such a huge increase in the numbers of women would bring a change to the 'yah-boo' culture of the Commons and with it a 'softer, more gentle style of politics'.[28] However, the election of so many women appeared to make little difference: in 2009, the *Times* remarked that the House of Commons 'with its baying and bellowing, remains a place of men, shaped by men'.[29] Anyone watching Prime Ministers' Question Time today will witness adults shouting and baying at each other across the floor of the House of Commons. Such conduct may be acceptable to members of the Bullingdon Club or the Piers Gaveston Society, but if teenagers behaved in this unruly way in school, they would be excluded from the class and reprimanded.[30] Appalled by the ill-mannered conduct of MPs in the Commons, a petition in 2018 asked for 'no shouting or jeering whilst an MP is speaking. We feel that this is unsatisfactory behaviour and unbecoming of a member of parliament. MPs should act in a manner that is expected in boardrooms and classrooms across the country'.[31] The petition was rejected, but the question remains: if so many MPs show such little respect to other politicians, how can the rest of the country in turn respect them?

Historically, the Labour Party has rarely wavered in its commitment to women's equality: it appointed the first-ever female Minister, the first-ever female Cabinet Minister and resolved women's under-representation in Parliament by positive action. Given its commitment to women's equality, it is surprising that no woman has ever been elected Leader, let alone Prime Minister. Between 1918 and 2000, there were 156 female Labour MPs and eleven Cabinet Ministers, yet no woman reached the very top position in politics. Three of the first five women Cabinet Ministers—Barbara Castle, Judith Hart and Shirley Williams—were tipped by newspapers to become Labour leader and Britain's first female Prime Minister. None of the three achieved this. In fact, not one of these women put herself forward to stand as Labour leader, an obvious prerequisite for the premiership should the party be elected.

In 1994, the tragic death of John Smith swept Margaret Beckett into becoming the Labour Party's first female leader, albeit in an acting capacity. It was an accident, rather than a job she seemed destined to take, and her chance of seizing the ultimate prize was seen as slim. When the elections took place, Beckett became the first-ever woman to stand for the leadership of the party: she came third, beaten by John Prescott and Tony Blair. At the time, the Labour Party Leader was chosen by three separate electorates: MPs, affiliated societies, which were mainly trade unions, and constituencies. In the first category, only thirteen out of 37 women MPs and 28 men out of 327 voted for Beckett.[32] Twenty women and 178 men voted for Blair, 4 women and 60 men for Prescott. Overall Beckett only received 18.9% of the MPs vote. Beckett also did badly in the other two electorates, receiving 19.3% of the vote from the affiliated societies and only 17.4% from party members. Tony Blair won 57% of the overall vote.

In 2007, when Blair stood down, Gordon Brown was elected uncontested. After an electoral defeat in 2010, Brown resigned and five MPs: Diane Abbot, Ed Balls, Andy Burnham, David Miliband and Ed Miliband stood for election. Abbot, who was the first black woman to take her seat in the House of Commons, stood in the leadership election only to be eliminated in the first round, winning only 7 votes from MPs, whereas David Miliband won 111.[33] Only two female MPs—Katy Clark and Linda Riordan—voted for Abbott. Ed Miliband, who had garnered more trade union votes, won and became

Leader of the Labour Party. His tenure was not to last. In May 2015 when Labour lost yet again, Ed Miliband stood down, Harriet Harman became Acting Leader, and new leadership elections were held. For the first time in Labour history, two women, Yvette Cooper[34] and Liz Kendall,[35] stood as candidates. Harriet Harman did not. This time only members of the Labour Party, registered supporters and affiliated supporters could vote. The two women came bottom of the poll—Yvette Cooper with 71,928 votes and Liz Kendall with 18,857—probably rejected as much for their close association with Blairism than because they were women. Jeremy Corbyn won overwhelmingly with 251,417 votes, the first leader to be elected by one member, one vote. The power of the PLP and the trade unions to choose the leader of the Labour Party had disappeared.

A year later, Corbyn's leadership was challenged by Angela Eagle[36] and Owen Smith. Eventually, Eagle stood down leading to a contest between two white men. Some criticised the Labour Party for allowing a strong female contender to withdraw in favour of Owen Smith. A toxic masculinity was blamed. One female journalist insisted that 'the lingering backwash of the patriarchal world of industry, trade unionism and smoke-filled constituency rooms, which did for Barbara Castle all those years ago, had one more outing, felling a candidate who would have stood head and shoulders above her rivals in any general election'.[37] However, this analysis is inaccurate as trade unions, and the Labour Party had jointly led the way in advancing women's political participation throughout the centuries. Moreover, in 2017 electoral procedures had changed dramatically, giving individual members overwhelming command and the PLP and trade unions a drastically reduced role in leadership elections. Once more, principles rather than gender prevailed: Labour Party activists—men and women—wanted a leader willing to return to what was they saw as a purer version of socialism. Corbyn was re-elected with an overwhelming majority.

This is a story without an ending. In 2018, Harriet Harman suggested that the next leadership election should be a woman-only contest in order to give the Labour Party its first female leader. Her comments were ridiculed, just as woman-only shortlists had been in the twentieth century and just as the suggestion that women could vote and even become MPs had been in the century before that. Despite being mocked, women had always fought for justice and equality: the many unknown women who campaigned and suffered to win the vote for women set the drama of women in politics in motion, a drama that will never, can never be finished. But what is certain is that the five women Cabinet Ministers in this book stand proud in the Labour tradition of trying to create a more fair and equal society. Collectively, they helped make Britain and other parts of the world a better place for all, not just for the privileged.

NOTES

1. Fran Abrams, *The Independent*, May 3, 1997, p. 8.
2. In contrast, only 13 Conservative women were elected.
3. *Women Candidates May 1979—General Election*, Private and Confidential Memo, NEC July 25, 1979.
4. *Women Candidates May 1979—General Election*, Private and Confidential Memo, NEC July 25, 1979.
5. Clare Short, 'Women and the Labour Party' in Joni Lovenduski and Pippa Norris, *Women in Politics*, OUP, 1997.
6. Judith Squires 'Quotas for Women: Fair Representation', in Joni Lovenduski and Pippa Norris, *Women in Politics*, 1997.
7. As Secretary of State for Trade and Industry and President of the Board of Trade (later Lord President of the Council and Leader of the House of Commons).
8. As Secretary of State for Social Security and Minister for Women.
9. As Secretary of State for Northern Ireland (later Cabinet Office Minister and Chancellor of the Duchy of Lancaster).
10. As Secretary of State for International Development.
11. As Lord President of the Council and Leader of the House of Commons (later Chief Whip).
12. Florence Horsburgh 1953–1954, Margaret Thatcher 1970–1954, Lady Young 1981–1953, Gillian Shephard 1992–1997 and Virginia Bottomley 1992–1997.
13. Janet Young, Baroness Young was created a life peer in 1971 and so sat in the House of Lords. She joined the Cabinet in September 1981 and remained there until June 1983.
14. 'Makers of the Labour Movement', *The Labour Magazine*, October 1923.
15. She attended Blackheath Grammar School in spite of the fact that her father had promoted comprehensives.
16. Margaret Beckett has said she was a feminist and regards the term as a 'title of honour'; both Clare Short and Harriet Harman have championed women's rights; Ann Taylor pushed through legislation to change working hours in the House of Commons, a policy which was seen to help women. There were exceptions: in 1998, Baroness Jay insisted that she was not a feminist. She was roundly condemned by feminist journalists who saw her as betraying women who had transformed the political landscape and in doing so had helped Jay succeed.
17. Quoted in Helen Jones, *Women in British Public Life, 1914–1950*, Longman, 2000, p2.
18. Jesse Phillips, 'Conclusion: Kicking Away the Stumbling Blocks', in Sally Keble (editor), *This Woman Can*, Fabian Society, 2017, p. 89.
19. Jesse Phillips, 'Conclusion: Kicking Away the Stumbling Blocks', in Sally Keble (editor), *This Woman Can*, Fabian Society, 2017, p. 89.
20. In 1968 Barbara Castle set up a committee to examine the introduction of a minimum wage. If Labour had passed a law about 75% of women would have benefited and 10% of men.

21. See Sarah Childs, 'The New Labour Women MPs in the 1997 British Parliament: Issues of Recruitment and Representation', *Women's History Review*, Vol. 8, No. 1, 2000 for an analysis of this.
22. Germaine Greer, 'Women in Parliament', in Andrew Duff (editor), *Making the Difference: Essays in Honour of Shirley Williams*, Biteback, 2010, p. 32.
23. Ibid.
24. Sally Keble (editor), *This Woman Can*, 2017.
25. *The Guardian*, April 15, 1995, p. 23.
26. Lesley Abdela, *The Guardian*, June 30, 1989, p. 11.
27. Ibid.
28. Sarah Childs, 'The New Labour Women MPs in the 1997 British Parliament: Issues of Recruitment and Representation', *Women's History Review*, Vol. 8, No. 1, 2000, p. 67.
29. *The Times*, April 29, 2009, p. 2.
30. The Bullingdon Club is an all-male dining club for Oxford University students. Many local restaurants refuse to host their dinners because of its reputation for vandalising properties and creating mayhem. In 2005, members of the club smashed 17 bottles of wine, every single piece of china and window at a pub near Oxford. Since 1927, when it smashed 400 windows in Christchurch College, it has been banned from meeting within a 15-mile radius. The Piers Gaveston Society is an exclusive men-only club, known for its ostentatious decadence. While being initiated into the Piers Gaveston Society, David Cameron was accused of putting a private part of his anatomy into a dead pig's head.
31. Petition submitted February 2, 2018.
32. Diane Abbott, Margaret Beckett, Jean Corston, Angela Eagle, Maria Fyfe, Mildred Gordon, Helen Jackson, Lynne Jones, Alice Mahon, Dawn Primarolo, Barbara Roche, Clare Short and Audrey Wise voted for Margaret Beckett.
33. Diane Abbott was first elected in 1987 for Hackney North and Stoke Newington. Born to parents from Jamaica—her father was a welder, her mother a nurse—she gained a place at grammar school and then at Cambridge University where she read History.
34. Yvette Cooper was part of the Labour elite. Her father was General Secretary of the Prospect trade union; her mother was a maths teacher. She attended a comprehensive school before going to read PPE at Oxford, where she gained a first-class honour. In 1997, she became an MP for Pontefract and Castleford. In 2008, she was appointed to the Cabinet as Secretary of State for Work and Pensions.
35. Liz Kendall's father was a senior Bank of England official; her mother was a primary school teacher. She attended grammar school, then Cambridge where she read History. In 2010, after a time working in government departments, she was elected MP for Leicester West.
36. Angela Eagle's father was a print worker and her mother a factory worker. She attended a grammar school and then read PPE at Oxford University. In 1992, she was elected as MP for Wallasey. In 1997, her twin sister joined her in the Commons.
37. Anne Perkins, *The Guardian*, July 19, 2016.

Bibliography

Archival Sources

Barbara Castle Papers, Bodleian Library, Oxford.
Cabinet Papers, National Archives, Kew.
Ellen Wilkinson Papers, People's History Museum, Manchester.
Hansard's House of Commons Parliamentary Debates.
Home Office Papers, National Archives, Kew.
Judith Hart Constituency Papers, Glasgow City Archives.
Judith Hart Papers, People's History Museum, Manchester.
Labour Party Conference Reports, People's History Museum, Manchester.
Margaret Bondfield Papers, People's History Museum, Manchester.
Margaret Bondfield Papers, Ross Davies Collection, The Women's Library, LSE London.
Margaret Grace Bondfield Papers, Archives and Special Collections Library, Vassar College Libraries, Poughkeepsie, New York.
National Conference of Labour Women Reports, People's History Museum, Manchester.

Newspapers, Journals and Periodicals

Birmingham Post.
British News (Uganda).
Burnley Express.
Cassell's Weekly.
The Christian Science Monitor.
Clitheroe Advertiser and Times.
The Common Cause.
The Courier and Advertiser.
The Daily Herald.
The Daily Mail.

© The Editor(s) (if applicable) and The Author(s), under exclusive license to Springer Nature Switzerland AG, part of Springer Nature 2019
P. Bartley, *Labour Women in Power*,
https://doi.org/10.1007/978-3-030-14288-9

The Daily Mirror.
Daily News.
Daily Sketch.
Daily Telegraph.
Derby Daily Telegraph.
Dundee Courier.
Dundee Evening Telegraph.
East Kilbride News.
The Economic Journal.
Economist.
Empire News.
Evening Chronicle.
Evening Dispatch.
Evening Telegraph.
Exeter and Plymouth Gazette.
Express and Star.
Glasgow Herald.
Gloucester Citizen.
Gloucester Journal.
The Guardian.
Hamilton Advertiser.
Hastings and St Leonard's Observer.
The Herald.
Hull Daily Mail.
Illustrated London News.
The Independent.
The Labour Magazine.
The Labour Outlook.
Labour Weekly.
Lanark Post.
Lanark and East Kilbride Post.
The Lancashire Daily Post.
The Leader.
Leeds Mercury.
The Listener.
Liverpool Daily Post.
The Liverpool Echo.
Liverpool Evening News.
London Daily News.
Morning Star.
Newcastle Journal.
The New Dawn.
New York Times.
Northampton Labour Gazette.
Northampton Mercury.
The Northern Whig and Belfast Post.
Nottingham Evening Post.
Nottingham Guardian.

The Observer.
The Outlook.
The People.
Preston News.
The Scotsman.
Scottish Miner.
Shepton Mallett Journal.
The Shop Assistant.
Stonehouse News.
South Wales Daily.
The Standard (Tanzania).
The Stage.
The Sun.
Sunday Express.
Sunday Sun.
The Sunderland Echo and Shipping Gazette.
Thames Valley Times.
The Times.
Tribune.
Uganda Argus.
West Africa.
Western Gazette.
Western Times.
Yorkshire Evening Post.

Published Sources

Abdela, Lesley, *Breaking Through the Glass Ceilings*, Metropolitan Authorities Recruitment Agency, 1991.

Adonis, Andrew, and Keith Thomas, *Roy Jenkins: A Retrospective*, Oxford University Press, 2004.

Alexander, Douglas, *Judith Hart Memorial Lecture*, May 13, 2013.

Alexander, Philip, 'A Tale of Two Smiths: The Transformation of Commonwealth Policy, 1964–70', *Contemporary British History*, Vol. 20, No. 3, September 2006, pp. 303–321.

Andrews, Maggie, *The Acceptable Face of Feminism: The Women's Institute as a Social Movement*, Lawrence and Wishart, 1997.

Andrews, Maggie, and Janis Lomas, *The Home Front in Britain*, Palgrave Macmillan, 2014.

Attlee, C. R., Ellen Wilkinson, Philip Noel Baker, and John Dugdale, *We Saw in Spain*, Labour Party, 1937.

Bartley, Paula, *Ellen Wilkinson: From Revolutionary Suffragist to Government Minister*, Pluto, 2014.

Barton, Dorothea M., 'The Course of Women's Wages', *Journal of the Royal Statistical Society*, Vol. 82, No. 4, July 1919, pp. 508–553.

Beard, Mary, *Women in Power: A Manifesto*, Profile Books, 2017.

Beers, Laura, *Red Ellen*, Yale University Press, 2016.

Bellamy, Joyce, and John Saville, *Dictionary of Labour Biography*, Vol. 11, Macmillan 1974.

Benson, John, *The Rise of Consumer Society in Britain, 1880–1980*, Longman, 1994.

Bew, John, *Citizen Clem*, Riverrun, 2017.

Bondfield, Margaret, 'Conditions Under Which Shop Assistants Work', *The Economic Journal*, Vol. 9, No. 34, June 1899, pp. 277–286.

Bondfield, Margaret, *Socialism for Shop Assistants*, The Clarion Press, 1909.

Bondfield, Margaret, *Shop Workers and the Vote*, The People's Suffrage Federation, 1911.

Bondfield, Margaret, *A Life's Work*, Hutchinsons, 1948.

Bondfield, Margaret, and Teresa Billington-Greig, *Sex Equality Versus Adult Suffrage*, Verbatim Report of Debate, December 3, 1907.

Bowlby, John, *Maternal Care and Mental Health*, World Health Organisation, 1951.

Branson, Noreen, *Britain in the Nineteen Twenties*, Wiedenfeld and Nicolson, 1971.

Brinson, Charmian, *The Strange Case of Dora Fabian and Mathilde Wurm: A Study of German Political Exiles in London During the 1930s*, Verlag Peter Lang, 1996.

Brittain, Vera, *Testament of Experience*, Victor Gollancz, 1957.

Brittain, Vera, *England's Hour*, Continuum, 1970.

Brittain, Vera, *Chronicle of Friendship, Diary of the Thirties, 1932–1939*, Victor Gollanz, 1986.

Brookes, Pamela, *Women at Westminster*, Peter Davies, 1967.

Bryant, Christopher, *Stafford Cripps: The First Modern Chancellor*, Hodder and Stoughton, 1997.

Bullock, Alan, *The Life and Times of Ernest Bevin*, Heinemann, 1960.

Butler, David, and Gareth Butler, *Twentieth Century British Political Facts, 1900–2000*, Macmillan 2000.

Callaghan, John, Fielding Steven, and Steve Ludlam, *Interpreting the Labour Party*, Manchester University Press, 2003.

Campbell, Beatrix, and Anna Coote, *Sweet Freedom: The Struggle for Women's Liberation*, Blackwell, 1987.

Campbell, John, *Nye Bevan: A Biography*, Hodder and Stoughton, 1994.

Campbell, John, *Roy Jenkins*, Vintage, 2015.

Castle, Barbara, *The Castle Diaries, 1974–1976*, Weidenfeld and Nicolson, 1980.

Castle, Barbara, *The Castle Diaries, 1964–1970*, Weidenfeld and Nicolson, 1984.

Castle, Barbara, *Fighting All the Way*, Pan Books, 1993.

Catlin, George, *For God's Sake, Go*, Colin Smythe, 1972.

Chase, Susan, and Elisa Wilkinson, 'What Happened to Integrated Rural Development?', *The Hunger Project*, August 11, 2015.

Childs, Sarah, 'The New Labour Women MPs in the 1997 British Parliament: Issues of Recruitment and Representation', *Women's History Review*, Vol. 9, No. 1, December 2006, pp. 55–73.

Clarke, Peter, *The Cripps Version: The Life of Sir Stafford Cripps*, Allen Lane, 2002.

Coggins, Richard, 'Wilson and Rhodesia: UDI and British Policy Towards Africa', *Contemporary British History*, Vol. 20, No. 3, September 2006, pp. 363–381.

Cooke, Colin, *The Life of Richard Stafford Cripps*, Hodder and Stoughton, 1957.

Coote, Anna, and Polly Pattullo, *Power and Prejudice*, Wiedenfeld and Nicolson, 1990.

Cowman, Krista, *Women in British Politics, C1689–1979*, Palgrave, 2010.

Cox, Pamela, and Annabel Hobley, *Shopgirls*, Arrow Books, 2014.

Crines, Andrew, and Kevin Hickson, *Harold Wilson: The Unprincipled Prime Minister*, Biteback, 2016.

Crossman, Richard, *The Diaries of a Cabinet Minister*, Vol. I, Trinity Press, 1975.

Crossman, Richard, *The Diaries of a Cabinet Minister*, Vol. II, Trinity Press, 1976.

Currell, Melville, *Political Woman*, Croom Helm, 1974.

Dale, Iain, and Jacqui Smith, *The Honorable Ladies, Profiles of Women MPs 1918–1996*, Biteback, 2018.

Dalton, Hugh, *The Fateful Years: Memoirs 1931–1945*, Frederick Muller, 1957.

De'Ath, Wilfred, *Barbara Castle*, Clifton Books, 1970.

Donoughue, Bernard, *Downing Street Diary*, June 28, 1974, Jonathan Cape, 2005.

Donoughue, Bernard, and G. W. Jones, *Herbert Morrison*, Phoenix Press, 2001.

Drake, Barbara, *Women in Trade Unions*, Virago, 1984.

Duff, Andrew, *Making the Difference: Essays in Honour of Shirley Williams*, Biteback, 2010.

Dyhouse, Carol, *Feminism and Family in England, 1880–1939*, Blackwell, 1989.

Estorick, Erick, *Stafford Cripps. A Biography*, The John Day Co., 1949.

Foot, Michael, *Aneurin Bevan*, Vols. 1 and 2, Davis-Poynter, 1973.

Friedan, Betty, *The Feminine Mystique*, W. W. Norton, 1963.

Gavron, Hannah, *The Captive Wife*, Penguin, W. W. Norton, 1966.

Graves, Pamela M., *Labour Women: Women in British Working-Class Politics, 1918–1939*, Cambridge University Press, 1994.

Hamilton, Mary Agnes, *Margaret Bondfield*, Leonard Parsons, 1924.

Hamilton, Mary Agnes, *Uphill All the Way*, Jonathan Cape, 1953.

Hannam, June, and Karen Hunt, *Socialist Women*, Routledge, 2002.

Harman, Harriet, and Judith Hart Memorial Lecture, *Daily Record*, May 14, 2009.

Harris, Robert, *The Making of Neil Kinnock*, Faber & Faber, 1984.

Harrison, Barbara, *Not Only the 'Dangerous Trades': Women's Work and Health in Britain, 1880–1914*, Taylor & Francis, 1996.

Harrison, Brian, *Prudent Revolutionaries, Portraits of British Feminists Between the Wars*, Clarendon Press, 1987.

Harrison, Brian, *The Transformation of British Politics, 1860–1995*, Oxford University Press, 1996.

Hart, Judith, *Aid and Liberation: A Socialist Study of Aid Politics*, Victor Gollanz, 1973.

Hazlehurst, Cameron, and Whitehead Sally with Christine Woodland, *A Guide to the Papers of British Cabinet Ministers, 1900–1964*, Cambridge University Press, 1996, pp. 57–58.

Holden, Katherine, *The Shadow of Marriage: Singleness in England, 1914–60*, Manchester University Press, 2010.

Hollis, Patricia, *Jennie Lee: A Life*, Oxford University Press, 1997.

Hosgood, Christopher P., '"Mercantile Monasteries": Shops, Shop Assistants, and Shop Life in Late-Victorian and Edwardian Britain', *Journal of British Studies*, July 1999, Vol. 38, No. 3, pp. 322–352.

Hunt, Cathy, *The National Federation of Women Workers, 1906–1921*, Palgrave Macmillan, 2014.

James, Simon, *British Cabinet Government*, Routledge, 1999.

Jenkins, Roy, *A Life at the Centre*, Macmillan, 1991.

Ireton, Barrie, *Britain's International Development Policies, A History of DFID and Overseas Aid*, Palgrave Macmillan, 2013.

John, Angela V., *Unequal Opportunities: Women's Employment in England 1800–1918*, Basil Blackwell, 1986.

Johnson, Neil, *The Labour Church: The Movement and Its Message*, Routledge, 2017.

Johnston, J., *A Hundred Commoners*, Herbert Joseph, 1931, p. 109.

Jones, Helen, *Women in British Public Life, 1914–1950*, Longman, 2000.

Jones, Mervyn, *Michael Foot*, Victor Gollanz, 1994.

Judge, Tony, *Margaret Bondfield*, Athlone Press, 2018.

Keble, Sally (Editor), *This Woman Can*, Fabian Society, 2017.

King, Anthony, 'The Rise of the Career Politician in Britain—And Its Consequences', *British Journal of Political Science*, Vol. 11, No. 3, July 1981.

King, Anthony, and Nicholas Allen, '"Off with Their Heads": British Prime Ministers and the Power to Dismiss', *British Journal of Political Science*, April 2010.

Klein, Viola, *Britain's Married Women Workers*, Routledge, 1965.

Koch, Stephen, *Stalin, Willi Munzenberg and the Seduction of the Intellectuals*, HarperCollins, 1995.

Kramer, Ann, *Women and Politics*, Wayland Press, 1988.

Law, Cheryl, *Suffrage and Power*, I.B. Tauris, 1997.

Liddington, Jill, *The Long Road to Greenham: Feminism and Anti-Militarism in Britain Since 1820*, Virago, 1989.

Lovenduski, Joni, and Pippa Norris (Editor), *Women in Politics*, Oxford University Press, 1996.

Lovenduski, Joni, and Pippa Norris, 'Westminster Women: The Politics of Presence', *Political Studies*, 2003, Vol. 51, pp. 84–102.

Mann, Jean, *Women in Parliament*, Odhams, 1962.

Manning, Leah, *A Life for Education*, Victor Gollancz, 1970.

Marquand, David, *Ramsay MacDonald*, Jonathan Cape, 1977.

Martineau, Lisa, *Barbara Castle*, Andre Deutch, 2000.

McDougall, Linda, *Westminster Women*, Vintage, 1998.

McDougall, Linda, *Westminster Women*, Vintage, 1998.

McMeeken, Sean, *The Red Millionaire: A Political Biography of Willi Munzenberg*, Yale University Press, 1974.

Meredith, Stephen, 'A "Brooding Oppressive Shadow?" The Labour Alliance, the "Trade Union Question" and the Trajectory of Revisionist Social Democracy, c1969–1975', *Labour History Review*, December 2017,

Miliband, Marion, 'Margaret Bondfield' *Dictionary of Labour Biography*, Vol. 11, 1974.

Middleton, Lucy, *Women in the Labour Movement*, Croom Helm, 1977.

Miles, Jonathan, *The Nine Lives of Otto Katz*, Bantam Books, 2011.

Mitchell, Juliet, *Woman's Estate*, Verso, 1986.

Morgan, Kenneth O., *Michael Foot*, Harper Perennial, 2007.

Morrison, Herbert, *The Communist Solar System*, Labour Publications, 1933.

Myrdal, Alva, and Viola Klein, *Women's Two Roles Home and Work*, Routledge, 1956.

North Tyneside Fabians, *A Celebration of Pioneering Labour Women*, Cullercoats, 1995.

Oxford Dictionary of National Biography, Oxford University Press, online edition, May 2012.

Robert Pearce, *Britain: Domestic Politics, 1918–1939*, Hodder and Stoughton, 1992.

Peel, Mark, *Shirley Williams: The Biography*, Biteback, 2013.

Perkins, Anne, *Red Queen: The Authorized Biography of Barbara Castle*, Macmillan 2003.

Perry, Matt, '*Red Ellen' Wilkinson*, Manchester University Press, 2014.

Phillips, Melanie *The Divided House*, Sidgwick and Jackson, 1980.

Pimlott, Ben, *Hugh Dalton*, Macmillan, 1986.

Pimlott, Ben, *Harold Wilson*, HarperCollins, 1992.

Prescott John, and Charlie, *Not Wanted on Voyage*, NUS Hull Dispute Committee, June 1966.

Pugh, Martin, *Women and the Women's Movement in Britain*, Macmillan, 2nd ed., 2000.

Pugh, Martin, *Speak for Britain: A New History of the Labour Party*, Vintage 2011.

Randall, Vicky, *Women and Politics*, Macmillan, 1982.

Reeves, Rachel, *Alice in Westminster*, I.B. Tauris, 2017.

Reeves, Rachel, *Alice in Wonderland: The Political Life of Alice Bacon*, I.B. Tauris, 2017.

Reeves, Rachel, *Women of Westminster: The MPs Who Changed Politics*, I.B. Tauris, 2019.

Riddell, Peter, *Honest Opportunism*, Hamish Hamilton, 1993.

Rowbotham, Sheila, *Dreamers of a New Day*, Verso, 2011.

Rubinstein, David, 'Ellen Wilkinson Re-Considered', *History Workshop Journal*, March 1979.

Ryan, Michelle K., and Alexander S. Haslam, 'The Glass Cliff: Exploring the Dynamics Surrounding the Appointment of Women to Precarious Leadership Positions', *Academy of Management Review*, Vol. 32, 2007,

Seaman, L. C. B., *Post-Victorian Britain 1902–1951*, Methuen and Co., 1966.

Shore, Peter, *Labour Solidarity*, March 1981.

Silver, Eric, *Victor Feather T.U.C.*, Victor Gollancz, 1973.

Sked, Alan, and Chris Cook, *Post-War Britain, A Political History*, Penguin, 1979.

Skidelsky, Robert, *Politicians and the Slump: The Labour Government of 1929–1931*, Macmillan, 1967.

Smith, Andrew, and Chris Jeppesen, *Britain, France and the Decolonisation of Africa*, UCL, 2017.

Smith, Harold (Editor), *War and Social Change*, Manchester University Press, 1990.

Snowden, Philip Viscount, *An Autobiography*, Vol. 2, 1919–1934, Ivor Nicolson and Watson, 1934.

Sutherland, Duncan, 'Hart, Judith, Baroness of South Lanark (1924–1991)', *Oxford Dictionary of National Biography*, Oxford University Press, 2004.

Taylor, A. J. P., *English History, 1914–1945*, Penguin, 1965.

Thomas-Symonds, Nicklaus, *Nye: The Political Life of Aneurin Bevan*, I.B. Tauris, 2016.

Tracey, Herbert, *The British Labour Party: Its History, Growth, Policy and Leaders*, Caxton Publishing Company, 1948.

Tyler, Richard, '"Victims of our History?" Barbara Castle and *In Place of Strife*', *Contemporary British History*, September 2006, pp. 461–476.

Vallance, Elizabeth, *Women in the House*, The Athlone Press, 1979.

Vernon, Betty D., *Ellen Wilkinson*, Law Book of Australasia, 1982.

Walker, Peter, *Ernest Bevin*, Routledge, 1981.

Webb, Beatrice Diaries 1929–1943, LSE Digital Library.

Webb, Sydney, *What Happened in 1932: A Record*, The Fabian Society, 1932.

Whitehead, Phillip, *Dictionary of Labour Biography*, Palgrave, 2001.

Wilkinson, Ellen, and J. F. Horrabin, *A Workers' History of the Great Strike*, Plebs League, 1927.

Wilkinson, Ellen, *The Terror in Germany*.

Wilkinson, Ellen, *Peeps at Politicians*, P. Allan, 1930.

Wilkinson, Ellen, *The Division Bell Mystery*, 1932.

Wilkinson, Ellen, *The Town That Was Murdered*, Victor Gollanz, 1939.

Wilkinson, Ellen, *Plan for Peace*, Labour Party, 1945.

Wilkinson, Ellen, *The Clash*, 1930, Reprinted Trent Editions, 2004.

Wilkinson, Ellen, and Edward Conze, *Why Fascism?* Selwyn and Blount, 1934.

Wilkinson, Ellen, and Edward Conze, *Why War?* NCLC, 1934.

Wilkinson, Ellen, et al., *Condition of India—Being the Report of the Delegation Sent to India by the India League*, Essential News, 1932.

Williams, Shirley, *Politics is for People*, Penguin 1981.

Williams, Shirley, *God and Caesar, Personal Reflections on Politics and Religion*, Continuum 2003.

Williams, Shirley, *Climbing the Bookshelves*, Virago, 2009.

Wilson, Elizabeth, *Only Half-Way to Paradise, Women in Postwar Britain: 1945–1968*, Tavistock, 1980.

Wilson, Harold, *The Labour Government 1964–1970*, Pelican, 1974.

UNPUBLISHED MANUSCRIPTS

Davies, Ross, Unpublished Biography of Margaret Bondfield, Women's Library, LSE.

Erswell, Christopher, *UK Aid Policy and Practice, 1975–90*, PhD, University of Liverpool, 1994.

Parker, James, *Trade Unions and the Political Culture of the British Labour Party, 1931–1940*, PhD thesis, Exeter University, 2017.

Parker, Kristy, *Women MPs, Feminism and Domestic Policy in the Second World War*, DPhil, University of Oxford, 1994.

Tyler, Richard John, *'Victims of Our History', the Labour Party and in Place of Strife, 1968 to 1969*, PhD thesis, Queen Mary College, 2004.

Winkler, Barbara, *The Intractable Million*, Senior Essay, Vassar College, Unpublished Manuscript, April 1974.

INDEX

© The Editor(s) (if applicable) and The Author(s), under exclusive license to Springer Nature Switzerland AG, part of Springer Nature 2019
P. Bartley, *Labour Women in Power*,
https://doi.org/10.1007/978-3-030-14288-9

Printed by Printforce, the Netherlands